A practical handbook for software development

A practical handbook for software development

N. D. BIRRELL
Logica Pty Limited, Sydney, Australia

M. A. OULD
Logica UK Limited, London, UK

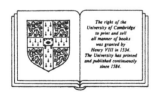

CAMBRIDGE UNIVERSITY PRESS

CAMBRIDGE

LONDON   NEW YORK   NEW ROCHELLE

MELBOURNE   SYDNEY

Published by the Press Syndicate of the University of Cambridge
The Pitt Building. Trumpington Street, Cambridge CB2 1RP
32 East 57th Street. New York, NY 10022, USA
10 Stamford Road, Oakleigh, Melbourne 3166, Australia

First published 1985
Reprinted 1986

Library of Congress catalogue card number: 84-9403

British Library cataloguing in publication data
Birrell, N.D.
A practical handbook for software development.
1. Electronic digital computers-programming
I. Title II. Ould, M. A.
001.64'25   QA76.6
ISBN 0 521 25462 0 Hardback
ISBN 0 521 34792 0 Paperback

Transferred to digital printing 2003

Contents

Contents

Foreword

The cost of software development is now the dominating cost in computer systems. As hardware costs decline, improved efficiency of software production becomes the key target if further reductions in computing costs are to be achieved. Accordingly the Alvey Committee identified software engineering as one of the four underlying technologies for the UK national programme of cooperative research in information technology.

Coming as it does at the start of the Alvey programme, I welcome this book by Martyn Ould and Nick Birrell, for it presents a picture of software engineering techniques that are already in existence and can therefore be exploited now. If the techniques set out in the book are widely applied we can look forward to a very significant improvement in the efficiency of software production.

Brian Oakley, Director, Alvey Programme
London, Autumn 1983

Preface

With the accelerating pace of work being done in the field of software engineering, it is becoming increasingly difficult to see the range of available techniques against a common background. Individual techniques are accessible throughout the literature but generally each is described in isolation. Comparison is difficult unless one has a strong idea of what one is looking for.

Our purpose in writing this book has therefore been to bring together, within a single framework, a variety of methods from all stages of software development and, in this way, to assist software engineers in particular in finding and evaluating the techniques appropriate to their own working environments. This should be regarded principally therefore as a book of signposts, leading the reader out into the field with a map, a compass and some reference points. By combining pointers to a selection of modern development practices with practical hints and checklists, all within one framework, we hope to fill the need for a vade-mecum to the software developer.

Managers with responsibility for software production will also, we hope, find much to stimulate their ideas about what modern practices have to offer and how their departments' efficiency and effectiveness could benefit. Students of computing science will be able to complement their more theoretical work by seeing the software development process as a day-to-day activity, a process that has managerial and sociological as much as purely technical aspects. As software developers we need to be aware of the work that has been done already in the software engineering field and that is ready for us to exploit.

Much of the flavour and content of this book naturally derives from our work for Logica and Logica's own philosophy and practice, and we would like to acknowledge both this contribution and the encouragement and facilities that Logica has given.

We would very much like to thank the following people for their advice and help:

John Cameron (Michael Jackson Systems Limited)
Deborah Cooper and John Scheid (System Development Corporation)
Tony Curry (DMW Group Europe)
Dave Forsyth (British Aerospace)
R. P. Loshbough (TRW)
Pieter Mimno (Higher Order Software Inc.)
Peter Neumann (SRI International)
Martyn Thomas (Praxis Systems Limited)
Tony Ward (British Aerospace)
Robert Worden (Logica Limited)

Suzanne Wallace and her word-processing team (particularly Cheryl Taylor) at Logica receive our particular thanks for their sterling work through all the drafts, reworkings and re-arrangings.

Finally, we welcome the opportunity of acknowledging all those whose work this book reports on; many of their names appear in the text and the bibliographies.

N. D. Birrell and M. A. Ould
London, November 1983

1

The choices facing the system developer

Given the task of developing a software system, how *does* one go about it? To start the building of a system of a thousand or maybe a million delivered lines of source code is a daunting (if exciting) prospect. No one should begin without a very clear idea about how the development is to be undertaken and how the quality of its output is to be assessed.

Turning this around we can say that anyone undertaking software development, on no matter what scale, must be strongly advised to establish a methodology for that development – one or more techniques that, by careful integration and control, will bring order and direction to the production process.

To paraphrase Freeman 1982: *every* software development organisation already has *some* methodology for building software systems. However, while some software is developed according to modern practices of software development, most of it is still built in an *ad hoc* way. So it is best to talk about software development techniques and methodologies in terms of *changing* current practices, replacing them with new techniques that improve the process of software development and the quality of the resulting products.

There is of course a dilemma here for us as system developers: technique X may offer us potential gains such as reduced development time, reduced costs, increased reliability, quality etc, but in adopting it we also incur the risks arising from the fact that we may be unfamiliar with technique X, it might not be suitable for the system we have to develop, and it might not suit our staff and their skills. And yet we must resolve this dilemma if the efficiency of development is to improve and the quality of our products is to increase.

The questions that need always to be asked are: what techniques are there, which are appropriate to our problem, and how can we monitor the quality of the products? Just as the builder of aircraft is constantly looking for new materials and new production processes so we as builders of software systems should be constantly searching, constantly choosing and constantly refining.

This is in fact largely a book about choice. One of its central messages is: look at the different techniques you can apply to the development process (and here are some examples), make your choice for your own situation and make a resolute decision to support that choice.

A second message is: establish a management framework within which you can apply the techniques you choose in a controllable fashion. This is essential. You must be able to define how you will mark your progress against tangible milestones.

The third message is that management of *technical* development requires the planning and monitoring of more than just the traditional *managerial* indicators – budget and timescale. Technical indicators – particularly the various symptoms of complexity – need to be managed at all stages of development to ensure that the right techniques are being used in the right way.

So, carefully selected and appropriate techniques, an appropriate development framework and monitorable technical indicators are necessary to improve software development.

The introduction of new techniques is however not solely a technical matter. It has a sociological impact in that it requires software engineers to change their working practices and there may be a temptation to feel that the newer, more formal and more mechanised techniques will devalue the software engineer's skills. On this topic Michael Jackson says that 'there is still misunderstanding about the impact of development methods on skill. The development method, certainly if it is any good, must enlarge your skill, it must make you able to do things that you could not do before and instead of reducing skills on the job it increases it.' We believe that even a cursory glance through the following chapters will convince doubting software engineers that the scope for increasing their skills and abilities is vast.

Once they have used this book as a primary input to their decision on what techniques to use, we urge readers to move to the authoritative texts for the detailed input. An important feature of the succeeding chapters is therefore the bibliographies. These concentrate on literature that is in the public domain either in book form, in international journals or in the proceedings of major conferences. In some cases, material published by software companies is included where it can be obtained easily.

Each technique that we describe is given its own bibliography of both central and supporting material. Furthermore, at the end of the book you will find 'Other bibliographies'. Each of these contains references to literature on a subject area that does not have a bibliography of its own earlier in the book.

All references whether appearing in the text or in bibliographies are given in an abbreviated form such as Pode 1982. Where an item has more than one author only the name of the first appears in references. You can find the corresponding full bibliographic references in the 'References' section just before the Index.

At various points we have included exercises for the reader. These are not tests on the comprehension or memory nor do they have simple answers such as '42'. They are more intended to provoke thought about some key idea in a technique, again with the aim of illuminating what sort of problems different techniques set out to solve, whether your problem is related and so on.

Finally, some words on the structure of the book.

In chapter 2 we set out the managerial framework necessary for the remaining chapters: the Work Breakdown Structure which gives a framework of activities and deliverable items resulting from them, the estimation of resources to be allocated to the activities, the use of a variety of managerial and technical indicators of progress and quality, and finally the control of the products of development – 'configuration control'.

The remainder of the book is then built on this framework. First of all each of the development techniques that we describe is summarised in chapter 3. This is to allow you to scan the spectrum relatively quickly. Chapters 4 to 8 then take each phase of development in turn. Chapter 4 on Project Inception and chapter 8 on System Acceptance and Post-Acceptance Development bracket the three major chapters that are principally concerned with system development: System Definition, System Design and System Production. In those three chapters the framework of activities and deliverables is expanded to further detail, the techniques of use in that phase are given more detailed treatments, the indicators relevant to the products of the phase are described, some general words of wisdom are collected under the heading of memorabilia, and checklists for various topics appear.

Finally, chapter 9 ('Project Debriefing') returns us to the idea that the introduction of new techniques needs itself to be monitored if we are to find and make the best use of those that are the best for us. We need to record and learn from our own mistakes and successes.

In a similar sense we hope that our readers will treat this as an open-ended book, one to which they can add their own experiences with techniques, their own indicator data, memorabilia, checklists and so on.

2

The software development process

The transformation of your client's ideas about his proposed system into the physical, delivered system is a long one. If this transformation is to be at all manageable, it needs to be tackled as a sequence of stages, each bringing you closer to your destination.

The simplest model of the software development process is a purely sequential one with each succeeding stage following on in serial fashion from the previous one. Such a model could serve for a small one-man project but a better approximation to reality is contained in the so-called 'cascade' or 'waterfall' model suggested in figure 2.1. This recognises that it is generally necessary – even desirable – for the stages to overlap and even repeat.

It is normally customary at this point to talk of the software development 'lifecycle' and to draw a diagram along the lines of figure 2.2. This custom is based on the premise that the original development of a system from scratch has the same underlying sequence of events as the enhancement or correction of a system: inception, definition, design, implementation and acceptance. Superficially this is true but the similarity is slight and the generalisation at times unhelpful.

In this book we prefer to talk about the 'development path' and 'maintenance cycles' and to draw the 'b-diagram' along the lines of figure 2.3. This reflects reality more closely. The development path, starting from nothing more than a desire for a system, stands alone. At its termination, the maintenance cycle, and possibly several simultaneously, take up the resulting system together with ideas for enhancements and in their turn produce new systems, but always as developments from the initial system

Since the evidence points strongly to the fact that maintenance consumes the greater part of software budgets we can deduce that we should expend the greater part of our effort on improving the efficiency of the maintenance activity. Our contention here is that efficiency is largely predetermined by the quality (in many senses) of the

Fig. 2.1. The cascade model of software development.

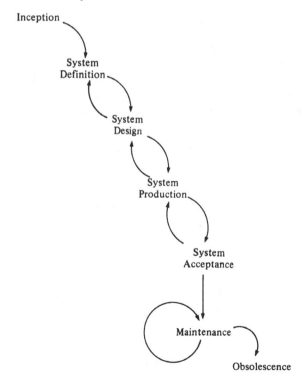

system being maintained, i.e. by the quality of the output from the development path. Given also that the initial development has to be successful in the first place for there even to be further maintenance we have placed the emphasis of this book on the development path alone so we remain with the simple cascade model of the development path.

Once we have established a simple model of the software development process we will have a basis for planning and managing. This will be necessary for two critical activities:

- estimating the task in hand – how it will be split up amongst staff, how long will be allowed for each activity and how the activities will be co-ordinated;
- monitoring the task, as it proceeds, against the original plans and estimates.

In this chapter we

- develop the concept of the phases and stages into which a software development project can be broken,
- look at the techniques for allocating effort, and
- describe the 'indicators' that can be monitored during a project to check its progress against plan.

These three items constitute the model of the software development process that underlies the remainder of the book. As you start off the development of your own system it is important to decide on the subset of the complete model that matches your situation. Establishing that subset is one of the most important management decisions you will make as it determines all of your planning and monitoring.

The model of the software development process is also the ideal background against which to see the great variety of development methodologies that are available. In chapter 3 we describe some of these individually in sufficient detail that you can decide which might be appropriate to your own project. Chapters 4 to 9 deal individually with the successive project phases discussing in further detail what each methodology means for that phase and for the stages within the phase. First then, let us investigate those phases and stages.

2.1 Phases and stages

There is no single breakdown of the development path. The one presented here works in practice but you may wish to change it to fit your own purposes or preconceptions. The essential property of any good breakdown is, however, *completeness*. The aim is not to forget anything. The model must describe all the steps required in producing

Fig. 2.3. The b-model of software development and maintenance.

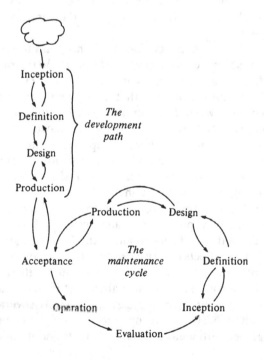

Fig. 2.2. The traditional software development lifecycle diagram.

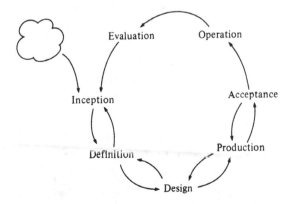

the deliverable items, typically software, hardware, manuals, training and support.

We must, therefore, be able to identify in our model (and in any real life plan based on it) the point at which we can deliver each of the items that we have contracted with our client to supply and to see a network of activities culminating in those deliverables.

The first level of breakdown that we have adopted is into these phases:

- project inception,
- system definition,
- system design,
- system production,
- system acceptance,
- post-acceptance development, and
- project debriefing.

These phases have a very natural serial progression:

- decide to do something for some reason,
- agree on what is to be done,
- work out how to do it,
- do it,
- have it accepted,
- look after it following delivery,
- look back at how it all went.

We shall see that the individual techniques available to improve your product and its production rarely span more than a couple of these phases and need preparation in earlier ones. So you will need to put together a coherent set of techniques which carry you through from inception to debriefing. It is the purpose of this book to help you choose that set and also to keep you reminded at each phase of its inherent dangers and pitfalls and how to avoid them by preparation.

We can hope that, in time, more comprehensive tools will become available that integrate the development process from definition to acceptance. Steps have been taken in this direction and some are described later in the book, but in the meantime we must rely on a synthesis of lesser tools.

2.1.1 Delineating the phases – deliverables

We said above that the phases have a 'natural serial progression'. This is true, but it is not a truth that we should feel bound to. For instance, it is a brave person who defines a system without being certain they can build it, or, in other words, without doing sufficient (albeit high-level) design to satisfy themselves that they are setting a soluble problem. There will be design done during definition; equally there will be some software production during design, and so on. In fact, taking a realistic viewpoint, we can consider this iteration between phases as being symptomatic of that very same foresight which makes projects flow smoothly, that ability to see early on in the project the groundwork that should be done now for the activities that come later.

There is, of course, a danger here, namely that of iterating so much between phases that the boundaries between them become blurred and indistinguishable. If this happens, two results are unavoidable. Firstly, progress becomes impossible to monitor and hence management becomes impossible. Secondly, development takes place on shifting foundations, and this is a situation that leads to errors, frustration and finally failure.

The solution to this is simple. Each phase (and – we shall see – each stage) must have a clear start and a clear end, and to give the start and end precise and material meaning we define them in terms of *deliverable items*. In general, these deliverable items will be documents. Often those documents will be agreed and signed by the parties to whom they will be important, as an indication of everyone's commitment to them as definitive statements. In the coming chapters we shall circumscribe each phase by defining the deliverable items that are its *inputs* – i.e. without which the phase cannot start – and those that are its *outputs* – i.e. those without whose completion the phase cannot be said to have finished.

These measures will allow you to tell when you have finished a stage or phase. When drawing up your plans for the project these deliverable items must be identified for each phase and stage. They are the subgoals on the way to producing the final goal – successful delivery of a working system. With this scheme of deliverables it also becomes possible for you to iterate between phases in a manageable way – an important ability if you are working in a new area with new problems and innovative techniques.

2.1.2 The phase profile

Figure 2.1 showed some phases overlapping in time. Provided we maintain the safeguards introduced with the notion of deliverables, this overlapping can be successfully handled. Indeed, it is often essential that this overlap or iteration take place for technical reasons.

With this in mind we go on to examine the profile in a little more detail – to take each phase apart and identify the stages that compose it. The stages in a phase form a mini-network of their own, sometimes overlapping and interdependent but finally coming together at the deliverable item(s) of the phase.

To some extent the different techniques that you can adopt will determine which stages are relevant. You should therefore regard the network that is built up in this chapter as a basic matrix on which you can plug the detailed sub-networks appropriate to the techniques you choose (where these exist). These sub-networks are given with the techniques in chapters 5–8.

2.1.3 The Project Inception Phase

This is the starting phase in the development of a system; the phase in which you conceive of the need for the system, justify that need and decide on system requirements. The deliverable item from this phase is a Requirement Specification for the system upon which a decision to proceed with system development has been based.

In reaching the point where a decision to proceed can sensibly be made you may need to carry out a great deal of analysis such as market research, cost–benefit analysis, operations research and tender analysis. All such activities are aimed at producing a Requirement Specification which defines a system that will meet your needs and which can be developed with the resources available.

2.1.4 The System Definition Phase

This phase has two purposes: to define *what* is to be produced and to define *how* it is to be produced. There are four deliverable items each associated with one of the following stages:

- Produce Functional Specification;
- Produce Project Plan;
- Produce Quality Management Plan;
- Produce Acceptance Test Specification.

The Functional Specification is the document that will be your bible for the remainder of the project. It describes what you are contracting to produce. The Project Plan and Quality Management (QM) Plan describe how you will produce it.

The Project Plan is your statement of what managerial steps you will take to ensure that the product is delivered on time and within budget. The Quality Management Plan is your statement of what technical and managerial steps you will take to ensure the quality of your product. We will not be telling you in this book exactly what should appear in these two plans as this is largely an organisational matter. You will find in this book useful references in the bibliographies plus checklists of items that should appear in the Plans and that are essential if you want to exploit the ideas and techniques in this book.

Your Quality Management Plan will give clear instructions to staff of what they are required to produce whilst the Project Plan tells them the resources they have been given to do the job – time, computers, budget etc.

As we shall see later on, a prime quality in the Functional Specification of a system is that it should be testable. Now is the time, therefore, to ensure this quality by writing down and agreeing with your client the strategy that he will use to test the system before accepting it. This Acceptance Test Specification and the Functional Specification will together be the inputs to a document – the Acceptance Test Description – that will be written during the Design and Production Phases and that will describe those Acceptance Tests in full detail.

We can add another stage to the phase:

- Perform System Modelling.

Now is the time during the project to carry out what we will call 'modelling' of the system. 'System model' is a generic term for any object that allows you to assess some quality of the system being built. As examples, you may wish to model the proposed user interface so that the future users of the system can assess its friendliness; stringent performance requirements may require you to simulate the system in some fashion to see whether the proposed hardware and software will have the throughput/speed/reliability/resilience that is being written into the Functional Specification; you may need to do some preliminary high-level design to check the very feasibility of the system you are soon to agree to produce by signing the Functional Specification. In summary, you can see that the System Definition Phase also has System Models as deliverable items.

2.1.5 The System Design Phase

The central task of this phase is clear: to take the agreed Functional Specification and derive from it a design that will satisfy it. Precisely how this transformation is made will depend on the methodology you choose from the ones available. The process may be wholly manual or it may be automated to some extent, but the deliverable item remains the same – a System Design Specification. This is the seminal document that is the basis for your Production Phase. It may take any one of a number of forms – each methodology has its own bias and its own output documents. The essential points are that your Quality Management Plan should have defined what the System Design Specification should contain and what it should look like, and that the System Design Phase will not be complete until it is produced.

Whichever technique you adopt to generate the System Design Specification, its production will give you a far more detailed breakdown of the work to be done in subsequent phases than you have had so far. You should therefore take the opportunity to refine your Project Plans and possibly to review your Quality Management Plan in the same way. In addition to the Specify System Design stage in this phase we can, therefore, also identify two other stages:

- Refine Project Plan, and
- Refine QM Plan.

It may be appropriate to consider either re-running the System Models produced during System Definition or building new ones testing out features of the design. Typical examples are load and throughput models using mock-ups of the proposed program structure or overlaying mechanism, or benchmarks for the timing of critical computa-

tions. To cover these we introduce the stage Refine System Models.

2.1.6 The System Production Phase

It is a sad fact that this phase is often mistaken for the entire development project. It is certainly the largest phase – something like half of pre-acceptance development in terms of effort – but without adequately resourced System Definition and Design Phases preceding it, it is very likely to fail. It has one major deliverable item – a System Ready for Trials – and a number of minor but nevertheless important ones:

- User Documentation;
- User Training Schedules;
- Acceptance Test Description;
- System Conversion Schedule.

Your choice of software development procedures will determine the stages within the phase. Those stages are typically

- Design in Detail (Modules),
- Code Modules,
- Test Modules,
- Integrate Subsystems,
- Integrate System.

The Test Modules activity may then be broken down further, each subordinate activity relating to the modules for a particular subsystem, and may possibly contain activities covering the development of test software.

The last stage will deliver the System Ready for Trials. The other deliverable items will come from

- Prepare User Documentation,
- Prepare Training Schedules,
- Prepare Acceptance Test Description,
- Prepare System Conversion Schedule.

2.1.7 The System Acceptance Phase

This short phase is the last opportunity for detecting and removing errors in your system before it goes into full use or parallel running prior to cutover. Just like the earlier phases of a project, System Acceptance is receiving increasing attention with regard to thoroughness and rigour in the approaches made to it. Formalised and exhaustive tests are becoming the norm, and it is for this reason that we have stressed the need for the early production of the Acceptance Test Specification (the strategic document) and the Acceptance Test Description (the detailed tactical document). These two are the principal inputs to the first stage of this phase, together with a System Ready for Trials out of the System Production Phase. The output deliverable item is the Accepted System.

The second stage is that of installing the system. This takes as its inputs

- the Accepted System,
- the System Conversion Schedule,
- the User Documentation,
- the Training Schedules,

and produces as its deliverable item the Running System. Exactly where the boundaries lie between the System Ready for Trials, the Accepted System and the Running System cannot be defined for the general case but it is important that you should identify the actual progression for your own system. The Install System activity can range from immediate full use to a prolonged process of parallel running, gradual cutover, pilot testing and so on – almost an extension of the acceptance process.

2.1.8 The Post-Acceptance Development Phase

It is now common knowledge that delivery and installation of the first version of a system often only mark the beginning of a long process of enhancement, bug-fixing and reworking that continues until the system becomes obsolete. We must therefore place emphasis on two areas:

- firstly, building longevity into the system right from the start through good design and implementation practices;
- secondly, managing the post-acceptance development in a way that preserves the integrity of the system, thereby delaying the decay that would otherwise set in.

The inputs to the phase arising internally from the project are:

- the Accepted System;
- the Functional Specification;
- the System Design Specification;

- all detailed design documentation;
- all source code;
- all test records;
- the full archive of working papers, discussion documents, and early versions of specifications, in other words, not just the system itself and all the final specifications but also all the background documents that record implicitly what design decisions were made and why. Ideally, these 'second-order facts' should appear in the primary documents, but, like polished mathematical theorems, the final specifications all too rarely show the route taken to them. This is unfortunate as the maintenance team's task of preserving the system's overall integrity will often need the second-order facts to appreciate just what form that integrity takes. Hence the importance of a definition and design archive.

Once underway, the phase also takes inputs from external sources and we can group them generically under three headings:

- enhancement requests,
- environment changes,
- error reports.

All of these will probably cause changes to the internal inputs in some way so that the outputs of the phase are clearly new versions of those internal inputs.

2.1.9 The Project Debriefing Phase

This is possibly the most neglected phase in the whole development process, and yet it has a great deal to offer. One of the main themes of this handbook – the use of indicators – is designed, amongst other things, to maximise the value of the debriefing exercise by ensuring that throughout development you are recording your experience both quantitatively and qualitatively. The aim is to crystallise that experience in a form that will make it of use both to yourself and to others in your organisation in subsequent software development projects. To this end, the phase has a single deliverable item – the Project Debriefing Report (PDR).

In addition to collecting indicator statistics throughout the project, you should aim to be continuously recording all the successful *and* unsuccessful decisions and actions of the project. Once the system has been accepted you will have all the raw material necessary for a PDR.

A good PDR will act as a beacon for future projects and a collection of PDRs within an organisation will allow it to capitalise on its experience in software projects far more rigorously than by simply relying on the memories of those who took part in them. The PDRs can be salutary reminders for the experienced, handbooks for the novice and, if properly handled, the basis for a corporate policy of planning, estimating, quality management and technical practices. Do not pass up this opportunity – include a Project Debriefing Phase in your plan.

2.1.10 The Work Breakdown Structure

We have now dissected a project and broken it down into a network of co-operating activities. In doing so we have supplied ourselves with a structured breakdown of all the work that needs to be done during the project. This Work Breakdown Structure (WBS) can be written down in words with the indentation that software engineers rely on to show a hierarchy:

```
1000  Project Inception
      1100  Project Inception Management
2000  System Definition
      2100  System Definition Management
      2200  Produce Functional Specification
      2300  Produce Project Plan
      2400  Produce Quality Management Plan
      2500  Produce Acceptance Test Specification
      2600  Perform System Modelling
3000  System Design
      3100  System Design Management
      3200  Specify System Design
      3300  Refine Project Plan
      3400  Refine Quality Management Plan
      3500  Refine System Models
      3600  Prepare Acceptance Test Description
4000  System Production
      4100  System Production Management
      4200  Produce System for Trial
      4300  Prepare User Documentation
      4400  Prepare Training Schedules
      4500  Prepare Acceptance Test Description
      4600  Prepare System Conversion Schedule
      4700  Refine Project Plan
      4800  Refine Quality Management Plan
```

```
5000  System Acceptance
      5100  System Acceptance Management
      5200  Perform System Acceptance
      5300  Install System
6000  Post-Acceptance Development
      6100  PAD Management
      6200  Correct Bugs in System
      6300  Enhance System
      6400  Adjust System to Environmental Changes
7000  Project Debriefing
      7100  Write Project Debriefing Report
8000  Overall Project Management
      8100  General Management
      8200  Liaise with Client and Suppliers
      8300  Control Quality
      8400  Train New Staff
```

Figure 2.4 shows the basic dependencies between these activities and their relationship to the deliverable items defined earlier.

We have adopted a style of numbering scheme most commonly used for a WBS. It forms a convenient shorthand when planning and reporting – particularly if automated tools are used. Some of the estimating models described in section 2.2 contain algorithms for deciding what proportion of the total effort budget should be allocated to each phase and stage – in other words, how that budget should be mapped onto the WBS.

Once your project is under way you will want your staff to report how much time they are spending on the activities assigned to them and you will naturally want to have them do this against the WBS for comparison with the original targets.

Each activity in your WBS can be broken down to as low a level as you need. We call an activity at the lowest level a *work package*. It corresponds to a single area of work that can be allocated to one or more individuals, so you should expect to decompose the WBS until you end up with appropriately sized lumps.

You will see from the WBS that Project Management and Quality Management activities appear at phase level and at project level. It is up to you whether you have one or both of these. You should consider phase-level management on a large project with team leaders and group leaders reporting to a project manager. On a small project, the single manager may not be able to sensibly separate his management activities between phases and hence a project-level management work package would suffice.

Whichever work packages you leave in or leave out, you should bear in mind that completeness is the most important property of a WBS. Projects frequently overrun their budgets and timescales for two reasons:

(i) they take longer to do the things that they expect to do;
(ii) they completely forget to plan for other things.

Careful compilation of the WBS is your way of avoiding the second trap. For instance, if you expect system integration to be a major activity requiring its own full-time integration leader then you will need to budget them into your WBS at the planning stage – probably as a management work package during System Production Phase.

One of the central recommendations of this book is that during the course of development you should collect data about certain 'indicators' of status and progress. In time you will begin to collect the statistics and indicator behaviour data from a number of projects and you will want to be able to contrast and compare them. This is now the time, therefore – before you start the next project – to decide on a *standard* WBS, one that is comprehensive, whose activities are well-defined by

their deliverable items, in other words, a WBS that you can use consistently (either in whole or in part) on all projects in your organisation or even just on your own. The usefulness of the statistics you collect will be greatly enhanced and your understanding of the whole development process will deepen.

2.1.11 Prototyping

Prototyping of new products has been commonplace in the hardware engineering community for years. Hardware prototypes are produced to demonstrate quickly and at relatively low expense the viability and utility of a product and to find and solve problems in the product before it is cast into its final form.

Although the same arguments can be applied to software prototyping as for hardware, the practice of producing software prototypes is far less common. The reason for this is twofold. Firstly, there tends to be a belief that software prototyping is not cost-effective. Secondly, the tools for software prototyping are not as readily available or as obvious as for hardware prototyping.

The belief that software prototyping is not cost-effective is almost certainly misguided (e.g. Boehm 1975). Large numbers of projects that have run into very expensive difficulties could have saved themselves a lot of trouble by a relatively

Fig. 2.4. The network of activities and deliverable items.

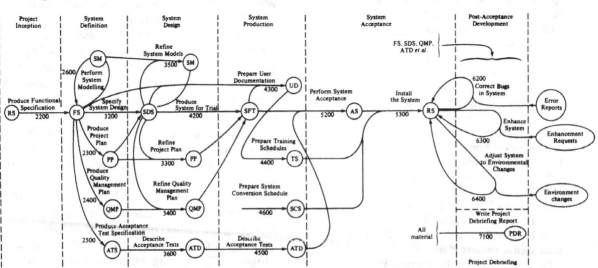

inexpensive amount of prototyping. For example projects that find themselves in trouble when the users finally get to see their system and find that it does not live up to their expectations could well have avoided this problem by producing an early prototype of the user interface to the system. An example of such a prototype is described in Gomaa 1981. As another example, projects that discover in their final stages of testing that the key algorithm on which the design of the system has been based does not meet its performance criteria could often avoid this problem by early prototyping of the candidate algorithms. An example of such key algorithm prototyping is described in Dreyfus 1976.

The second reason for not producing software prototypes, namely lack of appropriate tools, is perhaps slightly more valid although it is becoming less so. Hardware prototypes are very often made from materials which are more easily manipulated than those of the final product. For example an electronics engineer who wishes to prove a newly designed circuit will probably produce a wire wrapped prototype before committing his design to a printed circuit board. A wire wrapped board can be made reasonably quickly and inexpensively and, most importantly, it is easily modified. What are the equivalent, easily manipulated 'materials' for a software engineer?

The answer must be the ever-increasing number of very high level languages (VHLL). These range from general purpose VHLLs, such as APL used in the prototype described by Gomaa 1981, through special purpose VHLLs, such as GPSS (IBM 1970) for simulation, through special packages such as program generators, report generators, database query languages, screen formatters and so-called fourth generation languages, to VHLLs associated with particular methodologies, such as RSL (see section 5.4.6). All of these, if properly used, allow the rapid production or support of prototype code that accurately reflects the current plan for the actual system and which may be easily changed to allow for experimentation.

Software prototyping is most effective if it is carried out within a (definition or design) framework which supports it. Consequently, in subsequent chapters we do not deal with prototyping

in isolation but rather mention it in connection with other supporting methodologies.

By its nature we can expect it to require a variation of our simple cascade model for the development path. Since a prototype is a vehicle for experimentation we can also expect that variation to take the form of a prototyping cycle appended to the main path along the lines of figure 2.5. At some point a decision to prototype will be made and this will cause the cycle to be entered. How many times it is traversed will vary from situation to situation but the essence of a prototype is that it must be cheap and quick to produce and evaluate if the amount learned from it is to be maximised by repeated cycling.

Once the prototype has been squeezed for all it can efficiently yield the main development path is re-entered, generally at the point it was left unless the experimentation with the prototype has itself pushed development further on. In a sense, we can view a prototype as a major system model that is developed during System Definition and/or Design.

In this book we adopt the traditional development path corresponding to what James Martin calls 'prespecified computing' (Martin 1982). Martin contrasts this with 'user-driven computing' which is more appropriate where users do not know in detail what they want until they use a version of it and then want to modify it quickly and often.

Fig. 2.5. The development path augmented by a prototyping cycle.

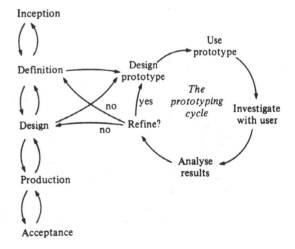

User-driven computing will, says Martin, increasingly become the norm for the bulk of data processing applications where better suited and more flexible applications can be built more quickly and cheaply through the use of database query languages, application generators and so on. Such tools will move into the hands of end-users themselves as well as DP professionals and traditional programmers.

However, Martin is clear that, for the foreseeable future, the production of complex computer applications (of the sort that will concern us in this book) will still require programmers and the sort of development techniques described in this book. The lesson is that, even for such applications, we need to be ready to adapt the traditional development path to incorporate prototyping, experimentation and modelling wherever they are necessary to avoid the pitfalls that Martin points out in prespecified computing.

Bibliography

Appleton 1983, Boehm 1975 and 1983, Dearnley 1983, Dodd 1980, Dreyfus 1976, Zelkowitz 1982.
(See also the bibliography for SREM, section 5.4.6.)

2.2 Quantitative software development models

2.2.1 Introduction

In the preceding section we discussed the qualitative aspects of the software development lifecycle but made no mention of quantitative attributes such as development costs, resources required and development time. A model which helps predict, or estimate, such attributes is clearly essential if a development project is to be completed on time and within budget.

Until fairly recently, software cost estimation has been very much a black art with many consequent disasters. (For an amusing and salutary collection of disasters see Glass 1977.) The realisation of the importance of accurate estimation has since led to a great deal of effort being spent on developing accurate quantitative models of the development lifecycle. In chapter 3 we shall describe some of these models in a little more detail. In this section, we discuss the general aspects of such models and consider in more detail what numbers you need to estimate and how you might go about estimating them.

If the amount of manpower per day being devoted to a given phase of a project is plotted against time, graphs very much like those in figure 2.6 typically result (Putnam 1978). The 'project curve', given by summing the curves for the individual phases, is also shown. Graphs of this form can be well approximated by the so-called Rayleigh distribution and other, similar, theoretically derived functions (e.g. Parr 1980).

It has also been noted empirically that software development activities typically end near the point at which the Rayleigh curve reaches its maximum (i.e. the point at which most people are

Fig. 2.6. Project effort usage rate by phase (after Putnam 1978).

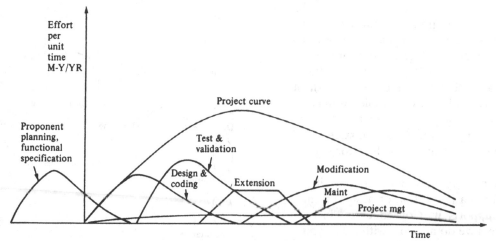

working on the project) and that after this point the project is mainly involved in extension, modification and maintenance activities. If we denote the time for software development by TD then this empirical evidence implies that TD is approximately given by the time at which the Rayleigh curve reaches its maximum. The error in this approximation is likely to be a small percentage of the total lifecycle duration, even if it is a quite large percentage of TD.

The area under the Rayleigh curve up to a given time gives the total manpower used on the project up to that time and has a graph as shown in figure 2.7. The total effort expended over the entire project lifecycle is denoted by E.

The project attributes that we need to be able to estimate are:

- the development time TD,
- the total effort E,
- the distribution of the development time between the phases and stages,
- the distribution of the total effort between the phases and stages.

2.2.2 Approaches to estimating

There are essentially two approaches to the estimating of quantitative project attributes: top-down and bottom-up.

In the top-down approach estimates are made (by some means) of the total development time and total effort for the entire project and then these quantities are divided up over phases, stages and finally work packages.

Fig. 2.7. Accumulation of effort expended over the life of a system.

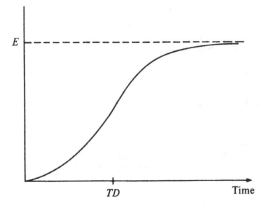

In the bottom-up approach, quite the opposite method is used. The effort and development time for each work package are individually estimated and the results combined to give the total effort and total development time.

In either approach, some method is required to allow the estimates to be made. There are many such methods available but nearly all can be placed in one of three classes:

- estimation by expert judgement,
- estimation by analogy,
- algorithmic estimation.

Other methods such as 'Parkinsonian estimation' and 'Cost-to-win estimation' (see for example Boehm 1981 and Zelkowitz 1979) are not recommended for serious software development efforts.

Experts
Estimation by expert judgement relies on one or more 'experts' making essentially an educated guess at the required project attributes. The accuracy of such estimates clearly depends both on the experts' understanding of the qualitative properties of the project being estimated and on their experience with previous projects. In the latter respect, estimation by expert judgement is similar to estimation by analogy.

Analogies
Estimation by analogy in the top-down approach relies on making a direct comparison between the global properties of the project being estimated and similar historical projects. In the bottom-up approach it involves making analogies between similar historical work packages; for example, 'it took Tom three months to design, code and test the line driver for computer A on project X. Dick is less experienced than Tom so we'll estimate that Dick will take four months to design, code and test the line driver for computer B on project Y.'

Algorithms
The danger with both estimation by expert judgement and estimation by analogy is that they rely on uncontrolled, subjective assessments of the nature of the project being estimated. The aim of algorithmic estimation is to control the subjective

judgements that must be made in arriving at an estimate.

There are essentially two types of algorithm used in estimation:

- those that are theoretically derived;
- those which are obtained empirically.

The theoretically derived algorithms are generally related to Halstead's software science theory (Halstead 1977). Such models are still in their infancy compared with those using empirically derived algorithms and are still subject to some debate (e.g. Coulter 1983 and Hamer 1982).

The second class of algorithms empirically relate the quantities estimated to a number of variables. The variables used vary from model to model but in the case of software cost estimation (in which case they are often called cost drivers) they are typically drawn from the list given in table 2.1. The relations between the quantities being estimated and the cost drivers are determined empirically using historical data, of the sort that you will be recording during your project. Of course, in using algorithmic methods, it is still necessary to estimate values for the cost drivers and expert judgement and estimation by analogy are still applicable here.

2.2.3 Algorithmic estimation methods

To demonstrate an algorithmic method and to illustrate some of the potential pitfalls of estimation methods in general, it is worth considering the very simplest, realistic algorithm for estimating development effort.

Table 2.1. *Cost drivers that possibly affect the results of cost models*

System size
1 Estimated number of instructions
2 Number of delivered machine language instructions
3 Number of delivered source language instructions
4 Percentage of new instructions
5 Percentage of clerical instructions
6 Number of decision instructions
7 Number of non-decision instructions
8 Percentage of information storage and retrieval instructions
9 Percentage of code for delivery

Data base
10 Number of words in the data base

System complexity
11 Grade for estimated overall complexity
12 Complexity of interfaces
13 System uniqueness
14 Degree of difficulty
15 Hardware–software interfaces
16 Program structure considerations
17 Number of files, reports and application programs
18 Total lifecycle manpower, total development manpower, total test and validation manpower
19 Total lifecycle time and total development time
20 Job type (number of system interactions)

Type of program
21 Type of application (business/non-business)
22 Program categories (control, I/O, pre/post-processor, algorithm, data management, time-critical)
23 Real-time/non-real-time

Documentation
24 Documentation in pages
25 Number of document types for customer
26 Number of documents for internal use

Environment and project attributes
27 System development environment
28 New or old computer
29 Number of display consoles
30 Special displays (used/not used)
31 Random access devices (used/not used)
32 Language used
33 Memory occupancy constraints
34 Computer system speed and memory capacity
35 Time sharing or batch processing
36 Programmer familiarity with language, compiler, etc
37 Programmer experience in programming
38 Programmer participation in design
39 Personnel continuity
40 Number of locations for program development
41 Productivity (lines of code/unit time)
42 Concurrent hardware development
43 Number of personnel
44 Programmer applications experience
45 Customer interface
46 Requirements definition
47 Requirements volatility
48 Maintenance requirements
49 Customer applications experience
50 User participation in requirements definition
51 Number of miles travelled
52 Frequency of operation after delivery of software
53 Degree and time phasing of simulation
54 Intent to prototype code
55 Fault tolerant computing
56 Reliability
57 Safety
58 Single CPU/multi-CPU application environment
59 Growth requirements – maintainability

Source: After Mohanty 1981.

Nearly all algorithmic methods use the number of instructions, I, to be produced in the project (or some closely related quantity) as one of their cost drivers. The simplest way of relating this to manpower, M, is by an algorithm of the form

$$M = I/p \qquad (2.1)$$

where p is a constant having, for example, the units 'instructions per man-day'. This constant is used to calibrate the model against data obtained on previous projects and can be considered as a measure of productivity on a project (e.g. Jones 1978, Howard 1980).

Since, in reality, the value of p is likely to depend on I (large projects progressing at a slower rate than small ones), equation (2.1) should only be regarded as a crude, but useful, first approximation.

When using the algorithm (2.1), one is still faced with the problem of estimating I, the number of instructions produced, and this must be done using expert judgement or analogy. In the top-down approach the total number of instructions and an average value of p for the entire system under development must be used. In the bottom-up approach the number of instructions in each system component is estimated separately and possibly different values of p are used for different types of component. For example, the value of p used for a device driver written in assembler would be different to that used for a report generator written in COBOL.

This leads us to consider a potential pitfall of algorithmic methods, namely, inaccuracies due to imprecise definition of terms. For example, in relation to algorithm (2.1) we could ask the following questions:

- Is I the number of source instructions or object instructions?
- Does I include a count of comments and data definitions?
- Is I a count of card images or executable instructions, possibly extending over several card images?
- Does I include instructions which are not delivered to the client?
- What phases of the development lifecycle are accounted for in M with a given value of p? Is requirement definition included? Are quality assurance and project management included?
- Does M make allowance for weekends, vacations and sick leave?

Without answers to these and other questions, model (2.1) is useless. In other words, the applicability of the algorithm, the cost drivers and the estimated quantity produced must be very clearly defined for an algorithmic method to be of practical benefit.

Power law models

Despite the simplicity of (2.1) a number of studies have found that a small modification to (2.1) can produce an algorithm which gives very good agreement with observed data.

The algorithm can be written as

$$ED = rS^c \qquad (2.2)$$

where ED is the total development effort in man-months (i.e. effort expended up to time TD) and S is the number of source instructions (nominally card images excluding comments but including data declarations and format or similar statements). The constants r and c are used to calibrate the model against historical data. If S is measured in thousands and E is in man-months, r typically ranges between 1 and 5, while c is typically between 0.9 and 1.5. These ranges are quite small given the various definitions (or non-definition) of terms in the different studies and the widely differing types of projects covered.

2.2.4 Allocating effort to phases

Once the total effort has been estimated you need a model of its distribution between phases. The percentage of effort expended in a given phase must be determined empirically from historical project data. Here again the records you keep during development will add to that stock of data and improve subsequent estimating. A typical effort distribution over the entire lifetime of a system is illustrated in figure 2.8 while the distribution of effort up to TD is shown in figure 2.9. Typical ranges of figures for the distribution of development effort are given in table 2.2. One point especially worth noting in figure 2.8 is the

Table 2.2. *Distribution of effort by activity over the development phases of a system*

Phase/stage	Percentage of development effort
Requirements	5–12
System design	10–20
Detailed design	15–30
Code and unit test	15–50
Integration and test	15–50

predominance of effort spent on maintenance over that expended in initial system development. This point should prompt us into designing into a system those features that aid maintenance.

2.2.5　Deriving the development schedule

The next quantity which needs to be dealt with is the development schedule. It would be useful if *TD* could be used as a variable that is altered at will along the lines: 'We've estimated the total development effort to be *ED*. We need the system to be ready in time *TD*, so we had better have an average of *M* = *ED*/*TD* people working on the project'. Unfortunately, the effort and development time for a project cannot be used as

independent variables as in the above equation (e.g. Brooks 1975, Gordon 1977, Putnam 1978). A most extreme manifestation of this observation is summarised in Brooks' Law (Brooks 1975): 'Adding manpower to a late software project makes it later.'

The development time must be estimated in a similar way to the effort. A number of studies have shown that the development time can be quite accurately related to the development effort by an equation of the form

$$TD = a(ED)^b \qquad (2.3)$$

where *a* and *b* are empirically determined constants. If *ED* is measured in man-months and *TD* in months, *a* and *b* are typically in the range 2 to 4 and 0.25 to 0.4 respectively.

Equation (2.3) gives a nominal development time. Some models also indicate how the development effort will change if it is desired to change the development time from its nominal value. For example, in Putnam's (1978) model, this relationship goes as the inverse fourth power of the development time, implying a very heavy cost penalty for a small shortening of the development time. Additionally, some models give a lower bound below which the development schedule cannot be compressed, no matter how much extra effort is added to the project. For example, in Boehm's (1981) COCOMO model, this maximum compression is to 75% of the nominal value of *TD*.

Fig. 2.8. Distribution of effort by activity over the life of a system.

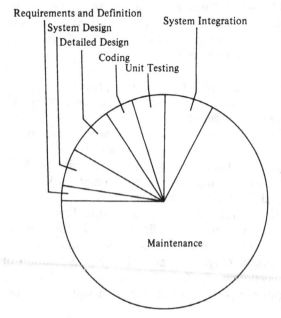

Fig. 2.9. Distribution of effort by activity over the development phases of a system.

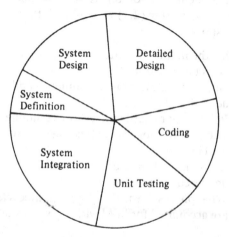

Any effort that is added to try to reduce this lower bound is lost in overheads such as those involved in maintaining communication between project members (Gordon 1977).

The division of the development schedule between phases must again be determined empirically from historical data. Typical percentage values are shown in table 2.3.

(You will find a bibliography on cost estimation models in section 3.2.)

Table 2.3. *Division of the system development schedule over phases*

Phase	Percentage of development schedule
Requirements	10–30
System design	17–27
Production	25–60
Integration and test	16–28

2.2.6 Is reliability quantifiable?

So far we have only dealt with quantitative modelling of the length and cost of a software development project and have said nothing about modelling any of the attributes of the software being developed. To a large extent the detailed aspects of many such attributes are not directly relevant to modelling the development process and accordingly are not dealt with until later in the book.

There is, however, one general class of software attributes which should have a considerable effect on how the development process is run and which have an even greater effect on the subsequent maintenance phase of the lifecycle. This is the class of attributes dealing with software quality, or more specifically, software reliability.

While software quality in general is a highly subjective matter and numerous studies have been made into methods of quantifying software reliability (for a bibliography see Anderson 1978 and Dunn 1982), the principal quantities of interest in modelling software reliability are:

- the number of errors remaining in the software;
- the mean time between failures (MTBF) of the operational software.

An estimate of the former is very useful as a guide to the efficiency of the debugging techniques that are being employed in the development process. An estimate of the MTBF is useful, not only as a means of checking that the reliability of the software will be operationally acceptable, but also as a method of estimating maintenance work load.

As in the case of software cost estimation, there are two distinctly different approaches to estimating the number of errors remaining in a piece of software: namely, theoretical and empirical methods.

Error count estimation models based on the metrics of software science (Halstead 1977) have been studied with some good results (e.g. Ottenstein 1979). As with the software science approach to cost estimation, these models have the disadvantage of not taking into account many of the qualitative features of the project at hand.

Empirical methods rely simply on estimation of remaining error count by comparison with figures collected on similar projects. In this respect they are similar to cost estimation by analogy rather than by algorithmic methods. No empirical algorithmic methods of error count estimation of similar detail to the cost estimation methods are known to the authors.

Models of the MTBF of software are most often based on error counts and error detection times. A certain amount of controversy still surrounds such models (e.g. Littlewood 1980, Goel 1980) but they are at least a useful guide to the reliability of software. Misra 1983 presents empirical data suggesting good fit with the Goel–Okumoto model.

The basic historical data which are required to calibrate nearly all empirical models of software reliability are:

(i) the number of errors detected per number of lines of code;
(ii) a measure of the time of detection of the error (e.g. in which development phase).

Other useful data are:

(iii) the type of error;
(iv) the method of detection (e.g. during module test, or due to catastrophic system failure).

Once such historical data has been recorded it can

be used in monitoring and predicting the quality of software under development, as we discuss in later sections.

2.2.7 Using historical data

This leads us on to the importance of historical data in all the aspects of estimating considered above, and hence to the importance of the Project Debriefing Report. Well-structured and accurate statistics can be used directly in estimations for a new project if the similarities are great enough. If they are not, then earlier statistics can often still provide upper or lower bounds for quantities being estimated and the opportunity to check estimates against such bounds must not be neglected.

As the statistics from earlier projects accumulate you will find yourself in a position to construct a cost estimating model (along the lines of Boehm's COCOMO method for instance) that encapsulates the productivity and quality of software development in your organisation. The importance of the Project Debriefing Report cannot therefore be over-emphasised.

2.3 Indicators

2.3.1 Why indicators?

In the previous two sections we have discussed how a project should typically progress through the development lifecycle. In this section we examine means by which actual progress can be monitored so as to determine the 'health', or otherwise, of the project.

Monitoring of a project's progress can take place at a number of levels. Commercial (or line) management will be interested in monitoring the overall progress of a project against its budget and timescale. A quality assurance function will be interested in monitoring the quality of the product being produced. The project manager will be interested in monitoring the detailed progress of individuals or teams within the project and using this information to provide input to line management and quality assurance monitoring functions. At the lowest level, individual programmers should be interested in monitoring their own progress and the quality of their produce.

In a project involving a number of people and developing thousands of lines of code over an extended period, informal monitoring of the progress of the project is generally unsatisfactory. By informal monitoring we mean, for example, line management asking the project manager for a qualitative assessment of how his project is going, or the project manager asking a programmer how long it will be until work package X is completed.

The disadvantages of such informal methods are twofold. Firstly, there is a strong psychological barrier to individuals admitting that work in their charge is going less well than was planned. Secondly, in a complex development project it is very difficult for an accurate qualitative assessment of progress to be made. For example, one section of a project may be finished a long way ahead of schedule, giving cause for optimism, but at the same time, perhaps unknown to the project manager, another part of the project may be heading towards severe schedule problems.

The method of monitoring that we advocate here and elaborate throughout the remainder of the book is based upon quantitative *indicators* of the health of the project. The main purpose of such indicators is to give an objective early warning of risk of problems related to budget, schedule or product quality. In other words, they help you to identify anomalous or unexpected behaviour in your project.

In order for an indicator to be objective it must be measurable and it must be capable of comparison against a previously established plan or against historical data. In order that the measurement error be small and that the indicator data be available sufficiently regularly to provide timely warnings, indicators must be measured over reasonably small sections of the project. The most suitable basis for such measurement is the project Work Breakdown Structure, the work package being the section of project over which indicators are measured.

We can summarise the above by the following definition: an indicator is a measurable project attribute recorded or accumulated on the completion of work packages and used in monitoring the progress of the project against its plan or against historical data.

2.3.2 Monitoring indicators

The definition of indicators makes a distinction between indicators which are compared against plan and those which are compared against historical data. This distinction is worth examining by considering some simple examples of indicators.

The most obvious measure of the progress of a work package against plan is the difference between the actual date of completion of the work package and that required by the project plan. The sum of this measure over all work packages in the project gives a measure of the overall health of the project. This indicator is formalised in, for example, the United States Air Force 'earned value' system (see, for example, Boehm 1981).

As a second example of an indicator let us consider a work package which involves the detailed design of a particular part of the system's software. On completion of detailed design, it will be possible to measure the amount of design documentation produced – for example, the number of lines of program design language. It is possible that the project plan (or the calculations which led to the plan) made an estimate of the amount of design documentation that should result from this part of the system. In this case the measure of design documentation can be used directly as an indicator. If the actual amount of design documentation is considerably greater than that estimated then this provides an early warning of possible budget and schedule problems as well as, for example, possible memory occupancy difficulties.

It is, however, unlikely that the plan will directly provide an estimate of the amount of design documentation. Rather, it is much more likely that the cost estimation model which was used to arrive at the plan will have used an estimate of the number of lines of code for each part of the system. To compare our measured indicator with this estimate we need to use historical data to convert amounts of design documentation to amounts of code (for example, a historical value for lines of code per line of program design language). The indicator can then be used as before.

As a final example we consider an indicator which is only compared with historical data. Consider a work package which involves the module testing of a part of the system. During the testing process each error detected is recorded. Upon completion the total number of errors detected per line of code is recorded as an indicator for this work package.

Although the project plan is most unlikely to include a 'planned number of errors' for each part of the system, this indicator can be compared against historical data similar to that contained in the sample Project Debriefing Report in chapter 9 (see figure 9.5). If the error count is very low compared with data collected in the development of software of similar complexity, then this might indicate inadequate testing. If, on the other hand, the count is too high, then it might indicate that the programmer is getting into difficulty with this part of the system. In either case a technical review of the work package is indicated.

These examples illustrate:

  (i) an indicator that can be compared directly against plan;
 (ii) an indicator that can be compared against plan by the use of historical data;
(iii) an indicator that can only be compared against historical data.

The distinction between the three cases is entirely dependent upon which attributes are included in the plan or are used to arrive at the plan. In the examples above it was assumed that:

  (i) expected work package completion dates are included in the plan;
 (ii) numbers of lines of code were used in arriving at the plan;
(iii) the amount of design documentation and the number of errors were not used in arriving at the plan.

Assumption (i) is fundamental to good project control, but assumptions (ii) and (iii) may not hold in every project. For example, the expected number of errors might be used to estimate the amount of manpower required in the testing activities of the project.

We see that there are three classes of indicator:

  (a) those which are fundamental to all projects;
  (b) those which are related to attributes used in arriving at the project plan of a given project
  (c) those which belong to neither category (a) nor (b).

Indicators in category (*b*) are especially important as they indicate the accuracy of the assumptions which went into planning the project. Such indicators will be related to attributes (cost drivers) drawn from table 2.1, the exact choice of attributes depending on which estimation scheme was used to model the project.

For each phase we discuss how you should go about selecting a suitable set of indicators, describe individual indicators in more detail, discuss how to measure them and suggest how you can use them in project monitoring. In chapter 9 you will find an example Project Debriefing Report containing indicators recorded during an actual software development project. For a general bibliography on software metrics you will find Cook 1982 useful.

2.4 Configuration management

2.4.1 Introduction to the problem

In setting the scene for the rest of the book, this chapter has dealt largely with management matters, describing a basic management framework within which the technical activities can be carried out efficiently. Having looked at the management of activities and of quality, we now extend the framework one step further in this section by considering the management of the deliverable items themselves.

The flow diagram proposed earlier for the deliverable items that will be generated during and after development can really only be considered to be a summary: the System Design Specification may in fact be a number of separate documents or a hierarchy of diagrams; the System Code will consist of the source code of hundreds or even thousands of modules plus their corresponding object files; during System Integration there will be command files for the build process, integrated systems, PROMs containing blown-in software, and so on; in the Post-Acceptance Phase different versions and releases of the system, its components and its documentation will arise out of the process of enhancement and correction.

It is not difficult to see that a development team can produce hundreds or thousands of discrete deliverable items. The entire set of them forms a web of interdependencies with items generally relying on the correctness of superior or preceding items. Moreover, with the constant need for reworking, correction and enhancement at *all* stages of development and maintenance, any item may exist in a number of different versions, any one version of an item being related to particular versions of other items.

Preventing this delicate complex of related items from disintegrating is the problem attacked by the disciplines of System Configuration Management.

The problem can assume such proportions and the machinery necessary to solve it be so extensive that you may find a need for a separate Configuration Management Plan that concentrates precisely on the topic and supplements the Quality Management Plan in giving instructions to your staff as to how they are to carry out and control their work.

2.4.2 Baselines

Throughout development and after delivery, the system will be subject to change: because errors are discovered and corrected, because design or implementation decisions are overturned in favour of others, because the requirement on the system changes. The natural outcome of these perturbations along the development path is that any deliverable item might, at any one time, exist in a number of versions.

It therefore becomes essential for us to be able to identify out of the entire collection which items together form a consistent subset – often referred to as a *baseline*. A baseline should not be seen as a 'snapshot', a time-slice of what exists at a particular moment. It is a selection of one version of each deliverable item, versions that will typically have been produced at different times but that have this property of being mutually consistent – of referring to the same state of the system, at a particular stage of development.

How can the baseline idea help us? Firstly, a baseline serves as a form of checkpoint, particularly during development. Should things go wrong after the baseline has been taken, we can always return to the most recent and appropriate baseline – there at least we knew where we were. Secondly, it can act as a clearly identified starting point for two or more diverging development paths – this much they had in common when they started on their separate ways, a common design for instance. Thirdly, being internally consistent, a baseline is an ideal object for formal review by your development team and perhaps by your client. Fourthly, a baseline that includes a tested system can be formally issued: for evaluation, for training, for use as a test aid on other related systems, or finally for putting to use in its real role with your client.

'Taking a baseline' is clerically a simple task. Two things need to be done:

- making a list of the component deliverable items that are to form the baseline and which version of each is required;
- ensuring that copies of each baselined version of the deliverable items are placed in the project archive where they will remain inviolate.

The crucial activity is of course determining which versions of all the deliverable items are required. It is here that the consistency of the baselined components is ensured. Table 2.4 contains a checklist of the different deliverable items that may need to come under formal control.

When you intend taking baselines is something that you should identify early on, either in your Project Plan, in your Quality Management Plan or, if you have one, certainly in your Configuration Management Plan. There are a number of standard places where baselines are appropriate though circumstances may change this list. Figure 2.10 shows in matrix form which deliverable items might typically appear in which baseline.

2.4.3 Issuing deliverable items

Whilst baselining is largely a matter of the development team's keeping control of its own output, there is an orthogonal need to issue deliverable items to parties outside the team or for special purposes within the team.

Typical deliverable items that are issued, especially to people outside the team, include:

- specifications of hardware/software interfaces,

Table 2.4. *A checklist of potential candidates for configuration control*

Requirement Specification
Functional Specification
System Design Specification
Software Interface Specifications
Hardware Interface Specifications
Subsystem Specifications
Database Specifications
Module Specifications
Module Code files
Macro definitions
Module object files
Unit Test Descriptions
Linked subsystems
System Build command files
System binary files
PROMs containing software
PROM maps
Acceptance Test Specification
Acceptance Test Description
Job control language procedures
Operators' manuals
Training material
Project Plan
Quality Management Plan
Configuration Management Plan

Fig. 2.10. Sample baseline contents.

Deliverable item	Baseline 1	2	3	4	5	6	7	8+
Functional Specification	Y	Y	Y	Y	Y	Y	Y	Y
System Models	Y		Y	Y				Y
Project Plan	Y							
Quality Management Plan		Y	Y					
Acceptance Specification	Y							
System Design Specification			Y	Y	Y	Y	Y	Y
Acceptance Test Description			Y	Y	Y	Y		
Module Specifications				Y	Y	Y	Y	Y
Module Code					Y	Y	Y	Y
Unit Test Descriptions					Y	Y		Y
User Documentation						Y		Y
Training Schedules						Y		Y
System Conversion Schedule						Y		
Running System							Y	Y
Error Reports								Y
Enhancement Requests								Y
Environment Changes								Y

Note: Baselines 1 to 7 are taken along the development path.

Baselines 8+ are taken in the maintenance cycles.

- specifications of software interfaces,
- early prototypes,
- early versions of the system for performance measurements,
- early versions of the system in a form suitable for checking correct meshing with the hardware.

Invariably, it is vital that we know which version of a deliverable item has gone to someone else. The same is true even when items need to be issued within the team. There is an obvious need therefore for all deliverable items to have a clearly recorded status – a version number or creation date or whatever, something that can uniquely place that version in the development history of the deliverable item. How often an item has its version number incremented is a question for your local situation but as a general rule we can say that as soon as a deliverable item changes after it has entered a baseline or been issued it should be up-versioned.

Recording a baseline clearly requires us to list every item included together with its version number. It can sometimes be convenient to create the baseline physically by copying all the constituent deliverable items and keeping them together in a single binder, on a single disc pack or in a single disc directory. The aim always is to be in a position to re-create the baseline should the need arise.

2.4.4 The mechanisms of configuration control

The sophistication of your configuration control will be governed by the size of your project and by the extent of your interface with the outside world. As the number of concurrent activities in a project increases the chances of getting the products of the development process into an inconsistent state also increase. If you are producing software products your problems will be greater than if you are producing a single site system.

In product development, configuration control will often require to be on such a scale that it must be resourced and managed much as quality management or project management are. Bersoff 1981 emphasises the need in product development for investment, organisation, planning and man-

agement of configuration control. You may need to employ databases or commercial packages to support it. Roles may need to be defined and staff made responsible for the tasks: librarians in particular.

If version control is not a significant problem in your environment much simpler mechanisms may suffice, possibly as a minimum consisting of some forms and simple procedures. In this case descriptions of these mechanisms could be covered in your Quality Management Plan without the need for a separate Configuration Plan.

It is important to separate two sides of configuration management: the way in which items are placed under configuration control and thereafter changed (the organisational aspect), and how configuration control activities are recorded, especially in the deliverable items themselves (the physical aspect).

Before a baseline is taken or an item is issued it should be subjected to some form of review that has as its aim determining and recording the precise status of the item or set of items. This is a matter for local management procedures but one can expect that the greater the level of 'exposure' generated by the issue (e.g. to an external body) or the greater the importance of the baseline being taken (e.g. one embodying some major design decisions) the greater the level of authority you might demand for making the issue or taking the baseline.

By definition, a baseline never changes. However, you might take a new one with the same components if you want to capture some significant changes that have been made to components within it after the first baseline had been taken. The need for prior review and careful recording remains.

It makes sense to extend this idea to issued deliverable items. That is, having issued version 10 you cannot re-issue it. You can only issue version 11. Review and recording are again necessary but there is a further requirement here: that of determining which other deliverable items are affected by the change to the issued item. The obvious example is that of a change to an issued program source module. All issued systems containing the changed module should be re-issued at a new version level.

There is a clear case for a formal procedure to control changes to issued deliverable items especially where those changes could have cost and/or timescale implications for your project. You could well be obliged (let alone wise) to obtain approval for new funding or extended timescales before agreeing to make changes (to a Functional Specification for instance). This process generally takes a few basic steps that can be elaborated to fit local practices:

- a change request is raised perhaps to report a suspected bug or to request some change in functionality,
- the implications of the change are established and reviewed,
- the cost and timescale implications are evaluated and presented for approval to the appropriate body,
- iterations possibly occur in order to find a compromise between the ideal change and the incurred cost changes,
- the authorising body approves the change,
- the project manager schedules the required changes,
- configuration control procedures are followed in order to capture the change and its ripple effects clearly.

Establishing the extent of the ripple effects of a change is a critical part of this process. What other items need to be reworked, re-assessed, rebuilt, recompiled, etc? This requires that the relationships between deliverable items are carefully recorded either manually on forms and lists or perhaps via database facilities. Whichever way the record is kept, it must make the complete listing of (possibly) affected items foolproof.

In addition to ensuring that inter-relationships are recorded, your procedures should ensure that each deliverable item contains or carries with it in some way its version and change history. This will detail the dates when new versions were created and how they differed from the preceding one. Module source code is a simple example where change histories can be kept inside the item, here as comment in the module header. Commercial operating systems often provide help in this simple case but in the more general configuration management area you may need to fall back on clerical methods and old-fashioned discipline.

3

Development techniques

3.1 Introduction

Having established the framework for the phased development of a system we now go on to look at the techniques that are available to you during those phases.

The purpose of this chapter is not to present all known techniques in an encyclopaedic way. Rather, it is to present sufficient information on a representative selection to allow you to make a first selection of a subset for your own project. As you read each précis, you can decide which of the techniques presented are not of interest and those that might be.

In the subsequent phase-orientated chapters each technique is presented with further detail in the context of the phase or phases where it is of use. Thus techniques applicable to, say, the System Definition Phase can be read and compared. Should you still feel that a particular technique is or may be of use, you can refer for complete information to the source material listed in the bibliography.

Similarly, all of the descriptions of the techniques in later chapters are necessarily simplifications. Remember that they are given not so that you can learn how to use the technique – for that you must turn to the authoritative references and suppliers. The purpose is solely to give you sufficient flavour of each technique for you to judge whether further evaluation could be worthwhile.

For each candidate technique you should aim to adopt, adapt or reject it. For your project as a whole you should aim to put together a coherent set of techniques, each either in its original form or adapted to suit your own purposes. You might find it a useful exercise to record for each candidate technique why you adopted/adapted/rejected it, and to place that record in your Project Debriefing Report.

You should remember that techniques are not necessarily mutually exclusive and you may choose to bring several to bear on your problem area, each attacking one part of your problem. Figure 3.1 summarises the phases where the techniques that we cover are principally applicable. Again, two techniques may overlap in their phase coverage, but this does not necessarily mean that they clash.

No list of computing methodologies can ever be complete and to find a place in this book each methodology has had to satisfy a number of criteria:

(i) it has had to come to our notice at some time prior to publication,
(ii) sufficient information must be publicly available for potential users to make an initial judgement of its value in their own situations,
(iii) it must either be commercially supported (for example, through courses or the sale of software) or be reasonably well described in the literature.

Though generally *necessary* these are not *sufficient* conditions and the absence of a methodology should not in any way be construed as a comment on it.

There have been many locally produced 'home-brew' techniques and systems that will be of interest for the ideas they contain to any one developing a software development environment, but that do not satisfy any of the above criteria. For these you will need to refer to bibliographies such as Hausen 1981*b* and those within the text. There are also many other proprietary systems that overlap or are similar to those we present here. Whenever possible we have included bibliographies for these so that you can include them in your own surveys.

With the increasing interest in making software development into an engineering discipline, comparisons and critiques of the available techniques often appear in the literature: e.g. Basili 1981, Bergland 1979 and 1981, DoI 1981, Freeman 1980*b* and 1982, Glass 1980 and 1982, Hausen 1981*b*, Horowitz 1975, Jensen 1979, Lewis 1982, McGowan 1977, Marmor-Squires 1977*a* and 1977*b*, Miller 1979*b*, Peters 1977 and 1979, Pressman 1982, Ramsey 1979, Riddle 1978*b* and 1980*c*, and Yeh 1977 and 1979.

Two recent reviews in particular have investigated the extent to which certain techniques fit in with concepts embodied in Ada (Ada is a registered trademark of the US Government, Ada Joint Program Office) and the APSE (Ada Programming Support Environment). Despite this apparently specialised approach both reviews contain valuable guidelines on the techniques, outside the Ada context, and also on the criteria that can be used in evaluating and comparing techniques.

Freeman 1982 contains a short paper that 'identifies requirements for software development methodologies'. You will find checklists based on this paper later in this chapter. In addition, Freeman 1982 also contains the results of a questionnaire-based survey of 48 methodologies. The survey gathered general facts about them and, relying solely on the questionnaire returns, aimed to determine how each could be used in an Ada development environment.

The questionnaire produced data on 24 methodologies and this is presented in a number of ways, including

Fig. 3.1. The coverage of phases by the techniques discussed.

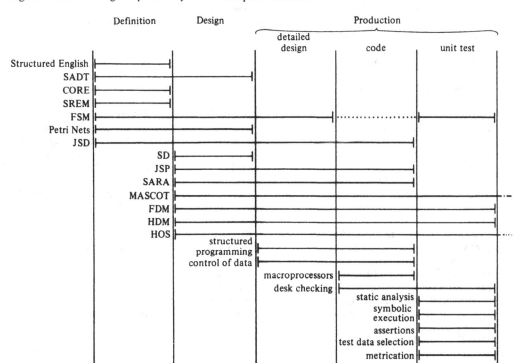

- which phases of the development process are covered,
- which methodologies are applicable to which application types,
- which technical concepts are supported,
- what deliverable items are produced and what form they take,
- what quality assurance methods are invoked,
- to what extent the methodology is supported with automated tools.

Table 3.1. *Techniques canvassed in Freeman 1982*

Methodology mnemonic	Full name of methodology
ACM/PCM	Active and Passive Component Modelling
DADES	DAta oriented DESign
DSSAD	Data Structured Systems Analysis and Design
DSSD	Data Structured Systems Development
EDM	Evolutionary Design Methodology
GEIS	Gradual Evolution of Information Systems
HOS[a]	Higher Order Software
IBMFSD-SEP	Adaptation of IBM Federal Systems Division Software Engineering Practices
IESM	Information Engineering Specification Method
ISAC	Information Systems work and Analysis of Changes
JSD[a]	Jackson System Development
MERISE	
NIAM	Nijssen's Information Analysis Method
PRADOS	PRojekt Abwicklungs und DOkumentationsSystem
REMORA	
SADT[a]	Structured Analysis & Design Technique
SARA[a]	System ARchitect's Apprentice
SD	System Developer
SA-SD[a]	Structured Analysis and Structured Design
SDM	System Development Methodology
SEPN	Software Engineering Procedures Notebook
SREM[a]	Software Requirements Engineering Methodology
STRADIS	STRuctured Analysis, Design and Implementation of information Systems
USE	User Software Engineering

[a] Described in this book.

Of these 24 techniques six are explicitly described in this book and references are given to a number of others. You may find amongst them techniques that suit your own application area and organisational environment. Not all of them are to any extent in the public domain or fully developed as methodologies. However, when you are carrying out your own evaluations you may find the criteria and questionnaire in Freeman 1982 a useful starting point. Table 3.1 lists the 24 methodologies for which data was obtained.

The UK Department of Industry funded a study published in 1981 (DoI 1981) that took a more pragmatic approach to the comparison business and, in looking at candidates for an 'Ada-based system development methodology', applied four of the techniques covered in this book –

Table 3.2. *Techniques described in DoI 1981*

CADES	Computer Aided Design and Evaluation System
CORE	COntrolled Requirements Expression[a]
Fagan inspections[a]	
GAMMA	
HDM	Hierarchical Development Methodology[a]
HOS	Higher Order Software[a]
The Rigorous Approach	
JSD	Jackson Structured Development[a]
JSP	Jackson Structured Programming[a]
MASCOT	Modular Approach to Software, Construction, Operation and Test[a]
PSL/PSA[a]	Problem Statement Language/ Problem Statement Analyser
SADT	Structured Analysis and Design Technique[a]
SARA	System Architect's Apprentice[a]
SDL	System Definition Language
SDS	Software Development System[a]
SPECK	
SREM	Software Requirements Engineering Methodology[a]
Structured Systems Analysis[a]	
VDM	Vienna Development Method
Warnier–Orr[a]	
WELLMADE	

[a] Described in this book.

CORE, MASCOT, JSD and SARA – to the same problem, generating programs in Ada via each. In addition, brief assessments based on the available literature were given for the techniques shown in table 3.2.

Ramsey 1979 reports on an analysis of Structured Design, Jackson Structured Programming, Higher Order Software and Warnier's Logical Construction of Programs, looked at particularly from the human factors viewpoint. Comparisons of the techniques and their relative strengths and weaknesses were carried out and recorded.

Matching technique characteristics with problem characteristics

The methods you choose will be determined by two factors:

  (i) the problem to be solved;
  (ii) the project environment.

The first of these factors concerns relating methods and tools to the technical characteristics of the problem. The second concerns relating methods and tools to the managerial and commercial characteristics of the environment in which the problem is being solved.

This suggests that we need to determine the possible characteristics of problems and projects and to determine the areas of appropriateness and applicability of techniques and tools. Such a two-sided analysis would allow us to make a rational choice of technique in any given situation. This requires having the ability to categorise both techniques and projects with some measure of precision to identify and match their characteristics.

The act of choice is in a sense a two-way process. Not only will the choice of techniques available and the characteristics of the project determine which techniques are used. The characteristics of a project might be changed by management to accommodate a particular technique. This can only happen for characteristics that can be changed by management – budget, staff quality, computer resource levels and so on – and one does not generally have the luxury of being able to change the characteristics of the problem.

Is the decision to use/not use a method or tool a commercial or a technical decision? Do the technical answers form only part of the input to the commercial decision making process? Assessing in hard cash terms the benefits of using technique X is probably as difficult a process currently as assessing how much code is to be written. And yet many *tools* are used without much of a conscious decision – perhaps out of habit, perhaps by chance. Most development projects use compilers, editors, OS filing systems . . . We 'know' they are a good thing. We sometimes even develop our own for a given project. But nobody could *prove* their worth unequivocally, particularly when it comes to choosing PASCAL over C, or buying a screen editor to supplant the line editor supplied by the computer manufacturer.

Projects hand-build their own tools and techniques too. Most projects build some more-or-less general 'module test harness' to suit their own purposes. Development of such a beast may well be planned in from the beginning on the grounds that you know you'll need one and end up building one whether or not you put time in the plan for it. The need for a simulator for some special hardware is more often recognised earlier on and budgeted for.

The idea of planning to do something because you will do it anyway extends into adoption of new techniques. Good designers use 'their own' design techniques, for instance. It would be interesting to see how often they have invented through trial and error some amalgam or subset of the publicised 'proprietary' brands. We believe that this is so commonly the case that it makes great sense to invest in tools and techniques in the same frame of mind that one budgets for a simulator or buys a C compiler.

In the following two checklists we have collected some of the characteristics that we feel it is important to establish about your project and your problem before thinking about choosing techniques and tools. These questions will suggest characteristics that you should look for in new techniques when looking for a match with your problem. The third checklist then lists the characteristics you should examine in each technique when looking for that match. As a minimum, your answers to the questions should show you where you may need to bring some technique to bear on particular problem areas.

Your research into the different candidates

should take you on to the literature via the bibliographies, to suppliers (in the cases where the techniques are commercially supported), to the originators of techniques, to existing users and to reviews and analyses frequently carried out by various organisations. As examples, the Department of Industry in the UK and the National Bureau of Standards in the USA have both carried out surveys of definition and design techniques and tools in the last few years. (See DoI 1981 and NBS 1981 for example.)

One of the crucial characteristics that one needs to identify in any technique is the point where users must exercise intuition, experience or whatever – in other words, where they are on their own. This is the point where the technique isolates the non-mechanical decision making. Knowing where this point is will allow you to concentrate your efforts where they will be most effective. It is not always readily identifiable!

A checklist of project characteristics

- What is the overall budget? Is there an allocation in the budget for the procurement of tools and methods, training in their use, purchase and support of the necessary support hardware etc.? What are the cost savings that one is looking for in using them?
- What is the likely team size? What communications problems could therefore arise? What should one expect of a technique in such an environment?
- What is the quality of the staff? Are they up to mathematical design techniques, VHL languages, etc.? How much could they take after some training? What does this say about the 'difficulty' of technique that could be accommodated?
- What is the experience and background of the staff? Have they used similar techniques before? Are they receptive or would some persuasion be necessary? What does this say about the introduction of new techniques?
- Do the team members have appropriate skills? Do they have those necessary for the techniques appropriate to the problem in hand?
- What levels of quality control and quality

assurance are being required of the project? What demands do they make on techniques and automated tools, for instance as regards auditability, traceability, visibility?
- What form will maintenance and enhancement take after delivery? Do the tools and techniques square with continuing support of the system in the evolutionary phase?
- What is the project's delivery date? Will the tools and methods make achievement more or less likely? For instance, might they impose an unacceptably long learning time and/or set-up time?

A checklist of problem characteristics

- How big is the problem? How many levels of decomposition could one expect in a top-down approach? How many constraining features are there, such as different peripheral types, databases, complex man/machine interfaces, complex timing relationships, complex data interactions? How much of a problem will design control be? In terms of volume and the communication problems implied?
- What level of reliability is required? Must the system be algebraically proven correct or will traditional testing suffice? What are the implications for analysis of test coverage, path coverage and other forms of static analysis? How much will the tools and methods help here?
- What are the properties of the host environment? How high a level does the virtual machine offered by the hosting OS achieve? Do any packages or middleware assist? What power is devolved to peripheral processors? How many arithmetic and logical processors are there? Does the virtual machine offer atomic semaphore, queue, stack, list . . . actions? Are multiple processes supported? Are processes allowed to share code, share data, communicate formally . . .? In summary, what are the primitive operations that can be assumed in design? Does the technique allow you to map onto the virtual machine that they define?

- What are the space constraints imposed by the target system? Is it tight? Is there plenty of room? Is smallness therefore a prime consideration? How much does the technique take this into account?
- What are the time constraints on the system? Is it time-critical, e.g. loss of life if too slow? Are the time constraints localised and severe or general and normal (e.g. high speed response to sensor as opposed to terminal response within one second)? Can the system take 'as long as it needs' within reason, on the other hand? What are the throughput requirements? Can these be devolved onto system components during design? How well does the design/ requirements technique handle this?
- Do parts of the system interact with varying temporal order? I.e. is synchronisation of components to be considered or does the system single-thread its way through time? Thus, should techniques be considered that handle such interactions explicitly? Is the system real-time or off-line in nature?
- Is the system a data processing or control processing system primarily? How much can these two aspects be clearly separated? To what extent can different techniques be applied to the two aspects separately? Can time be factored out first, leaving a collection of data-processing sub-problems?
- Will the system appear in a number of different versions? Will it be used at more than one site? Will it be enhanced continually, with the resulting proliferation of different release levels at perhaps many different sites? What is the likely scale of this configuration control problem?
- To what extent is the system forming the kernel for a series or collection of related products? How much will there be a problem of resolving conflicting demands on its functionality, performance and maintenance? What will this mean for the configuration control problem?
- What is the lifetime of the system to be and what level of change can be expected? Who will do this work and will all the original development facilities be available to them?

How much of a d... techniques and tools getting locked into environments or requiring special should those technique? How much specifically support or ... tools evolving design for insta... supporting an

- Is the system to interact or ... with other systems or devices ...municate developed? What are the impli...ng specially special handling of interfaces, p...ons for etc.? What are the implications fo... the need for simulations etc.?
- Has early prototyping been considered important? To what extent do the tools and techniques specifically or potentially support model making and prototyping?
- Is there in existence a fully worked through functional description of the required system? Is it in a form amenable to machine processing? Does it need to be transformed into a more acceptable form first? If it does not exist, does there need to be a preliminary stage in which the full form is produced? How many different parties would be involved in such an exercise? How will the tools and techniques help here?

A checklist of technique characteristics (based on Freeman 1982)

The first group of questions relate to the technical aspects:

- How understandable are the deliverable items of the technique by someone without expert knowledge of using it?
- How easily can the use of the techniques be passed on to others?
- To what extent could the deliverable items (or parts of them) be used in other developments?
- What level of computerised support is available (or could be developed easily)?
- What phases and stages of the lifecycle are supported?
- What range of applications is the technique claimed/proven to be appropriate for?
- What level of usage has it seen within the industry?
- How well does the technique highlight where

decisions are [m]ade and what the alternative c[o] [consequ]ences are?
- How repeat[ably is] the output of the technique [when] used by different people?
- How stra[ight]forwardly can changes be made to the de[rived] able items in response to changes [at a] higher level?
- What [have] other workers' experiences with the te[chn]ique been?
- Doe[s th]e tool or technique affect the timing or [sizi]ng of the system in an acceptable or de[sir]able way?

The second group of questions relate to managerial aspects:

- How well does the technique mesh with and support managerial activities: scheduling, estimating, planning, monitoring and so on?
- Does the technique help or hinder teamwork?
- Does it produce clearly identifiable deliverable items? In particular, are there clear criteria for telling when they are complete?
- Does the technique fit with the regime for configuration management?
- What benefits can one expect from using the technique in the phase(s) where it is useful?
- What are the net benefits given the relative importance of these phases and the deliverables produced?
- What will it cost to acquire and use the technique?
- What will be the overhead costs for management of the technique?
- Is the tool or technique available for use now?
- Can it be made available for delivery to the client as part of the maintenance package?
- Are sufficient, good quality documentation and training available?

Information sources on techniques and tools

This book is necessarily a selection of some of the techniques generally accessible to the software practitioner at the time of writing. Techniques evolve, some die away, some are born, software companies put new tools on the market.

To keep your knowledge current you should scan the following journals for relevant material:

ACM Computing Surveys (ACM)
Acta Informatica (Springer-Verlag)
Bell System Technical Journal (Bell Labs)
BIT (Nordisk Tidskrift for Informationsbehandling)
Communications of the ACM (ACM)
Computer (IEEE)
Computer Journal (British Computer Society)
IBM Systems Journal (IBM)
IEEE Transactions on Software Engineering (IEEE)
Journal of the ACM (ACM)
Journal of Systems and Software (Elsevier Science Publishing)
SIGPLAN Notices (ACM SIGPLAN)
Software – Practice and Experience (John Wiley)
Software Engineering Notes (ACM SIGSOFT)

A number of international conferences are held regularly and the proceedings of these are useful sources of interesting developments:

AFIPS National Computer Conference (AFIPS Press)
ACM Annual Conference (ACM)
COMPCON (IEEE Computer Society Press)
COMPSAC (IEEE Computer Society Press)
International Computing Symposium (North Holland)
International Conference on Software Engineering (IEEE)

This book is principally about techniques for software development rather than about the tools that exist to support the techniques. Although we give indications of where tools are available, the market place changes too quickly to make any greater detail sensible. Up-to-date catalogues and surveys can be obtained from bodies such as the Department of Industry and the Computing Services Association in the United Kingdom, and Reifer Consultants, Software Research Associates and the National Bureau of Standards in the USA.

(See Reifer 1981, SRA 1981, DACS 1979, Houghton 1980, 1981, 1982, 1983.) In the USA, tools in the public domain can be obtained from public repositories such as the National Technical Information Service (see Houghton 1983 again).

3.2 Cost estimation models

In this section we give very brief descriptions of some of the better known cost estimation models. You are referred to the original literature or to the reviews listed in the bibliography at the end of this section for more details of these and the other models for which only references are given.

IBM

The IBM model of Walston and Felix (Walston 1977) is based on data from 60 projects undertaken by the IBM Federal Systems Division. The best fit to the data gave an estimation algorithm of the form (2.2) with $c = 0.91$, that is, an almost linear relationship of the form (2.1). In attempting to account for fluctuations about this best fit, the model uses a productivity index, I, obtained from 29 cost drivers using the equation

$$I = \sum_{i=1}^{29} W_i X_i$$

where $X_i = -1, 0$ or $+1$ depending on how the ith attribute is likely to affect the project (e.g. low, average or high effect). The weights W_i are given by

$$W_i = 0.5 \log_{10}(PC_i)$$

where PC_i is the ratio of productivities resulting from a change from a low to high rating for the ith cost driver (as determined from historical data). The actual productivity in deliverable lines of code per day is taken to be linearly related to I.

SLIM

Putnam's work on Rayleigh curve models of the software development lifecycle (Putnam 1978, Putnam 1979) has led to a commercially available cost estimation model known as SLIM. The principal estimation equation in SLIM is

$$S = CK^{1/3}(TD)^{4/3}.$$

Here S and TD are respectively the number of deliverable source instructions and development time (as defined in section 2.2), K is the total lifecycle manpower effort (which can be approximately related to the development effort ED of section 2.2.3 by $ED = 0.4K$) and C is a constant which must be determined from historical data and which is representative of the level of sophistication of the development technology available.

The SLIM computer program, which is available in the United States and from PACTEL in the UK, provides in addition to development time and cost estimates information on risk, feasibility, estimated CPU time requirements and several other quantities of use in project planning.

PRICE-S

The RCA PRICE-S model of Freiman 1979 is another commercially available cost estimation model. The PRICE-S computer program is based on an unpublished heuristic algorithm which takes as input a number of cost drivers, principal of which is the number of source or object code instructions to be produced, and produces cost and schedule estimates as well as other optional project management data as output.

A second program, PRICE-SL can be used to estimate system maintenance costs. The program uses outputs from PRICE-S as inputs along with a number of user supplied parameters such as the expected life, growth and usage of the software.

COCOMO

The COCOMO (Constructive Cost Model) developed at TRW is one of the most refined and most accessible cost estimation methodologies, being described in considerable detail in the important book Boehm 1981.

Boehm defines 'basic', 'intermediate' and 'detailed' COCOMO models. The basic model is defined by power law relations such as those given in equations 2.2 and 2.3, where different values of the historically determined constants r and a are used depending on the overall type of project ('organic', 'semidetached' or 'embedded'). The intermediate model goes one step further in detail by introducing effort multipliers for r based on the value assigned to 15 cost drivers. For both the basic and intermediate models, effort and schedule are distributed across the project phases using percentages based on historical data and on the overall type and size of the project.

The basic and intermediate COCOMO models apply the estimation equations to the system as a whole and effort is distributed amongst activities in a top-down fashion. Detailed COCOMO, on the other hand, applies a bottom-up approach, first dividing the system into a three-level hierarchy of system, subsystem and modules and then building up the total effort by first applying the estimation algorithms at the module level and then at the subsystem level. Additionally, detailed COCOMO uses different effort multipliers for the different phases of the lifecycle.

COCOMO has been calibrated using a database of 63 TRW projects which are listed in Boehm's book, where details of how to calibrate the model against your own database can also be found.

Bailey–Basili meta-model

Bailey and Basili describe a meta-model which allows the development of effort estimation equations which are best adapted to a given development environment. The resultant estimation model will be similar to that of IBM and COCOMO.

Schneider model

All of the models described above are purely empirically derived. Schneider 1978 has derived estimation equations based on Halstead's 1977 software science theory. The resultant effort equation is of the power law form (2.2).

Bibliography
Reviews of cost estimation models
Boehm 1980, Boehm 1981, Mohanty 1981, Shooman 1979, Zelkowitz 1980.

Descriptions of specific estimation models
Aron 1969, Bailey 1981, Black 1977, Boehm 1981, Buck 1971, Farr 1965, Frederic 1974, Freiman 1979, Halstead 1977, Herd 1977, James 1978, Kustanowitz 1977, Nelson 1966, 1976, Putnam 1978, Putnam 1979, Ruby 1975, Schneider 1978, Walston 1977, Wolverton 1974.

3.3 Structured English

Structured English is a simple notational technique that enables you to write Functional Specifications with increased precision and testability. It relies on the use of a number of sentence templates to which the writer must limit himself and which are hierarchically structured to reflect the successive levels of refinement of the system's functions.

The technique is essentially manual although simple tools can easily be developed to support it. It bears a close similarity to PDL – Program Design Language – but is specifically orientated to describing requirements. It can also be seen as a manual analogue of PSL/PSA.

It is appropriate to small systems where the establishment of automated methods would not be cost-effective, and where the number of entities and relationships is low. It represents the minimal amount of formality that can be brought to System Definition, just above no formality at all.

By suitably 'disguising' the templates, a Functional Specification in structured prose should be acceptable to clients if they are prepared to accept the stilted prose and hierarchical breakdown of the statements.

3.4 PSL/PSA

PSL/PSA is a toolkit for the systems analyst and designer – essentially a computer-aided technique for documentation. The results of each of the activities in the system development process are recorded as statements expressed in the Problem Statement Language (PSL). PSL statements are machine-processable and are maintained in a database. Reports and analyses can be derived from the descriptions of the problem held in the database using tools in the Problem Statement Analyser (PSA). It is generally used to greatest effect during Project Definition and System Design.

PSL/PSA is available commercially in several countries including the UK and the USA. It is a *support* tool; in other words you need to have a methodology with which you wish to use it. It has been used to support a variety of other methodologies in the System Definition and Design Phases – CORE, MASCOT, and Structured Design amongst others. It is an evolving system that many users have made the starting point for their own techniques.

It is unlikely that the cost of acquiring and using PSL/PSA can be justified for the occasional small project. Its strengths are best realised on large projects, particularly those consisting of more than one major subsystem, where the numbers of entities is large or where their interrelationships are complex. In these situations it gives the designers a more secure hold on the system than would be obtainable by purely manual means.

PSL/PSA recognises the importance of accessibility of documentation during all the phases of the development lifecycle. It sees the development of a system from initial concept to operational form as consisting of a number of activities each of which makes the concept more concrete, the output from one stage becoming the input for the next.

Users might not find PSL/PSA's terminology immediately comprehensible but with appropriately designed report tools in the PSA this problem can be circumvented.

3.5 Structured Analysis – SA

Structured Analysis is a generic term for analysis methodologies which approach system definition in a 'structured' way. Much has been written about Structured Analysis (see the bibliography in chapter 5) and courses on its practice are available from companies such as Yourdon Inc.

Many of the ideas of Structured Analysis are included in or are related to other methodologies (such as SADT and SREM) which are described elsewhere in this chapter. Here we take Structured Analysis to mean explicitly the methodology described in De Marco's book (1978) which provides an excellent basis for learning Structured Analysis techniques.

De Marco describes a methodology for progressing from a user requirement through to a Structured Functional Specification using the following tools of Structured Analysis:

- Data Flow Diagrams,
- Data Dictionary,
- Structured English,
- Decision Tables,
- Decision Trees.

Data flow diagrams are used to show the movement of data through the existing or proposed system. The data dictionary is used to define the data flowing through the system while Structured English, decision tables and decision trees are used to describe the processes which act on the data flows.

As the name implies, Structured Analysis can be used right from the earliest part of the Inception Phase for analysing, possibly vague, user requirements. This is done by modelling existing systems in terms of 'physical' data flow diagrams and transforming these through logical data flow diagrams of the existing system to logical data flow diagrams of the proposed system and thence to potential 'physical' data flow diagrams of the proposed system. Alternatively the Structured Analysis tools can be used simply as a means of transforming a user Requirement Specification for the proposed system into a concise and easily verified Functional Specification which will serve as a firm base for the use of structured design techniques during the Design Phase.

Structured Analysis is aimed largely at projects involving commercial data processing where there is a high correlation between data flows within an organisation and those in a proposed data processing system. It may, however, prove useful as one of your specification methods for any system involving substantial flows of data.

Structured Analysis can be applied in a purely manual fashion or it can be automated to varying degrees. (PSL/PSA and SDS/RSRE are two possible routes to the automation of Structured Analysis.) This gives you the opportunity to try Structured Analysis at very little cost and to postpone any investment in automated tools until you have shown it to be a success. In this latter respect, De Marco provides many useful hints on selling Structured Analysis to your client.

3.6 Structured Analysis and Design Technique – SADT

SADT (SADT is a trademark of SofTech Inc.) is a graphical language for describing systems, together with a methodology for producing such descriptions. It can be applied on a variety of systems (computer-based or otherwise) and is of particular use during requirements analysis and software design. It works on the divide-and-conquer principle.

On the procedural side SADT provides methods for:

- handling complex problems in a structured fashion through rigorous decomposition,
- defining and managing the roles and relationships of the personnel involved (author, commenter, reader, expert, instructor, librarian etc.),
- recording and presenting the results of decisions,
- recording and presenting the results of interviews, analysis and design,
- ensuring quality (e.g. accuracy and completeness) through review.

SADT works with *models*. Each *model* consists of a hierarchy of diagrams describing a system from a particular *viewpoint*. Thus a given system might be represented by a number of models corresponding to different viewpoints. This approach is also adopted in CORE. Such models might, for instance, be from the operator's viewpoint, the manufacturing viewpoint or the sales viewpoint.

As a graphical language, SADT uses diagrams with well-developed syntax, semantics and pragmatics.

Models may share common detail. Consistency between them (and hence their respective viewpoints) can be verified in the SADT diagrams for each model and via the SADT concept of a mechanism – a (sub-)model that is to be shared by other models or whose implementation may be changed. Typically a mechanism encapsulates a major design decision. By definition it describes something which can be separately specified, designed and implemented.

As a notation, SADT can be operated manually, but in large projects some level of automation is necessary. To this end, a combination of SADT and PSL/PSA has been used successfully. UNIX-based tools that assist diagram methods are available from SofTech Inc. It can also be used in conjunction with design reviews and Structured Walkthroughs with which it has much in common.

During design, the technique gives graphical support towards the safe delaying of detailed decisions. It does this by allowing mechanisms to remain undeveloped and by recording potential parallelism which may or may not be exploited later. This means that during the Design Phase SADT can be used in conjunction with other techniques that operate on a decomposition basis such as Structured Design.

SADT is available commercially from SofTech Inc.

3.7 Controlled Requirements Expression – CORE

In the phraseology of this book, CORE is a procedure for determining the functional requirements of a system and drawing up a Functional Specification.

The technique starts from the premise that the requirements of a system need to be analysed from a number of different 'viewpoints', for instance

- that of the environment of the system, e.g. its user interfaces and physical environment,
- that of its operators, i.e. the interfaces with those responsible for running it,
- that of reliability, e.g. the system's MTBF and its action under different failure conditions,
- that of the overall lifecycle, i.e. how the system fits into an organisation's plans and environment.

CORE analysis proceeds iteratively, each iteration decomposing the viewpoints at a certain level. In this way a top-down expansion of the viewpoint hierarchy is produced. (Compare this with the viewpoint models of SADT.)

It is the responsibility of an experienced analyst to extract from all the parties concerned the relevant viewpoints, at each step, and the relationships they have with each other and with the hierachy of which they form part. CORE defines how the analyst should propose, define and confirm these relevant viewpoints. The 'confirmation' of viewpoints means their successful combination into a coherent system, the addition of reliability actions and data to the combined viewpoints, and their acceptance by the users.

The results of the analyst's work are recorded in the CORE diagrammatic notation for which a set of rules is laid down. This notation will be accessible to most clients. For anything but very small projects, manual support of CORE is likely to be unwieldy and an automated tool such as PSL/PSA or SDS/RSRE is required.

The basic CORE procedure and notation can be continued into the Design Phase of system development, though other design methods can be used, taking the CORE diagrams as input to the design stage.

Commercial support for the technique is available in the UK from Systems Designers Limited. British Aerospace have successfully combined CORE with PSL/PSA, MASCOT and CORAL in their SAFRA project.

3.8 Software Requirements Engineering Methodology – SREM

SREM was originally developed as an automated aid in the requirements definition for software for United States Ballistic Missile Defence Weapons Systems (Alford 1978a). As such it formed part of the much broader Software Development System (SDS) which addressed all development phases of ballistic missile software (Davis 1977). It has since been marketed by TRW in the United States and has been used by a range of organisations (Alford 1980).

SDS has evolved into the Distributed Computing Design System (DCDS). DCDS incorporates research into system level requirements, software requirements, distributed design, module development, and test requirements. Thus, the results of this research will integrate with SREM to produce a total inter-related set of methodologies, languages, and software tools to support the entire software development path.

In DCDS, which is mainly applicable to large systems, a first stage of system level requirements

definition is carried out before the use of SREM. This stage, known earlier as Data Processing System Engineering and now called System Requirements Engineering Methodology (SYSREM), provides the system level requirements of each subsystem with the emphasis on Data Processing Subsystem Performance Requirements (DPSPR).

SYSREM applies disciplined functional decomposition rules designed to recognise the time sequences of function inputs and outputs so as to take advantage of opportunities for parallel data processing in meeting system requirements. Decomposition continues until a level is reached where each of the functions to be allocated to the software utilises single inputs. This yields a natural transformation into the SREM stimulus–response construct described below. In smaller systems this stage may not be necessary.

Although SYSREM provides a direct means to arrive at the information required to initiate SREM, any analysis technique which can identify and define the input messages the DP system will receive is acceptable. The identification of the input messages is central to the SREM technique since, unlike any other software engineering approaches which utilise a functional orientation, it describes the software requirements in terms of how the DP responds to each of these inputs under all conditions. This stimulus–response approach is unique to SREM.

SREM provides a methodology for systematically progressing from the Data Processing Requirement Specification to the Software Functional Specification and Performance Requirements.

The methodology is supported by an automated tool system known as the Requirement Engineering and Validation System (REVS) (Bell 1977).

The steps involved in applying SREM are as follows.

1 For each of the input messages to the system, the required sequence of processing is translated into a graphical form – an R-NET – showing the requirements as a network of processing paths between system inputs and outputs. The processing along these paths is described as a sequence of small functions

which input and output the data flowing on that path. The conditions under which these paths may branch to lead to conditional processing is also depicted. Thus, both data flow and control flow are depicted on the R-NET.

Because all the stimulus–response paths of processing that the DP will encounter are described in the R-NETs, there is no need for the software designer and the test designer to 'thread' the software specification, as is the case for the more traditional functional requirements approach.

R-NETs can also be represented in a machine-readable Requirements Statement Language (RSL) which is translated into abstract form in the REVS relational database. REVS provides tools for examining the database to check the static consistency and completeness of the requirements.

2 The requirements in the form of RSL stored in the REVS database are refined until all processing required to satisfy the system requirements has been incorporated. Validation points at which performance requirements must be met are included in the specification.

3 Performance requirements are allocated to paths in the R-NET. Functional simulations of the system, automatically generated by REVS, may be used to evaluate performance and to provide dynamic consistency checking of the requirements.

4 Algorithmic simulations of parts of the system may also be carried out. Once again this step uses REVS simulation generation facilities.

Although parts of SREM can be applied manually, such use lacks some of the principal benefits of the SREM/REVS combination, namely:

- automated traceability of RSL statements to the originating system requirement,
- interactive graphics flow path specification and display,
- automated completeness and consistency checking,
- automated requirements documentation,
- automated generation of simulations.

You are likely to find SREM most cost-effective for use in the specification of large, embedded, real-time systems. Although there is a learning curve to be considered in their application, SREM and REVS provide an exceptionally sophisticated methodology and tool set which should be useful in the requirement specification of any data processing system.

3.9 Finite State Machines – FSM

Finite State Machines (FSMs) can be used in all phases of the development lifecycle from System Definition through to Production.

An FSM is defined by the following elements:

I – a set of inputs
O – a set of outputs
S – a set of states
f – the next-state function which, given an input and a state, gives the new state which the FSM moves to
g – the output function which, given an input and a state, gives the output that the FSM produces.

A system described by an FSM can be thought of as a 'black box' into which inputs from the set I are fed and from which, in response, outputs from the set O emerge. To specify or implement this black box behaviour, one must specify S, f and g, which are mechanisms hidden within the box.

Specification of a system in terms of FSMs allows a great deal of mechanical checking of the correctness of the specification to be carried out. For example, it is not difficult to check that each state can be reached and that each output can be produced. Moreover, algorithms which provide sequences of inputs to test the FSMs in some optimal way either in the definition stages or following implementation are readily available (see, for example, Chow 1978, Braun 1981).

As far as we know, no tools for the analysis of

FSM designs as described above are commercially available. This is probably because they are so easily implemented and tailored to the specific needs of the user. On the other hand, state machine descriptions form a part of several larger design methodologies (such as FDM and HDM) which provide sophisticated analysis tools.

The principal role of FSMs is to define or implement the control structure of a system. The definition of data and data flows requires the use of other methods. In particular, in the Definition Phase, FSMs are best used to describe overall system operation prior to application of one of the other methodologies for specifying the system in more detail. This is one approach used in the Software Development System (see SREM), in which FSMs can be used to provide system level requirements prior to the use of SREM for detailed subsystem requirements (Salter 1976).

3.10 Petri Nets

Petri Nets are designed specifically to model systems with interacting concurrent components. Though principally of use during design, they can be applied to good effect in the definition of systems. (In particular, the first stage of requirements analysis in SREM can use Petri Nets as a notational medium.)

The importance and usefulness of Petri Nets lie in their use as an auxiliary analysis tool. As such you should consider adopting them even though you may have chosen a more all-embracing technique.

Conventional techniques can be used to investigate and propose a system, the resulting proposal then being modelled and analysed in the form of a Petri Net. The process proceeds iteratively: a model is proposed, it is drawn as a Petri Net, the net's properties are analysed, the model is revised and redrawn, and so on. Continuing theoretical work on Petri Nets is orientated towards developing *automatic* techniques for the modelling and analysis stages.

Carl Petri's original work (Petri 1962) was concerned with the description of the causal relationships between events that characterise communication between asynchronous components of a computer system. His work and the subsequent theoretical and practical development of it can be applied to any system (hardware, software, social . . .) where events trigger each other in a well-defined way.

The modelling of a system starts with the identification of *events* that can occur, the pre-conditions (inputs) necessary for them to occur, and the *post-conditions* (outputs) resulting from their occurrence. The output post-conditions form the pre-conditions of other events.

Once a Petri Net model has been drawn up the modelled system can be analysed with the aim of obtaining insights into its behaviour. The topic of Petri Nets is far from exhausted theoretically and many problems remain unresolved. However, analysis techniques exist for certain classes of Petri Net and models restricted to these can be valuable.

The results from the analysis of the Petri Net model can be used to refine the model. Additionally, a model can be used to generate simulations of the system. Though not *proving* anything about the system, a Petri Net simulation can provide insights into the system's behaviour under specific circumstances and for different values of parameters. For example, loading patterns in a multi-process system can be investigated given different execution times for the processes.

3.11 Jackson System Development – JSD

JSD is one of the few techniques that cover development from Definition, through Design and into the Production Phase. It is intended to be used to produce entire systems starting from the analysis of the real world situation in which the required system is to work and finishing with code.

Under JSD the developer

- models the real world processes upon which the system functions are to be based,
- determines the required functions and inserts them into the model,
- transforms the resulting specification into one realisable in the target environment.

This is done in six steps.

(i) The entity action step: the total potential functionality of the system is delimited by listing the entities involved and the actions they cause or suffer.

(ii) The entity structure step: here, the life-span (structure) of each entity is modelled by showing the ordering of actions which the entity can cause or suffer during its lifetime.

(iii) The initial model step: this step produces a model of the real world in terms of communicating 'model processes' that correspond to the actions in the entity structures; time ordering is carried through.

(iv) The function step: not until now are the required functions inserted into the model in the form of 'function processes'; system outputs appear for the first time.

(v) System timing step: during this step the timing constraints in the system are recorded for use in the next step.

(vi) Implementation step: the ideal multi-process system constructed so far is now semi-mechanically transformed into a form in which it can be realised on the target operating system, computer etc.

The final output of this procedure can be compilable source code.

Amongst the key features of JSD are the following:

- traditional functional decomposition without the preceding modelling stage is seen as over-constraining, in particular making the subsequent introduction of new functions during the maintenance phase potentially very difficult,
- code is seen as something that can be derived mechanically from design,
- the development technique does not constrain design by early decisions on the implementation mechanisms (e.g. scheduling),
- the problem of the co-ordination of processes (and timing in general) is given a formal solution,
- traditional top-down working is seen as dangerous in as much as it forces the designer to make the most crucial decisions at the time of greatest ignorance.

JSD is supported by Michael Jackson Sys-tems Limited and its licensees world-wide. Automated tools are becoming available.

3.12 RSRE Software Development System – SDS/RSRE

SDS/RSRE (not to be confused with the SDS associated with SREM) is a database system developed for the UK Royal Signals Research Establishment (RSRE) for storing information on all phases of the software development lifecycle. It is commercially available from its implementers, Software Sciences Limited, on a variety of computers.

The database stores data related to three principal areas of concern on a project, namely

- project control,
- design control,
- documentation control.

A hierarchical breakdown of data of each type is supported and links between related items of data of different types are maintained, as are relationships between data of a given type. For example, under the heading project control, a hierarchy of development activities can be stored, possibly related to one another by 'before'/'after' relationships and linked to the design control information on the component of the system which the activity is producing.

SDS/RSRE does not provide a specific methodology for any phase of development but rather provides a tool for the support of a wide range of methodologies (such as Structured Analysis and Structured Design). It does this by allowing the user to specify architectural rules for the methodology being used and subsequently by checking data entered into the database against these rules. It also provides utilities for extracting data from the database and producing reports. In the area of project control, a critical path scheduler is provided for use in producing project plans from data in the database.

You should particularly consider the use of SDS/RSRE for the application of otherwise non-computerised methodologies to large projects, which are likely to produce volumes of data that are uncontrollable by manual means alone.

3.13 Structured Design – SD

Structured Design (also called Composite or Modular Design) concerns itself with the structure of programs. More explicitly it addresses the structure of the modules, data and processes that make up a program or system and the interfaces between them. The ideas of SD are embodied in some of the more elaborate methodologies that we discuss (e.g. JSP, HOS) and it could be argued that SD is the minimal design technique that should be applied to any system. As such a minimal technique, SD provides a graphical method of documenting structured designs (*structure diagrams*), criteria and heuristics for evaluating structured designs and a method for producing good structured designs.

A structure diagram shows the structural ('calling') relationships between *modules* and describes the interfaces between modules. The evaluation criteria are used to judge the 'goodness' of this structure in terms of two principal concepts, *module strength* and *module coupling*.

Module strength is a measure of how well a single module hangs together, while module coupling is a measure of the degree of interconnection of different modules. In general, the greater the module strength and the weaker the module coupling the better the design. SD provides means of judging module strength and coupling which can equally well be used as indicators of design goodness for designs produced with other methodologies.

The method of producing a structured design for a system is a natural progression from the Structured Analysis process. The method provides a means of deriving a system structure diagram from the system data flow diagram. Thus, if your Functional Specification has been produced using Structured Analysis, then SD is a good, basic choice of methodology to apply in transforming it to an Overall Design Specification.

As mentioned above, SD only concerns itself with the structure of a system and not with the detailed function and logic of modules making up the structure. These latter aspects of the design need to be documented using some other 'structured' methods such as Structured English or more detailed pseudo-code/PDL, HIPO diagrams (IBM 1975) or Nassi–Shneiderman charts (for which see 'Other bibliographies').

3.14 Jackson Structured Programming – JSP

JSP is a technique intended mainly for designing programs for data processing applications though having wider use. It has its roots in the general principles of structured programming but goes further by removing much of the reliance on intuition and inspiration. This is done by presenting a step-by-step approach that leads from the structure of the data in a problem to the structure of a program that will solve it.

JSP is principally orientated towards the sequential processing of data defined in terms of hierarchical structures to produce similarly defined structures. By modelling the problem environment through its data structures and then deriving the program structures from them, JSP helps ensure that programs are correct, intelligible and easy to maintain.

In JSP the serial file is fundamental because, although it might take many forms (e.g. records in a tape file or commands from a terminal user), it models the chronological ordering of the environment. JSP's strengths therefore work best when applied to systems or parts of systems where there is a simple ordering that can be dealt with in a sequential fashion. Where problems of co-ordination and synchronisation arise between programs, it could prove advantageous to 'factor out' time using a procedure that is explicitly designed to do this and then use JSP to design the resulting sequential processing.

The basic design procedure is summarised in Jackson 1975 as follows:

(i) consider the problem environment and record our understanding of it by defining structures for the data to be processed;

(ii) form a program structure based on the data structures;

(iii) define the task to be performed in terms of the elementary operations available, and allocate each of those operations to suitable components of the program structure.

The technique recognises that programs must handle erroneous data as well as good data and that this error handling needs to be designed into a program. This means in turn that we must design data structures that 'recognise' erroneous data, or that model bad as well as good data.

An elaboration of the basic technique allows you to deal with data structures that do not allow you to decide how to process a component without knowing its context.

A final elaboration caters for the common situation where there is no direct sequential transformation of input data structures into output data structures.

The technique is widely practised in the industry. Training material and courses are available from Michael Jackson Systems Limited in the UK and from licensees elsewhere in the world. The books in the bibliography give an excellent guide to the technique.

Tools are commercially available for generating source code (e.g. COBOL) from the design expressed in schematic logic (a form of PDL) and for handling structure diagrams in graphical form.

3.15 System Architect's Apprentice – SARA

SARA is a collection of language processors and tools developed at the University of California at Los Angeles (UCLA) for use in the design of both hardware and software systems.

The SARA design methodology involves modelling the system and its components in conjunction with their environments. The *structure* of the system is modelled as a hierarchy of *modules* connected via *sockets* and *interconnections*. This structure can either be shown graphically or be represented in a machine-processable language, SL1. Each module has associated with it functional requirements which, in our terminology, map to the Functional Specification.

The *behaviour* of the system is modelled using a Graph Model of Behavior (GMB). This consists of a control flow graph (CG), a data flow graph (DG) and a description of the processes associated with the nodes of the DG. The CGs are very similar to Petri Nets, while the DGs are similar to those of Structured Analysis. Processes in the DG can be initiated by the firing of nodes in the CG. As well as being graphically representable, both the CG and the DG can be described in a machine-processable form. The functions of processes in a DG are described in a pre-processed form of PL/1 called PLIP which allows a smooth transition to PL/1 code.

The final design consists of the SL1 description of structure, the GMB and a mapping of the GMB onto the structure. SARA will support the development of such a design by either top-down decomposition or bottom-up re-use of existing modules.

The SARA methodology is well suited to the design of concurrent real-time systems. The tools support analysis of the CG for potential problems such as deadlocking and simulation of the behaviour of the DG.

SARA is still being developed and experimented with and, although accessible to authorised users via ARPANET, TELENET and TYMNET to MIT-Multics, it should mainly be considered as an excellent example of a good integrated design methodology and tool-set.

3.16 MASCOT

For our précis of the MASCOT design procedure we turn to the definitive document (MSA 1980):

MASCOT is a Modular Approach to Software Construction Operation and Test that:
  a defines a formal method of expressing the software structure of a real time system which is independent of both computer configuration and programming language;
  b imposes a disciplined approach to design which yields a highly modular structure, ensuring a close correspondence between functional elements in design and constructional elements for system integration;
  c supports a program acceptance strategy based on the test and verification of single modules and larger collections of functionally related modules;
  d provides for a small easily implemented executive for the dynamic control of program execution at run time;
  e provides for a straightforward and flexible method for system building;

f can be applied through all stages of the software lifecycle from design onwards;

g can form the basis of a standard system for software procurement and management.

MASCOT is a design method supported by a programming system. It is neither a language nor an operating system although it includes elements that are related to both these aspects of programming. MASCOT brings together a coordinated set of tools for dealing with the design, the construction (or system building), operation (or run time execution) and testing of software.

MASCOT can be applied in a wide range of application areas. It is however aimed particularly at real time embedded applications where the software is complex and highly interactive.

MASCOT is therefore aimed at all stages of development from System Design to Acceptance. You can use the design method independently of the programming system or a subset of the latter can be implemented should you find it convenient and appropriate.

MASCOT identifies two types of data object:

- *pools* of reference data;
- *channels* containing queues of datasets.

Activities process data from pools and channels outputting their results to other pools or channels. Activities are potentially able to run concurrently and hence can be treated as single thread programs. This is made possible by encapsulating all synchronisation matters into the *access mechanisms* by which activities access data in pools and channels. These mechanisms handle contention problems.

The resulting modularity aids design structuring and all levels of testing.

A MASCOT *machine* is defined that controls the run-time configuration and operation of the system. A *monitor* is geared to testing MASCOT designed systems. This MASCOT infrastructure for the Production Phase is not inconsiderable and will generally be composed of standard tools together with special purpose software.

MASCOT derived originally from work at the UK MoD Royal Radar Establishment (now the Royal Signals and Radar Establishment) in the early 1970s. It is now considerably developed and is supported in the UK by members of the MASCOT Users Forum.

3.17 Formal Development Methodology – FDM

FDM is a highly rigorous design and implementation methodology devised by System Development Corporation. FDM design specifications are written in a non-procedural language called Ina Jo (Ina Jo is a trademark of the System Development Corporation) which is based on first-order predicate calculus. The specification describes the system as a number of levels of decreasing abstraction, each level being designed as an abstract state machine.

The top-level specification contains correctness criteria which must be satisfied by the entire system. The Ina Jo language processor checks the specification for syntax errors and generates theorems which must be proved to assure the correctness of the specification. An interactive theorem prover is used in the construction and documentation of the required proofs.

The bottom-level specification is the program design specification which maps onto implementation language constructs via an implementation specification. Given the implementation specification the Ina Jo processor produces entry and exit assertions for the procedures that implement the state transitions of the program design specification. Satisfaction of these assertions ensures that the implementation maintains the correctness proved for the design specification.

Finally code level theorems are generated using language-specific verification condition generators. These theorems, if proved, guarantee that if a procedure satisfies its entry condition then it will satisfy its exit condition. These theorems are also proved using the interactive theorem prover.

The high level of rigour that FDM brings to design and implementation must be paid for. The non-procedural nature of Ina Jo may mean that staff used to procedural programming languages will require a long learning period (although this is less likely to be the case if languages such as Prolog become more widely taught). The rigorous proving of correctness theorems takes time and staff should have a good command of propositional and predicate calculus. You are thus most likely to consider using FDM on systems requiring an extra high degree of reliability. Typical past applications have been secure operating system kernels and secure network components.

3.18 Hierarchical Development Methodology – HDM

HDM has been developed by SRI International as a formal development methodology that integrates the important ideas of a number of computer scientists and supports the application of these ideas with special languages and tools. In particular, principles due to the following authors are included:

Dijkstra (1972) – Use of abstraction in the form of a hierarchy of machines.

Parnas (1972b) – Use of modules to encapsulate facilities which are (largely) independent of one another.

Hoare (1972a, b) – Abstract specification of data.

Floyd (1971) – Proof of consistency between specification and code.

Many of the concepts employed in HDM have also been adopted by the originators of FDM which has already been discussed. We therefore concentrate on the differences between the methodologies and the special features of HDM.

The design of a system is based on a hierarchy of abstract machines from the top-level machine, which provides the user interface, to the bottom-level, primitive machine, which is typically the target virtual machine (hardware plus operating system etc.). The abstract machines are divided into modules each of which contains data and operations that together typically define a single abstract data entity.

The structure of the hierarchy of abstract machines and their component modules is defined using one of the HDM languages, HSL (Hierarchy Specification Language). The modules and thus the abstract machines are specified using another language called SPECIAL (Specification and Assertion Language). SPECIAL is also used to represent data in upper-level abstract machines

in terms of data in the machine directly below them.

The next step in the HDM development approach as originally published involves implementing the specification in terms of an abstract implementation language ILPL (Intermediate Level Programming Language) which is then translated to compilable code. In practice the SPECIAL specification is implemented directly in Pascal and (at the time of writing) there are plans to support Ada.

At each stage of development, HDM facilitates formal verification of the design and implementation. Tools to assist in this process include specification checkers for the various languages, a multilevel security verifier and theorem prover and Modula and Pascal code level verification tools.

HDM has been used in the development of a number of complex systems including (see Neumann 1983):

- PSOS, A Provably Secure Operating System;
- KSOS, A Kernelised Secure Operating System;
- SCOMP, A Secure Communications Processor;
- TACEXEC, A Real-Time Tactical Executive;
- SIFT, A Software-Implemented Fault-Tolerant System.

As in the case of FDM, learning HDM involves a considerable investment of time. Such an investment is likely to be well justified in cases where software faults could cause loss of life or large sums of money.

3.19 Higher Order Software – HOS

HOS is a software development methodology conceived by Hamilton and Zeldin (Hamilton 1976, 1979) as an outcome of their involvement in the production of software for the Apollo space programme. It is now marketed by their company, Higher Order Software Inc., and by distributors.

Taking as its input the client's Functional Specification, HOS applies rigorous, mathematically correct engineeering techniques to prove the correctness of a design represented in a hierarchy of graphical design specifications. These specifications are finally converted automatically into program code and consistent documentation. In its commercially supported form, HOS is used by the designer via an interactive applications generator called USE.IT.

The approach involves a development path model that is radically different from the traditional series of phases that we use in this book as a framework for the more traditional techniques. Analyst and client work together in specifying the application in the form of a top-down structure – a hierarchical 'control map' – using an iterative graphics editor that forms the first component of the USE.IT development tool. The tree structure produced must satisfy a simple set of rules that allow it to be analysed automatically for logical correctness and consistency. This analysis is carried out by the second component of USE.IT – the Analyser. Once the specifications have been corrected and proven to be logically consistent by the Analyser, the third USE.IT component – the Resource Allocation Tool – translates them into the target language. (At the time of writing, FORTRAN is supported and COBOL and Pascal support is in preparation.)

The benefits of the approach are that:

- specifications are proven to be logically consistent and correct,
- code is automatically generated,
- there is considerable scope for the re-use of major or minor segments of systems,
- resulting systems possess high reliability and integrity,
- the whole development path is covered by a single technique and supporting tools,
- one specification of a system can be targeted at different machines and languages.

Despite its mathematical foundations, HOS does not require the user to have a mathematical background. A knowledge of the principles of functional decomposition is sufficient.

Given the way HOS departs from our standard development path and the fact that the production of code is an automatic process, we treat HOS in a single section in chapter 6.

3.20 Structured programming

We have brought together a number of ideas and threads under the umbrella term 'structured programming'. They are stepwise refinement, program proving, program design languages, program families and structured programming itself.

As a group, structured programming techniques drop loosely into the tactical design and coding stages of production. In other words they take in high-level design and produce code. In some cases, particularly small problems with no time element (e.g. programs rather than systems), structured programming may be sufficient as a total design process in itself, taking as its starting point some form of functional specification for the program.

As techniques they regularly appear embedded within other, more extensive methodologies – JSP and JSD for instance – and the principles form some of the few points of agreement in the software world.

One of the central ideas of structured programming is the idea that the construction of a program (its detailed design and coding) should take place through a process of 'stepwise refinement'. Successive refinements of the solution are produced, each being more detailed than the last. At each layer a number of solutions may be devised, the programmer using one and rejecting others, and possibly returning to an alternative if one fails at a lower level.

Central to this process is the fact that only three constructs are used. Traditionally, they are *sequence* (do X then Y), *selection* (do X or Y depending on C) and *iteration* (as long as C is true, do X). By restricting our designs and programs to using these constructs we make it possible to *prove* the correctness (or otherwise) of the solution. The ability to know that something is correct because of the way you have built it is immeasurably more valuable than the ability to test it in the hope of finding the errors you let in. Programs also become easier to understand and easier to modify correctly.

Structured programming gives you criteria for telling whether your design or your code is good, and guidelines on how to produce the design and the code in the first place.

The literature is well provisioned with material on the subject and some tools are available commercially. Training courses and seminars in the various aspects appear regularly from organisations that supply educational services to the industry.

3.21 Control of data

There are a number of techniques that can be used during the Production Phase to specify and implement the data used by a system in such a way as to minimise development and maintenance problems. These techniques can be classified under headings of:

- formal specification,
- data abstraction,
- information hiding.

You will see from the bibliography in section 7.4.8 that they have quite a long history.

Formal data specification techniques recognise the fact that it is difficult, if not impossible, to give precise natural (English) language definitions of data. Consequently they propose more mathematical approaches to the specification process. Such techniques generally define data in terms of abstract objects represented by the data and the operations that act upon these objects. This data abstraction approach might, for example, lead you to specify abstract data objects 'chess board' and 'pawn' in terms of operations 'move up', 'take left' etc., rather than describing a two-dimensional array of integers representing a chess board with the integer 1 representing a pawn.

The information hiding principle involves hiding the detailed implementation of the data in a module. To users of the module, access to the data is only granted via procedures (or similar) that implement the operations on the abstract object represented by the data.

Designers of programming languages are increasingly recognising the importance of data abstraction and information hiding and are beginning to provide language features that support these concepts. In particular the Ada language provides very complete support for both techniques.

Whatever programming languages you use you should consider rigorously applying data abstraction and information hiding techniques. Formal data specification is likely to be a more difficult technique to introduce and will require a certain level of mathematical skill amongst the staff applying it. For systems requiring a high level of reliability the investment in training should be worth making.

3.22 Coding techniques

Although coding was once *the* act of software production, its relative importance is constantly decreasing. In the long run we can hope that manual coding will, like the manual laying-out of printed circuit boards, be displaced by faster and surer mechanical methods. Steps have been taken in this direction with report generators, data dictionaries, program generators of various sorts and so on. However, much code is still written by hand and we therefore look at two aspects in keeping with our general approach.

The first relates to the choice of language to be used. The world's data processing software is almost exclusively written in COBOL, scientific and military software in FORTRAN, and hobbyist software in BASIC, whilst languages with their foundations in the more modern 'structured' school (C, Pascal, Ada, JOVIAL, FORTH, Occam, Modula) and the functional languages (LISP, PROLOG, etc.) share the remaining few per cent. Should you therefore follow the old or the new traditions and what should determine your choice?

The second aspect relates to what should be a long-term aim of the industry – to reduce software costs through the re-use of existing software. Little headway has been made in this area although the aim has been recognised for years.

In the short term we must make do with relatively simple re-use mechanisms. Macroprocessors, whilst generally being used as ways of extending languages, also allow the importing of existing code and mechanisms into a system. Libraries of re-usable software modules can, if properly standardised, save much re-inventing of wheels.

Finally, there is always the opportunity of using bought-in packages – database management systems, screen menu systems, graphics systems, etc. You should remember these as ways of significantly reducing technical risk in areas that otherwise often require considerable specialist skills.

3.23 Unit testing techniques

We can look forward in the future to improved techniques that, in increasingly large areas of application, will allow us to be certain of the *correctness* of our code simply because of the mathematical correctness of those techniques. The act of coding and the need for testing will be removed with the advent of design methodologies that allow the automatic generation of correct code. Steps are already being taken in this direction but until such methodologies are commonplace we will need to learn from work done in the field of verification and validation.

We can divide testing techniques into two major groups: static and dynamic. The static group covers techniques relying on some form of inspection of the source code, whilst the dynamic group covers techniques involving actual execution of the program. Under the static group we describe *static analysis, symbolic evaluation* and *program proving* (the last of these being covered in the section on Structured Programming as it more closely belongs to the tactical design and coding activities). As for the dynamic group, we investigate the different forms of *test data selection*, the use of *assertions*, and *software metrication* (including test coverage analysis).

None of these different techniques *compete*. They each have their benefits and disadvantages and you will be well advised to look for some 'mix' that matches your own environment and that gives you a cost-effective level of error detection.

Above all you must remember that only in the very simplest of cases can any amount of testing be guaranteed to reveal all errors. Testing *proves* nothing – it only finds the bugs it finds. It is this realisation that should make you think hard about adopting techniques earlier on during development that allow you to know a program is correct because you designed it correctly and transformed the design into code correctly.

(Myers 1979 gives a good guide to the whole field of software testing, openly describing the topic as 'an art'.)

3.24 System integration

The approach taken to the assembly of the components of a system can have a most important effect on the success of a system development project. It is during the integration stage, which usually occurs near the end of the development lifecycle, that many projects get into difficulty when it is found that interfaces do not match or that an important system function has been omitted or does not work properly. You are thus well advised to carefully consider the procedure that you use for integration.

We discuss three approaches to integration, namely, bottom-up integration, top-down integration or development, and sideways integration or development. These approaches differ mainly in the order in which software is assembled and possibly developed. Of the three, bottom-up integration is probably the most commonly used in practice although top-down development has received the most attention and acclaim.

If you have used good System Definition and Design methods the choice of approach may not be as clear cut as some of the advocates of, say, top-down development would claim. Rather the choice of approach should be guided by the particular circumstances of your project such as the need for early user visibility, the desire to test complex hardware interfaces early or the late availability of a development computer.

3.25 Structured Walkthroughs

Some of the techniques prescribed in this book include their own review procedures under which the product of the technique – specification, code module or whatever – is submitted to more or less formal review. The primary aim is to detect and correct faults as early as possible.

Yourdon's Structured Walkthrough (Yourdon 1979*a*) can be used to bring this review concept to any stage in the development process. A *walkthrough* is defined as the peer group review of a product of development, for instance a module specification, a Functional Specification, or a piece of source code. The technique concerns itself only with the conduct of walkthroughs and is independent of what is being reviewed and of how it was produced. This means that you can use Structured

Walkthroughs to supplement or complement any other procedure you might decide to use.

The technique sets down roles to be taken by those involved in a walkthrough, what their responsibilities are before, during and after a walkthrough, who should be considered for participation, how far walkthroughs concern line management, and how they can be performed most efficiently.

The key guideline is that the purpose of a walkthrough is to *detect* errors and not correct them. This, like other guidelines described by Yourdon, takes into account the psychology of technicians and especially teams of technicians, stressing the need to carry out technical criticism without causing personal conflict.

Whatever other procedures you are using, you should consider adopting Structured Walkthroughs at all stages of development. Being a 'social' discipline it is independent of application area and needs no automated support (beyond a word processor, perhaps). Courses on the technique are available from Yourdon Inc.

3.26 Fagan inspections

This is a general inspection procedure that has been developed and used within IBM. The overall principles of a Fagan inspection are very similar to those of the Structured Walkthrough. However, Fagan sets his inspections in the wider context of planning, measurement and control and gives their functions in the latter two areas.

Fagan inspections serve two purposes: to find errors in a product of development and to give greater control over error detection through the collection of error statistics. As in the Structured Walkthrough, the purpose is detection and not correction. But, in addition, errors are classified by type and severity so that profiles can be maintained showing the most common types and how they should be looked for.

Some combination of Fagan inspections and Structured Walkthroughs should give you the best of both worlds: the feedback control and the social organisation. For comparison, chapter 5 contains detail on Structured Walkthroughs and chapter 6 on Fagan inspections.

4

Project Inception

4.1 The purpose of the Inception Phase

The Inception Phase is that part of the development lifecycle in which you will decide to embark on the development project. This is the time in which you will make a large number of crucial decisions regarding the need for and nature of the proposed system. The questions that must be asked in this phase will depend on particular circumstances, but may include the following:

- Why is the system needed?
- Are there better alternatives?
- Will the system be acceptable to its users?
- At what price will the system be marketed?
- Is there a market for the system?
- What are the legal implications of the system?
- What are the Trade Union implications of the system?
- What is the intended lifetime of the system?
- How reliable should the system be?
- Can management approval be obtained for system development?
- Will sufficient resources be available for system development?
- Will sufficient resources be available to run the system?
- Will the system be developed 'in-house' or will its development be put out to tender?
- How will tenderers' responses be assessed?

Although this phase is not directly involved with software development, it is vitally important that you ask the correct questions and obtain the correct answers to lead to a firm system requirement. These answers will affect all subsequent phases and ultimately the usefulness of the entire project. It is essential that software development should commence with a stable requirement. Introduction of large numbers of requirement changes during development is a sure way of leading to schedule and budget overruns. Even worse, it is possible to produce a beautifully engineered system based on a requirement which bears no relation to what the user needs. When such a system is put into active service it will not be long before it is decided to scrap the system entirely or carry out large scale, costly modifications. A major mistake made in the Inception Phase can easily be the most expensive mistake of all.

4.2 The starting point of the Inception Phase

The Inception Phase commences as soon as the possible need for a system is identified. The need can arise from a wide variety of circumstances, for example, the arrival of new technology on the market, the introduction of new operational requirements, the identification of a 'hole' in the market or the desire to exploit a new invention.

However the need has arisen, its existence should be documented in the form of an Inception Paper. This paper should consist of two major parts. The first part should identify the need and its reason, and the second part should give a plan for the remainder of the Inception Phase.

The amount of detail given in the first part of the paper will depend on the author's view of how difficult it will be to have the second part of the paper approved. For example, it might be sufficient to have the first part of an Inception Paper say simply 'there is a need for a new or modified payroll system because the current system will not handle the new tax laws'. On the other hand an Inception Paper saying 'there is a need to replace the manual payroll system by a computerised system', would almost certainly require rather more elaboration.

The second part of the Inception Paper should set out what questions need to be answered, a plan for answering them and a summary of methods to be used. Preliminary answers to some of these questions may have to be given in the first part of the Inception Paper, although invariably a more detailed analysis will be required once the Inception Paper has been accepted.

4.3 The finishing point of the Inception Phase

The Inception Phase is complete once a decision has been made as to whether or not to proceed with system development. It is to this end that the plan in the second part of the Inception Paper should lead.

The deliverable item available at the end of the Inception Phase is the Requirement Specification. This is the document which describes to the development team what they are meant to produce. It is a distillation of the findings of all the studies carried out during the Inception Phase and is the major document upon which a decision to proceed is made. The entire process is shown in a somewhat simplified form in figure 4.1.

It should always be remembered that the main purpose of the Requirement Specification is as input to the System Definition Phase. As such it must be written so as to facilitate its use in this phase. This is the case irrespective of whether the Requirement Specification is to be immediately handed to a team for implementation or, alternatively, put out to tender.

In the latter case, the tenderers have to carry out a certain amount of definition and design work

Fig. 4.1. The Inception Phase summarised.

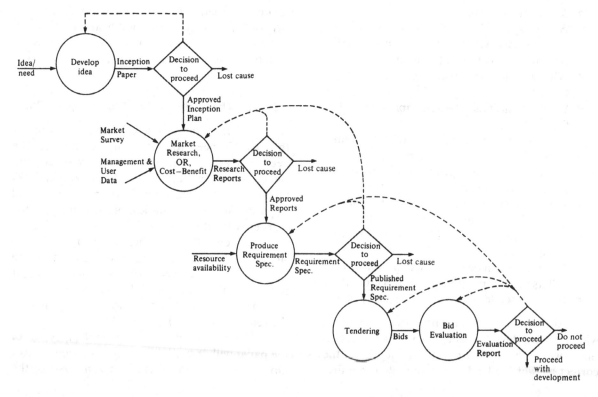

before they can propose a viable system (see section 4.5.2). A Requirement Specification which is useful to designers in an implementation team will be equally as useful to tenderers in this respect. For the same reason it is important to separate system requirements from the requirements for the tenderer's response to the Requirement Specification. For example, the statements:

> 'the system shall have an availability of 95%' and
> 'the tenderer shall discuss how the required availability of 95% will be met'

should appear in separate parts of the Requirement Specification with cross references to one another. When the tenderers are deciding on the best solution to propose to meet all the requirements they are not interested in what has to be written in their response, and when they are writing their response, they do not want to have to read through pages of system requirements to find what is required in the response. For the same reason, general background discussion about the requirement should be separated from detailed requirement descriptions and requirements for the tenderer's response.

Given the need to separate the different types of requirements, the overall contents of a Requirement Specification might be as follows:

Part 1 Background to the Requirement
Part 2 System Requirement Definition
Part 3 Implementation Requirements
Part 4 Requirements for the Tenderer's Response.

Part 3 should cover any requirements affecting the way in which the project shall be carried out – for example, project reporting methods. The only difference between a Requirement Specification that is put out to tender and one that is not is that the latter does not include Part 4.

We must next ask how the requirement definition in Part 2 should be written so as to facilitate System Definition. To this end we must look ahead to what is produced as the main deliverable item of the System Definition phase; namely the Functional Specification. The Functional Specification is a specification of the functions to be performed by the system and the constraints within which it must work. These functions are one particular solution to meeting the requirement presented in the Requirement Specification and will be the basis for system design.

The Requirement Specification should not attempt to replace the Functional Specification by proposing a particular solution (unless of course there are strong reasons for requiring such a solution). However, as the functions in the Functional Specification must map onto Part 2 of the Requirement Specification, these two documents can have similar structures. For this reason, many of the techniques used for writing Functional Specifications described in the next chapter can be applied to writing Requirement Specifications.

4.4 Techniques available during Project Inception

We now note those methods that can be used in progressing from the idea expressed in the first part of the Inception Paper to the point at which the Requirement Specification can be produced. This involves deciding which questions to ask and then answering them, or in other words deciding upon the plan in the second part of the Inception Paper and putting it into action.

Methods for undertaking these activities include market research, cost–benefit analysis and operations research. They have been the subject of a vast body of literature in a wide range of disciplines over a large number of years and since few of them are specifically involved with the software development process you are referred to that literature.

4.5 Looking forward

4.5.1 Tender evaluation

If your requirement specification is being put out to tender, now is the time to decide how the tenderers' responses will be evaluated. In Part 4 of the Requirement Specification you will have asked for sufficient information to provide useful input to your evaluation process. The detailed form of the evaluation process should be decided upon well in advance of receipt of any of the tenderers' proposals.

The form of evaluation can range from simple methods such as subjective preference or acceptance of the cheapest bid through to sophisticated figure of merit analysis and related methods. A wide variety of methods are dealt with in the literature and we only note here that it is well worth investing a relatively small amount of time in using one of the more sophisticated methods, if it means that you will end up with a system that can really meet your needs over a number of years.

4.5.2 Tender preparation

If you have written a Requirement Specification it is unlikely that you will also be preparing a tender in response to that Requirement (although it has been known to happen). This is, however, the most appropriate point at which to make a few observations about the preparation of a Proposal in response to a Requirement Specification. In particular, in writing a Requirement Specification you should be aware of what will be involved in responding to it.

A Proposal normally has two sides to it: a technical aspect and a sales aspect. The technical aspect details the proposed solution, describes how it meets the Requirement, gives its cost and how long it will take to implement. The sales aspect involves selling the solution to the potential purchaser. Needless to say, however, a technically sound solution is easier to sell than one which is technically tenuous.

The preparation of a technically sound Proposal can require the use of techniques drawn from almost any of the phases of the development life-cycle. Especially important are the methods used in the System Definition Phase to decide what the system should be like, how much it will cost to produce and how long it will take.

The use of accurate cost modelling methods in obtaining answers to the 'how much' and 'how long' questions is particularly important to the success of the Proposal. If you are confident in the accuracy of your cost model then you will not need to add such a large contingency factor into a tendered fixed price, thus perhaps giving yourself an advantage over your competitors. Moreover if you can demonstrate the accuracy of your cost model to the potential purchaser then you are likely to engender more confidence than a competitor who

has a suspiciously low price that might have been obtained by 'pricing to win'.

In summary, the techniques presented elsewhere in this book are highly relevant to the production of competitive Proposals.

4.6 Checklist for the Project Inception Phase

PART 1 Background to the requirement

- Are the following items included?
  - Description of any existing system,
  - reason for replacing an existing system,
  - overall description of the required system,
  - overall description of implementation requirements,
  - overall description of the tendering procedure,
  - a contact name for queries.
- Does this part confine itself to purely descriptive background and not state any mandatory requirements?

PART 2 System Requirement Definition (see also section 5.5)

- Are all system requirements included?
- Are all requirements phrased in such a way as to be testable?
- Is there sufficient data to allow accurate system sizing (e.g. daily throughput requirement, response time requirement)?
- Are mandatory requirements for the initial system clearly separated from required enhancement capability and desirable options?
- Have necessary requirements affecting the following areas been included?
  - Operating environment,
  - maintenance and warranty,
  - availability,
  - documentation,
  - lifetime,
  - development facilities,
  - testing facilities,
  - compatibility with other systems.
- Does this part confine itself to purely system requirements and not include requirements for the implementation process or the tendering activity?

PART 3 Implementation requirements

- If necessary, are the following requirements included?
  - To interview implementation team members,
  - to apply specific project reporting standards,
  - to apply specific implementation standards,
  - to apply specific security standards,
  - to undertake implementation in a specific place (e.g. contractor's premises or purchaser's premises),
  - to provide certain deliverables by specific dates,
  - to undertake specific acceptance testing,
  - to produce the system within a given budget,
  - to produce the system by a certain date.

PART 4 Requirements for the tenderer's response

- If necessary, are the following requirements included?
  - To respond by a given time,
  - to provide a specific number of copies of the response,
  - to provide the response in a given format,
  - to provide a compliancy statement for each requirement of Parts 2 and 3 of the Requirement Specification,
  - to detail pricing in a specific way (e.g. itemised in some way, with or without taxes, valid on a specific date, with or without inflation allowance, fixed price or 'time and materials').

4.7 Memorabilia during Project Inception

Recording successes and failures

Remember that to get the most out of your experiences you should record them both for your own benefit and for that of others. Make an entry in your Project Debriefing Report at the end of the phase listing the successful things and the failed things. For example:

- Could the evaluation of tenders be speeded up by improving the questions posed?
- What items need to be added to the Requirement Specification checklists for next time?
- Which techniques proved successful?
- Which were unsuccessful?
- Why were others untried or omitted?
- Were these good reasons in retrospect?

If at first you don't succeed . . .

All the decision points in figure 4.1 show feedback loops as possibilities when it is decided not to proceed. You should not necessarily give up just because your idea has not succeeded first time around or is having difficulty getting over one of the hurdles. You should learn from the decision making process and, if you think it appropriate, modify your ideas taking into account the reasons for rejection and try again. The key to success in this respect is lateral thinking; tackling the problem from an entirely different angle. To sharpen up your powers of lateral thinking we strongly recommend the books of Edward de Bono (e.g. de Bono 1971).

Thorough consultation – the key to success

The earlier you talk to everyone who might have an interest in the system that you are proposing the better. You can then incorporate their ideas at an early stage and are less likely to find them an obstacle when it comes to decision making.

You should take particular pains to ensure that you have identified all interested parties. This avoids the particularly embarrassing and costly situation of having some previously unconsulted part of your organisation emerge, for example, part way through the tendering activity and insisting that the Requirement Specification be changed to suit their needs.

4.8 A sample case-history – VISTA

4.8.1 Introduction

Throughout the remainder of the book we give examples of the application of most of the techniques that we describe. Rather than use a different system as the subject of the examples for each stage of the system lifecycle or even for each method, we concentrate on one particular system and follow its development through its lifecycle.

The choice of a system which is suitable for such an example is quite difficult. A prerequisite is that all of the methodologies discussed must be sensibly applicable to it or some part of it. This means that parts of the system should be amenable to treatment with methods that are generally considered most suitable (and certainly are most used) for 'commercial data processing' applications, while other parts should demand treatment with methods most often used in 'real-time' applications.

The system that we use as an example is called VISTA. It is a fictitious image processing system based in part on a real system with which the authors were involved (Ould 1982). Although image processing is a highly specialised applications area the system satisfies the prerequisites given above. As we shall see, on the one hand it involves time critical real-time treatment of television images and on the other hand it has a conventional, if special purpose, filing system, user interface and data processing aspect. Moreover, as with so many application areas, the applications specialist or system user speaks a quite different language from the computer systems designer. While the former might be talking of pels, chrominance, luminance, YUV and RGB, the latter might be talking of bytes, hexadecimal values and ADC chip characteristics. Bridging the gap between the user's conception of the system in his language and a working computer system built by computer specialists is what a great deal of the following chapters is about.

To set the scene for the examples in following chapters, we give here a brief overall description of VISTA. This may be thought of as an example of an inception paper, although, to make it meaningful to the non-specialist, we have not used image processing terminology profusely (and certainly not without explanation) and, to avoid further explanation later, we have gone into design characteristics rather more than would be desirable in an inception paper.

4.8.2 Image processing background

Television pictures as you see them on your TV screen consist of *frames* of video information which appear on your screen at a fixed rate of 25 or 30 frames per second (depending on where in the world you happen to be watching TV). A frame is composed of a number of lines (of the order of five or six hundred depending again on where you are) which become visible as an electron beam hits the TV screen (see figure 4.2). The information which controls the formation of a monochrome picture is contained in an analogue signal which looks very roughly like that shown in figure 4.3.

Image processing in the VISTA system consists of inputting one or more TV frames in an analogue form, changing them by user-specified image processing algorithms and then outputting the changed analogue signal to allow visual examination of the effects of the processing. Since digital computers cannot readily process analogue signals, the image is first digitised.

Digitisation consists of taking samples of the analogue signal at a fixed rate and at each sample converting the signal strength to a digital value. Typically, the sampling rate might be 16 MHz (16 million samples per second) and each sample would consist of one byte of data giving a range of 0–255 for the intensity. If the time duration of a line is 64 microseconds then, when sampled at 16 MHz, 1024 samples result. Each sample is called a *pel* (picture element) or *pixel*. Thus a digitised frame can be considered as an array of say 625 lines consisting of 1024 pels with each pel being in the range 0–255. It is on such an array that digital image processing is performed.

Fig. 4.2. The lines forming a TV picture ('frame').

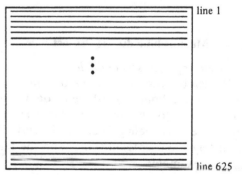

Fig. 4.3. The TV analogue signal.

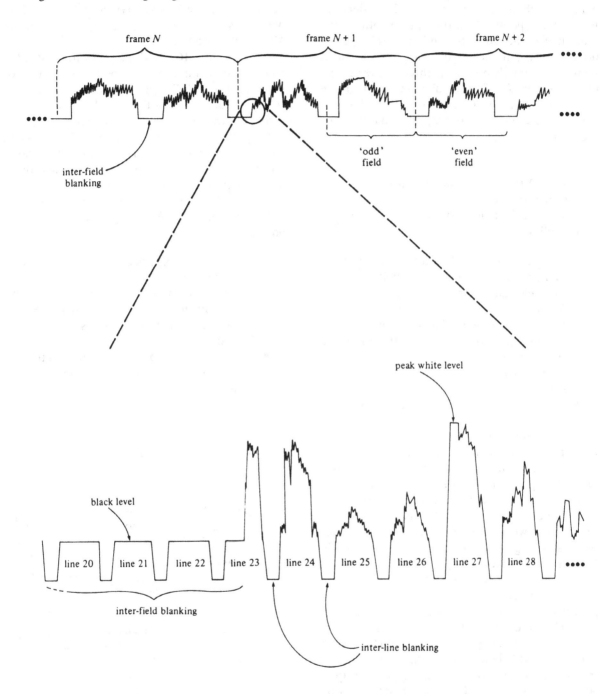

If the TV picture is colour, then a frame is made up of three analogue signals, which, depending on the type of television input, might be the intensities of the red, green and blue (RGB) components of the frame. In this case each signal is sampled separately producing three arrays of samples called *bands*. Thus, a colour frame might be made up of a red band, a green band and a blue band. These can be processed separately or together.

4.8.3 VISTA functionality and hardware configuration

The principal functions of the VISTA system are the following:

- to input analogue colour television signals,
- to digitise the analogue signals with a user-selectable range of sampling frequencies,
- to store one or more digitised frames in real-time (i.e. to store them at the same rate as they arrive),
- to provide a means of image processing the stored digital frames,
- to allow real-time replay of stored frames.

The function of storing a sequence of digitised frames in real-time is technically difficult to achieve. Assuming a frame consists of 512 visible lines (as opposed to lines which are not displayed, such as those that carry teletext information) and each line consists of 1024 pels, then every $\frac{1}{25}$ of a second (say) we need to store $512 \times 1024 \times 3$ bytes of data, giving a data transfer rate of about 39 Mbytes/second. Moreover, to store a sequence of any useful length requires a considerable storage capacity. For example, 30 seconds of video sampled as above requires over a gigabyte of memory.

The solution to this storage problem in VISTA is to use a high speed disc (HSD) on each band; each HSD being capable of sustaining data transfer rates of up to 13 Mbytes/second for up to 30 seconds. The three HSDs are front-ended by some special microprocessor controlled hardware which we shall call Video Capture Equipment (VICE). A VICE digitises analogue TV signals and stores up to a frame of data in a local frame-

store before transferring it to the HSDs. A VICE need not necessarily have HSDs attached to it in which case one frame can be captured into the VICE and stored there.

Both the VICE and the HSD are controlled from a mini-computer (the host) which can have several sets of VICEs and HSDs attached to it. A VICE is connected to the host by a slow speed serial link for the transfer of commands and by a high speed parallel link for the transfer of image data. An HSD is connected to the host by a parallel link for the transfer of both commands and data. The configuration is shown in figure 4.4.

We can now elaborate on the functions of the VISTA system. The following functions are supported:

- capture and replay of a single frame or part of a frame to or from the VICE framestore;
- capture and replay of sequences of frames to or from an image sequence file on the HSDs;
- maintenance of an image filing system on the HSDs;
- transfer of (parts of) frames between the VICE framestore and the host's local disc filing system;

Fig. 4.4. The VISTA system configuration.

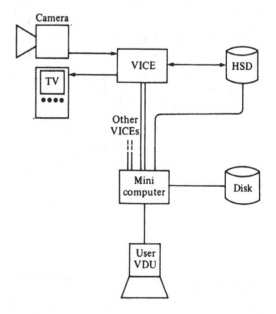

- transfer of sequences of frames between the HSD filing system and the host's local disc filing system;
- processing of images stored in the host's local disc filing system;
- capture and replay of a sequence of part frames into the VICE framestore in 'animation' mode (see below);
- control of all functions from a number of users' visual display units;
- control of allocation of devices to users, allowing a user to reserve a VICE so that another user cannot overwrite the frame stored in it.

The animation mode function requires some explanation, especially as it will provide one of the most useful examples of real-time operation. A VICE's framestore contains enough memory to store one complete frame (say 1.5 Mbyte). Alternatively it can be used to store a sequence of partial frames. For example, we could store 50 part frames of 100 lines by 100 pels. Once captured the 50 frames could be placed back in a continuous fashion, looping back to frame 1 following the replay of frame 50.

To achieve such a function, the microprocessor in the VICE must, between each frame (i.e. during the frame blanking period – typically 1.4 ms), instruct the VICE hardware to start capturing or replaying the next frame from a new address in the framestore memory. The VICE microprocessor knows that a frame has ended because of an interrupt generated by the occurrence of a *frame synchronisation pulse*, which is part of the analogue input signal. If, on replay, the start address is only updated every Nth frame synchronisation pulse then each frame in the sequence will be replayed N times, allowing a slow motion replay function (the slow down factor being N). The use of animation mode allows moving sequences to be captured, processed and replayed with VICEs which do not have HSDs attached to them.

5

System Definition

5.1 The aims of the System Definition Phase

Once the decision has been made to proceed, this is the most important phase of development. Decisions made here influence the rest of the project. Time spent here is rarely less than well-spent, if properly directed. On the other side of the coin, this is one of the most difficult stages as regards knowing where you start, knowing when you have finished and knowing how to go about it.

The purpose is clear however, namely to decide the following:

- what is to be produced,
- when it is to be produced by,
- what resources will be required to produce it.

These latter two may already have been determined for you. If so, you must regard them as constraints that limit what can be produced. In other words you will need to decide additionally that the system can actually be produced in the time with the resources.

Every project manager at this stage of his project needs to be reminded that there is a strong empirical correlation between failure to define a system adequately and failure to produce it. The temptation to short-circuit the Definition Phase is all the easier to succumb to, given the momentary feeling of an increased rate of progress.

5.2 The starting point of System Definition

It is most likely that you will start with some form of Requirement Specification. This document, produced by your client or some agency on his behalf, will sometimes be no more than a few pages, sometimes tomes. It will hopefully restrict itself to requirements and avoid solutions. It will rarely be any sort of firm basis for system design and it is the purpose of this phase to produce from it something that is.

In the case where budgets and timescales have been set then these too are inputs to this stage and the resulting definition of the system to be produced will be a compromise between your client's desires as expressed in his Requirement Specification and the resources he is prepared to commit towards its realisation.

It is important therefore to see the Requirement Specification more as a target to be aimed for than as an inalienable expression of your client's desires. Compromise will be necessary not only because of budget constraints but also because of technical constraints. Investigation may prove that parts of the Requirement Specification are technically impossible as they stand.

5.3 The finishing point of System Definition

As in all other phases we must first identify the deliverable items of this phase and then plan to produce them.

5.3.1 The Functional Specification

There is one major document that marks completion of the System Definition Phase – the Functional Specification, signed and agreed by you and your client. This is the most important document of the project and its influence permeates design, production and testing. Getting it right is therefore critically important.

The average Functional Specification is unsuccessful despite the best intentions of all those involved – generally in fact because of all those intentions. It is too frequently seen or expected to act as:

- .a document justifying the project and its cost,
- a training manual,
- an operational handbook,
- a brief history of the project,
- a design document,
- a publicity document,
- a management summary,
- a sales handout,
- an expression of hopes for the future.

It must be none of these. It is purely a specification of the functions to be performed by a system and the constraints within which it must work. Any compromise made at this stage can only represent a possible risk later.

This is not to say that the above documents are not needed. Some or all generally are, but in this case they should be written separately and aimed at their own specific audiences.

An important step finally is to get the Functional Specification agreed by all concerned and signed by them as their commitment to seeing it implemented. However, a signed Functional Specification should not be regarded as a tablet from on high. It will occasionally need to be changed and to this end it is important to agree a change procedure at the same time. Functional changes often will involve a change to the implementation cost or timescale and this implication needs to be recognised and again accepted by everyone involved. It is all too easy to take on board new or altered functions in the optimistic hope that they can be 'absorbed' within the existing budget and schedule.

5.3.2 The Project Plan

How you plan your project is a matter that this book does not cover. It will depend on your organisation's standards. What we do present, however, is an indication of what should appear in your plan – in whatever form – to allow you to

make the most efficient use of your resources and the techniques you use.

The most important feature of your plan is the complete and detailed breakdown of the work to be done in the form of a WBS. The level of detail in your WBS will increase as the project proceeds. At this stage you will not necessarily know the software to be produced to module level but you will probably have identified major components and costed them.

Each item in your WBS will have a target manpower figure – the amount of effort you estimate it will need. As work progresses you will record the actual effort consumed. These two numbers represent one of the most important indicators on the project.

Your plan will also contain definitions of a number of *milestones* – points during development that represent significant achievements such as completion of strategic design, demonstration of the first prototype and so on. The essential properties of a milestone are that it should be clearly identifiable, and likely to survive the project life and any replanning except the most radical. Your plan should show the forecast dates for such milestones, whilst your progress reporting will show your progress against these planned dates. In this way milestones can give a quick at-a-glance summary of a project's overall progress against plan.

5.3.3 The Quality Management Plan

This is a critical document. It describes how you intend to ensure that you are producing a system of the necessary quality, i.e. one that will work and behave according to the Functional Specification. If you cannot write it you presumably have no strategy for your technical approach to the project.

System Definition might seem an early stage at which to talk of Quality Plans. Remember however that you should have such a plan for this phase itself as it has a highly technical content and is critically important. Again, the exact form and content of your plan will depend on your own organisation. But you should include in it, in whatever form, a statement as to which techniques you expect to use at each phase and stage of the project. You should relate the techniques to specific work packages and deliverable items so that team members know how to go about individual activities when they are allocated to them.

It may be necessary to postpone the choice of some techniques – e.g. for unit testing – until a later stage when more information is available about the development environment. For this reason you should regard your QM Plan as an evolving thing which is successively reviewed and refined as the project proceeds. You will find therefore that each phase includes a stage for precisely this purpose.

In a sense, your QM Plan describes the choice of techniques and indicators you have made after reading this book and others. It will say how you intend going about building the system and how you propose to monitor progress during that building process. Whereas your Project Plan is a statement of intent to your own line management, your Quality Management Plan is the way you pass work instructions to your staff.

Within your organisation you may well have Quality Control and Quality Assurance functions. The distinction is generally that Quality Control consists of the actions you take to build in and ensure the level of quality in your product, whilst Quality Assurance is the (external) activity of checking that Quality Control procedures exist and are visibly (provably) in operation. You will see that our requirement for a Quality Management Plan is that it should concern itself with Quality Control since that is something that you as system developer or project manager are responsible for. We prefer to talk about 'quality management' as it includes the notion of *planning* as well as that of control.

Your QM Plan could be a substantial document – albeit cut-and-pasted from the plans of earlier, similar projects! You should ensure that it covers every aspect of your project from project management to standard link editing programs. One of the checklists later in this chapter gives you some headings that you might find appropriate.

Like Project Debriefing Reports, QM Plans have a usefulness beyond the project for which they were originally created. The practices, techniques and various forms of control that prove successful should be retained in the plan, whilst inappropriate or unsuccessful ones are deleted. If your organisation's work is uniform in nature, one all-purpose delete-where-inapplicable QM Plan could be appropriate.

Because of the importance of a QM Plan to the successful execution of a project a number of organisations have drawn up standards for them: for instance the IEEE 'Standard for Software Quality Assurance Plans' (ANSI/IEEE Std 730-1981) and the US Department of the Army 'Standard for Software Quality Assurance Programs' (MIL-S-52779) (see also Buckley 1979, Cho 1980 and Dunn 1982).

5.3.4 The Acceptance Test Specification

Before your system is actually put to work or sold as a product your client will wish to check that it actually carries out the functions defined for it. The precise details of the Acceptance Test that contains those checks are the subject of the Acceptance Test Description, but a prerequisite is an agreement on the 'terms and conditions' under which the Acceptance Test will be carried out: who will define the tests?, who will carry out the tests?, how failures will be treated, whether concessionary changes will be allowed to the system, what level of retesting will be required after correction of a fault and so on. A checklist at the end of the chapter includes these and other points.

Laying down these ground rules is vital if the Acceptance Tests are to proceed smoothly and without conflict. All the parties involved will therefore need to agree both the Specification and the Description – with a signature.

5.4 Techniques available during System Definition

As in all the subsequent phases of development there is no panacea for the Definition Phase. Indeed, Functional Specifications are often produced with no underlying method in their production. But the risk is then great that the document's single central purpose is forgotten and it attempts to become all those other documents rolled into one.

The approaches tried to date have concentrated, not surprisingly, on bringing a level of formalism to the document and its production. The success of this approach in other parts of the development cycle suggests we should apply computing techniques such as high-level languages, databases, query languages and so on to this phase as to others.

Above all, good structuring improves the quality of the Functional Specification. Long, discursive prose permits ambiguity, contradictions, omissions and irrelevancy to creep in during changes. Reluctance to do without such prose is generally traceable to a desire to view the Functional Specification as one of the documents listed above, i.e. something it is not. You should therefore aim as a minimum at a more or less formal approach to your Functional Specification; the techniques covered below range from manually driven techniques right up to fully computerised mechanisms (though formalism does not necessarily imply automation).

Which you choose of these and the others available will be determined by the size and nature of the product you are defining.

To get some idea of how important the use of reliable techniques at this stage of the project is, consider the data in figure 5.1. You will see that the cost to correct a Functional Specification fault at the end of the project could be 100 times as much as it would if it were found now. Your approach should therefore be to adopt a technique that allows you to produce with reliability a document of high quality, and that also allows you to check that quality. In section 5.6 there is a checklist of

Fig. 5.1. Software validation: the price of procrastination. (From Boehm 1977.)

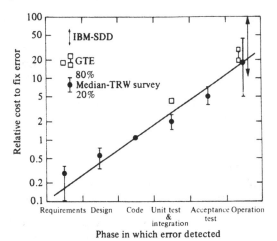

properties one would expect to find in a high quality FS, that is, one likely to contain as few errors as possible.

One extra benefit to be reaped from a formal Functional Specification is that the document becomes an ideal starting point for the Design Phase. For, although the Functional Specification must not contain statements about implementation (unless certain techniques are contractually required), the system designer wants a clear, complete and unambiguous definition of the system to be produced as much as the user. It is in their common interest to generate a good Functional Specification.

You will need to be prepared to engage in some design work whilst drafting your Functional Specification. Not because design will need to be put in the Functional Specification – on the contrary, you should not constrain yourself in this way. Instead, you will want to be sure that you are describing a feasible system. The closer you are working to the edges of technology (or even your own knowledge) the more important the iteration between defining functions and designing systems becomes and the more you must be prepared to budget time for this. The implication is that whichever technique(s) you use should allow you (if not actively encourage you) to iterate between definition and design in a controlled fashion.

A further quality you should look for in the techniques concerns your relationship with your client. It is vital that the client should be actively involved with the analysis and drafting process. It is not sufficient to present them suddenly with a four volume specification and expect useful constructive comment. Your techniques should ideally allow you to go to the client regularly with the next level of breakdown in the definition – ideally all on just a couple of sheets of paper – and get approval for each level before going on to the next.

A taxonomy of System Definition techniques

Before giving descriptions of each of the techniques that are appropriate to System Definition, we first give a crude taxonomy. This is intended to reveal where techniques complement one another. Always bear in mind that, as in all the other phases, it is a matter of horses for courses.

The first table – 5.1 – shows whether each technique can be considered to be a 'methodology' and/or a 'notation' and/or an 'analytic technique'. A 'methodology' gives you a prescribed technique for generating the definition of the system – the Functional Specification – whatever form this may take. A 'notational technique' gives you a way of recording the definition, i.e. a way of writing or drawing the Functional Specification. An 'analytic technique' supplies algorithms (of a more or less formal nature) which allow you to analyse the properties of the definition at any given stage.

The perfect technique for System Definition could be seen as one that gives you all three handles on the definition process. But, again, other techniques will prove highly effective in certain aspects and on particular types of system, so a combination makes good sense.

When you have read the outlines of the various techniques below you will see that a common feature is that they all in some way *model* the system being defined. What varies from technique to technique is which *aspect* of the system is being modelled. It is important therefore to identify which aspects of your system appear to be central – data flow, process synchronisation etc. – and to choose techniques accordingly. To help you, table 5.2 gives a summary of the techniques we discuss and the system aspects they model. If you are interested in modelling more than one aspect consider choosing more than one technique.

(See Ohno 1982 for papers on recent work in the field of 'requirement engineering environments'.)

5.4.1 Structured English

This technique is appropriate if you wish to derive (or possibly just draw up retrospectively) your Functional Specification by stepwise refinement. At each level of refinement a single statement of function is expanded into a number of definitions and smaller functions. At the bottom level (whose depth can vary with the complexity of the function) *sentence templates* are used to bring precision and clarity to the (*atomic*) statements of function. We look first at one set of templates that can be used.

Inputs to the system are defined by **define** statements that include all the properties of the input – range, default value, checks, type, scale, units etc. Terms needed for use within the Functional Specification are defined by **let** statements. The names of both inputs and terms are preceded by an asterisk when used.

The system's actions are either unconditional:

do (action)

or conditional on a term:

while status-term **do** (action)
for every value-term **do** (action)
whenever event-term **do** (action)
if term **then do** (action)
else do (action).

Table 5.1. *A first taxonomy of System Definition techniques*

Technique	Methodology?	Notation?	Analytical method?
Structured English	no	yes	no
PSL/PSA	no	yes	yes
SA	yes	yes	no
SADT	yes	yes	no
CORE	yes	yes	no
SREM	yes	yes	yes
FSM	some	yes	yes
Petri nets	some	yes	yes
JSD	yes	yes	no
SDS/RSRE	some	yes	yes

Table 5.2. *The principal aspects of a system that are modelled by the different techniques*

Technique	Data structure	Data flow	Control flow
Structured English	some	could	some
PSL/PSA	could	could	could
SA	yes	yes	no
SADT	yes	yes	yes
CORE	no	yes	yes
SREM	no	yes	yes
FSM	no	no	yes
Petri nets	no	no	yes
JSD	yes	yes	yes
SDS/RSRE	could	could	could

Steps within an action can be ordered:

> . . . action 1 **then** action 2 **then** action 3 . . .

or unordered

> . . . action 4 **and** action 5 **and** action 6 . . .

or mixed

> . . . **then** (action 1 **and** action 2) **then** action 3 . . .

Statements of function above the lowest level (i.e. *composite* statements) are in a sense redundant as the atomic template statements contain the entire specification. However, composite statements serve two purposes. Firstly, during the drafting of the Functional Specification, they allow the analyst to control and record the process of stepwise refinement. (There is an analogue here with stepwise refinement as applied to the Design and Production Phases.) Secondly, once the Functional Specification has been drafted, the composite statements make the Functional Specification readable and give it structure.

In the following example, part of the VISTA Functional Specification relating to one of the major requirements has been drafted using the templates suggested above.

A To capture and replay single frames and sequences of frames of television

> **let** a digitised-part-picture (DPP)
> **be** the result of digitising a rectangle within the viewable video picture
> **let** DPP-width
> **be** the number of pixels in each line of a *digitised-part-picture

> A1 To provide a mechanism for a user to request the capture of a single *DPP in a framestore

>> A1A **define** single-shot-capture-request (SSCR)
>> **to be** a user request for the capture of a single *DPP in a framestore
>> **parameters**
>> framestore-id: **range** MSS or SFS
>> **default** SFS

>>> **type** alphanumeric string
>> *DPP-width: **range** 16 . . . *max-DPP-width
>> **default** 512
>> **type** numeric
>> *DPP-height: **range** 1 . . . *VP-height
>> **default** 512
>> **type** numeric
>> **checks** specified framestore is not reserved by another user

> A1B **whenever** a valid *SSCR is received
>> **do** (reserve the specified framestore for the user until explicitly released
>> **then** capture a single frame *DPP of the specified dimensions in it
>> **then** display the captured *DPP on the analogue outputs of the framestore)

> A1C **whenever** an invalid *SSCR is received
>> **do** (. . .)
> A1D **constraint** the analogue-to-digital conversion performed in the framestores shall be carried out by CHIPTEK AB2345 class components

⋮

> B3E **while** a framestore is reserved to a user
>> **do** (light lamp RSV on the framestore
>> **and** ignore button RESET
>> **and if** user is privileged
>>> **then** ignore button OFF
>>> **else** light lamp ENABLE)

For a small system the technique offers

- readability, which is particularly important for training and for the less technical reader,
- traceability, since each atomic function is uniquely labelled,
- the opportunity for manual (and possibly

some automated) consistency and correctness checks,

- a means of cross referencing around the Functional Specification,
- conciseness and accuracy of statement.

It can be seen as a simple cut-down version of more formalised techniques such as PSL/PSA and SDS/RSRE and as such is appropriate in simple systems where a manual procedure is acceptable. Since it is essentially a notational technique (albeit one that informally embodies and hence encourages the ideas of functional decomposition and interface specification) it does not allow you to draw up any further detail for activity 2200 (Produce Functional Specification) in your WBS. If however the technique is appropriate you may choose to adapt the mechanisms of production and analysis used in other procedures and to use Structured English as your recording medium. Thus SADT's methodology could be used to determine and agree functional requirements whilst a Structured English scheme is used to give a word-processable record instead of manual diagrams.

Exercises

1 Using the templates described above, write a Functional Specification for a drinks dispenser with which you are familiar. Be sure to identify the inputs and their permissible values. Go on to describe the dispenser's actions in response to different stimuli.

2 Write down a procedure for producing a hierarchical Functional Specification that involves your client in agreeing each successive level of refinement. Write it in a form that will convince them that they should be involved in this way.

3 Return to your Functional Specification from exercise 1 and categorise each action under one of the following headings:

- functionality from the user's viewpoint,
- functionality from the maintenance department's viewpoint,
- functionality from the accountant's viewpoint,
- functionality from the safety inspector's viewpoint.

4 Scan your Functional Specification and identify

precisely what the dispenser is defined to do in combinational circumstances such as:

- 'coin reject' pressed during drinks delivery, and
- water pressure fails after selection accepted but before drinks delivery.

5 Write a short paper to your clients that will convince them that it is to their benefit to have the Functional Specification of their system expressed in Structured English.

5.4.2 PSL/PSA

A common feature of more formal techniques (SADT, SARA and SREM for instance), whatever stage of development they relate to, is that they involve the generation of considerable detail and, if used manually, considerable paperwork. The maintenance of this material during definition or design iteration, changes and updates can become a major clerical task and the benefits that we would like to get from our techniques – consistency, completeness etc. – can be lost in the cost of supporting the output.

One commercially available solution to this problem is PSL/PSA. Originally developed within the ISDOS project at the University of Michigan, PSL/PSA provides a language (PSL) for the representation of a system, a database within which the representation can be stored and a tool set (PSA) providing mechanisms on the contents of the database.

Though we have included PSL/PSA as a technique it is strictly speaking a notation and a tool.

PSL is a language for describing systems. A *system* contains *objects*. Objects have attributes which in turn have *attribute values*. Objects can be connected by *relationships*.

The Problem Statement Language, PSL, therefore has facilities for:

- naming objects in a system,
- assigning one of a number of types to that object (e.g. INPUT, PROCESS, INTERFACE, CONDITION, EVENT),
- assigning relationships between objects concerning for instance:

system boundaries: RECEIVES,
                       GENERATES
data hierarchy: CONTAINED IN,
                       ORDERED BY
data derivation: USES,
                       DERIVES,
                       MAINTAINS
system control: COMES
                       BEFORE,
                       UTILIZES
system dynamics: CAUSES,
                       TRIGGERS,
                       INTERRUPTS
project management: RESPONSIBLE
                       PROBLEM
                       DEFINER

- assigning values to properties (attributes) of objects, new properties being DEFINEd by the user.

PSL is a neutral language in that it prescribes no particular methodology or procedure, though it is somewhat constraining in that the model must be in terms of the available objects and relationships and their semantic content. However, there is considerable richness to be exploited and the properties mechanism represents an open-ended mechanism of description.

A PSL description is a combination of formal statements and text annotation.

In the following partial example of PSL we start the description of the part of the VISTA system expressed in Structured English in the previous section. The paragraphs in the Structured English are traced through into the PSL using the in_func_spec_para attributes. A number of the objects in the example are not defined and if, in actual use, we omitted their definition we would be told so by PSA.

```
DEFINE ATTRIBUTE     in_func_spec_para;
DEFINE PROCESSOR     single_frame_working;
   SYNONYM IS        SFW;
   ATTRIBUTES ARE    in_func_spec_para "A";
   PERFORMS          single_DPP_capture,
                     single_DPP_display;

DEFINE PROCESS       single_DPP_capture;
   PERFORMED BY      SFW;
   ATTRIBUTES ARE    in_func_spec_para "A1"
   RECEIVES          DPP_capture_request;
   DERIVES           captured_DPP USING video_input;
```

```
DEFINE INPUT         DPP_capture_request;
   ATTRIBUTES ARE    in_func_spec_para "A1A";
   CONSISTS OF       framestore_id,
                     DPP_width,
                     DPP_height;
   RECEIVED BY       single_DPP_capture;

DEFINE ELEMENT       DPP_width;
   VALUES ARE        16 THRU max_DPP_width;
   ATTRIBUTES ARE    default 512;
```

We have defined the SFW PROCESSOR to be the processor (possibly physical) that carries out, *inter alia*, the capture and display of single digital_part_pictures (DPPs). These PROCESSes RECEIVE inputs such as DPP_capture_requests and DERIVE outputs such as a captured_DPP.

All such facts are expressed in PSL and entered via PSA into a database capable of supporting properties and relationships efficiently. PSA tools then allow the production of, for instance,

- database modification reports, identifying changes made chronologically and highlighting resulting or potential errors and problems,
- perspective reports, presenting the information in the database from different angles, such as the Formatted Problem Statement Report which shows all the properties and relationships for a particular object,
- summary reports, presenting the database contents in summary form, such as the Structure Report which might show the complete hierarchy of processes in a stored design,
- analysis reports, deriving facts about the system from the stored data, such as the Data Process Interaction Report which can be used to detect gaps in the information flow or unused data objects.

The database approach to the storage and analysis of system or design descriptions – whether through PSL/PSA or using general relational databases such as RAPPORT (RAPPORT is a registered trademark of Logica UK Limited) – offers a number of benefits:

- simple and complex analysis become possible and in particular qualities such as completeness, consistency and coherence can be more easily ensured and checked for,

- the communication of ideas between staff and with users is made easier, more thorough and thus up-to-date,
- the implications of changes can be quickly and completely established,
- the qualities noted above can be preserved in the specification despite changes,
- the clerical responsibilities of skilled staff are reduced.

Bibliography
Basili 1978, Falla 1977, Freeman 1979, Hershey 1975*a* and 1975*b*, ISDOS 1981, Ramamoorthy 1977, Teichroew 1977, Wig 1978, Winters 1979*a* and 1979*b*.

Exercises

1 Taking a system design that you are familiar with, identify the entities in it, their attributes and relationships. What generalisations of these can you make that it would be useful to express the system in terms of? – In other words invent a syntax for describing your system and others.

2 Does your syntax support the hierarchical definition of functions and data? If not, work this concept into the syntax, e.g.

   [function] IS_MADE_UP_OF [subfunctions list]

3 Does your syntax support consistency checking between layers? For instance is the IS_MADE_UP_OF statement mirrored by an IS_PART_OF statement?

4 Does your syntax support the notion of cause and effect? If not, work this concept into the syntax, not forgetting to incorporate 'mirror statements' (TRIGGERS *and* IS_TRIGGERED_BY)

5 List the types of report/analysis you could (or would like to) get from a database built according to your syntax.

5.4.3 Structured Analysis – SA

The tools of Structured Analysis

Structured Analysis is primarily involved with the application of a particular set of tools to the production of a Structured Functional Specification. In particular, De Marco (1978) and Gane and Sarson (Gane 1979) have defined a methodology for applying these tools from the early stages of the Inception Phase through to the completion of the Functional Specification.

You may decide that De Marco's methodology is quite appropriate and adequate for your project, or you may wish to modify it to suit your needs. Whatever the case, the Structured Analysis tools should be of use to you in most projects. For even if you do not use them in the documentation of your Functional Specification, they are extremely useful thinking aids in the analysis process. Consequently, we first briefly discuss each of the tools in their own right before turning to a description of De Marco's method for using them.

Data Flow Diagrams Data Flow Diagrams (DFD) provide a graphical representation of the movement of data through a system. A DFD is comprised of named vectors (data flows) which connect bubbles (processes), straight lines (files) and boxes (sources or sinks of data). Figure 5.2 shows the overall DFD for the VISTA image processing system. In this case the primary data flows are of television pictures and information about them. Control information is not shown on a DFD.

It would be impossible to represent all of the detailed data flows of a large system in a single diagram. Consequently a hierarchy of levels of DFD (levelled DFDs) is introduced. Levelling of DFDs follows naturally from a top-down analysis of a system. Thus, for example, having arrived at figure 5.2 as a top-level decomposition of the system, we proceed to further decompose each of the processes 1–3 in turn. This further decomposition is aimed at providing greater detail concerning the transformation of the process's inputs to its outputs. Such a decomposition of process 1 of figure 5.2 is shown in figure 5.3.

DFDs can be extremely useful in clarifying the thinking of both analysts and users. This is particularly the case if they are used in Structured Walkthroughs. A Structured Walkthrough using a DFD is a walk through the system as seen from the point of view of the data. This point of view tends to represent the lowest common denominator between the points of view of the analyst, the designer and the different types of user.

For example, a user–analyst walkthrough of

Fig. 5.2. Level 1 data flow diagram for the VISTA system.

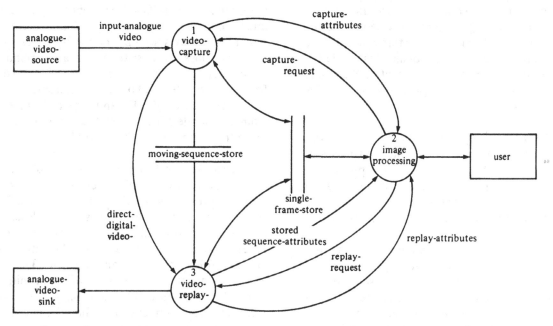

Fig. 5.3. One of the level 2 data flow diagrams for the VISTA system.

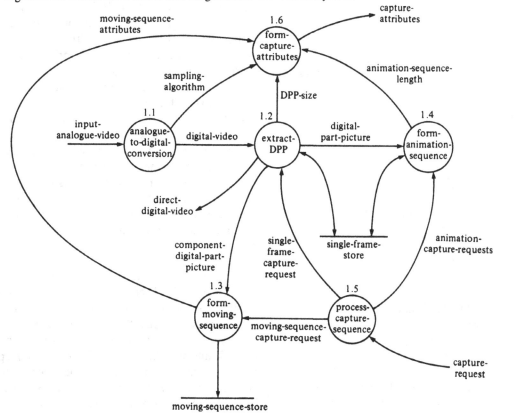

the DFD in figure 5.2 would very quickly reveal to the user that if he wants to perform image processing on a moving sequence of video frames he must transfer it a frame at a time through the single frame store. If the user does not like this restriction then he can say so early in the Definition Phase and be told of the likely cost implications of changing the requirement.

Data Dictionary The Data Dictionary (DD) is used in defining the data flows, files and processes that appear in the DFDs. The DD provides a top-down decomposition of the data in the system just as the DFD provides a top-down decomposition of the transformation of system inputs to outputs.

DD definitions are given in terms of a minimal set of relational operators representing 'sequence', 'selection' and 'iteration' (see also the section on JSP) plus an 'option' operator which is added for convenience. Each of these operators is used in figure 5.4 in which some of the data flows of figure 5.3 are partially defined.

Fig. 5.4. Sample data dictionary entries from the VISTA Functional Specification, produced using Structured Analysis.

SEQUENCE
Dpp-Size = Dpp-Height + Dpp-Width

SELECTION
Capture-Request = [Moving-Sequence-Capture-Request|
Animation-Capture-Request|
Single-Frame-Capture-Request]

SEQUENCE
Digital-Video = {Digital-Video-Picture}
Digital-Video-Picture =
1 {Digital-Video-Line} 625

OPTION
Digital-Video-Line = (Digitised-Colour-Burst)
+ Digitised-Active-Line

Use of a DD should ensure that every term in the Functional Specification is defined and that the inter-relations between data flows and their component data-items are understood by all. In practice, ensuring such consistency in a large, manually maintained DD can be very hard work and some form of automated DD becomes desirable.

An automated DD can range in complexity from a good file editor through to systems such as those that support PSL/PSA and SREM.

Process description tools The bubbles in the lowest level DFDs of the hierarchy of levelled DFDs represent what are called Primitive Processes (or primitives). Primitives are not described in terms of further DFDs and so require some other means of definition. Structured Analysis uses Structured English, Decision Tables and Decision Trees for this purpose. For each of the primitives, a so-called *mini-spec* is written using these tools. The mini-specs form entries in the DD. De Marco gives a particular set of templates for constructing Structured English mini-specs in terms of 'sequence', 'repetition' and 'decision' constructs.

An example of a decision construct is shown in figure 5.5. This piece of Structured English forms the mini-spec of one of the primitives which make up process 1.3 of figure 5.3.

The mini-specs of some primitives are given more clearly in terms of decision tables, or decision trees than in Structured English. An example of a decision table definition of a primitive of process 1.3 of figure 5.3 is given in figure 5.6. This decision table defines the moving sequence store access control policy. By representing this primitive as a decision table the analyst can be certain that all cases are covered while the user is able to check that all cases are defined in the way which he desires.

Using Structured Analysis tools
The tools discussed in the previous subsections can be used in a variety of ways from being simply aids to your thinking about the system through to being the mainstay of a well-defined analysis and specification methodology and a principal communication medium between yourself and your client. Structured Analysis as described by De Marco involves the latter approach.

De Marco describes a number of activities which use the Structured Analysis tools to transform user needs into a Structured Functional Specification (see Dickinson 1980 for a structured specification of how to use the techniques). In general terms these activities can be mapped onto the System Definition Phase WBS as follows:

2210 Study the current situation; produce 'physical' DFD.
2220 Derive logical equivalent DFD.
2230 Model new logical system; produce DD and primitive descriptions.
2240 Establish man–machine interface; produce a selection of possible new physical DFDs.
2250 Quantify each option in terms of cost, risk etc.
2260 Select one option.

Fig. 5.5. A Structured English description of a primitive from the VISTA Functional Specification, produced using Structured Analysis.

Primitive 6 of process 1.3

Moving Sequence Storage Allocation
Select the case which applies:
  Case 1: (Best-Fit-Sequence-Length is equal to 0):
          Set Capture-Status to Moving-Sequence-Store-Full.
  Case 2: (Best-Fit-Sequence-Length is equal to Moving-Sequence-Length):
          Set Moving-Sequence-Start-Address to Best-Fit-Sequence-Start-Address.
          Set Capture-Status to Perfect-Allocation.
  Case 3: (Best-Fit-Sequence-Length is less than Moving-Sequence-Length):
          Set Capture-Status to Not-Enough-Space.
  Case 4: (Best-Fit-Sequence-Length is greater than Moving-Sequence-Length):
          Set Moving-Sequence-Length to Best-Fit-Sequence Length.
          Set Moving-Sequence-Start-Address to Best-Fit-Sequence-Start-Address.
          Set Capture-Status to Extended-Allocation.

2270 Package and publish the completed Functional Specification.

Depending on the firmness of the description of user needs, you may be able to omit some of the above steps. In particular the first, second and parts of the third steps are typically carried out in the Inception Phase and result in what we have called a Requirement Specification. Even if the Requirement Specification is not presented in terms of DFDs, it usually presents, in some form or

Fig. 5.6. A decision table description of a primitive from the VISTA Functional Specification, produced using Structured Analysis.

Primitive 2 of process 1.3

Moving Sequence Store Access Policy

	RULES							
CONDITIONS	1	2	3	4	5	6	7	8
1 System Manager	Y	Y	Y	Y	N	N	N	N
2 Pack Owner	Y	Y	N	N	Y	Y	N	N
3 Sequence Owner	Y	N	Y	N	Y	N	Y	N
ACTIONS								
1 Create Pack Control Entry	Y	Y	Y	Y	N	N	N	N
2 Delete Pack Control Entry	Y	Y	Y	Y	Y	Y	N	N
3 Create Sequence	Y	Y	Y	Y	Y	Y	N	N
4 Delete Sequence	Y	Y	Y	Y	Y	Y	Y	N
5 Write Sequence	Y	Y	Y	Y	Y	Y	Y	N
6 Read Sequence	Y	Y	Y	Y	Y	Y	Y	Y

Fig. 5.7. The client's initial conception of VISTA.

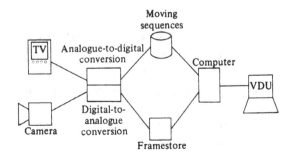

the other, the user's perception of the logical or physical model of the required system. This model can be translated into logical DFDs which are used in activity 2230 onwards. As an example, figure 5.7 shows a user model of the required image processing system which led to figure 5.2.

Bibliography
De Marco 1978 (a detailed and instructive text book), Dickinson 1980 (the project lifecycle defined by Structured Analysis), Gane 1979, Gildersleeve 1970 (an introduction to the use of decision tables), Weinberg 1978.

Exercises
1 In our example we started with a level 1 DFD. De Marco recommends drawing a level 0 *context diagram* which represents the system to be analysed as a single process interacting with sources and sinks in its environment which are not to be analysed. Draw the context diagram for the VISTA system.
2 The VISTA system assumes a particular physical incarnation of the logical DFD in figure 5.2. Can you devise another physical hardware configuration?
3 Choose a set of methodologies from the chapters of this book that cover the complete system development path. Carry out a structured analysis of how these methodologies would interact and progress the system development through its various phases. You should produce a physical DFD, English Language process descriptions and brief DD entries. Once the physical DFD is complete produce a logical DFD from it and see if you can use it to invent a new physical DFD which represents your own integrated development methodology.
4 Use decision tables as an aid in drawing up an argument to present to your bank manager to convince him that you are capable of handling a bigger overdraft.

5.4.4 Structured Analysis and Design Technique – SADT
SADT has two sides:

- a methodology for controlling the analysis and design of a system;
- a diagramming technique for recording the results.

The methodology is based on *functional decomposition* that takes place in a structured or controlled way. The control is exercised through the rules governing the formal diagramming technique and well-defined procedures for the production and review of the diagrams. That is, SADT tells you *what* to produce and *how* to produce it.

Functional decomposition

Functional decomposition (which is not peculiar to SADT) forces you to concentrate on small problems with well-defined boundaries, viz. objectives and interfaces. It also promotes the putting off of implementation decisions (e.g. those concerning efficiency) with all the benefits this brings. In SADT decomposition proceeds by working downwards through a hierarchy of diagrams – a *model*. Figure 5.8 shows a number of model hierarchies appropriate to system development stages. Each level of diagrams is derived from the level above according to rules that ensure that each level describes the same system. Each diagram in a level is drawn according to an extensive rule-book designed to make errors more apparent and the reading of SADT diagrams easier.

The strictness with which decomposition takes place allows controlled iteration back and forth in the analysis–design–implementation process. The more classical separation of these three stages is dissolved in SADT but in a way that allows you to retain a handle on the overall process.

Diagrammatic notation

A hierarchy of SADT diagrams forms a model or *viewpoint* of the system. You may draw a number of models during definition of the system – from the user's viewpoint, from the system manager's viewpoint, from the viewpoint of the operations team, and so on. The collection of viewpoints defines the system in all its aspects.

Suppose we are applying SADT to our VISTA system. At some stage in decomposition the user's viewpoint will contain the notion of free space on the HSD that they may allocate to a file. This will coincide with the viewpoint of the system manager who will see free space on the HSD resulting from fragmentation and require it to be made contiguous by compaction of files up to one 'end' of the HSD. Where such intersection occurs, models from different viewpoints can share sub-models by means of 'mechanisms'.

A SADT diagram contains a small number of boxes connected by arrows. In *activity models* the boxes represent activities ('capture frame of video', 'reserve framestore'); in *data models* they represent data structures ('framestore attributes', 'HSD directory'). The SADT diagram captures all the constraints on the flow of activities or data where they are *true* constraints; otherwise no specific ordering is implied.

An activity box has arrows entering it for

- inputs,
- control,
- mechanisms,

and arrows leaving it for

- outputs.

Decomposition involves taking a single box and its attached arrows and expanding it on its own diagram into smaller activities/data structures connected by arrows. One of the diagramming rules states that the arrows entering and leaving the diagram must be the same as those entering and leaving the box being decomposed.

A SADT diagram can carry explanatory notes (within certain limits) and can be supported by separate text. This would generally be read *after* the diagram has been inspected by a reader, since the definitive description of the system is the diagram alone.

A rigorous numbering system ensures that all boxes and arrows that appear on more than one diagram are uniquely identified in a natural way.

Sequencing constraints can be added to the model by putting *activation rules* on diagrams. Activation rules override the normal interpretation of activity boxes, viz. that an activity produces *all* of its outputs only if the contents of all of its input and control arrows are present.

Thus activity 5 on diagram 6 might generate output O2 only if input I1 is present and control C3 is absent:

$$6/5: \text{I1 \& } \overline{\text{C3}} \rightarrow \text{O2}$$

The arrow separates the *precondition* list from the *postcondition* list. Either list may reference inputs, controls or outputs or their negation (absence).

Methodology

A major element of SADT is the infrastructure it defines to produce, review, monitor and archive the diagrams as work proceeds. A number of roles are defined, including 'authors' who are responsible for carrying out the analysis and for modelling the system in SADT diagrams, 'commenters' responsible for reviewing and making

Fig. 5.8. SADT models appropriate to system development stages. (From Dickover 1978.)

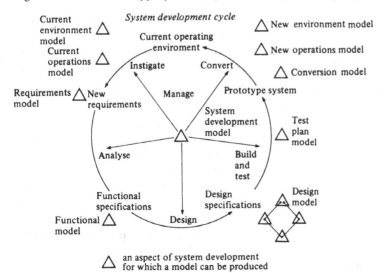

written comment on the output of authors, 'experts' from whom system requirements are extracted through interviews with authors, and a 'librarian' who keeps the archive, distributes material and so on.

The method prescribes their relationships and hence the information flow around the team: an author interviews the experts and draws up a level of SADT diagrams; these are filed by the librarian in the archive and distributed to commenters and non-commenting readers in the form of a 'kit'; annotated copies of the kit are returned to the author by the commenters and filed in the archive by the librarian; the author revises the diagrams and repeats the cycle until all problems are resolved at that level. The individual diagrams then pass to authors for decomposition at the next level. The first author might be one of these or perhaps a commenter on this lower level.

This reader/author cycle is supported by reviews by a technical committee which also has the task of resolving technical issues where necessary.

Although in the above we have identified a number of roles there need not be as many people since the roles could be mapped onto a smaller number of staff – two people can use SADT successfully.

We can summarise the procedure for the entire analysis–design–implementation path crudely as follows:

(i) The reader/author cycle model is started for the activity model(s).

(ii) Once this has settled down (but before design decisions start being made) a reader/author cycle is set going for the data model.

(iii) When the cycles for the two models are stable they can be tied together – they must describe exactly the same system and in a sense be 'duals'.

(iv) At the current activity model level, *mechanisms* are identified that would need to exist in the computing system if the level were to be implemented directly from the diagrams.

(v) These mechanisms are inserted on the diagrams.

(vi) The reader/author cycle is started at this new

level on the mechanism and decomposition proceeds.

(vii) When all boxes are represented by mechanisms the system can be coded from the diagrams together with the data specifications resulting from the data model.

(viii) Once it is working, the system can be inspected for inefficiencies which can be optimised out by iterating back in a controlled fashion.

An audit trail is kept of the design process by storing the results of all iterations in the library – diagrams, text and commenter's comments. The need to record design decisions and the reason for them must not be neglected.

Finally, your Functional Specification will consist of the complete collection of consistent viewpoint models, each being a hierarchy of SADT diagrams and explanatory text. Since your client has been involved at each step in the iterative process it should be ready for their signature without further ado.

Example Here we show the results of this procedure had it been applied to the question of the allocation of space for sequences of TV frames on the HSD in VISTA (see figure 5.9).

After the highest level diagram for the viewpoint, the next level diagram (A1) of the activity model analyses the functions expected of the system from the viewpoint of space allocation on the HSD. We want the system to

- implement commands relating to HSD space from the user,
- generally manage that space effectively,
- print a map of the files on certain occasions.

Note the inputs, outputs and controls on these activities.

In diagram A1.2 we expand box 2 of diagram A1. Note how the controls and outputs of A1 are decomposed on A1.2. When box 2 of A1.2 is decomposed the pure functional structure starts to disappear and the constraints of data begin to dictate a control flow. At this point, implementation decisions would come into the picture having been put off for as long as possible. Up to this point we have also left open our options on parallelism and concurrency of the different activities.

Work Breakdown Structure

From this outline description of SADT we can expand our WBS for the System Definition activity (2000) along the following lines:

2000 System Definition
    2100 System Definition Management
    2110 Manage reader/author cycles and iterative progress
    2120 Maintain archive (librarian)
2200 Produce Functional Specification
    2210 Identify viewpoints to be modelled
    2220 Elaborate viewpoint models (authors)
    . . .
        222*n* Elaborate acceptance model
        222*m* Elaborate quality requirements model
    2230 Review diagrams (readers, commenters)
    2240 Review models (technical committee)
    2250 Reconcile performance requirements and models
2300 Produce Project Plan
2400 Produce Quality Management Plan
2500 Produce Acceptance Test Specification
2600 Perform System Modelling

Although modelling of the system is implicit in SADT, we have left activity 2600 in place as you might still wish to perform simulations based on your analysis using SADT.

SADT extends naturally, as we have seen, into the Design Phase, in fact almost dissolving the separation between the two. Since the process in that phase is not significantly different we finish our coverage of SADT at this point noting simply that SADT is a useful approach in the planning, analysis and design phases, leading naturally to PDL or, if a more formal approach is required, into VDM.

Bibliography

Connor 1980, Dickover 1978, Pedersen 1978, Ross 1977*a* and 1977*b*, SofTech 1976, Thomas 1978.

Exercises

1 Consider the benefits and dangers of delaying design decisions. In particular, what justification is there for ignoring the problem of efficiency for as long as possible? In his Structured Programming, Jackson recommends that optimisation is the last thing you do to a system. Do you agree?

2 You have to come up with a Requirement Specification for an air-conditioning system.
    Analyse the different viewpoints you would need to model:

- the user,
- the maintenance man,
- the building regulations officer,
- the architect,
- the builder,
- the heating engineer,
- the window cleaner.

Decompose their viewpoints and identify where they intersect. Also, identify the point in each viewpoint model where you start to make design decisions.

3 SADT relies on formal diagrams. What characteristics would you require of a graphics system that supported SADT interactively?

4 SADT has been used in conjunction with PSL/PSA. Consider how SADT diagrams might be recorded in terms of PSL's entities, relationships and so on.

5 From the descriptions in this book, identify the parallels between the SADT methodology and Structured Design.

6 Draw up a programme of Structured Walkthroughs (in the Yourdon fashion) to monitor and review an SADT development, ignoring SADT's own mechanisms.

7 Draw an SADT diagram hierarchy for system development itself based on the WBS in section 2.1.10 from the viewpoint of project managers.

5.4.5 Controlled Requirements Expression – CORE

Overview of the procedure
As a technique, CORE offers you

- a methodology for determining and temporally ordering the requirements of a system,
- a notation for representing the requirements in an easily comprehensible way,
- some quality control measures allowing you to check out consistency and so on.

CORE is closely related to SADT and, like SADT, can be enhanced by using an automated notation and analysis tool such as PSL/PSA. In actual implementations it has been used to develop requirements to the point where a natural transi-

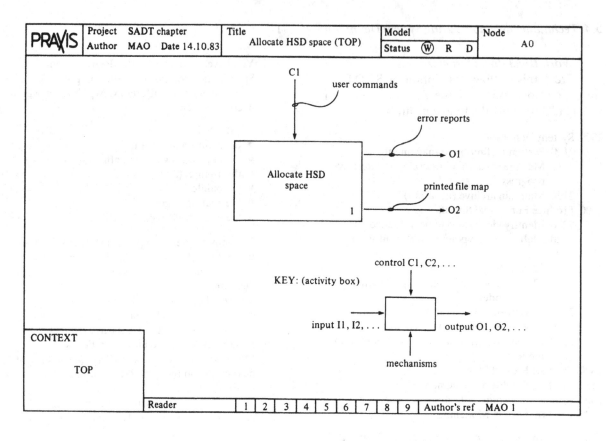

	Project	SADT chapter	Title		Model			Node	
PRAXIS	Author	MAO Date 14.10.83		Allocate HSD space (TOP)	Status	(W) R D			A0

C1
user commands

Allocate HSD
space
1

error reports → O1

printed file map → O2

KEY: (activity box)

control C1, C2, . . .

input I1, I2, . . .   output O1, O2, . . .

mechanisms

CONTEXT

TOP

Reader | 1 | 2 | 3 | 4 | 5 | 6 | 7 | 8 | 9 | Author's ref MAO 1

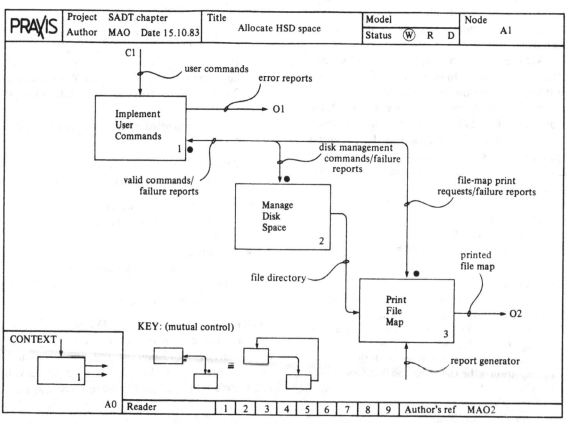

	Project	SADT chapter	Title		Model			Node	
PRAXIS	Author	MAO Date 15.10.83		Allocate HSD space	Status	(W) R D			A1

C1
user commands
error reports

Implement
User
Commands
1

O1

valid commands/
failure reports

disk management
commands/failure
reports

file-map print
requests/failure reports

Manage
Disk
Space
2

file directory

printed
file map

Print
File
Map
3

O2

report generator

KEY: (mutual control)

CONTEXT

1

=

A0 | Reader | 1 | 2 | 3 | 4 | 5 | 6 | 7 | 8 | 9 | Author's ref MAO2

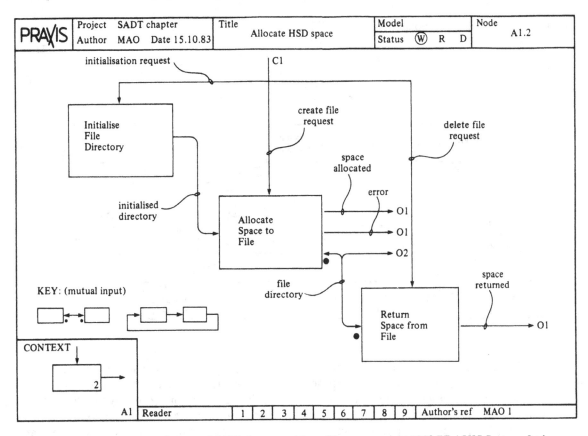

Fig. 5.9. The diagram output from an SADT decomposition. (Form copyright 1983 PRAXIS Systems Ltd, Bath.)

tion to design can be made using the MASCOT design approach.

The technique is an iterative one, each level of iteration producing a new level of refinement of the requirements. Each level of iteration has three stages each itself carried out iteratively:

(i) gather information,
(ii) propose data–process relationships,
(iii) prove data–process relationships.

These three steps, repeated at successive levels, are designed to ensure that at each stage the expression of requirements is consistent with the user's expectations and with itself.

One of the principal concepts in CORE is that of the *viewpoint*. A viewpoint is an area that directly affects or comprises the requirement. Typical viewpoints are

- system manager,
- QA department,
- customer withdrawing cash,
- weapons control officer,
- external environment.

Refinement of the requirements then becomes synonymous with refinement of viewpoints and via the iterative procedure we are led to a *viewpoint hierarchy*. Figure 5.10 shows part of a possible viewpoint hierarchy for our VISTA system as an example. Once the viewpoint hierarchy has been drawn up, however tentatively, the iterative refinement can start at the top layer.

Information gathering

The first stage of analysis for a new level in the viewpoint hierarchy is to gather information at that level by consultation whenever possible with representatives of the various viewpoints, to order that information and to do some first-line checking. Information may also be derived from relevant documentation or indeed be generated by the analyst. The four steps are as follows:

Fig. 5.10. A CORE viewpoint hierarchy for VISTA.

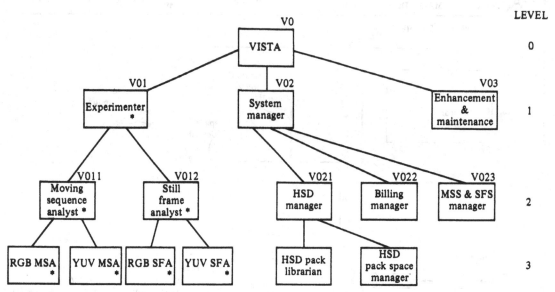

A1. Select the viewpoints at this level In collaboration with the user, the analyst decomposes the viewpoints at the previous, higher level to form the viewpoints to be considered at this level. Thus in VISTA, 'experimenters' fall into two groups: those working with stills and those using TV sequences.

A2. Analyse the viewpoint data flows The analyst must now extract from viewpoint representatives descriptions (possibly in informal terms) of the requirements of each viewpoint in terms of the data flows through it. These descriptions are then transferred into the more formal form of data flow tables similar to the one in figure 5.11 which has

Fig. 5.11. A partial CORE viewpoint analysis for viewpoint V011.

		Viewpoint: moving-sequence analyst V011		
source	input	action	output	destination
ENV	analogue video	capture-moving-sequence on MSS	captured sequence	V011
V023	MSS status		updated MSS status	V023
USR	CMS request		rejected request	USR
V021	HSD file		logged request	V022
USR	DMS request	display-moving-sequence on MSS	rejected request	USR
V011	captured sequence		analogue video	ENV

key:
ENV = system's environment
USR = user of the system (formally part of the environment)

been partly filled in for the 'moving sequence analyst' viewpoint. Internal consistency checks are carried out on each table:

- Does each input have a source viewpoint?
- Does each output have a destination viewpoint?
- Are all the actions for this viewpoint shown?

A3. Reconcile the data flows Once all the analysis tables for all the viewpoints at the current level have been completed and individually checked they can be checked collectively by asking such questions as:

- Do all sources and destinations match?
- Are the tables at this level consistent with those at the level above, of which they are a decomposition?
- Do the users see the tables as representing their requirements at this level completely and correctly?
- Are all data names used on the tables consistent?

A4. Draw up data decomposition Throughout the iteration a record is kept of the database

being defined and refined by the flow tables. The data structures are recorded using a notation similar to that used in Jackson Structured Programming.

Propose data–process relationships
Having tabulated the viewpoint data at the current level we then go on to draw diagrams showing the data–process relationships that exist between viewpoints. We do this in two steps.

B1. Draw isolated threads Loosely speaking, a *thread* can be defined as a tightly coupled flow of data through the processes of a viewpoint. Identifying a thread is therefore an exercise that is aided by the data decomposition. Threads represent the second major concept of CORE.

This step produces diagrams that detail the individual functions in each viewpoint separately. Figure 5.12 shows the notation used for a function or process in such diagrams. (Note the strong similarity with the notation used in SADT activity diagrams.) In figure 5.13 we show the isolated thread diagram for the capture-moving-sequence function in the moving-sequence-analyst viewpoint (V011).

Fig. 5.12. Notation for CORE activity diagrams.

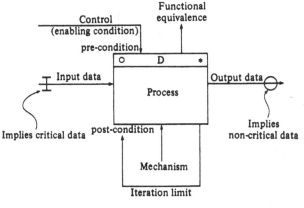

Key:
o = mutual exclusion
   (with adjacent process)
D = lower level detail available
* = iteration

Fig. 5.13. Capture-moving-sequence thread in the moving-sequence-analyst viewpoint.

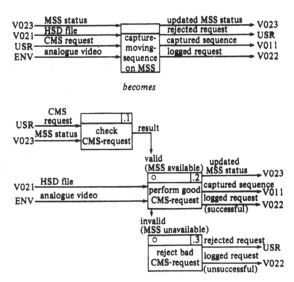

B2. Draw isolated operational view This means drawing up a single diagram for each viewpoint showing how all the individual functions – i.e. the isolated threads from B1 – operate together. As such it is a composite of the B1 diagrams with threads grouped into functional areas.

Prove data–process relationships

The final stage of the analysis of one level of the viewpoint hierarchy is to check out the relationships between threads and between viewpoints in the level.

C1. Draw combined threads A new set of diagrams is now drawn up showing how the threads in a viewpoint interface with the threads of other viewpoints. Each diagram shows related isolated threads combined in their correct temporal order. For our capture-moving-sequence thread, the diagram would show the creation of the HSD file in viewpoint V021 as a necessary pre-condition for sequence capture and the corresponding threads would be combined.

Drawing this diagram forces us to check the consistency between viewpoints, i.e. the consistency in our requirements.

C2. Draw combined operational view This results in a single diagram showing how the viewpoints at this level operate together, i.e. how the overall requirement operates. Figure 5.14 shows the combined operational view in a crude form for VISTA.

C3. Review requirements This final step in the processing of the level requires the analyst to check the diagrams for requirements such as reliability, cost, integrity, error handling and so on, and to modify the diagrams as necessary. Any review technique could be used, Structured Walkthroughs for instance.

Iteration to higher levels may be necessary but if this is so it can be undertaken in the framework provided by the diagrams. Such questions as the following can be asked:

- In the operational system what can go wrong here?

Fig. 5.14. Sample diagram of the combined operational view.

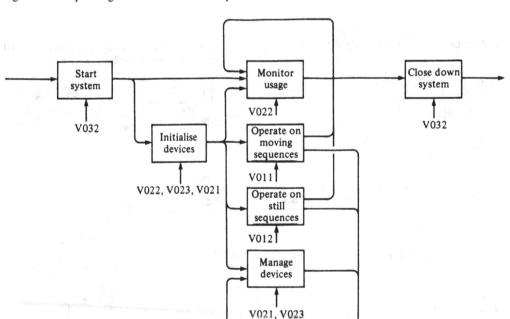

- How can it be prevented/detected/repaired?
- What extra actions, mechanisms or data are required to achieve the required reliability here?

The Functional Specification in CORE

If you use the CORE technique in System Definition the deliverable item – the Functional Specification – will be composed of the final versions of the following:

- the viewpoint hierarchy,
- the viewpoint analysis tables,
- the isolated thread diagrams for all viewpoints,
- the isolated operational view for each viewpoint,
- the combined thread diagrams,
- the combined operational view.

The inherent structuring in the technique will give a corresponding structure to all these items.

Work Breakdown Structure

CORE does not directly contribute much to the WBS segment for the System Definition phase except to expand the section on preparing the Functional Specification. Also, as it is an iterative technique, we need to remember that each sub-work-package has a component at each level of iteration. Nevertheless the following sample WBS segment would be a useful framework for planning and recording given that once the viewpoint hierarchy has been drafted one will have a good idea of the likely depth of iteration.

2200 Produce Functional Specification
    2210 Derive viewpoint hierarchy
    2220 Gather information at current level
        2221 Select viewpoints
        2222 Analyse viewpoint data flows
        2223 Reconcile data flows
    2230 Prove data relationships at current level
        2231 Draw isolated threads
        2232 Draw isolated operational view
    2240 Prove data relationships at current level
        2241 Draw combined threads
        2242 Draw combined operational view
        2243 Review requirements

Bibliography

DoI 1981, Mullery 1979, Ward 1981.

Exercises

1 Carry out an informal viewpoint analysis of a system with which you are familiar along the lines of steps A1–A4.
2 In common with other definition techniques CORE places emphasis on mechanisms that allow the consistency of a Functional Specification to be checked at different points in the iteration. Consider how much value is to be gained from this and relate this to the cost of manual checking and automatic checking.
3 CORE offers a smooth transition into the Design Phase. How much of this is in fact desirable? Do you think that there is anything to be said for a clear boundary between the *requirements* on a system and its *design*? Looking ahead a little, do you think one should have a clear boundary between the logical *design* of a system and its *implementation*?

5.4.6 Software Requirements Engineering Methodology – SREM

Work Breakdown Structure

As described in chapter 3, SREM and its support environment, REVS, provide a sophisticated, automated requirements definition and analysis tool. A description of the steps involved in applying SREM was given in chapter 3. These steps can be mapped onto a WBS for the Definition Phase in a number of ways. For the purpose of exposition we adopt the following partial mapping:

2000 System Definition
    2100 System Definition Management
        2110 Management of Requirement Specification Problem Reports
        2120 Review of Definition Phase Plans
    2200 Produce Functional Specification
        2210 Translation of Requirement Specification
        2220 Review of Requirement Specification
        2230 Correction of Requirement Specification Problems
        2240 Decomposition of requirements
        2250 Review of decomposition
        2260 Allocation of performance requirements
    2300 Produce Project Plan
    2400 Produce Quality Management Plan
    2500 Produce Acceptance Test Specification
    2600 Perform system modelling
        2610 Functional simulation
        2620 Analysis feasibility demonstration

Fig. 5.15. SREM R-NETs resulting from the requirements.

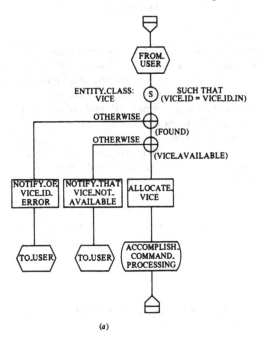

(a)

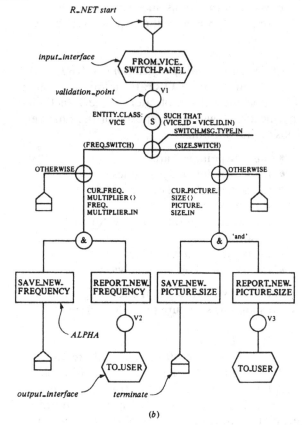

(b)

```
...
INPUT_INTERFACE FROM_USER.
   CONNECTS SUBSYSTEM USER_CONSOLE.
   ENABLES R_NET PROCESS_USER_COMMANDS.
OUTPUT_INTERFACE TO_USER.
   CONNECTS SUBSYSTEM USER_CONSOLE.
   PASSES MESSAGE VICE_ERROR_MSG_OUT
          MESSAGE FREQ_MULTIPLIER_CHANGE_MSG_OUT
          MESSAGE PICTURE_SIZE_CHANGE_MSG_OUT.
...
ALPHA ALLOCATE_VICE.
   DESCRIPTION
          "Assigns VICE to requesting user by linking the Console
           ID to the (instance of the ENTITY-CLASS) VICE which has
           been allocated.".
   INPUTS DATA CONSOLE_ADDRESS_IN.
   OUTPUTS DATA USER_TO_WHICH_VICE_ALLOCATED.
DATA VICE_AVAILABLE.
   TYPE BOOLEAN.
R_NET PROCESS_USER_COMMANDS
   DESCRIPTION
          "Upon receipt of a legal command, the DP shall check the
           legality of the requested VICE ID. If an incorrect VICE
           ID is input the user is notified of the VICE_ID error. If
           the VICE_ID is legal, the VICE's availability is checked.
           If not available, the user is notified of its nonavail-
           ability. If available, it is allocated to the user and
           User Command is executed.".
```

```
STRUCTURE
   INPUT_INTERFACE FROM_USER
   SELECT ENTITY_CLASS VICE
      SUCH THAT (VICE_ID = VICE_ID_IN)
      IF (*CHECK FOR PROPER VICE ID ENTERED*)
         (FOUND)
         IF (*CHECK IF VICE IS IN USE*)
            (VICE_AVAILABLE)
            ALPHA ALLOCATE_VICE
            SUBNET ACCOMPLISH_COMMAND_PROCESSING
            TERMINATE
         OTHERWISE
            ALPHA NOTIFY_THAT_VICE_NOT_AVAILABLE
               (*INDICATES THAT VICE IS IN USE AND
                NOT AVAILABLE TO PROCESS USER's COMMAND*)
            OUTPUT_INTERFACE TO_USER
         END
      OTHERWISE
         ALPHA NOTIFY_OF_VICE_ID_ERROR
            (*SENDS ERROR_MSG TO USER INDICATING THAT INPUT
             ID WAS IN ERROR*)
         OUTPUT_INTERFACE TO_USER
      END
END.
...
```

(c)

In the following subsections we consider in more detail the stages involved in the production of the Functional Specification and consider their relation to other System Definition activities.

Translation of Requirement Specification

The aim of this stage is to translate the Requirement Specification, whatever its form, into the SREM notation of R-NETs which are themselves translated into the language RSL and to enter this baseline requirements description into the REVS database.

Traceability of the Functional Specification to the originating requirement in the Requirement Specification is an important concept in SREM. Consequently a summary of each of the Requirement Specification's requirement paragraphs is fed into the REVS database as an RSL ORIGINATING-REQUIREMENT element.

```
R_NET UPDATE_VICE_CONFIGURATION
  DESCRIPTION
          "Whenever the frequency or picture size switch on the
          VICE switch panel is changed, the VICE information
          concerning the change is stored (in the ENTITY-CLASS:
          VICE) and the user is notified of the change.".
  STRUCTURE
  INPUT_INTERFACE FROM_VICE_SWITCH_PANEL
  VALIDATION_POINT V1
  SELECT ENTITY_CLASS VICE
    SUCH THAT (VICE_ID = VICE_PANEL_ID_IN)
    CONSIDER DATA SWITCH_MSG_TYPE_IN
    IF (SIZE_SWITCH)
        IF (*COMPARE NEW PICTURE SIZE TO EXISTING PICTURE SIZE*)
           (CUR_PICTURE_SIZE < > PICTURE_SIZE_IN)
           DO
              ALPHA REPORT_NEW_PICTURE_SIZE
              VALIDATION_POINT V3
              OUTPUT_INTERFACE TO_USER
           AND
              ALPHA SAVE_NEW_PICTURE_SIZE
              TERMINATE
           END
        OTHERWISE
           TERMINATE
        END
    OR (FREQ_SWITCH)
        IF (*COMPARE NEW FREQUENCY TO EXISTING FREQUENCY*)
           (CUR_FREQ_MULTIPLIER < > FREQ_MULTIPLIER_IN)
           DO
              ALPHA REPORT_NEW_FREQUENCY
              VALIDATION_POINT V2
              OUTPUT_INTERFACE TO_USER
           AND
              ALPHA SAVE_NEW_FREQUENCY
              TERMINATE
           END
        OTHERWISE
           TERMINATE
        END
     END
  END
END.
```

(d)

The generation of a baseline set of R-NETs proceeds via the following steps (e.g. Alford 1980):

(i) Identification of all interfaces to the data processor, the messages that cross the interfaces and the message contents.

(ii) Objects about which data must be stored globally are identified. Each such class of objects defines an ENTITY-CLASS. The DATA which is associated with each instance of the ENTITY-CLASS is also defined.

(iii) Elements of a particular ENTITY-CLASS may be in different states which require different subsets of data to be maintained. Any such states are identified as ENTITY-TYPEs associated with their unique sets of DATA.

(iv) R-NETs are drawn which show the processing logic for each input message. These may involve transformation of global information such as that defined for ENTITY-CLASSes and/or they may produce output MESSAGEs as a result of the processing.

(v) The R-NET structures are entered in the REVS database using RSL.

(vi) Data that must be maintained to meet the requirements and processing steps that are needed to perform the input-to-output transformations are identified and entered in the REVS database as RSL DATA and ALPHA elements respectively.

The results of applying these steps are best discussed by way of an example from VISTA. Consider the following requirement paragraphs:

A The VICE shall, upon receipt of any user command, implicitly allocate the VICE to such user if available (not allocated to another user). If it is not available, a message will be issued to the user and no further processing of the user's command shall occur.

B2 When the VICE configuration is changed, the VICE configuration information will be modified to reflect the new configuration, and the user shall be informed.

Figure 5.16(*a*) shows how these requirements might be expressed in RSL.

Fig. 5.16. SREM material derived from the R-NETs.

```
ORIGINATING_REQUIREMENT VICE_ALLOCATION
  DESCRIPTION
          "The VICE shall, upon receipt of any user command, implicitly
          allocate the VICE to such user if available (not allocated
          to another user). If not available a message will be issued
          to the user and no further processing of the users command
          shall occur.".
  DOCUMENTED SOURCE PARA_A.
  TRACES MESSAGE USER_VICE_COMMAND_MSG_IN
          R_NET PROCESS_USER_COMMANDS
          MESSAGE VICE_ERROR_MSG_OUT
          SUBSYSTEM USER_CONSOLE
          ENTITY_CLASS VICE
          INPUT_INTERFACE FROM_USER
          OUTPUT_INTERFACE TO_USER.
ORIGINATING_REQUIREMENT VICE_CONFIGURATION_CHANGE_NOTIFICATION.
  DESCRIPTION
          "When the VICE configuration is changed, the VICE
          Configuration information will be modified to reflect
          the new configuration, and the user shall be informed.".
  DOCUMENTED SOURCE PARA_B2.
  TRACES R_NET UPDATE_VICE_CONFIGURATION
          INPUT_INTERFACE FROM_VICE_SWITCH_PANEL
          OUTPUT_INTERFACE TO_USER
          MESSAGE FREQUENCY_SWITCH_MSG_IN
          MESSAGE PICTURE_SIZE_SWITCH_MSG_IN
          SUBSYSTEM USER_CONSOLE
          ENTITY_CLASS VICE
          VALIDATION_PATH FREQ_CHANGE_REPORT_PATH
          VALIDATION_PATH PICTURE_SIZE_CHANGE_REPORT_PATH
          MESSAGE FREQ_MULTIPLIER_CHANGE_MSG_OUT
          MESSAGE PICTURE_SIZE_CHANGE_MSG_OUT.
```

(a)

```
CRADX COMMAND=
  SET UNAUTHORED_ELEMENTS = PRIME_ELEMENTS        WITHOUT ENTERED_BY
          (*INDICATES KEY ELEMENTS WHOSE AUTHORSHIP IS UNKNOWN.*)
--------------------------------------------
SET COUNT = 14

CRADX COMMAND=
LIST UNAUTHORED_ELEMENTS
--------------------------------------------

  ENTITY_CLASS: VICE
  INPUT_INTERFACE: FROM_USER
  INPUT_INTERFACE: FROM_VICE_SWITCH_PANEL
  MESSAGE: FREQUENCY_SWITCH_MSG_IN
  MESSAGE: FREQ_MULTIPLIER_CHANGE_MSG_OUT
  MESSAGE: PICTURE_SIZE_CHANGE_MSG_OUT
  MESSAGE: PICTURE_SIZE_SWITCH_MSG_IN
  MESSAGE: USER_VICE_COMMAND_MSG_IN
  MESSAGE: VICE_ERROR_MSG_OUT
  OUTPUT_INTERFACE: TO_USER
  R_NET: PROCES_USER_COMMANDS
  R_NET: UPDATE_VICE_CONFIGURATION
  SUBSYSTEM: USER_CONSOLE
  SUBSYSTEM: VICE_SWITCH_PANEL

CRADX COMMAND=
SET DATA_WITH_SINK_BUT_NO_SOURCE = SINKS MINUS SOURCES
                  (* IF A DATA ITEM HAS A SINK, THEN IT MUST HAVE
                  A SOURCE *)
--------------------------------------------------------------------
SET COUNT = 2

CRADX COMMAND =
          LIST DATA_WITH_SINK_BUT_NO_SOURCE
--------------------------------------------------------------------

  DATA: VICE_AVAILABLE.
  DATA: VICE_ID.
```

(c)

```
CRADX COMMAND=
ANALYZE DATA_FLOW PROCESS_USER_COMMANDS
-------------------------------------------------------
  R_NET: PROCESS_USER_COMMANDS
    REFERS TO
      ALPHA: ALLOCATE_VICE
        INPUTS
            DATA: CONSOLE_ADDRESS_IN
        OUTPUTS
            DATA: USER_TO_WHICH_VICE_ALLOCATED
      ALPHA: NOTIFY_OF_VICE_ID_ERROR
        INPUTS
            DATA: CONSOLE_ADDRESS_IN
        OUTPUTS
            DATA: ERROR_TEXT_OUT
            DATA: USER_ADDRESS_OUT
        FORMS
          MESSAGE: VICE_ERROR_MSG_OUT
            MADE BY
                DATA: ERROR_TEXT_OUT
                DATA: USER_ADDRESS_OUT
      ALPHA: NOTIFY_THAT_VICE_NOT_AVAILABLE
        INPUTS
            DATA: CONSOLE_ADDRESS_IN
        OUTPUTS
            DATA: ERROR_TEXT_OUT
            DATA: USER_ADDRESS_OUT
        FORMS
          MESSAGE: VICE_ERROR_MSG_OUT (*)
      DATA: FOUND
      DATA: VICE_AVAILABLE
      DATA: VICE_ID
      DATA: VICE_ID_IN
      ENTITY_CLASS: VICE
        ASSOCIATES
            DATA: CUR_FREQ_MULTIPLIER
            DATA: CUR_PICTURE_SIZE
            DATA: USER_TO_WHICH_VICE_ALLOCATED
            DATA: VICE_AVAILABLE
            DATA: VICE_ID
      INPUT_INTERFACE: FROM_USER
        PASSES
          MESSAGE: USER_VICE_COMMAND_MSG_IN
            MADE BY
                DATA: CONSOLE_ADDRESS_IN
                DATA: SUPPORTING_COMMAND_INFO_IN
                DATA: USER_COMMAND_IN
                DATA: VICE_ID_IN
      OUTPUT_INTERFACE: TO_USER
        PASSES
          MESSAGE: FREQ_MULTIPLIER_CHANGE_MSG_OUT
            MADE BY
                DATA: NEW_FREQ_MULTIPLIER_OUT
                DATA: USER_ADDRESS_OUT
          MESSAGE: PICTURE_SIZE_CHANGE_MSG_OUT
            MADE BY
                DATA: NEW_PICTURE_SIZE_OUT
                DATA: USER_ADDRESS_OUT
          MESSAGE: VICE_ERROR_MSG_OUT (*)
      SUBNET: ACCOMPLISH_COMMAND_PROCESSING
*-*-*-*- ANALYZE DATA FLOW FOR R_NET: PROCESS_USER_COMMANDS
*ERROR 2800 REFERENCED SUBNET DOES NOT HAVE A STRUCTURE.
      SUBNET: ACCOMPLISH_COMMAND_PROCESSING

*ERROR 2820 INFORMATION PASSING INPUT_INTERFACE NOT USED.
      DATA: SUPPORTING_COMMAND_INFO_IN
      DATA: USER_COMMAND_IN.
```

(b)

The definitions identify two R-NETs, PRO-CESS-USER-COMMANDS and UPDATE-VICE-CONFIGURATION, that will result from the requirement paragraphs A and B2. Figure 5.15 (*a* and *b*) shows these R-NETs in graphical form whilst parts (*c* and *d*) of the same figure contain part of the RSL input that defines them and other items for the requirements database.

Review of the Requirement Specification

Once the baseline requirement definition has been fed into the REVS database, the requirements are checked for functional completeness and consistency and any requirement decisions which have been made are reviewed. This checking and review procedure is carried out with the aid of automatic REVS tools for data extraction and analysis.

Some of the problems found by checking the database will result from inadvertent errors that occurred in building the requirements database. These are immediately corrected and the checks are re-run on the corrected database. Other problems are often identified during this phase that are issues requiring client feedback. These result in problem reports defined as DECISIONs in the requirements database.

One of the principal project management roles during the Definition Phase is the management of such problem reports (Work Package 2110). This requires ensuring that all problems are reported, transmitting of the reports to the authority responsible for issuing the Requirement Specification, scheduling technical meetings necessary to resolve the problems and checking that all problems are resolved before they result in schedule slippage.

Returning to the example given above, a number of problems would be detected with the aid of REVS. For example, the DATA-FLOW ANALYSIS (reproduced in figure 5.16(*b*)) shows two errors.

The first reports that the SUBNET: AC-COMPLISH-COMMAND-PROCESSING has not yet had its structure defined. The second reports two data items that were in the input message but which were not used anywhere in the R-NET. These data items will actually be used in the undefined SUBNET when its structure is finally defined. At that point, if the DATA-FLOW

ANALYSIS were re-run, none of these reported errors would then exist. A more serious problem exists, however, because the requirements do not include any discussion of what processing is required for user commands. The undefined SUB-NET cannot be completed until those requirements are known. This problem would result in a problem report which would be issued to the client along with appropriate recommendations. Possibly following meetings with the client to discuss the problem, change requests would be issued, the Requirement Specification augmented and new RSL added to the database (Work Package 2230).

REVS allows a great many other reports and consistency checks to be carried out on the requirements database: key elements in the database must have assigned authors, REVS will check that this is so; data items with sinks but no source will be flagged. Figure 5.16(*c*) shows the REVS output that might result.

Decomposition of requirements

In this step the Requirement Specification is refined until all processing steps required to satisfy the transformation of input to output messages have been identified. Further, an initial definition of performance requirements is made.

Performance requirements are defined in terms of VALIDATION-POINTS in an R-NET and data collected at these validation points. For example, to define the timing requirement in paragraph B2 of the Requirement Specification, VALIDATION-POINTS V1, V2 and V3 are included in the R-NET in figure 5.15. At these validation points timing data must be collected.

The assignment of performance requirements is reviewed to ensure that the mapping between such requirements in the Requirement Specification and those in the R-NETs is complete, correct and not over-constraining. This review is once again aided by automated REVS tools.

Allocation of performance requirements

Having established overall performance requirements for the paths through the R-NETs, the sensitivity of these requirements to the performance requirements of the Requirement Specification is determined. This allows optimal allocation of timing and accuracy requirements to be made and tolerances to be specified.

Functional simulations can be generated with the aid of REVS to accomplish dynamic consistency checking. The simulations are automatically generated in Pascal from the RSL in the database. Processing steps (ALPHAs) result in calls to Pascal procedures written by the person carrying out the simulation and entered in the REVS database as textual attributes of the ALPHAs. The interaction of these procedures (called BETAs) with other data in the database is automatically controlled by REVS.

The simulations allow the progress of externally introduced messages to be tracked and such performance factors as system loadings to be measured.

Following this verification, the Functional Specification can be extracted from the database and published. All performance requirements are now in the form of RSL and include tests for checking the requirements in terms of data collected at validation points. In this respect, much of the work of writing an Acceptance Test Specification has already been carried out.

Analytic feasibility demonstration

One further stage of system modelling may be desirable either before or immediately after the publication of the Functional Specification. This modelling is aimed at ensuring that algorithms do exist which meet the accuracy requirements of the Functional Specification.

Sample algorithms for the critical ALPHAs are selected and coded in Pascal into the REVS database. REVS can then be used to produce an analytic simulation of the system incorporating these sample algorithms (now called GAMMAs) in much the same way as functional simulations are produced. Such simulations are then used to check that the selected algorithms satisfy the Functional Specification performance tests and that these tests are sufficient to ensure that corresponding requirements in the Requirement Specification are satisfied.

Bibliography
Alford 1977 (gives the rationale for SREM and a good overview of the steps taken in applying it), Alford 1978a (provides a formal description of a methodology for allocating system requirements in a distributed data processing system), Alford 1978b (describes the status of SREM at the age of two giving an example of its use), Alford 1980 (describes the status of SREM at the age of four and gives an overview of Alford 1978a above), Alford 1981 (provides an overview and evaluation of SDS), Belford 1978 (describes the use of SDS), Bell 1977 (gives an overview of REVS and RSL), Davis 1977 (compares SREM with other requirements methodologies), Davis 1978 (gives a review of the problems of requirements engineering and of SREM), Ramamoorthy 1981, TRW (sales booklet for SREM containing extremely useful description of the methodology).

Exercises
1 Look at the sample RSL/REVS outputs and compare the entity types, their relationships and attributes with those in PSL/PSA.
2 Consider a system with which you are familiar and, in particular, its requirements. Would SREM have been effective? If not, why not? If so, what would the advantages have been?
3 How would you go about determining how the performance requirements on a system are to be devolved onto the software and hardware components that will satisfy them? How would you then *check* that the design will satisfy the performance requirements?

5.4.7 Finite State Machines – FSM

Introduction

In this section we concentrate on the method of applying FSMs to system definition given by Salter 1976. Salter was particularly concerned with the use of FSMs to specify data processing subsystem requirements when given the requirements for the overall system including non-data-processing subsystems. In the Software Development System (SDS) the data processing subsystem requirements would be further broken down using SREM. You may decide to follow precisely the SDS approach or, more likely, you may prefer to integrate some of the aspects of FSM definition with one of the other methodologies described in this chapter. You should, however, find FSMs one of the cheapest ways of producing an overall system definition which, in many respects, can be mechanically checked for correctness.

The basic ingredients

Salter presents his methodology in terms of three basic system ingredients:

- control,
- functions,
- data.

Overall system control is defined in terms of FSMs. The actions which take place when an input to an FSM occurs is a function performed by the system, while the functions act as transformations on data. Salter additionally defines the concept of a functional flow as the ordered execution of functions of the control FSM in response to a sequence of inputs.

The methodology considers the overall relationship between the ingredients in the definition of the system. It does not provide a means of defining functions and data so you will need to choose another technique for this purpose. The methods of Structured Analysis provide one possibility.

Control FSM

Salter prescribes the following approach to constructing the control FSM for a system.

(i) List a set of strategies that the FSM is to implement, expressing each strategy as a sequence of FSM actions. The FSM will execute a particular strategy in response to a particular sequence of inputs. For example, a particular sequence of inputs in the VISTA

Fig. 5.17. The top-level FSM for VISTA showing strata levels.

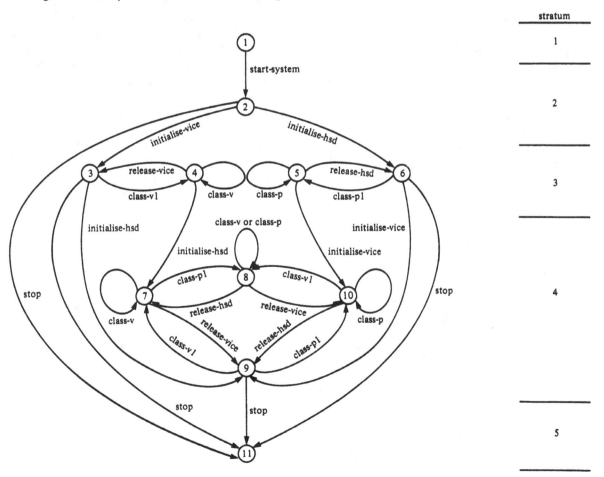

system consists of the following user commands: capture-moving-sequence, display-moving-sequence-cyclically, stop-moving-sequence-display, while the resultant strategy consists of a sequence of actions with the same names as the inputs.

(ii) Let each action in each strategy be a state.

(iii) Reduce the collection of state sequences to a minimal, or near-minimal FSM (FSM minimisation, which removes states that are equivalent to other states, is described in most books on FSMs; e.g. Gill 1962).

(iv) Modify the FSM to incorporate other strategies that may have been omitted from the original representative set.

(v) Repeat steps (i) to (iv) as often as required in order to expand individual states into detailed FSMs. For example, the state 'capture-moving-sequence' would be expanded in terms of an action to catch a single frame.

This process automatically leads to a hierarchy of sub-FSMs which make up the overall control FSM.

By way of example, the top-level FSM of the VISTA system is shown diagrammatically in figure 5.17. In this diagram the circles represent states and the arrows are the names of the inputs (user commands) or equivalence classes of inputs which cause the transition. In all cases, the names of the actions (functions) which take place when the transitions occur are the same as those of the inputs. Otherwise the arrows could also be labelled with the function names in upper case. Error actions which take place when an invalid input for a given state occurs are not shown.

The next level of FSM provides more detail of the composite states in the level above. For example, figure 5.18 shows part of the sub-FSM defining state 8 of figure 5.17.

Salter describes an alternative method of producing a hierarchy of FSMs based on *stratification* and *structuring* of the FSM resulting from the above process. Stratification of an FSM involves placing each state in a stratum such that any state transition either leaves the FSM in its original stratum or else moves it to a state in a stratum with a higher number. For example, in the five-stratum FSM in figure 5.17, a transition from state 9 either moves to a state in the level 4 cycle (made up from states 7, 8, 9 and 10) or else it moves *up* to level 5 state 11 (from which it cannot return to a lower level). Salter's paper describes an algorithm due to Warfield (1973) which can be used to stratify an arbitrary FSM. The next step involves transforming the stratified FSM to a structured FSM. A structured FSM is a stratified FSM for which inputs either leave the FSM in its original *state* or move it to a state in a higher stratum. A structured FSM can be produced from an arbitrary stratified FSM by factoring out all cycles. For example, structuring the FSM in figure 5.17 results in figure 5.19, where the composite states 3', 5' and 8' must be defined in terms of structured sub-FSMs.

Fig. 5.18. Part of the second-level FSM of VISTA.

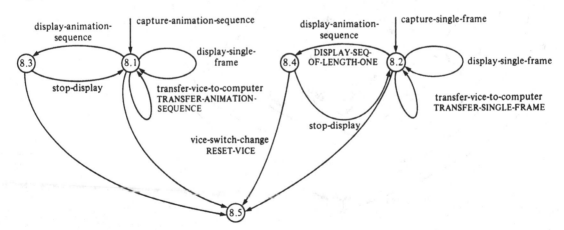

There are several advantages in presenting the definition of system control in terms of a hierarchy of structured FSMs, not least of which is visual clarity. Structured FSMs clearly show all the possible irreversible sequences of system operations in a way which should benefit both the system designer and the potential system user. For example, it is clear from figure 5.19 that once either a VICE or HSD has been initialised, the only way of de-initialising it is to stop the system and re-start it. If the user would like a facility for de-initialising a hardware unit without stopping the system it is much better to discover this now, on a paper model, rather than after the system is operational.

Another advantage of working with structured FSMs, described in more detail by Salter, is in checking performance requirements.

Once the control FSM has been defined it can be mechanically checked for properties which are important for a well specified system. These properties are:

- Consistency: an FSM is consistent if for any given state and any given input only one transition can occur.
- Completeness: an FSM is complete if for any given input and any current state a transition is defined.
- Reachability: a state of an FSM is reachable

if there is a path to it from a start state and there is a path from it to an end state.

Computer programs to carry out these checks can easily be written using the elementary properties of FSMs.

Functions

The functions that must be carried out by the system can initially be defined almost independently of the control structure. Salter's methodology involves drawing a data flow diagram for the functions of the system to show data from one function being input to another function. In this respect the methodology is identical to Structured Analysis and you could well use the Structured Analysis methods of defining data and functions (processes).

Salter goes on to suggest that Warfield's structuring algorithm be used to stratify the data flow diagrams in the same way as FSM transition diagrams. This allows structure to be more easily detected in the diagrams and conclusions to be more easily drawn concerning such matters as which processes could be executed in parallel. Figure 5.20 shows the stratified version of figure

Fig. 5.20. The VISTA data flow diagram (figure 5.3) following stratification.

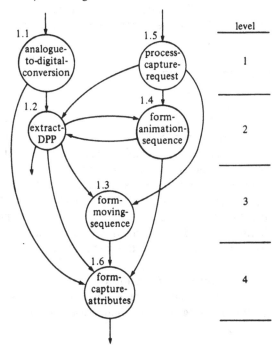

Fig. 5.19. The top-level FSM for the VISTA system following structuring.

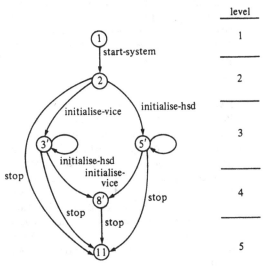

5.3 (without data flow labels and databases). You should find it much easier to walk through the data flows of the stratified diagram and also to spot potential problems. For example, it is clear that the analogue-to-digital conversion process could execute in parallel with the process-capture-request process, thus not allowing the capture request to influence the conversion process.

Finally, Salter defines properties of reachability and completeness for data flow diagrams as being requirements of a well-defined system.

Functional flows

A sequence of functions executed in response to a sequence of inputs forms a functional flow. Salter defines consistency, completeness and reachability for functional flows. He additionally suggests that, in order not to over-constrain the design of the system, the functions defined be the minimal set for the functional flows. That is, the set of functions is such that combining any two of them will not invalidate any of the functional flows.

Examination of a selected set of functional flows is a useful way of checking the system behaviour and presenting its operation to the user at a very early stage of the lifecycle. Algorithms for generating optimal sets of test input sequences for producing functional flows are readily available (e.g. Chow 1978). These algorithms can be automated and combined with an FSM test harness (i.e. the complete control structure but only dummy functions) to provide an early simulation of system operation.

Data

As for the other basic ingredients of the system definition, Salter defines desirable properties of consistency, completeness and reachability of data. Consistency and completeness refer to consistency between data and the data flow diagram and can be mechanically checked. An element of data is said to be reachable if it is defined before it is used. Mechanical tests of reachability of data are not covered by the methodology.

Summary of the method

Salter's recommended approach to system definition using the ingredients discussed above is as follows:

(i) Construct the control FSM and functions either in parallel or serially.
(ii) Use functional flows as a mapping of control onto functions guided by the data flow diagram.
(iii) Define in detail the data flowing in the system.

As mentioned in the introduction, these steps are likely to be integrated with one of the other definition methodologies, contributing such items as state transition tables or diagrams to the Functional Specification. Correspondingly, FSM definition activities are likely to be integrated with activities in the WBS of the other methodology. As an example, here is a possible WBS section for the Definition Phase of a project using Structured Analysis tools and FSMs:

```
2200  Produce Functional Specification
        2210  Construct control FSM
        2220  Analyse control FSM (for consistency etc.)
        2230  Specify data flow diagrams
        2240  Specify functions using Structured English
        2250  Specify data using data dictionary
      (2260)  Integrate control FSM and functions
2600  System Modelling
        2610  Simulate functional flows using test
              sequence generator
```

Bibliography

Birke 1972, Braun 1981 (describes a test sequence generation algorithm for FSMs), Chow 1978 (describes another algorithm for generating test sequences), Gill 1962, Henderson 1975, Salter 1976 (describes a methodology for the use of FSMs in System Definition), Sunshine 1982 and 1983, Warfield 1973.

Exercises

1 Produce a top-level state transition diagram specifying the operation of the user interface to your favourite operating system. Typical inputs might be 'log-on', 'password', 'edit command', 'run command', 'break in', 'abort'. Draw stratified and structured versions of the diagram.

2 Draw up a list of attributes of a problem that would make it most suitable for analysis using FSMs. Can you devise methods that make FSMs more suitable to problems that do not have these attributes?

5.4.8 Petri Nets

In contrast to Finite State Machines which are most appropriate for representing single process systems, Petri Nets are ideal where a number of independent but co-operating processes need to be co-ordinated or synchronised. Both techniques are principally of use in design but have found application during system definition as well. The reason for this is that both offer a formal representation of a system together with tools for analysing the properties of the system and this is clearly of interest to us during the drawing up of the Functional Specification.

Theoretical principles

Before the description of the use of Petri Nets we first outline the basic principles of the theory. A full understanding can be obtained from the literature – e.g. Peterson 1981. A number of different definitions and representations of Petri Nets exist but here we follow Peterson.

A Petri Net has four components:

Places — corresponding to system states
Transitions — corresponding to events in the system
Inputs — corresponding to the preconditions of transitions/events
Outputs — corresponding to the postconditions of transitions/events.

Fig. 5.21. A simple Petri Net Graph (PNG).

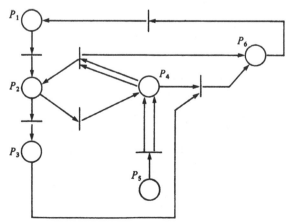

Formally speaking, the inputs and outputs are specified by functions that relate places and transitions, and Petri Nets can be investigated algebraically. For practical purposes however Petri Net graphs (PNGs) are drawn.

In a PNG, places are represented by circles, transitions by vertical bars, and inputs and outputs by directed lines connecting places and transitions. Thus, arrows leading into a transition represent pre-conditions for the corresponding event, whilst arrows leading out of a transition represent the post-conditions of the event.

Figure 5.21 shows a simple PNG. (Note that a place and transition can be connected by more than one arrow.) Such a PNG represents a system in a static fashion, showing simply the relationships. The full modelling of the system and its behaviour is performed by *executing* the Petri Net and to investigate this we introduce the notion of tokens.

Tokens can reside in places. In a bounded Petri Net only a (finite) limited number of tokens can reside in a place. A Petri Net with tokens is said to be *marked* and the disposition of tokens is called the *marking*. Figure 5.22 shows a marked PNG.

The execution of a Petri Net is controlled by the number and distribution of tokens. The net executes by *firing* transitions. A transition fires by removing a token from each of its input places (i.e. one per input arrow) and putting a new token in each of its output places (i.e. one per output arrow). A transition can only fire if it is *enabled*, i.e. if each of its input places contains a token.

Thus, in figure 5.22 transitions $t1$ and $t5$ are enabled and can fire independently resulting in the marked PNG of figure 5.23. Subsequently, after a number of transitions have fired, the PNG has the form shown in figure 5.24. (Exercise: which were those transitions?) Transition firing continues as long as there is an enabled transition and then the model halts. A model may however never halt.

Regarding transitions as events, we can see that enabled events can take place independently. The fact that parts of the PNG are executing independently indicates that the concepts of *parallelism* and *concurrency* are inherent in Petri Net modelling.

They can be simply introduced by appropriate combinations of Petri Nets. Thus, the paral-

Fig. 5.22. A marked PNG, *P*.

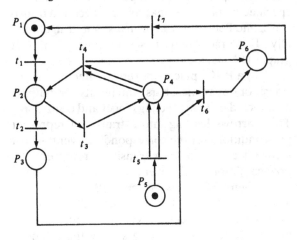

Fig. 5.23. PNG *P* after two transitions have fired.

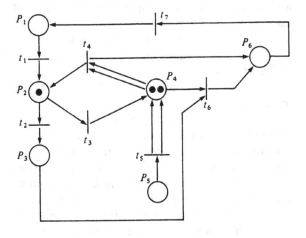

Fig. 5.24. PNG *P* after further firings.

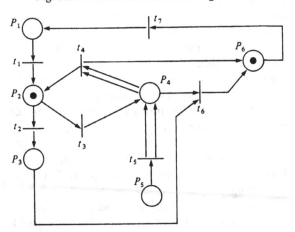

lel processing construct devised by Dijkstra (in Dijkstra 1968) has a natural representation; the fragment

> **parbegin**
>   S1 ; S2 ; S3 ; . . . ; Sn
> **parend**

takes the form in figure 5.25 in which each box is itself a Petri Net graph taking a single token to start and generating a single token on completion.

Petri Nets in their simplest form contain no inherent measure of time. As models they are asynchronous and yield only a partial ordering in time. They can therefore behave non-deterministically. (In the PNG of figure 5.24 either of *t2* or *t3* may fire next using the token at place *p2*.) Petri Nets are therefore an ideal modelling tool where events are independent and asynchronous.

Synchronisation between events is modelled explicitly only where it exists in the underlying system. For instance, the PNG in figure 5.26 shows a pair of processes only one of which can be in its critical section at a time. Once again the boxes represent Petri subnets.

So far the discussion has considered Petri Nets in isolation. If we wish to attach one to the outside world, the most convenient method is to have the net and the world communicate through places. The world creates tokens and deposits them in input places on the boundary of the net whilst taking output tokens from output places on that boundary.

Fig. 5.25. Parallel processes shown as a PNG.

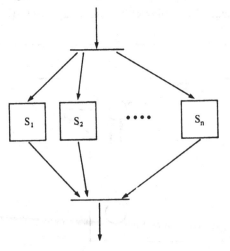

Analysing Petri Nets

There are a number of properties of Petri Nets that are of interest in that they parallel interesting properties of the underlying system. They include *safeness, boundedness, conservation, liveness, reachability, coverability* and *equivalence*. Below we briefly describe one of the analysis techniques and highlight how three of these properties can be investigated with that technique.

From a given marking of a PNG we can draw a *reachability tree*. The root of the reachability tree is the initial marking, say M. Each branch from M corresponds to the firing of one transition enabled in M and leads to the resulting marking. Branches then lead from this marking and so on down the tree. Markings in which no transition is enabled form *leaf nodes* and represent states of the model that are *dead*. As an example the marked PNG in figure 5.27 has the reachability tree shown in figure 5.28.

Although some Petri Nets can continue executing indefinitely (such as the one in figure 5.27), it is always possible, with a suitable notation, to represent the tree of reachable markings as a finite tree. Furthermore, there is a finite algorithm for drawing it. Where necessary, the notation treats as equivalent all markings in which one place acquires an indefinite number of tokens – an ω-place.

Fig. 5.26. A critical region implemented as a PNG.

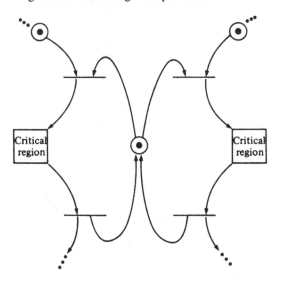

Fig. 5.27. A marked PNG, Q.

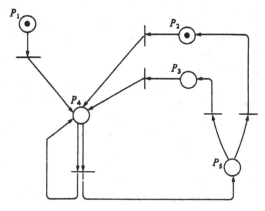

The marking of this net is (1, 1, 0, 0, 0)

As an example of the type of question that can be answered by the reachability tree, suppose we use a PNG to model a system with an embedded buffering mechanism. This buffer might be hardware registers or entries in a software table. We would like to check that the buffer will not overflow a certain size irrespective of the execution sequence of the system. In the PNG the buffer

Fig. 5.28. The reachability tree of PNG Q.

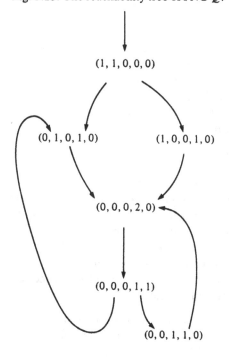

would be modelled by a place and the question becomes whether or not that place can receive more than *M* tokens. This question of *boundedness* can be answered directly from the reachability tree and can be handled automatically. The PNG in figure 5.27 is clearly *2-bounded*.

In a resource allocation system, the total amount of the resource generally remains constant whilst being consumed and released. If we model such a system with a PNG we might model units of the resource as tokens, and would therefore want the number (or value) of the resource tokens to remain constant, i.e. the PNG must exhibit *conservativeness*. Again this can be determined from the reachability tree. The PNG in figure 5.27 is conservative.

A Petri Net with marking M*a* is said to be *safe* with respect to marking M*b* if M*b* cannot be reached from M*a*. This can clearly be determined straight from the reachability tree. *Safeness* is often an important property for a system – certain states must not be reachable. For example, it might need to be impossible for two stages in the instruction pipeline of a processor to be writing to memory at the same time.

A vital property of many systems is that deadlock should be impossible. In Petri Net terms this means that there should be no leaf nodes in the reachability tree.

Developments of Petri Nets

Much theoretical work is available on Petri Nets and their properties, only a couple of which have been touched on here. The basic concept has itself been adapted by both restriction and extension. Among the variants we find

- different transition firing rules (*exclusive or* rather than *and*),
- *inhibitor arcs* as well as enabling arcs,
- *numerical Petri Nets* (see Symons 1982),
- *time Petri Nets* in which time constraints are imposed on transition firing,
- *priority transitions* where enabled transitions fire in order of priority,
- *trigger tokens* that vanish from places unless used 'immediately'.

All of these find application in modelling and algorithms are available in many cases for nets using them.

A simple Petri Net model

Suppose that in VISTA we wish to model the way that an HSD and a framestore are allocated between two users each wishing to replay a moving sequence. Figure 5.29 is a PNG for such a model. User inputs cause tokens to be placed in the double-circle places. By choosing a suitable value or 'weighting' to places as shown in the figure, we can see that the net is conservative, a property we can interpret to mean that the total resources in the system – one HSD and one framestore – remain constant. In a more complicated system this may be far from obvious.

Figure 5.30 appears on first inspection to be an equivalent solution. However, when we generate the reachability tree we find a marking that is a leaf-node, i.e. a state of the Petri Net where no further transitions are possible. We can interpret this as meaning that there is a sequence of events which leaves the system in deadlock. It is a simple example of the standard deadly embrace problem encountered when two resources are allocated separately.

Fig. 5.29. Two VISTA users wishing to perform sequence replay – a good PNG.

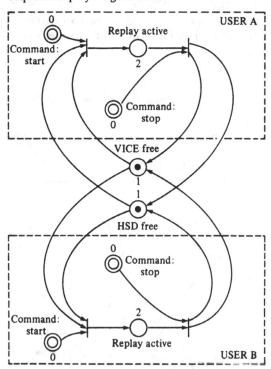

Figures next to places are weights

Petri Nets in the context of System Definition

We have seen how Petri Nets provide a powerful notational and analytical tool for defining systems with interacting concurrent components. They are probably best used by adopting them as such a tool in conjunction with a procedure that provides a methodology for developing the model initially. Whether Petri Nets are used in isolation or with another procedure the following iterative plan can be used:

(i) Identify discrete components of the system (places).

(ii) Identify the pre- and post-conditions for the activation of these components (transitions).

(iii) Identify the inter-relationships between the components in terms of the conditions (the PNG).

(iv) Determine the properties of the proposed system by analysing the PNG.

(v) Revise the model until satisfactory by repeating steps (i)–(iv) as necessary.

This plan falls within WP2200 (Produce Functional Specification) of the Work Breakdown Structure but does not itself give us any more useful detail.

Assuming that you use Petri Nets as an adjunct to a methodology you can expect the technique to contribute the following to your Functional Specification:

(i) a Petri Net Graph model of the system, possibly structured, possibly one of the variants described above;

(ii) the results of various analyses of the PNG in terms of properties of the modelled system, e.g. the unreachability of certain configurations or the impossibility of deadlock.

Bibliography

Alford 1981 (Petri Nets used in conjunction with SREM), Balkovich 1976 (Petri Nets in the investigation of data processing performance requirements), Celko 1982 (time-stamped Petri Nets), Nelson 1983 (putting Petri Nets into systems), Pagnoni 1983, Gouda 1976 (Petri Nets in protocols), Coolahan 1983 (time-driven systems with Petri Nets), Peterson 1977, Peterson 1981 (a primary source of Petri Net fundamentals with a full bibliography), Petri 1962 (Petri's original thesis), Symons 1982.

Exercises

1 How would you transform a Finite State Machine diagram into an equivalent Petri Net?

2 And the reverse?

3 Consider how you could introduce timing into Petri Nets and perform simulations of multi-process systems.

4 Draw up a Petri Net model of the annual round of activities in your vegetable garden. You should aim to be self-sufficient in vegetables *and* seed after the input of seed in the first year. Assume good weather and keep to a small set of vegetables. What is needed to regulate the speed at which the Net runs, i.e. how can one synchronise it to the seasons?

5.4.9 Jackson System Development – JSD

General principles

JSD extends across the Definition, Design and Production phases. Even though it is not top-down, it still fits our very general model. Its six steps spread roughly over the phases as follows:

entity action step ⎫
entity structure step ⎬ Definition ⎫
initial model step ⎭   ⎬ Design
function step ⎫ ⎭
system timing step ⎬
implementation step ⎬ Production

Fig. 5.30. An unsuccessful PNG that deadlocks.

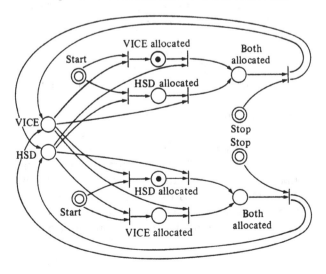

Before we delve into the six steps it is worth noting a number of features of JSD that mark it out from other techniques. Once you have read the three sections describing it you should re-read these features.

Firstly, JSD is not a top-down method. Jackson's view is that top-down development implies hierarchical decomposition and, although this may be a very reasonable approach for *description* of the already well-understood, this does not imply that it is reasonable for *development*. In fact, he argues, top-down is the worst possible way of proceeding when you do not already know the solution because you are forced to make the most far-reaching decisions at the time of greatest ignorance.

Secondly, JSD does not start with the functional requirements. Instead it first creates a model of the real world – a simulation. This abstract model implicitly defines and delimits the functions that can be supported. If you *start* with the functions then, it is argued, the addition of new functions later will be arbitrarily easy or costly. On the other hand, whilst functions may change, the model will prove more stable. We can equate building the model with understanding precisely and scoping exactly the relevant part of our client's business.

Thirdly, to a certain extent, JSD redefines the traditional roles in system development and at the same times moves the emphasis on certain topics to different phases:

- the user is involved right through the first four steps, rather than stepping out after the earliest stage,
- traditional 'design' (file design, decomposition of programs, etc.) becomes 'implementation' in JSD,
- traditional 'programming' is spread throughout the development activity,
- many of the steps are semi-mechanical.

In a JSD development there are three major activities:

- model the real world, excluding the functions required of the system (the first three steps),
- add the required functions to the real world

and pick up timing constraints (the next two steps),
- implement the system (the final step).

The real world model is, in principle, executable but would only simulate the real world. As functions are added to the model, it remains executable but would now operate on inputs and produce outputs. At the end of the function step we have 'designed' the system inasmuch as we have 'pseudo-code' for a network of inter-connected processes communicating in just two strictly defined ways. This design would be executable if we had a corresponding network of inter-connected processors communicating in the two ways via shared memory, or a general purpose scheduler on a single processor capable of supporting an almost unlimited number of processes. Since both are unlikely, the purpose of the last step is to transform the design into a form in which it can be placed on the hardware configuration that has in fact to be used. The final output of the whole process is then code ready to be compiled.

To keep it in step with less extensive procedures we have split the description of JSD over chapters 5, 6 and 7. You may wish to read them through consecutively now in order to get the flavour of the entire technique. Our division between Definition and Design Phases is somewhat artificial since the first four steps all involve the user and the second, third, fourth and fifth (and perhaps also the sixth) all involve design. However, our purposes will be served adequately provided you do not read any significance into exactly where we have made the split.

The entity action step

This is the first step. In it you draw a boundary around those aspects of the real world that are to be modelled. This means listing the real world *entities* involved and their *actions*. Actions are atomic and instantaneous; entities perform and suffer actions in a significant time-ordering.

The lists are drawn up from a wide-ranging analysis of the application area and should be as comprehensive as possible. They are then reduced by applying a number of criteria that filter out the entities and actions that are to form part of the model:

- an entity must retain its type throughout its life,
- entities within the system are deleted,
- actions or outputs of the system are deleted,
- actions and entities must be detectable by the system, and so on.

You will see from these criteria that any entities or actions that relate to the intended *function* of the system are explicitly deleted from the lists at this stage. The purpose here is to model the environment into which functions are to be fitted, and, for as long as possible, to avoid over-constraining the solution that is adopted. We are looking at the subject matter of the system rather than the system itself.

The resulting short-lists are of course provisional at this stage. They will be refined during later steps. But as in similar situations it will prove useful here to record in the project files the decisions that are made about the inclusion or exclusion of the entities and actions initially put forward, since these decisions will be amongst the most important you make.

The act of generating the lists constitutes an appraisal of the application area and any technique that offers a way of generating a rich and wide-ranging coverage should be considered. The viewpoint analysis of SADT or the real world modelling

implicit in Structured Analysis could for instance be brought to bear here provided again that only the *subject matter* of the system is investigated.

Once the full lists have been pruned to those that are essential to defining the boundary of the relevant part of the real world, each of the remaining actions is expanded a little with a brief text description and a tentative, incomplete list of its attributes. Figure 5.31 contains a fragment from the entity list analysis for the VISTA system. Figure 5.32 contains part of the action list and action descriptions that follow from it. These could have been derived after high-level SADT analysis of the User and System Manager viewpoints.

This analysis revealed, *inter alia*, that the System Manager wishes to discourage unfettered and inefficient use of the system through a simple charging system. To this end the 'account' and 'session' notions have been introduced into the model as reflections of his wishes.

The entity structure step

This step produces a model of the entire life-span of each real world entity in the entity list. Each model takes the form of a structure diagram showing the actions of the entity in terms of sequence, iteration and selection components –

Fig. 5.31. JSD entity list resulting from the Entity Action step.

Candidate entry	Reason, if rejected
User	
Video-frame (VF)	
Digitised-part-picture (DPP)	state of video-frame
VICE	
Processing algorithm	attribute of processing action
TV line	attribute of VF
Chrominance	attribute of pixel
Luminance	attribute of pixel
Sampling rate	
Terminal session	
Pixel	attribute of DPP
User account	
System manager	outside model boundary, i.e. our system only models human beings who are users

Fig. 5.32. JSD action lists and action descriptions.

Subject	Entity action	Object
User	captures	VF
User	processes	VF
User	obtains	account
User	closes	account
User	starts	terminal session
User	ends	terminal session
User	replays	VF
User	synthesises	VF
User	reserves	VICE
User	releases	VICE
Sampling rate	chosen	on a VICE
VICE	attached to system	
. . .	. . .	. . .

action descriptions
  capture: be snatched from incoming video signal between two consecutive frame syncs and digitised; attributes are window size, window location, . . .

the same notation as is used for data structure representation in JSP. Thus figure 5.33 shows the structure of the entity USER in VISTA and figure 5.34 shows that of the VICE entity.

A box containing a star represents an *iterated action*, one that is repeated zero or more times. Peer boxes containing circles represent *selected action*, only one of which takes place. Peer boxes containing neither stars nor circles are *sequential actions*, taking place in order from left to right in time. The diagram thereby shows the *time-ordered actions that constitute the lifetime of the entity* as far as our model of the real world is concerned. For instance, by tracing our way through the tree we can list in time-order the events/actions in the lifetime of a typical user.

Not all entities succumb to the simple handling of the USER entity and special mechanisms are required in certain cases. For instance, such a diagram cannot express concurrency (equivalent to an interleaving clash in JSP). Thus, a VISTA USER may have a number of asynchronous VF-processing actions active simultaneously, each action having its own lifecycle overlapping and interleaving those of others. To model this the interleaved action would be represented by its own so-called 'marsupial' entity with its own, independent structure.

The resulting *set* of entity structures can be checked for:

- formal correctness in that they do not infringe constraints imposed by the constituent structures;
- specification correctness in that they do not impose false constraints on the interleaving of constituent structures.

Fig. 5.33. JSD entity structure diagram for the USER entity.

Fig. 5.34. JSD entity structure for the VICE entity.

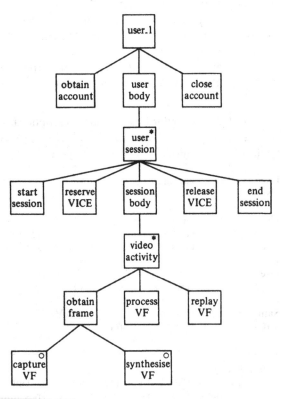

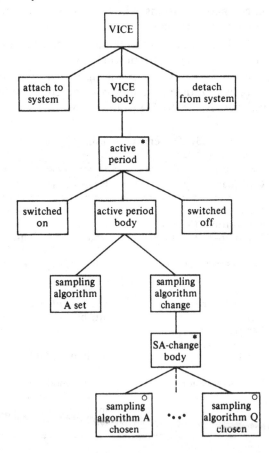

Note that leaf nodes in a structure diagram represent actions related to the entity concerned.

The outputs of the first two steps

To date we have produced the following deliverable items:

- a preliminary list of real world entities,
- a preliminary list of actions they suffer or perform,
- a time-ordering of these actions in terms of entity structure diagrams.

We clearly cannot call these a Functional Specification – the deliverable item that we normally get from a procedure in the Definition Phase. At most these documents represent an understanding of those parts of the user's world that bound the sorts of functions we wish to put into our system. However, this 'bounding' operation is strongly emphasised in JSD inasmuch as it determines which functions could be embedded naturally thereafter and it is sensible therefore to identify what we should perhaps call a Super-Functional Specification! Though this would not form the basis of a contract to produce a system (since it contains no functions) it could form an important basis of understanding between you and your client.

Bibliography

Jackson 1983 (an extensive description of the technique).

Exercise

1 Look back at a system or program, large or small, with which you have been involved. What subsequent enhancements to the system were easy to make and which were hard? Why was this so? Can you find entities that should have been identified during Definition and whose inclusion would then have increased the 'scope' of the system enough to make all the enhancements easy?

2 Imagine you have to define a simple stock-keeping system for a retailer. At the moment he just wants to keep up-to-date stock levels but in the future anticipates expanding the system to produce orders to his suppliers and to identify fast and slow selling lines. Consider how a system defined to fulfil his immediate requirements would need to change in the longer term. Look at the entities involved in the two cases and their life-histories.

5.4.10 Software Development System SDS/RSRE

Use of SDS/RSRE in the System Definition Phase

The standard SDS/RSRE (called SDS for the remainder of this section) database is comprised of nine files contained in three chapters as follows:

> Plan chapter
> > person file
> > assignment file
> > activity file
> > resource file
> Design chapter
> > component file
> > category file
> > requirement file
> Documentation chapter
> > document file
> > distribution file

The overall structure of the database is shown in figure 5.35 in which the lines represent relationships between the files. This standard structure can be varied to suit particular project needs using the SDS Data Definition Language (DDL).

During the System Definition Phase, all components of the database can be used and, if necessary, it is during this phase that the database should be modified or extended to support the methodologies of later phases. We consider each chapter

Fig. 5.35. The overall structure of the SDS database.

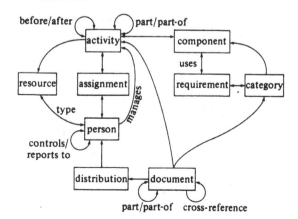

of the database in turn, starting with the design chapter, which is most related to the actual definition of the system to be built.

SDS design control and system definition

SDS can be used effectively to support almost any well structured definition methodology. The principal (non-mandatory) requirements of such a methodology are the following:

- the system is composed of *components* of various *categories*;
- components can *use* one another thereby imposing *requirements* on their usage;
- components can have other components as *parts* thereby creating one or more *classes* of hierarchy.

To illustrate these concepts let us choose Structured Analysis as our definition methodology. We need to define a *system architecture* for Structured Analysis. The categories of components that might be used in a Structured Analysis definition of a system are processes, primitives, data, files, sources, sinks. A component in the process category can make use of a component in the data category by reading it or writing it. A process thus imposes read or write requirements on the data components that it uses. This is shown in standard SDS graphical notation in figure 5.36 along with the Structured Analysis notation used in section 5.4.3. The existence of the requirement linking, for example, process P1 to data D2 in the diagram could be entered into the SDS database using the following piece of SDS Input/Update Language (IUL):

> COMPONENT : P1
> USES: D2, WRITE
> END:

The 'uses' relationship expresses a 'horizontal' link between components. A 'vertical' link is expressed by the 'part-of' relationship. For example, process P1 might have processes P1.1 and P1.2 as parts. This is shown in figure 5.37 and in the following IUL:

> COMPONENT: P1
> PART: (L) *P1.1, *P1.2
> END:

The asterisk indicates that SDS is to create a new component record for each of P1.1 and P1.2, having checked that they do not already exist. This 'part-of' relationship establishes one class of hierarchical structure corresponding to the levels of Structured Analysis and is indicated by the (L) in the IUL. At a later stage in the analysis, a second hierarchy might be established to show, for example, on which physical processor a given process will be executed.

Once the various categories of the architecture have been established, rules which specify the architecture are entered into the database. These rules take the form of relationships between the various categories.

For example one rule of our Structured Analysis architecture would be that 'a primitive is

Fig. 5.36. SDS graphical notation (top) for the Structured Analysis data flow diagram (bottom).

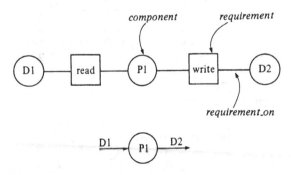

Fig. 5.37. SDS graphical notation for process P1 with processes P1.1 and P1.2 as parts.

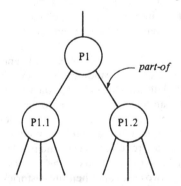

a valid part of a process'. Except in a few cases, where a special program must be run to check that the database complies with the rules, all updates to the database are automatically checked for compliance before they are carried out.

Checks of the type just described ensure that a system definition produced with the aid of SDS is consistent in its use of the architecture. The checking of the requirements that link components provides further assurance of consistency and is especially important when the links are between components in parts of the system being defined by different people.

At any time during System Definition, reports on the current state of the database can be produced using SDS facilities. These include a query language (QL) which can be used to look at selected data or to generate specific reports, a hierarchy printer which prints out hierarchical representations of data, and a network printer which produces network diagrams of the data in a user-specifiable format. These utilities can be used for the generation of a hard-copy Functional Specification.

SDS documentation control

The SDS database provides documentation control by way of *document* and *distribution list* records. A document record can represent any unit of documentation such as a volume (Functional Specification), section of a volume or a module of program design language or code. The structure of documents can be defined using the part/part-of relationships and cross references between documents can be recorded. Most importantly the relationships between design objects (components, categories etc.) and project control activities (see below) and their documentation are held in the database. The relationship between a document and distribution lists prescribes to whom releases of a document should be distributed.

During the System Definition Phase SDS documentation control provides the means of administering the documentation units that make up your Functional Specification (whatever methodology is used). In particular it can be used to ensure that as the system specification evolves all relevant documentation is kept up to date.

The System Definition Phase is also the time

to make an initial determination of the documentation schema for the remainder of the project, allowing a systematic approach to the documentation database to be adopted.

SDS project control

SDS provides powerful facilities for the management of projects, especially large ones. The database contains records relating to *activities, resources, persons* and *assignments*. An activity is any unit of work that must be completed (e.g. 'Produce Functional Specification'). Activities can be hierarchically related to one another using the part/part-of relationship (e.g. 'produce physical data flow diagrams' is part-of 'produce Functional Specification') and horizontally linked by before/after relationships which determine their sequence. Activities can also be connected to design components with which they are involved.

Resources such as computer time and programmers are stored in the database along with their times of availability. The assignment of a resource to an activity is represented by a link in the database. All persons working on a project represent particular types of resources and connections in the database represent this. When a person is allocated to an activity, an assignment record indicates this.

The SDS project planning process consists at the top level of the following steps:

(i)   identify major activities (from Work Breakdown Structure);
(ii) assign resources, duration and logical constraints to the activities;
(iii) apply the activity scheduler utility;
(iv) obtain resource profile;
(v)   derive any resource constraints.

Depending on the resource constraints, steps (iii) to (v) may be repeated until a satisfactory overall plan is obtained.

The activity scheduler utility carries out a critical path analysis on all or part of the project control database and either provides for each activity earliest and latest start and finish dates or indicates why it is not possible to arrive at such dates. The utility can produce a profile for each resource and a project bar chart.

Having established an overall project plan,

lower level activities are defined and staff are assigned to them. SDS can then be used to produce short term working schedules for distribution to each member of the project.

The final project control function of SDS is that of monitoring project progress. At regular intervals, the amount of each resource actually expended on a particular activity is entered into the database (from, for example, staff timesheets) and new estimates of activity completion dates are made. Using the Query Language and the Activity Scheduler, progress reports can be generated and, if necessary, the plans can be modified to account for changing circumstances.

The start of the System Definition Phase is the time to establish overall plans, refining them as the specification of the project becomes better defined. This is also the time to decide upon progress reporting mechanisms and report formats, especially taking advantage of SDS as a store and provider of project indicator data.

Bibliography
Falla 1977, SSL 1981 (SDS/RSRE support of project control), SSL 1982a (an overview of SDS/RSRE), SSL 1982b (SDS/RSRE support of design control), Stevens 1982 (an independent assessment of SDS/RSRE).

Exercise
Draw up a database schema that contains all of the files that have been mentioned as being contained in the SDS database. Decide upon the fields that should be associated with records of each file (e.g. start-date with activity record) and draw in the possible linkages between fields of different record types. (See Falla 1977 or SSL 1982b for the SDS schema.) How do these linkages relate to the sorts of ways you would want to analyse your database during software development?

5.4.11 Structured Walkthroughs
The Structured Walkthrough is a general purpose review technique that you can apply to any output of the development path. This being so, it is appropriate to present the technique in this very first phase of development. You will also find it mentioned in each of the subsequent chapters as a reminder of its general applicability.

A walkthrough is an event, attended by a number of interested parties, at which a piece of work – the *product* – is presented by its producer and subjected to scrutiny by the other attendees. A product can be any complete item of 'manageable' size – Yourdon suggests that this means that it can be reviewed in a period of 30–60 minutes and hence might be 5–10 pages of written specification, 3 diagrams or 50–100 lines of code.

The technique is structured insofar as it specifies a simple procedure for arranging, holding and following up a walkthrough, together with roles and responsibilities for the participants.

Yourdon identifies the following roles:

The *presenter:* the owner of the product and probably the person who produced it.

The *co-ordinator:* someone to organise the walkthrough and steer its execution.

The *secretary:* who is responsible for the paperwork and clerical aspects.

The *maintenance oracle:* representing those who will one day be responsible for maintaining the product being reviewed.

The *standards bearer:* who scrutinises the product for adherence to the standards defined for such products.

The *user representative:* there to check that the product conforms with the views of its user (who may be external or another person in the team).

Outsiders – any other team member who can contribute to the review.

The precise rules for walkthroughs can of course be decided within your own organisation. In the following summary we follow the suggestions in Yourdon 1979a.

Activities before the walkthrough
If a walkthrough is to be effective it is vital that all participants *prepare* for it. To this end the walkthrough is preceded by the following steps:

(i) The producer must give fair notice of his desire to walk through his product, choose a co-ordinator and other participants, supply copies of the product to the co-ordinator and ensure that the product is of a manageable size.
(ii) The co-ordinator must then confirm the time and place with attendees, circulate copies of

the product and finally ensure that people do attend.

(iii) Most importantly, the participants must agree to participate and hence to prepare by allocating some of their own time for studying the product and possibly for discussing it with the producer before the review.

Activities during the walkthrough

The walkthrough itself needs to be held to a set of rules of order amongst which the following in particular should appear:

- the aim is the detection and not the correction of errors;
- the review is of the product not the producer.

The action centres on the producer who presents his product to the assembled group. In response the reviewers in their various roles make comments, criticisms and suggestions which, besides clarification, are not argued over. The secretary records them in summary form. Finally the co-ordinator asks for a recommendation as to whether the product is accepted as it stands, is accepted with the provision that changes are to be made, or deemed to require changes followed by another walkthrough.

Activities after the walkthrough

The recorded comments are archived and circulated to the attendees to check for accuracy, whilst the producer acts on them, possibly preparing for the next walkthrough on the same or another product. Although the record of the walkthrough is in a sense a judgement on the performance of the producer, Yourdon is emphatic that the technical criticism of the review should be separated from the line management function of assessment of staff.

Besides its function of exposing error, the Structured Walkthrough can provide a regular communications channel between team members. This can help to ensure a commonality of purpose and the integrity of the system as well as spreading knowledge about the system around the team as a precaution against the possibility of loss of expertise should a team member leave.

Example

Yourdon 1979*a* gives sample forms for recording the results of a walkthrough. Figure 5.38 shows a similar form completed after a walkthrough of part of the Functional Specification for VISTA. Note that the form makes provision for the formal signing off of each comment once it has been actioned.

Bibliography
Yourdon 1979*a* (the technique described in an easily digestible form appropriate for training staff), Yourdon 1979*b* (the technique seen in the context of other 'structured' techniques), Freedman 1979 (an extensive and valuable manual describing the review process in the form of questions and answers coupled with checklists and examples).

Fig. 5.38. A sample Structured Walkthrough report.

VISTA WALKTHROUGH REPORT number 12 *dated* 17 April 1984

Subject reviewed:	SADT diagrams for HSD space allocation, diagrams A1 and its descendants.
Participants:	Presenter – NDB
	Coordinator – MAO
	Secretary – DG
	Maintenance Oracle – DB
	Standards Bearer – IHJ
	User Representative – DC
	Reviewers – JH

Subject was	accepted unchanged	☐
	revised, no further walkthrough	x
	revised, to be walked through again	☐

Action	Comment/criticism/error	Corrector
1	In diagram A1.2.2 no mechanism is specified for box 1, i.e. how is 'smallest suitable hole' defined?	NDB
2	The O3 output from box 4 is not labelled in diagram A1.2.2	NDB
3	Further expansion of Print File Map in diagram A1 is required	NDB

Exercises

1 How should the time spent walking through the various products of the development paths be budgeted for? What do you think are the pros and cons of having a special work package(s) allocated for the purpose, or of expecting people to absorb the time spent into the time budgeted for their work?

2 Do you think that the deliverable item of every work package should be walked through? If not, what criteria would you use to decide what to walk through?

3 The walkthrough reports that you generate are clearly good raw material for your Project Debriefing Report. What would you expect to be able to learn from them? Particularly in the System Definition Phase?

5.5 Indicators to be monitored during System Definition

5.5.1 Source code size estimate

When the system was originally budgeted or tendered for it is likely that schedule and cost estimates were based on some estimate of the delivered system's size, taken together with other factors such as complexity, staff quality and so on. As often as not the number of lines of source code forms the base input for the calculation.

If final delivered source size is such a strong indicator of the amount of work to be done you will be well advised to monitor it continuously throughout the project. At each stage you should make an estimate based on the information to hand, going to the greatest detail that is meaningful and in units appropriate to the phase of development.

At the end of the Definition Phase you should be in a position to make an estimate from the functionality of the system and an understanding of the crudely-formed design in the back of your head. Lines of code mean very little at this stage. We have found the 'page of annotated high-level language code' an appropriate unit. Such a page includes all in-line comments but not the module header. Over an entire system we find that comment lines account for about 40%–50% of the lines on such a page and this is sufficiently accurate to convert to 'lines of significant source code' – i.e. non-empty, non-comment lines. The density of comments and code varies from programmer to programmer, but at this stage a coarse average is

sufficient. Later in the project you can switch to estimating, and then measuring, in terms of actual lines of significant source code.

As you pass through the phases you will be estimating the value of this indicator repeatedly and with increasing accuracy. Its importance lies in the way it reveals trends in the growth (or even reduction) in size of the system and its components. Significant changes will lead you to reassess your schedule and resource allocations and perhaps your memory and time constraints in the delivered system.

In the sample PDR in chapter 9 we show a graph of the source code size indicator measured for a real project.

5.5.2 System size indicator

As software developers we are rarely blessed with so much memory at our disposal that the size of the system we deliver is of no consequence. Though with the comparatively low cost of memory it is often easier to solve a size problem with cash. Not infrequently however, memory capacity is limited by existing hardware, by the physical space available for the computer (on a satellite for instance) or by the fact that the equipment is going into mass-production and every penny counts. In such cases the final size of the delivered system (or at least the memory-resident part) is a critical parameter that needs to be constantly monitored.

You should be able to derive an estimate from the source code estimate (q.v. above). If you are producing software in a high-level language you will need a conversion factor giving the average number of bytes or words in your target machine that are generated by one line of source. This may require an experiment with the compiler to get a figure of useful accuracy or may be obtainable from the Project Debriefing Reports of other projects which have used that compiler. To this figure you naturally need to add the memory requirements of your data, the operating system and any graphics, communications, database or whatever packages you are also installing. You should turn to texts on system sizing for guidance.

If your estimates of the memory required exceed around half of the available memory you may find yourself incurring schedule and effort penalties as a result of the work that will be required to ensure the system fits. If your estimates suggest more than three-quarters, then the price of shoe-horning could become high. Cost estimation models such as COCOMO (q.v.) will help you get an idea of the effect space constraints can have.

5.5.3 Requirement Specification quality indicator

The quality of the Requirement Specification upon which you must base your Functional Specification is a good indicator of:

(i) how well the client understands what he wants;
(ii) how difficult it will be to complete and agree a Functional Specification of suitable quality (see section 5.6).

One means of objectively assessing the quality of a Requirement Specification is a count of the number of problems found in the specification. A list of likely categories of problems based on Bell 1976 is given in table 5.3.

A count of problems encountered on a first pass through the Requirement Specification should give a good idea of the amount of difficulty that can be expected in completing the Functional Specification, especially if historical data from other projects is used as a guide. Remember that many problem categories will require returning to the client for resolution and this can be time consuming.

5.6 Checklists for the System Definition Phase

5.6.1 Quality criteria for the Functional Specification

Each of the techniques discussed above will help to a greater or lesser extent in meeting the following criteria. You should aim for them not simply by relying on the technique or by trying to remember them occasionally but by actually reviewing your drafts against each – perhaps as part of a structured walkthrough. Look for:

1 Completeness
Everything your client requires is included – see the checklists in section 5.6.2 below.

Table 5.3. *A categorisation of possible problems with a Requirement Specification*

1	Requirement acceptable but not in current release of system
2	Missing/incomplete/inadequate features
	2.1 Elements of requirement not stated
	2.1.1 Decision criteria inadequate or missing
	2.1.2 Requirement paragraph to be determined
	2.1.3 Interface characteristics missing
	2.2 Description of physical situation inadequate
	2.3 Needed processing requirements missing
	2.3.1 Processing rate requirements missing
	2.3.2 Error recovery requirements missing
3	Requirements incorrect
	3.1 Requirement satisfaction probabilistic
	3.2 Timing requirement not realisable with present techniques
	3.3 Requirement not testable
	3.4 Accuracy requirement not realisable with present techniques
	3.5 Requirement (possibly) not feasible in real-time software
	3.6 Required processing inefficient
	3.7 Required processing inaccurate
	3.8 Required processing not necessary
	3.9 Requirement overly restrictive/allows no design flexibility
	3.10 Parameter units incorrect
	3.11 Equation incorrect
	3.12 Required processing illogical/wrong
	3.13 Required processing not/not always possible
	3.14 Requirement reference incorrect
	3.15 Requirement redundant with another requirement
4	Inconsistent/incompatible
	4.1 Requirement information not the same in two locations in specification
	4.2 Requirement references other paragraphs that do not exist
	4.3 Requirement information not compatible with other requirements
5	Requirement unclear
	5.1 Terms need definition or requirement needs restatement in other words
	5.2 Requirement does not make sense
6	Typographical
	6.1 Text typo
	6.2 Equation typo
	6.3 Requirement identifier typo

2 Relevance

Only those things required by the client are included. A simple scan by any independent person will generally show up all the removable noise in the Functional Specification.

3 Testability

It is no use making a requirement that cannot be tested. Words such as 'reliably', 'efficiently' and 'flexible' are generally the marks of untestable requirements. Sometimes, a way round such unquantifiable and untestable requirements is to replace them by specific tests that the system must pass to be considered acceptable in a particular area.

Thus it is no use saying that a system must 'correctly handle power failures' since this has a thousand interpretations. It is however valid to specify a test that involves switching off the mains supply in one or more specified situations and defining exactly what reaction is expected of the system.

4 Unambiguousness

There must be only one way of interpreting the specification, otherwise Murphy's Law will apply. This means in particular being absolutely rigorous in defining and consistently using terms. Also, Freedman 1979 contains a valuable checklist of keywords that are frequently used ambiguously and ways of transforming statements of requirement with the aim of revealing errors, ambiguities and inconsistencies.

5 Conciseness

Remove all background information, all history, all hopes for the future, all anecdotes. If absolutely necessary, put them elsewhere but out of the way.

6 Correctness

It is obvious that our Functional Specification should be correct, but what does this really mean besides that the user's requirements are correctly expressed? One area of danger is that individual functions may be correct in themselves but may lead to invalid or inappropriate combinations. In other words the parts may not fit together sensibly. This says that the Functional Specification must be fully worked through in all its facets and implications – perhaps via some form of prototyping.

7 Consistency

At the simplest level, terms must have the same meaning throughout the document. This requires either a good editor in the case of a manually supported technique or good supporting software where the Functional Specification is machine-processed. Above this, no two requirements should contradict each other, either directly or indirectly. The latter is, of course, the harder to check and means really thinking through the implications of each requirement.

8 Traceability into Design

This topic has already been mentioned under some of the techniques. Your Functional Specification should provide some means for referencing atomic requirements so that they can be clearly referenced on into the design documentation as a check that all of the requirements have been implemented.

9 Sound Basis for Design

It should be clear by now that criteria 1 to 8 will make life much easier for the design team in the next phase.

10 Clarity

If your Functional Specification (or any other document) has plain text in it try applying the Fog Factor test described on page 164.

11 Feasibility

You must be sure that each requirement can actually be implemented using the tools, techniques, people and budget at your disposal. This therefore means both *technical* feasibility and logistical feasibility. Being sure of the first means possibly working up high-level designs, experimenting or prototyping to a sufficient level to assure the practicality of implementing what is being promised. Being sure of the second means estimating the size and nature of the task to a sufficient level to know you have the right people and the right resources.

5.6.2 Contents of the Functional Specification

On any given system some of the items in this checklist will apply, others will not. The list should be considered minimal rather than exhaustive. It does not constitute a contents list for a Functional Specification but should stimulate thought about whether certain topics are to be covered in the Functional Specification or certain questions are to be answered:

1 Inputs to the System
- source of the inputs (standard peripherals, remote sensors, comms lines, human beings, other computers, mice, . . .)
- type of input (analogue – electrical, acoustic, optical – or digital)
- data format (range, units, scale, coding . . .)
- peak arrival rate, average arrival rate, arrival rate profile . . .
- validity checking required and action to be taken on discovery of an error
- time out periods
- separation into critical data (ie necessary for system operation) and non-critical data
- security measures
  - encryption by hardware and/or software
  - physical security of hardware (eg discs, processors, comms lines . . .)
  - security of incoming and outgoing media
  - access control (passwords, keys, authority codes and levels . . .)
- accuracy in input data to be expected by system or required for operation
- the effect of each and every input on the system's behaviour/database/output etc.

2 Outputs from the System
- screen layouts (are they standardised? ergonomic? appropriate?)
- screen input conventions (protected and unprotected fields, default values, use of inverse video and flashing fields, cursor movements, . . .)
- report layouts (are they standardised? informative? appropriate?)
- data channel physical characteristics
- output data format, scale, units, range, required accuracy and precision
- frequency of output and relationship to input (logical, temporal and functional)
- pre-emption of/by other output
- interruption of output for input (eg at a terminal)
- response time for all operations
- ways of requesting output
- security measures (as for input).

3 System Performance
- throughput of system under different loads (remembering to make the requirement precise and testable)
- response times in different circumstances
- precise reliability of hardware and software (how will this be checked?)
- system response to failures of software, hardware, power and so on
  - on different hardware units
  - in different circumstances
  - simultaneously on more than one unit
  - data and processing recovery thereafter when failure is cleared
  - operator intervention required and alternative course of remedial action
  - data integrity level required
- reduced operating capabilities after hardware/software failures
- redundancy of configuration, processing, data and so on for back-up
- checkpointing of data, files, transactions
- audit procedures
- compatibility with existing/proposed systems
- expansion capabilities (be precise)
- number of terminals (of different types/speeds) to be supported at given data rates
- permissible system degradation under load (be precise)
- fallback techniques (other computer, earlier software versions, manual processing)
- reaction of system to exception conditions such as disc offline, cartridge unavailable, Write Protect Ring missing on tape unit, video switched off, no paper in printer.

4 Constraints on the System
- maximum/minimum memory size

- maximum/minimum number for individual hardware units (disc drives, tape drives)
- development facilities required (separate computer system, modems, comms testers, sample databases, use of existing equipment eg new terminals or purpose-built equipment)
- proprietary hardware/software to be used/not used
- existing non-proprietary hardware/software to be used/not used
- interfaces with existing systems (be more precise than ever)
- hardware interfaces
- software interfaces
- data interfaces (shared files, shared databases, simultaneous access, data formats, validity checks required)
- techniques, tools, algorithms, formulae to be used/not used
- environmental constraints or capabilities to be met (temperature ranges, humidity ranges, electrical noise levels on power and signal lines)
- constraints imposed by maintenance requirements
  - both hardware and software.

5 Miscellaneous aspects of the System
- system start-up procedure:
  - automatic/manual
  - locally/remotely loaded
  - bootstrap technique
  - system media required
  - initial databases
  - load-time configuration
  - load-time data input (eg date, time, run number)
  - initial hardware states
- system close-down procedure
  - automatic/manual
  - locally/remotely triggered
  - database/file status (eg trailer records, tape unwinding, disc unloading)
  - final run statistics output or report
  - polite closure of service to users
    - warning of service closure
    - signing-off procedure
    - clearing VDU screens
  - security measures (disc erasing, memory flushing)
  - action with regard to connected systems/network
  - final setting of services under control (eg radar dish stopped, valves closed, doors locked)

- system statistics gathering
  - CPU usage
  - disc usage
  - line usage
  - task activations
  - peripheral activity/reliability
  - memory usage
- requirements for initial database creation, conversion from existing system.

(The above list has been reproduced, slightly modified, with permission from 'Formalised Functional Specifications', Logica Standard LS.062, M. A. Ould, copyright Logica UK Limited.)

5.6.3 Conduct of the Acceptance Test

Your Acceptance Test Specification lays down not so much the individual tests (these appear in the very detailed Acceptance Test Description) as the overall conditions and arrangements for the tests. The following checklist covers the sorts of topics that should be covered.

- Have representatives of the parties involved been identified and their roles defined? In particular, do they have authority to approve or disapprove of the results of a test?
- Has an overall schedule together with individual test timings been presented?
- Has a permitted failure rate (possibly zero) been defined across the entire test?
- Have procedures been laid down for in-flight corrections to software and hardware in the system being tested?
- Have representatives of the parties involved agreed in writing to the Acceptance Test Specification?
- Have the various parties been identified that are responsible for the provision of test software and hardware?

5.6.4 System Definition and maintainability

You cannot start early enough thinking about maintainability and building it into your system, so you should begin with the System Definition Phase. When thinking about the functional requirements of the system to be built now you should review possible future requirements and ask the following questions:

- What are the critical resources in the system and how might the demands on them change?
- What are the performance capabilities of the system and how might they need to grow?
- Which areas of requirement might become unnecessary and removeable?
- Is there the possibility of a need to have different versions of the system with different capabilities?
- What are the implications on manpower and computer resources if the identified changes come about?
- What impact will the new system have on existing operational systems?
- Which areas of function have the greater chance of requiring change in the light of experience with the system?
- Who are the system's future users?
- Who are the system's future maintainers?
- What are the future enhancements that the system's future users can identify as likely?
- How does the system fit into the user's overall plans and how are they expected to develop?

Answers to these questions will lead to specific orientation in the definition of the system's requirements and this in turn will feed into the Design Phase. However, there is a danger here. It is all too easy to write into your Functional Specification quite untestable requirements regarding maintainability, extensibility, flexibility and modifiability. Unless you are able to devise testable requirements for such topics you are best advised to adopt them as design *aims*, treated like contractual requirements, subjected to quality targets, reviews and so forth, yet not appearing as measurable and testable goals in the Functional Specification.

5.6.5 Contents of the Quality Management Plan

You may well have standards for QM Plans within your own organisation, but if not here is a suggested contents list loosely based on the IEEE Standard:

- Preamble: describing the project and system to which the plan applies and so on.
- Management: the organisational structure inside the team concerned with QM; the QM organisational structure outside the team and its relationship to the team (particularly with regard to any QM function that your client may wish you to interface with); the QM tasks involved; how they devolve on the internal structure.
- Deliverable items: what deliverable items are to be produced (your Project Plan will identify which activities produce which deliverable items); how each is to be checked for adequacy by reference to the next section . . .
- Standards, techniques, practices and conventions: which techniques you are going to use at each stage of development and for each deliverable item; whether you will be adapting them and if so how; the content and format of all deliverable items: documents, source code layout, directory structures, global data usage, document archiving, test result records, security back-ups of work in progress – in fact, all the rules and regulations necessary to standardise the work of your team to a consistently high level.
- Review and audits: what deliverable items will be reviewed/audited; when; by whom; how often; using what procedures (Structured Walkthrough, Fagan inspection, simple document reading . . .); levels of criticality; what records will be kept; what follow-up there will be.
- Configuration management: what deliverable items and others will come under formal control; how change on them will be controlled; how errors in deliverable items will be reported; how error correction will be controlled; how releases, issues and versions are defined and when they will be made; what baselines will be taken and when; how deliverable items, their issues and versions will be logically and physically labelled; what levels of authorisation are necessary for changes to the various deliverables once issued; what review and audit procedures will be applied to re-issued items; how master copies of items will be kept; how

copies will be made and distributed and to whom.

- Quality criteria: schedule; cost; memory occupancy; processor load; quality metrics and indicators to be applied; to which deliverable items; with what levels of acceptability.
- Quality tools: what techniques and automated aids are to be used to assess quality levels.

The form that your QM Plan takes will be a product of your own organisation's standards, your own experience and the particular project. We recommend however that, above all, somewhere in your QM Plan you should explicitly identify which development techniques you are intending to use and which indicators you will use to monitor effectiveness; it is these two aspects of development that you should be looking for in these pages. Your QM Plan then becomes a central document that tells your staff how to go about the tasks allocated to them and how to check the quality of their work.

The process of choosing the techniques you will use is discussed in chapter 3. The record of your choice in the QM Plan will probably take the form of references out to appropriate source material plus descriptions of how each technique will be adapted to your particular system and project.

The choice of indicators will be influenced from two directions: your own technical decisions on what is required and the quality requirements imposed on you by your client. In his essay 'Application of metrics to a software Quality Management (QM) Plan' (in Cooper 1979), G. F. Walters identifies a process for defining the required quality of a software product from the viewpoint of the 'acquisition manager'. This process generates requirements that go finally into the Functional Specification and actions to achieve those requirements that go into the QM Plan.

Cooper 1979 contains a number of essays on Software Quality Management, particularly from the organisational and contractual viewpoints. D. L. Wood's essay 'Department of Defense software quality requirements' gives a useful overview of the regulations, standards, guidebooks and so on that are mandatory for USA DoD contracts.

Finally, what of the techniques and tools that you will bring to bear on quality management? We discuss a number throughout this book and to bring them and others together refer you to tables 1 to 5 in D. J. Reifer's paper 'Software quality assurance tools and techniques' in Cooper 1979 (Reifer's paper also contains an extensive bibliography).

5.7 Memorabilia for the System Definition Phase

Manning the System Definition Phase

As in the Design phase, there are major benefits to be had from keeping the team responsible as small as possible, perhaps up to three or four experienced staff, one of whom will act as editor. The editor must make it his task to coldly check the Functional Specification against the checklists given above. A simple rule on manning is also to put your best people on this most critical work and not to dilute their strength with inexperienced staff. If you have the latter on the team already then they should be undergoing training and familiarisation.

Maintaining the information flow

Everyone with a hand in the Definition Phase needs to be kept up to date with the latest drafts. If you are using a scheme where the Functional Specification is held in a computer, you will need to have the software generate drafts or updates at regular intervals. If you are using a manual system, you will need someone to perform this secretarial task manually.

Keeping to the quality aims

You should resist the temptation to publish an incomplete Functional Specification simply because the plan says that design should have started.

Choosing good names for things

This is the phase when you will be choosing names for things. A major source of ambiguity, misconceptions and misdirection is poor naming. Objects often acquire names informally without anyone thinking too hard. So check all the jargon that has developed to date and consciously assess whether it is accurate. If it is not, change it – this is your last chance.

Identifying the functions to the lowest level

A major benefit will accrue if, during System Design and Production, you can easily check which parts of the Functional Specification are being designed or produced – i.e. traceability of function. To achieve this, aim for a representation of your Functional Specification that allows the smallest function to be uniquely identified, with a brief reference code say.

Limiting the scope of the Functional Specification

A useful view of the Functional Specification is as a document that defines the *boundaries* of the system. The question as to what lies inside those boundaries is the question of design and implementation, a question that is to be left unanswered until its time comes in the next phase.

Updating your Project Debriefing Report

Once again you should consider making an entry in your Project Debriefing Report. If you have been using some form of review and keeping records you should be able to answer some or all of these questions from your records:

- Which techniques were used?
- Were they successful?
- If so, how?
- If not, why not?
- Why were the other techniques not used?
- Were these good reasons in retrospect?
- What did your client think of the techniques you used?
- Did your client feel that they had a good grip on the situation?
- Did you?
- What new items can be added to the checklists?

Recording the process of definition

In this phase you will be making many strategic choices and tactical decisions. They are going to affect everything that comes afterwards. In the later stages of the project – in particular, during maintenance and enhancement – it will be difficult to remember why (or even that) these decisions were made. Make a point therefore firstly of keeping a chronological archive of all drafts and background material generated during definition, and secondly of recording those choices and decisions, even the 'obvious' ones – in fact, *particularly* them! This will all be invaluable source material later for those who were not involved in this phase but who need to avoid compromising the system's design and functional integrity because of ignorance.

Generalising facilities in the system

One approach worth considering if a facility is requested is firstly to refuse it and secondly to offer a higher level facility that allows the users to build the special facility themselves. Thus if I ask for a command that performs functions A, B and C in sequence you should consider refusing and offering instead a 'macro command' facility that allows me to string functions together in a general fashion. (You may wish to charge me more for this but I might be prepared to pay!) (Exercise: think of three reasons for not going about things in this way for commercial reasons, and three more for technical reasons. See Terrio 1981.)

Is English too good for Functional Specification?

English must be one of the most semantically rich languages available to the writers of a Functional Specification. It was certainly rich enough for Milton and Whitman. It is worth asking therefore whether richness is what you want when you write your Functional Specification. It's maybe significant that mathematicians don't use English or any other 'natural' language for that matter. (Exercise: what is the *nature* of the act of communication via a Functional Specification and hence what should we expect of the 'language' we use?)

What to expect from a model

You will have seen how the techniques available for defining systems are essentially about *making models*. You must not lose sight of the fact however that a model is only useful insofar as it enables you to answer questions about the thing being modelled, i.e. about requirements.

A good model is therefore one that is orientated towards answering the questions to be asked and that allows answers to be given that are within an appropriate level of tolerance.

Boehm's seven basic principles of software engineering

It is during the System Definition Phase, in drawing up your Project Plan and Quality Management Plan, that you should make a commitment to using 'good' software engineering methods. While most of this book is about such methods, it is worth having in mind a small number of guiding principles to 'good' software engineering. Boehm (1977) has produced what is aimed to be a minimal but complete set of independent principles of software engineering. These are:

- Manage using a sequential lifecycle plan. Use a plan based on the lifecycle model of chapter 2 (see section 5.3.2) and, most important, adhere to the plan.
- Perform continuous validation.
- Carry out structured walkthroughs and other, similar validation at all phases of the project. (See the relevant sections in chapters 5, 6 and 7.)
- Maintain disciplined product control. (See section 2.4.)
- Use enhanced top-down structured programming. (See the sections on structured programming.)
- Maintain clear accountability for results. Make individuals accountable for their work via work packages (section 2.1.10) and monitor progress with indicators (section 2.3).
- Use better and fewer people. This allows the communication overhead to be reduced (section 2.2.5) at the same time as gaining the considerably important advantage of having good people on the project.
- Maintain a commitment to improve the process. Keep track of the results of applying the principles so that you can improve on their use in the future (see section 2.1.9 and chapter 9).

It is well worth reading Boehm's paper on the motivation for the choice of each of these principles and certainly worth remembering them as you embark on your project.

Plan ahead for simulators

From the beginning, as soon as the full characteristics of your system's interfaces with the outside world are known, consider the need for the production of simulation software that can simulate the low-level (and preferably all of the) interfaces – whether to hardware or other software – plus the higher level functionalities and properties. For instance, you might need to simulate both the low-level protocol on a comms link and the high-level behaviour such as varying data rates, different frequencies of message type, sudden peaking, breakdown and so on.

Don't forget also to think about simulating interfaces to operating systems and other supplied software. In the early stages of testing you will want to both isolate the unit under test and exercise it against interface events to operating systems and other supplied software. In the early stages of testing you will want to both isolate the unit under test and exercise it against interface events that may be difficult or impossible to generate with the real software.

Having identified the need for interface simulators make sure you have budgeted and timetabled the work to mesh with your testing activities.

Interfacing with standard packages

It is likely that you will be incorporating someone else's software package(s) into your delivered system. It may be a hosting operating system, a graphics package, a database manager or a comms package. If you have never used it before, do not assume that because it is a package you will be able to just plug it in. You won't.

You will need to budget time and activities into your plan to find out about the package. Preferably you should also identify a person or persons who you want to become the centre of expertise on it. They will need familiarisation time to experiment with it and find out what its characteristics are, what it will and will not do, what it does quickly, what it does slowly, how you configure it, how much space it requires, and so on. You may also need to consider writing software to raise the level of the interface supplied with the package.

Errors made first are discovered last

And those discovered last are most expensive to correct.

Can your system be used?

Making a system usable in a pleasant, convenient, economical, non-patronising and fast manner means defining these properties at the outset. Too often, as system definers and designers we give too little attention to the ergonomics of our systems, in particular to the quality of the man-machine interface. The variety of mechanisms for interfacing with humans – VDUs, colour monitors, graphics, video, sound, voice, joysticks, keypads, rollballs, touch screens, light pens, digitising tablets with styli, and mice, to name the most common

– and the extensive work in the field of ergonomics should give us much material for making our systems more acceptable to our users.

An appropriate subject for a system model is often part or all of the user interface to a system. Using the model, early confidence can be gained that the system interfaces will be appropriate for its users through experimentation and feedback. You may also find it sensible for many reasons (exercise: list them) to prepare your User Documentation during the System Definition Phase. We have placed its production during the System Production Phase but that is simply because the fine detail of user interfaces is often not decided until then. However, this need not stop you drafting as much as you can now.

6

System Design

6.1 The purpose of the System Design Phase

6.1.1 Introduction

Although your main concern in the System Definition Phase will have been to decide *what* functions the system is to perform, you will also have given some thought as to *how* it is to perform them. During the System Design Phase you continue this process by deciding upon and documenting the overall strategy by which the system will perform the required functions. This involves mapping the system functions onto elements of software (and hardware) which can in the next phase be designed in detail and implemented.

The means by which this mapping is carried out can vary enormously, as can the designs resulting from different design approaches. The principal aim of the System Design Phase should, however, be the same no matter what design method is used; namely, to produce a system design which

- is easily implemented,

and which, when implemented,

- will provide all required functions,
- will operate within any required constraints,
- will be easily maintained.

Let us consider the implications of each of these goals for any potential system design methodology.

6.1.2 Ease of implementation

The process by which the system design will be implemented involves the following basic ingredients:

- the system design (in the form of design documents),
- the implementers (i.e. programmers etc.),
- the virtual machine (i.e. the hardware and supporting systems software).

The ease with which the implementation proceeds depends, in particular, on how well the system design interacts with the other two ingredients. What can be done to optimise this interaction?

On an implementation team involving more than one person, a very large percentage of the development time is spent in communication between implementers. As the size of a team increases, the amount of time spent in communication tends to increase at an even greater rate, contributing to phenomena such as the incompressibility of project schedules and Brooks' Law (see section 2.2). In relation to system design, most of this time is spent in:

(i) clarifying points of general design;
(ii) discussing parts of the system which are of mutual concern (i.e. interfaces).

Good system design methods aim at reducing the need for time spent in such communication by

(i) providing design documentation which is *complete*, *comprehensible* and *unambiguous* and by
(ii) paying particular attention to the *choice* and *definition* of interfaces between parts of the system that are likely to be implemented by different people.

The proper choice and definition of interfaces also has a considerable impact upon the integration of software produced by different programmers. The way in which the system's software is divided amongst programmers (i.e. the choice of interfaces) to a large extent determines the way in which the software must be integrated into the final complete system. Each interface that is brought into operation during integration is a potential source of 'interface mismatch' errors. The number of such errors can be reduced by reducing the number of interfaces, increasing the simplicity of the interfaces and by ensuring that the design documentation clearly and precisely defines the interfaces.

The final major way in which a good system design can ease the implementer's task is by minimising the amount of mental contortion and clever trickery that is required to cast the design into operational software. This aim can partially be achieved by ensuring that the design is as *logically simple* as possible. Precisely what is meant by logically simple is a question of concern to the originators of most design methodologies dealt with in section 6.4.

It is possible for a design to be logically simple and still be very difficult to implement on a given virtual machine. For example, a simple design involving recursion will be very difficult to implement in a programming language which does not support recursive function calls. A good system design will either carefully match the facilities of the target virtual machine or it will aim at being independent of the choice of virtual machine. The latter approach has the advantage of tending to improve the portability of the resulting software.

6.1.3 Functional completeness
The obvious goal of ensuring that the system design includes all required functions is not as easily attained as one might think. If the Functional Specification does not clearly identify each function or if the method of progressing from the Functional Specification to the system design is at all haphazard, it is all too easy for functions to be overlooked or incorrectly incorporated into the design.

If you have used one of the functional specification methods described in chapter 5 then you should have a good basis for the design process. An aim of a good system design methodology should be to transform this Functional Specification into a Design Specification in such a way that the presence of each of the system functions can be clearly identified in the final design. An added advantage of achieving this aim is that it facilitates functional testing during System Integration.

6.1.4 Compliance with constraints
The Functional Specification might impose constraints on the operation of the system in such areas as performance, security and reliability. During the Definition Phase you should have ensured that it is possible to meet these constraints, perhaps by carrying out some system modelling. The Design Phase continues this verification programme by ensuring that the particular design being produced will comply with the constraints. The extent to which a design methodology will assist in this process is a crucial factor in deciding whether it is suitable for your application.

The simplest way in which a design method can help in achieving compliance with tight constraints is by forcing the designer to consider the constrained area at each design step. This is most easily achieved by focussing upon the constrained area in the design documentation. For example, if overall system timing is an important constraint then the design documentation should emphasise timing relationships between system components.

At the other extreme, a design methodology can provide automatic tools for the verification of constraints. For example, timing constraints might be checked by a computer simulation of the design automatically produced from a machine-readable design language.

Whatever type of design method you use, it is most important that you verify the design against the constraints now, rather than waiting until system production is complete. Design flaws discovered late in the project will be much more expensive to fix than if they had been located during the Design Phase (see figure 5.1). It is well worth investing in learning, applying and, in some cases, purchasing an appropriate design methodology to help you in achieving this aim.

6.1.5 Ease of maintenance

Since about two-thirds of the total effort expended in the life of a typical system is devoted to maintenance work you should pay particular attention to the extent to which design methods can aid in this work.

There are two principal aspects of maintenance which must be borne in mind in choosing a design method, namely

- fault location and rectification,

and

- system modification and enhancement.

In any large system there are bound to be some bugs which remain undetected during the development phases, only showing up when the system is in service. Such faults must be fixed or by-passed rapidly so as to cause minimum disruption to system service and must very often be dealt with by a maintenance programmer who was not involved in system development. A good system design can be of both passive and active assistance in this fault location and rectification process.

The process of tracing the cause of a fault to a particular piece of software can be passively aided by a good design. For example, if a design results in software units each of which is responsible for performing a given system function, then a fault in a single function can almost certainly be isolated to that function's software unit. This process is further aided by good design documentation which is easily accessed by a maintenance programmer who was not involved in the system's implementation. In a similar way, good design documentation can assist in the rectification of faults by making clear any side effects of fixing a fault. The situation in which one or more new bugs are introduced into software in removing an identified fault is all too common.

A well designed system should also include active fault finding aids such as diagnostic tools and built in tracing and consistency checking. It is most important that these are designed into the system at an early stage and are not just thrown together when a fault has occurred. Early design of such maintenance aids allows maximum benefit to be obtained from them by having them fully integrated into the operational software. You should also be sure to include the development of maintenance aids in your resource estimation and project planning.

Many of the features of a good system design that ease the initial implementation process and the fault location and rectification process also assist when the system requires modification or enhancement. Moreover, a good design method should aim at producing software which is *stable* under changes of requirements. That is, a small change in requirements should necessitate a correspondingly small change in the software. It is very easy to design software for which this is not the case resulting all too often in a situation in which the easiest way to accommodate new requirements is to scrap the old software and start again. By careful system design you should be able to avoid this situation for all but the most extreme changes of requirements, thereby saving both time and money.

Exercises

1 Draw up a list of desirable features of design methods that will help to achieve the goals of the Design Phase as set out in the previous section. Compare each of the design methods described in this chapter using the list of features as a checklist. (Hint: as an example, see Griffiths 1978.)

2 Programmers need to be given manageable pieces of work to do during the Production Phase. Give a definition of 'manageable'. Is there any intrinsic reason why such manageability can only be reached by a process of decomposition?

3 What makes a design simple? Can a simple design be produced for a complex system?

4 What makes for a stable design? Under what conditions do changes to a design cause it to fall apart?

6.2 The starting point of System Design

The System Design Phase starts once the Functional Specification has been written and checked as described in the preceding chapter. Ideally the Functional Specification should also have been agreed to by the client before proceeding, although this may not always be possible. You should, however, strongly avoid expending any significant amount of effort on system design if you expect large scale changes to be made to the Functional Specification. Such premature embarkation on the System Design Phase is likely to lead to wasted effort in producing a design which does not match the ultimate Functional Specification and thus must be scrapped. Alternatively, the functional changes will lead to high-level changes in the design, the side effects of which may not be detected until much later in the project.

Although the Functional Specification is the major input to the System Design Phase, it is not the only one. Other inputs to the phase are

- the Project Plan,
- the Quality Management Plan,
- the results of system modelling and other technical investigations,
- the Requirement Specification.

The Project Plan will have been refined by taking account of the Functional Specification and should by this point provide very accurate estimates for the effort and timescales for the System Design Phase. The Quality Management Plan is relevant to this phase as it gives details of the design method(s) to be employed and the documentation that is required and the indicators that must be monitored.

The results of any system modelling that was carried out during the Definition Phase to ensure that certain functions or constraints are possible are of considerable importance in the System Design Phase where these functions and constraints must be accounted for in the software design. Since the modelling might need to be repeated or extended in this phase it is equally important that the methods such as computer simulations which were used to obtain the results are also well documented.

By this point the Requirement Specification should be of mainly historical interest as all of its requirements should now be dealt with in other documents, especially the Functional Specification. If however you are introducing new staff onto the project at the start of the System Design Phase, the Requirement Specification, or parts of it, can provide useful training material to ensure that these staff have a good understanding of the background to the project and the operational needs of the user. Needless to say, all staff involved in the System Design Phase should also be familiar with the other inputs to the phase. In particular, system design should not proceed until all designers are thoroughly knowledgeable of the Functional Specification, as this will be guiding them in the design process.

6.3 The finishing point of System Design

A detailed description of the finishing point of the System Design Phase, in terms of when to stop designing and what are the deliverable items, depends very much on the design methodology being employed. We can, however, provide a general description of the conditions at the end of the phase in relation to the following three major attributes of the design:

- structure,
- detail,
- validity.

6.3.1 Structure

The overall system structure must have been defined. The system has been successively subdivided into increasingly small components and the interfaces and interactions between the components defined. Irrespective of any other design aims this state must be reached in order that the design can:

- be mapped onto hardware in terms of tasks, processes, memory etc.;
- be mapped onto people in terms of work packages for the Production Phase.

6.3.2 Detail

The level of subdivision and detail of component design must be sufficient to ensure two conditions:

(i) functional completeness of the design can be verified without further subdivision or design;
(ii) implementation can proceed by reference to the design documentation only.

The transformation of the Functional Specification to a design satisfying these conditions is essentially the definition of the System Design Phase. The purpose of the two conditions is best illustrated by way of examples.

If a system design has as one of its high-level components one called 'handle all VDU input/output' with no subcomponents, then neither (i) nor (ii) is likely to be satisfied. For example, it would be impossible to verify a requirement such as 'each VDU shall be polled every 30 seconds'. The situation would arguably be better if the component were labelled 'carry out functional requirements 100–400 related to VDU input/output'. However, in this case condition (ii) would not be satisfied as the implementer would need to refer to the Functional Specification to implement the component and there would be a high chance of omitting some functions as the implementer concentrates on detailed design and coding.

In practice, condition (ii) is likely to be relaxed at the lowest level of detail. For example, a low-level component might have the function of 'displaying the data in the format of fig. 10 of the Functional Specification'. The principal purpose of condition (ii) is to allow the implementers to concentrate on getting the fine detail right, without having to concentrate on overall functionality.

6.3.3 Validity

Having specified a number of aims for the Design Phase in this and the previous sections, we now add one final goal which must be attained before the phase can be considered complete. This is that you must *verify that all design aims have been achieved*.

The principal aims to be checked are the functional completeness and compliance with constraints of the design. You should, however, also check aims such as those affecting ease of implementation and maintenance and any that are specific to a given methodology. Procedures for carrying out this verification process are given in the following sections, with section 6.6 giving some general checklists.

6.3.4 The deliverable item

The final, major deliverable item of the System Design Phase will be verified design documentation – which we call the System Design Specification. The form of the documentation will vary depending on the methodology used, but it should reflect the structure of the system software in so far as the latter is broken down into a hierarchy of components. Thus, for example, there may be an *Overall Design Specification* describing the overall system structure and *Subsystem Design Specifications* for each of the major components. Depending on the size of the system there may be further separate documents or else chapters within the Subsystem Design Specifications for each of the subcomponents and so on down to the smallest components considered in the design. The hierarchical structure of design documentation is very important both to development and maintenance programmers as it minimises the amount of information with which they must contend in order to both have a good overall understanding of how the system works and have a detailed knowledge of the design of the part of the system with which they are involved.

6.4 Techniques of use during System Design

Software design shares two characteristics with other creative acts:

- its success depends ultimately on the skills, intuition and experience of the designers;
- it involves a large amount of detail and a corresponding amount of slog to fill out the conceptual framework.

What does this tell us about choosing design techniques and the design process in general?

Firstly, our design technique must extend the designer's skill by making new designs possible and new problems soluble. A technique or methodology gives the designer a 'handle' on a problem – a way of looking at it and a way of developing a solution from the view obtained. Some handles fit some problems and not others. The solution to a problem may fall out 'naturally' if the problem is looked at in a certain way – i.e. by being approached with a particular technique – whilst another technique may confuse rather than clarify the problem.

The dangers here are clear: we can never assume that simply using a technique is enough to ensure success, nor can we hope that any one technique can solve all problems.

Now part of the designer's skill is to be able to understand the essential features of the problem to be solved and then to choose an appropriate approach. That skill can therefore be extended through increased familiarity with a variety of techniques, thereby lessening the dangers. These comments apply of course to techniques across the whole development path but are arguably most pertinent here in the Design Phase.

The second thing we can see from the similarity between software design and other creative acts is that given a mental tool in the form of a design technique we need to be able to answer the following questions:

- Where does the technique turn to us for the truly creative acts?
- Where does it expect us to generate and maintain detail?
- Where can we relieve the slog through the use of tools (whether pre-existing or built for the occasion)?
- What facts does the technique ask us to determine?
- What particular aspects of the problem does the technique concentrate on and is this appropriate in our problem?

When you study or experiment with the design techniques that we cover in this chapter and that are described elsewhere you should try to answer these questions for each technique. The selection we cover have their own principal con-

cerns, as suggested in table 6.1. We can also compare them in the same terms as we did the Definition Phase techniques in chapter 5, according to whether they provide a notation, a methodology and analytical techniques – see table 6.2. As usual there is no panacea and careful reasoned choice is important.

6.4.1 Structured Design – SD

The notation of Structured Design

At the most basic level, SD provides a means of documenting the structure of a system. This documentation takes the form of a structure diagram composed of three types of components:

- Modules shown as named boxes, representing bounded, contiguous sets of (code) statements that can be referenced by name from elsewhere in the system.
- Connections, shown as (directed) lines joining modules, and representing a reference from one module to another, usually via a 'CALL'.
- Interface descriptions, representing data moving between modules. These can be shown either as short named arrows or in a tabular form listing input and output data items on each numbered connection (see figures 6.2 and 6.3).

A complete set of SD notation can be found in Appendix A of Myers 1975.

Table 6.1. *The principal concerns of the design techniques described*

	Data flow	Data structure	Control flow/structure
Structured Design	yes		yes
JSP		yes	yes
JSD	yes	yes	yes
FSM			yes
Petri Nets			yes
SARA	yes		yes
MASCOT	yes		yes
FDM	could	could	could
HDM		yes	yes
HOS	yes	yes	yes

Table 6.2. *A simple taxonomy of the design techniques described*

	Notation	Methodology	Analysis
Structured Design	yes	yes	
JSP	yes	yes	
JSD	yes	yes	
FSM	yes	some	yes
Petri Nets	yes	some	yes
SARA	yes	yes	yes
MASCOT	yes	yes	
FDM	yes	yes	yes
HDM	yes	yes	yes
HOS	yes	yes	yes

From Structured Analysis to Structured Design

As a documentation method, structure diagrams can be of use for documenting designs produced using other methodologies. SD itself provides a methodology for designing a system structure starting from a system definition produced using Structured Analysis techniques. More precisely, SD gives guidelines for deriving a system structure diagram from the system data flow diagrams (DFD). SD is thus a data flow driven design methodology as opposed, for example, to JSP which is data structure driven or the FSM design method which is control flow driven.

Starting from a system's DFD, the SD methodology consists of the following principal steps:

(i) identify major input and output data flows,
(ii) determine the point of highest abstraction on each major data flow,
(iii) map the DFD to a structure diagram,
(iv) iterate steps (i)–(iii),
(v) refine and package the structure diagram.

Let us consider each of these steps in turn.

From a DFD one can usually identify one or more input and output data flows which are, in some respect, of primary importance and other flows which are of lesser importance. Step (i) involves identifying the former major data flows.

If we trace any of the major input flows into the DFD we find the form of the data becoming more and more abstract. Eventually a point is reached beyond which it is no longer possible to recognise the identity of the data flow. This point is called the point of highest abstraction for the input data flow. In a similar way, by tracing an output data flow back into the DFD, the point of highest abstraction for the output data flow is determined.

If we mark on the DFD the points of highest abstraction for each major data flow, we obtain a division of the diagram into three regions corresponding to input, transform and output. A typical DFD is shown in figure 6.1.

Having thus been divided into three regions, the DFD is mapped onto a structure diagram having one top-level module and a second-level module for each major input stream (source modules), each major output stream (sink modules) and for the central transform region (transform module). The structure diagram resulting from the first mapping of the DFD in figure 6.1 is given by the top levels of the structure diagram in figure 6.2. Note that the interfaces between modules are defined by the data flows in the DFD.

The fourth step involves iterating the steps above to expand the second-level modules into third-level modules and so on. This has been performed in the obvious way for the DFD in figure 6.1 to give third and fourth-level modules in figure 6.2. Lower levels beneath a transform module are obtained from lower levels defining the corresponding transform processes in the levelled sets of DFDs.

The final step consists of refining the structure diagram to make it a good design as judged by the SD evaluation criteria and then packaging the design for implementation in its target environment.

The steps described above lead to the following potential WBS for the Design Phase using Structured Design following on from use of Structured Analysis:

3000 System Design
    3100 System Design Management
    3200 Specify System Design
        3210 Produce environment-independent structure diagram from data flow diagram
        3220 Evaluate design
        3230 Package design for chosen environment

Fig. 6.1. A data flow diagram with the points of highest abstraction on the input and output data streams identified.

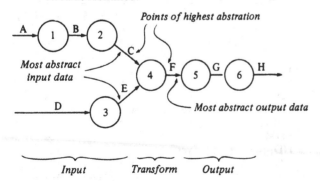

3240 Refine process descriptions to produce internal design of modules (this will require a documentation method such as PDL)
3300 Refine Project Plan
3400 Refine Quality Management Plan
3500 Refine System Models
3600 Prepare Acceptance Test Descriptions

Before describing the evaluation criteria we consider an example of the steps described so far.

An example

As the example giving figure 6.2 is fairly idealised we consider the slightly more involved example of transforming the VISTA DFDs in figures 5.3 and 5.4 into a structure diagram.

Examining figure 5.3 we see that there are two input data flows and two output data flows, corresponding to video and user I/O in each case. In performing the analysis that led to the DFD, the video data flows were the major driving force. In carrying out the SD we take the opposite view and consider the user data as forming the major data flow, arguing that it is the user who makes the system work (see exercise 2 below).

The point of highest abstraction on the user data flow is clearly before the data enters process 2. Each of processes 1, 2 and 3 may contribute to the transformation of the user input data to user output data (the system response). Thus one arrives at the top two levels of the structure diagram as shown in figure 6.3. The triangle at the point of interconnection of the three transform modules to the module 'VISTA' indicates a conditional call (i.e. a given transform module is not always called).

Subordinate modules for each of the transform modules are now decided upon using the lower level DFDs. In particular, figure 5.4 is used in decomposing the module 'Capture Video'. This further decomposition leads to an environment-independent structure diagram which we do not reproduce (see exercise 1). In producing this structure diagram, no attention is paid to the fact that two processors, the host and the VICE, are involved.

Having refined the environment-independent structure diagram with respect to the SD evaluation criteria, it is packaged to fit in the environment formed by the host and the VICE and

Fig. 6.2. The structure diagram resulting from analysis of the data flow diagram in figure 6.1.

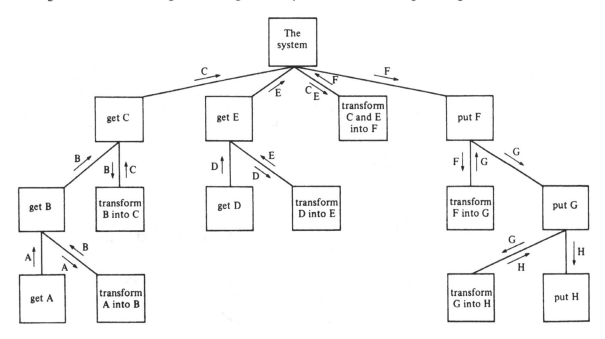

their respective operating systems etc. Figure 6.3 is the structure diagram for the host software after this packaging process. The remainder of the environment-independent structure diagram is subsumed by the structure diagram for the VICE, which we do not show (see exercise 1). The open circles in figure 6.3 are the SD notation for part of the operating environment. We have not defined all the interfaces in figure 6.3 but have given in figure 6.4 an example of the alternative method of defining data passing between modules.

Fig. 6.4. Definitions of some of the module interfaces in figure 6.3.

	In	Out
6	Moving-Sequence Capture-Request	Moving-Sequence-Attributes
7	VICE-Capture-Request	Sampling-Algorithm, DPP-Size, Animation-Sequence-Length

Fig. 6.3. Structure diagram for the VISTA Host Software resulting from an analysis of figures 5.3 and 5.4.

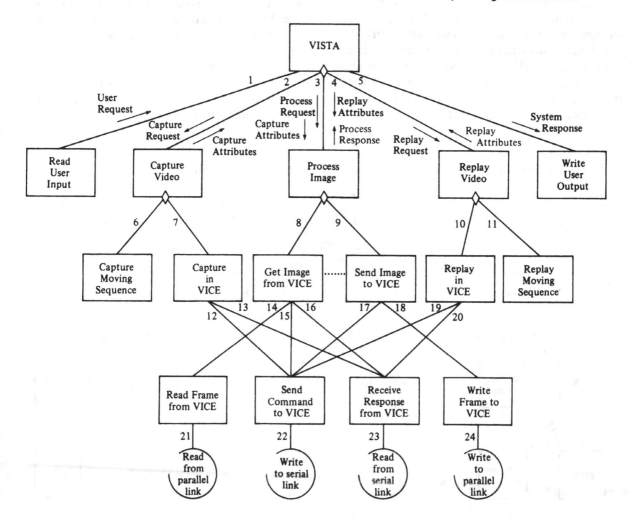

SD evaluation criteria

There are two principal criteria by which a structured design is judged: *module strength* and *module coupling*. Module strength is a measure of how strongly related are the elements within a given module, while module coupling is a measure of the strength of relationship between different modules. A structured design which maximises module strength and minimises module coupling is likely to be less susceptible to errors, more easily incorporated into other systems and less likely to be unstable under changes. This final quality of a design has been carefully analysed by Myers (1975), who has produced a model of program stability in terms of the SD measures of module strength and coupling.

Module strength Seven levels of module strength have been identified in the literature (e.g. Myers 1975). These are, in order of increasing strength:

- *Coincidental*, when instructions are together in a module for no apparent reason.
- *Logical*, when instructions in a module are logically similar (e.g. all input instructions).
- *Classical*, as for logical but all operations in the module are related in time (e.g. an initialisation module).
- *Procedural*, when all operations in a module are related to a problem procedure (e.g. plot *x*).
- *Communicational*, as for procedural but all elements of the module reference the same data.
- *Informational*, a module containing more than one functional strength module acting on a common database.
- *Functional*, all operations contribute to carrying out a single function.

The different levels of module strength are described in more detail in Myers 1975 who gives a checklist (figure 6.5) for deciding on the strength of a module.

Module coupling There are six levels of module coupling (e.g. Myers 1975) which are, in decreasing (improving) order of strength:

- *Content*, when one module makes direct reference to the contents of another.
- *Common*, when modules share a common data area (e.g. via FORTRAN COMMON statements).
- *External*, when modules reference the same external data items.
- *Control*, when one module passes elements of control (e.g. flags, switches) to another module.
- *Stamp*, when one module passes a data structure to another as an argument.
- *Data*, when one module calls another and none of the above couplings apply and all arguments are data elements (i.e. not control elements or data structures).

Once again, more details can be found in Myers 1975 where reasons can be found for considering the above to be in increasing order of goodness. Myers also provides the checklist given in figure 6.6 as a means of deciding on the type of module coupling.

Fig. 6.5. A checklist for determining module strength. (From Myers 1975.)

Difficult to describe the module's function(s)	Y	N	N	N	N	N	N	N
Module performs more than one function			Y	Y	Y	Y	Y	N
Only one function performed per invocation			Y	N	N	N	Y	
Each function has an entry point			N				Y	
Module performs related class of functions			N	Y	Y			
Functions are related to problem's procedure				N	Y	Y		
All of the functions use the same data					N	Y	Y	
Coincidental	×	×						
Logical			×					
Classical				×				
Procedural					×			
Communicational						×		
Informational							×	
Functional								×

Secondary evaluation criteria The following are other criteria and guidelines by which the goodness of a structured design can be judged:

- Simplicity.
- Manageable size: e.g. a module's statements should all fit on a single sheet of paper.
- Recursion: this is a design solution that often leads to crisp solutions, though sometimes at the expense of clarity.
- Predictability: a module is predictable if it behaves the same way every time it is called with the same arguments.
- Initialisation: do it in the module for which it is required, i.e. as far down in the structure diagram as possible without creating an unpredictable module.
- Decision structure: keep modules affected by a decision below the module in which the decision is made.
- Data access: minimise the amount of data a module can access.
- Restrictive modules: do not unnecessarily restrict the use of a module either by coding or documentation.
- Input/output isolation: a good thing.
- Internal procedures: do not use.

Fig. 6.6. A checklist for determining module coupling. (From Myers 1975.)

Direct reference between the modules	Y	N N N N			
Modules are packaged together	Y	N N N N			
Some interface data is external or global		Y Y N N			
Some interface data is control information			Y N N		
Some interface data is in a data structure			Y N	Y N	
Content coupling	× ×				
Common coupling		×			
External coupling			×		
Control coupling				×	
Stamp coupling					×
Data coupling					×

Bibliography
Basili 1978, Bergland 1981, De Marco 1978, Myers 1975 (a good introduction to SD), Myers 1978*a*, Orr 1977, Stevens 1974 (the seminal paper on SD), Stevens 1981, Troy 1981 (a recent study of SD indicators), Yourdon 1978, 1979*b* and 1979*c* (recommended reading).

Exercises
1 Use figure 5.4 to decompose the 'Capture Video' module in figure 6.3 to give an environment-independent structure diagram. Package this environment-independent structure diagram to give figure 6.3 as the structure diagram for the host and to determine the structure diagram for the VICE.
2 By considering the user data as the principal data flow in figure 5.3 we ended up with an environment-independent structure diagram the top levels of which, when packaged, ended up on the host and the bottom levels of which ended up on the VICE. If the Video data is considered to form the principal data flow then the opposite happens, namely, the top levels of the environment-independent structure diagram end up on the VICE. Try this approach to the design. Do you consider one approach to be in any sense better than the other?

6.4.2 Jackson Structured Programming – JSP
JSP is a technique that sees programs as means by which one set of data structures is transformed into another set of data structures. Program structures are derived from those data structures according to certain procedures.

The starting point for JSP design is therefore a full understanding of the data structures involved and this may well influence your choice of methodology during the Definition Phase.

We can develop the ideas in JSP in the following order, following Jackson 1975:

(i) the basic design technique with one data structure,
(ii) handling more than one data structure,
(iii) handling erroneous data in the data structures,
(iv) undoing decisions wrongly made,
(v) handling incompatible data structures,
(vi) optimisation.

The basic design technique

As we saw in the précis in chapter 3 the basic design technique has three steps:

(i)(*a*) identify and define the data structures involved,

  (*b*) form a program structure based on the data structures,

  (*c*) define the task to be performed in terms of elementary operations and allocate these to components in the program structure.

JSP is based on data structuring and for this reason a Functional Specification method that defines data carefully, such as Structured Analysis with its data dictionary, is a useful input to JSP design. It recognises four types of component in a data or program structure:

- elementary components,
- composite components
  - sequential – two or more parts occurring once each in a specified order;
  - iterative – one part occurring zero or more times;
  - selected – two or more possible parts, of which one and only one occurs once.

Thus a data structure such as a magnetic tape of records might take the form of a header record preceding a number of groups, each group containing a number of records which are of either type A or type B. The groups will be identified by a group number in each record. Each record will also bear a type identifier. In JSP notation this would be represented by the data structure diagram in figure 6.7. Asterisks identify iterated components and circles identify selected components.

Suppose we wish simply to count the number of groups and the number of each type of record on the tape, finishing by displaying the final counts. Since our program only needs to reflect the one input data structure it will have the structure in figure 6.8. Each component in the program corresponds to a component in the data structure. In such a simple case, step (i)(*b*) is trivial.

Step (i)(*c*) leads us to identify the following elementary operations:

(1) open file,
(2) close file,
(3) read file,
(4) display totals,
(5) zeroise group count (GC),

Fig. 6.7. A single JSP data structure diagram.

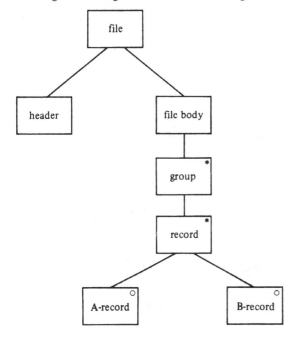

Fig. 6.8. A program structure diagram derived from figure 6.7.

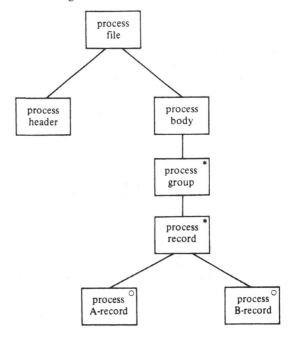

(6) zeroise A count (AC),
(7) zeroise B count (BC),
(8) increment GC,
(9) increment AC,
(10) increment BC,
(11) display file header,
(12) stop.

Allocating these operations to the program components is straightforward except for deciding when to read the tape file. A fundamental principle in JSP is to *read ahead* at least one record so that whenever decisions need to be made the data is always available. The single read ahead technique is summarised by Jackson in two rules for allocating the read operation:

- read the first record immediately after opening a file;
- read again at the end of each program component that processes an input record.

Fig. 6.9. Actions allocated to program components.

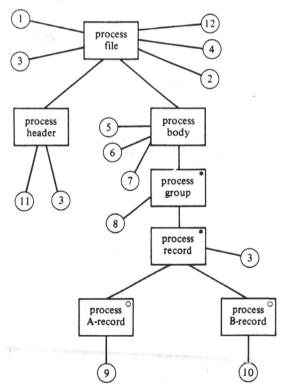

Taking into account rules for handling end-of-file (EOF), we can now allocate the 12 operations to components in the program structure with the result shown in figure 6.9. This diagram is then translated into Jackson's *schematic logic* to give the program shown in figure 6.10, which in its turn can now be worked up in detail and finally translated into the target language.

Handling more than one data structure

In the general case we need to construct programs that concern themselves with more than one data structure. A program taking one input structure and producing one output structure must have a program structure that corresponds to both. This is done by producing a composite of the two data structures. Thus, if the output from our program above had to take the form shown in figure 6.10 (rather than being structureless as we assumed above) then the program structure would have the form shown in figure 6.12 and we would have a new action:

(13) display group number.

A program taking more than one input structure is, in Jackson's terminology, *collating* – a merge of two ordered files is a typical example. For such programs the program structure is once again derived as a composite of the input data structures, but now with elementary operations that are selected according to relationships between the current record read from each file.

Fig. 6.10. JSP schematic logic for the program in figure 6.9.

```
PROC_FILE    seq  open file;
                  read file;
PROC_HEADER  seq  display file header;
                  read file;
PROC_HEADER  end
PROC_BODY    seq  zeroise group count (GC);
                  zeroise A count (AC);
                  zeroise B count (BC);
PROC_GROUP        iter while not EOF
                      increment GC;
PROC_REC              iter while not EOF
                          select type_A
PROC_TYPEA                    increment AC
                      or      type_B
PROC_TYPEB                    increment BC;
                          read file;
PROC_REC              end
PROC_GROUP        end
PROC_BODY    end
                  close file;
                  display totals;
                  stop;
PROC_FILE    end
```

Fig. 6.11. A simple output format.

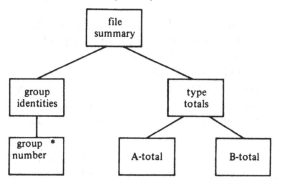

Fig. 6.12. A program structure diagram derived from figures 6.7 and 6.11.

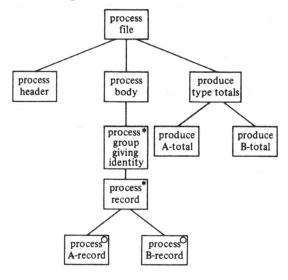

Fig. 6.13. A JSP data structure that makes selection difficult.

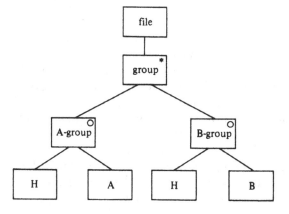

Common to both these situations is the aim of fitting the data structures together by identifying the one-to-one correspondences between them. This will ensure that the program structure corresponds to all the data structures. This is not always possible however and such 'structure clashes' need an additional technique for the derivation of the program structure. This is dealt with below.

Backtracking

So far the technique has assumed that, whenever we need to make a decision on a selection or iteration component we have available all the information necessary. This is not always true as you can see if you consider a program that handles a data structure where selection substructures have a lot in common and cannot be distinguished simply by looking at their first component. Consider the examples in figure 6.13. JSP has two techniques for dealing with this problem. The first – *multiple read ahead* – handles cases where the problem can be solved simply by reading enough of the file to ensure that the necessary information is available. The example in figure 6.13 would need two reads ahead.

In the more general case a more general approach is required – *backtracking*. The data structure causing the problem is drawn in the normal way and the program structure is derived from it on the assumption that the decision at the offending selection can actually be made. This will lead us to the following schematic logic for the data structure in figure 6.13:

```
PGROUP       select  A-group
    PA               seq
                     process H;
                     process A;
    PA               end;
PGROUP       or      B-group
    PB               seq
                     process H;
                     process B;
    PB               end
PGROUP       end
```

(Note that it is assumed that H is to be processed in the same way whether it heads an A-group or a B-group.)

We then transform this to allow the selection to be proved false and the decision to be 'backed-off' by backtracking our actions before choosing the other decision at the <u>select</u>. To do this, <u>select</u> is replaced by <u>posit</u> which lays down a hypothesis; <u>admit</u> then identifies the decision that should have been made if a <u>posited</u> hypothesis is shown to be wrong, and <u>quit</u> detects a false decision.

Our program fragment above thereby becomes

```
PGROUP     posit A-group (assume
                          A-group to
                          start with)
     PA        seq
               process H;
               quit PA if B next;
               process A;
     PA        end
PGROUP     admit      (must have
                       been B-group)
     PB        process B;
PGROUP     end
```

In this trivial case backtracking was easy. Often undoing the result of an erroneous decision at a <u>posit</u> may be problematical, particularly if the results involved input–output devices. JSP presents a number of techniques for solving this problem.

A similar approach is applied where the condition controlling an <u>iter</u> cannot be evaluated without entering the iterated section. As with <u>select</u>, backtracking may be required, this time to undo the results of the partially completed but unnecessary iteration.

Structure clashes

We saw earlier that in some cases it might be impossible to compose a program structure directly from two particular data structures. A simple example would be where we have an input file consisting of the rows of a matrix from which we wish to form an output file containing the columns of the matrix. This operation cannot be carried out sequentially by a single program and we have a structure clash.

Jackson 1975 identifies three types of structure clash:

- an *ordering clash*, such as the matrix problem,
- a *boundary clash*, where, although the data is in the same order in input and output files, it is broken up differently,
- a *multi-threading* clash, where, although input and output data are in the same order and in the same 'units', they run in parallel and overlap in the input file like individual threads in a rope.

The general solution presented for structure clashes makes use of *intermediate files*. Since the clashing data structures cannot be synchronised via a single program they must be processed by two or more programs that communicate via intermediate files. (In the matrix problem such an intermediate file could simply be a memory-held copy of the entire matrix.)

Program inversion

Although intermediate files will always provide one solution to clashes, implemented directly it could be very inefficient. In particular, as described so far, the technique would require us to write the entire intermediate file before the next sequential program can start. This could be avoided by multi-programming and organising a communications channel between programs but even this is likely to be resource consuming.

Instead, JSP adopts a technique called *program inversion*. Let us suppose that the processing of an input file IF to form an output file OF has been designed as two programs P1 and P2 communicating through an intermediate file IMF:

$$\text{IF} \text{- - - - - - -} \text{>IMF} \text{- - - - - - -} \text{>OF}$$
$$\text{P1} \qquad\qquad\qquad \text{P2}$$

Rather than running P1 and P2 in parallel we convert one so that it can run as a subroutine of the other. It does not matter materially which is made the subroutine. The intermediate file disappears to become instead the transfer of common units of data – the inversion is said to take place 'with respect to the intermediate file'.

The inversion process leaves the schematic logic of a program unchanged. It is performed on the source code (e.g. COBOL) derived from the schematic logic. The way in which the program –

now a subroutine of the other (main) program – gets its input changes, as it now expects data from the main program which acts as a form of window on the intermediate file.

An important feature of program inversion is that the process can be performed semi-mechanically thereby reducing the risk of error.

Optimisation

Jackson's attitude to optimisation is that it is something that is only done to a correct design, if it is done at all. It is claimed that the techniques used in JSP tend to produce the fastest possible programs though not the smallest. The optimisation methods described therefore involve transformations of program structure designed to reduce program size.

We can summarise the methods offered briefly as follows:

- simplifying data structures to contain fewer distinct components that need to be processed (though this is considered dangerous),
- amalgamation of identical processing ('common action tails'),
- generalising program components to serve more than one purpose.

Work Breakdown Structure

In as much as JSP produces schematic logic for programs it could be said to extend into the Production Phase. This is particularly so with the advent of preprocessors that generate (for instance) COBOL programs from the schematic logic. For our purposes here however we take the production of the logic as marking the completion of the Design Phase.

The production of schematic logic is a step that can be omitted unless there is a special problem such as difficult side-effects in backtracking. Tools are also becoming available that miss the step by carrying out the derivation of code from diagrams directly.

Our expansion of the WBS below assumes that if you have used some other technique as well as JSP during design – for instance to factor out the time element – then you will combine the two WBS fragments. It also assumes that you have a number of sequential programs in your system to design.

3000 System Design
  3100 System Design Management
  3200 Specify System Design
    3210 Establish all data structures for valid data
    $32n0$ Design program n (n greater than 1)
      $32n1$ Derive program structure from data structures
      $32n2$ Determine elementary processing operations and allocate to program components
      $32n3$ Draw schematic logic for program
      $32n4$ Introduce backtracking as necessary
      $32n5$ Optimise by transforming program structure

Note that we have been strict in not putting in an activity for program inversion – this is a transformation carried out on the source code of the Production Phase so you will find it in the WBS there.

Example

Since the above outline of JSP contains a number of examples we restrict ourselves here to giving in figure 6.14 the data structure diagram for a directory of the space allocation on the HSD in our VISTA system.

The directory contains information about the HSD itself, followed by a variable number of entries each describing either a 'hole' of unused space or a sequence occupying space on the HSD. The last (and ever-present) entry is a hole entry (possibly for a hole of zero length).

The data structure shown is intended as input to the problem in exercise 1 below. If the same data were input to a different problem it could require a different data structure.

Bibliography for JSP

Bergland 1981, DoI 1981, Hughes 1979, Ingevaldsson 1979, Jackson 1975 (the principal published description of the technique; contains a wealth of worked examples), Palmer 1979 (an example of an application outside traditional data processing: interrupt-driven microcode).

Exercises

1 Construct the schematic logic for a program to print the number of free blocks on an HSD using the basic JSP technique.

2 Suppose you wished to list the HSD files in chronological order of creation date. Identify the structure clash and define an intermediate file to resolve it.

3 Since the program structure is derived from the data structure, what does this say about producing a program that can detect and deal with data that is not in the correct form?

A related technique – LCP

If Jackson Structured Programming is of interest to you it may well be worth investigating Warnier's Logical Construction of Programs (LCP) and Logical Construction of Systems (LCS), and the Warnier–Orr Structured Systems Design technique, all of which share the same foundations.

In particular, LCP is like JSP in being data structure driven and is applicable to the same group of problems. It is a relatively mechanical design methodology with rather more specifically defined steps than JSP and a different notation (in fact one more amenable to standard typographical layout). From the definitions of the system inputs and the required outputs a program in the form of PDL is derived which can be translated into the target language.

We can summarise the procedure as follows. Firstly the input and output data structures are specified and decomposed into JSP-like hierarchies in terms of sequence, iteration and selection. The relationships between the data structures are then specified in terms of statements in boolean algebra – or equivalently as truth tables, Karnaugh Maps or decision tables. These relationship statements are then simplified using boolean algebra, with the subsidiary aim of increasing implementation efficiency (cf. JSP where optimisation is discouraged).

A skeleton program structure is then derived from the data structures. Where the boolean relationships are not simple, complex program structures may be necessary (cf. JSP's structure clashes), and a multipass design is used with intermediate data structures to resolve problems that involve JSP in backtracking.

Fig. 6.14. JSP data structure diagram for the HSD directory in VISTA allowing us to print the number of free blocks and the directory contents.

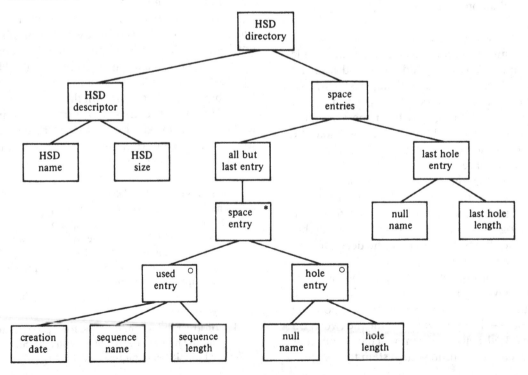

The various procedure operations to be inserted into the program skeleton are then listed and ascribed to the correct parts of the skeleton, according to a number of rules. The result is effectively a detailed flowchart in a pseudo-code of high-level, functionally orientated terms, equivalent to JSP's schematic logic. Once this has been verified it can be translated into the target language.

Like JSP, LCP leaves the initial formulation of data structures and their relationships to the designer, and then supplies the objective, syntactic methods for getting to the schematic logic.

For descriptions of LCP see Warnier 1974, Gardner 1981, Chand 1980, Higgins 1979, Orr 1977 and 1978 and Ramsey 1979; for LCS see Warnier 1981.

6.4.3 Jackson System Development – JSD

The major design steps of JSD

In chapter 5 we covered the first two steps of the six steps that make up JSD. In this chapter we cover the next three: the initial model, function and system timing steps. Although the first two still involve the user, there is a strong element of design in them.

You will remember that the entity action and entity structure steps basically identified the entities in the real world that are of concern, what actions they suffer or perform during their lifetimes and what the time-ordering of these actions is (the 'entity structure').

The initial model step

Each entity is now modelled by a 'model process' that appears as a box in a System Specification Diagram (SSD). This model process (or set of model processes) is shown as communicating with the corresponding entity in the real world. There are no outputs from the system as yet and the inputs to the system are simply messages that signal the occurrence of events in the real world so that they can be appropriately simulated in the model.

The communication between real world (so-called 'level-0') processes and system model (so-called 'level-1') processes will later manifest itself

as some form of input medium that informs the system of events occurring in the real world. Thus, the event of a new user opening an account with the System Manager will be notified perhaps by an on-line transaction. Such transactions constitute a data stream into the system. The event of a VICE being switched into sampling-rate-B state might however be notified by the subsequent status of a line on an interface card.

Processes can communicate therefore in two ways:

- by 'data stream', through a buffered queue of messages, with strict ordering and unblockable writing (cf. MASCOT 'channels');
- by 'state vector inspection', through the unbuffered, unblockable inspection by one process of the local variables (i.e. status) of the other.

Where necessary, a process can take and merge two or more data streams, the choice of next message being made according to fixed rules or the data contents of the messages or the availability of messages on the streams – the latter being known as 'rough merging'. An important form of rough merging is that which combines a data stream with another stream of 'Time Grain Markers' (TGMs) that indicate the arrival of particular points in real world time – end-of-calendar-month, 10ms-expired, or close-of-business, for instance.

Figure 6.15 shows the SSD for a subset of VISTA including the USER and VICE real world and model processes. We can see that the model

Fig. 6.15. A subset of the JSD SSD for VISTA.

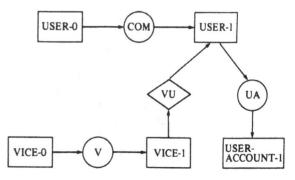

process for USER, USER-1, is attached to the real world USER entity, USER-0, via the data stream COM (probably of user commands); VICE-1 is connected to the real world VICE entity VICE-0 via the data stream V (probably of interrupts); the USER-1 process inspects the status of the VICE-1 process via state-vector VU; the USER-1 process generates a data stream to a third model process for the USER-ACCOUNT entity.

Given the connections between the model processes and the structures of the entities they model we can derive semi-mechanically the 'structure text' for each model process. As an example figure 6.16 contains the structure text for the USER model process. By comparing this with the USER entity structure you will see how:

(i) the structure has been transformed directly into the structure text, with sequential components being bracketed by a seq–end pair, iterated components by an itr–end pair, and selected components by a sel–alt–end structure;

(ii) the input command stream is read by a 'read COM' statement at the beginning of the entity structure and immediately after every component that consumes an input;

(iii) the status of the VICE is determined through a 'getsv VU' statement; by convention this returns the status of the VICE-1 process in terms of where it currently is within its

Fig. 6.16. JSD structure text for the USER entity's model process.

```
USER_1     seq  read COM;
               obtain account; read COM;
          USER_BODY itr (while new session)
               USER_SESSION   seq
                         start session; read COM; write UA;
                         reserve VICE; read COM;
                         SESSION_BODY  itr (while new activity)
                              VIDEO_ACTIVITY seq
                                        OBTAIN_FRAME sel (on request)
                                             getsv VU;
                                             capture VF; read COM;
                                        OBTAIN_FRAME alt
                                             synthesise VF;
                                             read COM;
                                        OBTAIN_FRAME end
                                        process VF; read COM;
                                        replay VF; read COM;
                              VIDEO_ACTIVITY end
                         SESSION_BODY end
                              release VICE; read COM;
                              end session; read COM; write UA;
               USER_SESSION   end
          USER_BODY end
               close account; read COM;
USER_1 end
```

structure, in particular which read, write or getsv it last executed.

Where a process merges a number of data streams the disposition of the read statements is determined by which type of merging is required: rough, data or fixed.

You may have noticed that the model entity is only prepared to accept a data stream of exactly the right form – i.e. one that agrees syntactically with the structure of the entity. What if something goes wrong and an unexpected message arrives? This is dealt with in two ways:

(i) firstly, the entity structure can be designed to handle certain incorrect but handleable streams;

(ii) secondly, Jackson interposes an 'input subsystem' between the real world and the model, one of whose tasks is to detect, and perhaps rectify, errors in the input data.

The function step

It is at this point that the required functions of the system are inserted into the model. They are added to the model in the form of 'function processes'. These receive inputs from model processes and sometimes extraneous data streams (time grain markers for example) and they produce outputs. Their connection to model processes is also via data streams or state-vector inspection, the choice being dependent on where the initiative for communication lies.

There are a number of different ways that a function process can be inserted into the System Specification Diagram. It can be embedded actually inside a model process if there is no change of structure between the inputs to the model process and the outputs required from the function process. If there is a structure clash (in the JSP sense) the function and model processes are separated and communicate via an intermediate data stream or state vector. The model process must, in this case, remain unelaborated. A function process might produce outputs that form inputs that are in turn rough-merged by the model process, thereby closing a feedback loop and producing an 'interactive' function.

Whatever its position in the system, a function process is always treated at this stage as having a long lifetime; it is never 'single-shot'. Thus, if we wanted to produce hourly status reports on the VICEs, the corresponding function process would be a sequential process whose output would be the *set of all* hourly reports produced during the lifetime of the system.

Let us take this hourly-status-report function further. Figure 6.17 shows the SSD elaborated to contain a function process PRODUCE-HR that rough-merges an hourly time-grain-marker data stream and messages on data streams from all VICE processes to produce an HOURLY-REPORT. By using principles similar to those used in JSP for determining program structures, we can draw a process structure for PRODUCE-HR – figure 6.18 – and derive the corresponding structure text from it – figure 6.19. The read statements have been organised to give preference to TGMs. It can be easily seen that no provision is made for initialisation or close-down. This is a direct result of the fact that in drawing up the structure for PRODUCE-HR we did not show its *entire* lifetime.

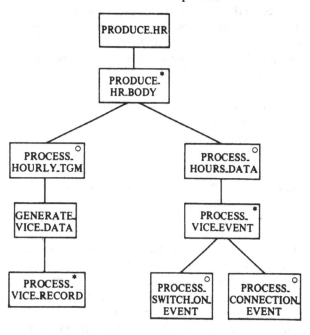

Fig. 6.18. JSD structure diagram for the PRODUCE-HR function process.

Fig. 6.17. Elaborated JSD SSD for hourly VICE status reports.

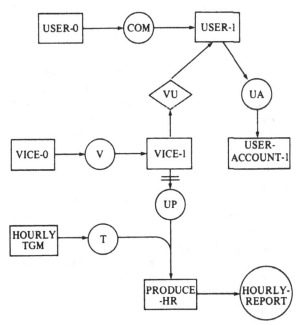

Fig. 6.19. JSD structure text for the PRODUCE-HR function process.

```
PRODUCE_HR itr read T; read UP;
    PRODUCE_HR_BODY sel (hourly TGM present)
        PROCESS_HOURLY_TGM seq
            GENERATE_VICE_DATA itr (for each VICE)
                PROCESS_VICE_RECORD seq
                    process switch-on count;
                    process connection count;
                    ...
                PROCESS_VICE_RECORD end
            GENERATE_VICE_DATA end
            read T;
        PROCESS_HOURLY_RGM end
    PRODUCE_HR_BODY alt (VICE event present)
        PROCESS_HOURS_DATA itr (for each event coming in)
            PROCESS_VICE_EVENT sel (switch-on event)
                increment switch-on count for VICE;
                read UP;
            PROCESS_VICE_EVENT alt (connection event)
                increment connection count for VICE;
                read UP;
            PROCESS_VICE_EVENT alt (select-algorithm-A event)
                ...
            PROCESS_VICE_EVENT end
        PROCESS_HOURS_DATA end
    PRODUCE_HR_BODY end
PRODUCE_HR end
```

The net result of the function step is therefore to produce a fully elaborated SSD plus structure text for all the functions involved. It is important to note that all the work done so far has been done without reference to the implementation and that the addition of functions to the model system has been left as late as possible.

The system timing step

In this step we look at the timing constraints to be satisfied by the implementation if the system is to do what is required. We therefore collect and document these before going on to the implementation step. Informal notes will suffice for subsequent reference.

It is worth noting that, so far, the techniques of buffered data streams and state-vectors have not forced us into any decisions on implementation; in particular we have not concerned ourselves with the target environment and its properties. The timing constraints are the last factor to be investigated prior to implementation. (This corresponds closely to Jackson's view on optimisation: do not, and (if you must) do it last.)

As examples of implications to be looked at in this step, we can imagine an implied need for a model process to check the status of a real world entity with a minimum frequency to be certain of noticing states of short duration, or the need to check the 'fairness' of a rough-merge algorithm to ensure that it does or does not favour a particular input stream.

The outputs of the process so far

It is worth summarising at this point what deliverable items have been produced by the first five steps of JSD. They are as follows:

- the list of entities refined in the light of the function step,
- the list of actions similarly refined,
- the System Structure Diagram showing all the model and function processes, connected to each other and to the real world via data streams and state vectors,
- for each process, structure text reflecting either (for a model process) the structure of a modelled entity, or (for a function process) the structure of its input and output data,

- a list of timing constraints to be satisfied by the system.

Collectively, these can be considered to form the System Design Specification which is the deliverable item of our Design Phase.

Exercises

1 Compare the SSD of JSD with the ACP diagram of MASCOT. In the latter, 'activities' (processes) communicate through 'channels' (data streams) and 'pools' (that typically contain state-vectors in some form). Where are there differences and how might they be significant in terms of constraining the designs the two techniques permit?

2 MASCOT activities derive from a consideration of how system inputs are to be transformed into system outputs. Compare this process with JSD's Function Step.

6.4.4 Finite State Machines – FSM

In section 5.4.7 we saw how FSMs can be used as part of the system definition process, probably in conjunction with some other methodology. If this other methodology does not provide a means of transition to a system design then FSMs can be used for this purpose.

The System Design procedure using FSMs continues from where the System Definition process described in section 5.4.7 stops. In particular, the hierarchical decomposition of the system FSM is continued until a sufficient level of detail has been defined (see section 6.3.2).

The system data flow diagrams (preferably stratified as described in section 5.4.7) are then used to make decisions regarding, for example, the division of the system into tasks, the allocation of tasks to processors, possible concurrency of tasks and the assignment of databases. Finally, the structure of the system (in the meaning of Structured Analysis) can be defined directly from the hierarchy of FSMs.

The final step can be carried out in a number of ways, one of which we illustrate by continuing the example of section 5.4.8. The level of decomposition given in this example is probably already sufficient to allow an Overall Design Specification to be produced but further decomposition into lower level sub-FSMs would be required for sub-system specification.

The top two levels of the system structure diagram follow directly from figure 5.17 and are shown (along with part of a lower level) in figure 6.20. The module called 'Control' inputs commands and, where necessary, determines to which equivalence class a command belongs (e.g. class V). It also keeps track of the current top-level state (1 to 11) of the system and uses this and the input to determine (from tables based on figure 5.17) the new state and the action to be performed to get to this state. The action is performed by 'calling' the appropriate next level action module and passing to it data determined from the data flow diagrams.

For example, if the top-level state is 10 and a 'capture-animation-sequence' command is input, then Control determines that this is of class V1 and thus (see figure 5.17) changes the top-level state to 8 and calls module Class V1, passing it the command and any other data required by it. Module Class V1 reserves the VICE and activates the second-level FSM.

The second-level modules collectively implement the second-level sub-FSMs by keeping track of the second-level state (i.e. the top-level state qualified by a substate, e.g. 8.1) and by responding to inputs according to the second-level state transition diagrams. Thus for example, if the second-level state is 8.1 and module 'Class V' receives the (class V) input 'display animation sequence' then it

will move to state 8.3 and call module 'Display Animation Sequence' (see figure 5.18). This module may well exist as a separate task on the host computer or as a task running on the VICE.

As with Structured Design, some supplementary method will be needed to document the action carried out by each module and the precise nature of each input.

Exercise
There is a danger that designs produced using FSMs will be 'bad' designs when judged by the criteria of Structured Design. Why is this the case and does it matter? What steps can be taken to ensure that the FSM design approach produces a 'good' design when judged by these criteria?

6.4.5 Petri Nets
We have already seen how Petri Nets provide a powerful modelling tool for systems involving independent co-operating processes. Part of their power derives from the fact that the behaviour of a system modelled by a Petri Net can be determined analytically from the net's graph (PNG). The technique therefore extends naturally into system design where it is of particular use in real-time environments.

It offers a way of recording and analysing a design, and the resulting model can generally be

Fig. 6.20. Structure diagram of the VISTA system resulting from a design using FSMs.

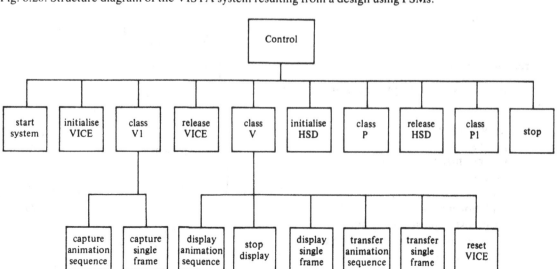

translated directly into software terms. Since the basic principles about Petri Nets are described in chapter 5 we restrict ourselves here to illustrating how that translation can be made and to giving an example.

One technique is as follows:

(i) decide what activities are to take place,
(ii) decide what inter-relationships exist between these activities, i.e. what dependencies they have on each other,
(iii) draw the PNG showing activities as transitions and places as events on which activities are dependent,
(iv) analyse the properties of the PN and adjust the model to give the required behaviour,
(v) repeat steps (i)–(iv) as necessary,
(vi) translate the PN components back into design terms.

Suppose that we wish to design the VICE software to capture M frames of television in succession on command from the host. In, say, a simple micro we could design a single process with the following logic:

> wait in idle state for capture request from host;
> process request (e.g. initialise hardware)
> wait for next frame sync;
> process first frame sync (e.g. start counting);
> do M times
> > (wait for next frame sync;
> > process frame just captured (e.g. count it)
> >);
> process last frame (e.g. reply to host);
> return to idle state.

If we wished to use a multi-process solution the steps would take the following form:

1 the activities are
> process-request
> process-first-frame-sync
> process-frame-just captured
> process-last-frame
2 their relationships are
> **once** host request arrives **and**
> > previous sequence capture has terminated
> **then we can** process-request

> **once** process-request is done **and**
> > one frame sync has arrived
> **then we can** process-first-frame-sync

> **once** (process-first-frame-sync is done **or** process-frame-just-captured is done) **and** one frame sync has arrived
> **then we can** process-frame-just-captured

> **once** process-last-frame is done M times
> **then we can** process-last-frame

> synonyms are
> > previous sequence capture has terminated
> > process-last-frame is done.

3 figure 6.21 represents the PNG for these activities and relationships
4 analysis of this PNG (for instance through its reachability tree or simply by 'dry-running') reveals that frame capture continues without stopping even after M frames have been captured because of the $p3/t3$ feedback loop; we correct this by making $p3$ an input place of $t4$
4° further analysis shows that tokens can accumulate embarrassingly in $p6$, i.e. there is no mechanism for discarding unneeded frame syncs; the result of this is that $t2$ is enabled incorrectly when the next request arrives from the host; we correct this by

Fig. 6.21. A PNG design for VISTA animation mode.

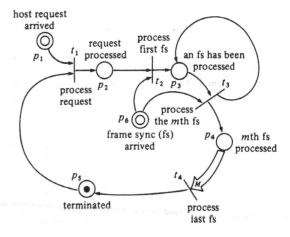

consuming frame syncs through *t*5 whenever there is a token in *p*5, i.e. whenever the system is waiting for the next host request

5 the resulting PNG is then as in figure 6.22.

Our analysis has shown that we need a new activity (*t*5) that absorbs unnecessary frame syncs and that when processing the last frame sync we needed to 'consume' the event that the previous frame sync has been processed.

What we have still not analysed are the timing constraints in our model. Frame syncs arrive widely spaced and regularly and to ensure correct sequence we may wish to place priorities on transitions, for instance giving *t*4 higher priority than *t*3 to ensure correct termination of sequence capture.

Having finally determined that our PNG correctly models the system we require, we can consider extending our analysis by simulating the system, building it with dummy programs of adjustable duration and using the operating system or scheduler of the final implementation. This would allow us to investigate loading levels, maximum program durations and so on.

Other requests in the VICE can be similarly modelled with PNGs, the set being combined in a hierarchical fashion and analysed as a super-PNG, though it may be preferable to perform the analysis in a top-down fashion, developing and analysing the global PNG first and then decomposing composite places into their own (subordinate) PNGs.

Exercises

1 You have to design the software for a microprocessor-controlled car park with two entry and two exit barriers.

There is of course a maximum number of parking spaces and in practical terms the maximum number of cars in the car park should always be kept a few lower than this.

The entry barriers will take season tickets or coins. The proportion of places allocated to each type of payment can be arranged at any time. An entry barrier must not accept either form of payment unless there is space available so the system needs to be able to enable both barriers when this happens.

Design a PNG model of the system and use it to investigate the possible deadlock and overcrowding situations.

2 Carry out a similar exercise for a two-lift system serving four floors of a building. Look at possible ways of combining PNGs and Finite State Machines in the solution of the problem. (Finally, look at Jackson 1983 for a worked through solution to a similar problem using Jackson Structured Development).

3 Design a 'Petri Net Scheduler' that would allow you to host an arbitrary PNG on an operating system with which you are familiar, so that you could watch the PNG model run under different inputs.

6.4.6 System Architect's Apprentice – SARA

The SARA design methodology

The SARA design methodology is requirements driven and can proceed in a top-down or bottom-up fashion. The procedure is summarised in figure 6.23 (Campos 1978*a,b*).

The requirements of the system and its environment are mapped onto a model composed of a number of types of building blocks. If building blocks already exist that can be used to meet the requirements then the design can proceed bottom-up, using these building blocks to construct the system. Otherwise, if there are no predefined building blocks then the design must initially proceed by top-down partitioning.

Two types of model are produced: a structural model and a behavioural model. The structure of the system is modelled by *modules, sockets* and *interconnections* (see figure 6.24). The requirements of the system are mapped onto the

Fig. 6.22. A correct design from figure 6.21.

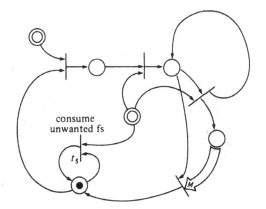

consume
unwanted fs

t_5

modules which are to implement them. Thus, the highest level of SARA documentation could consist of a structure diagram with references to sections of the Functional Specification written into the modules.

The behaviour of the system is modelled by control flow graphs (CG) and data flow graphs (DG). The DGs are composed of *data processors, datasets* and *data arcs* (see figure 6.25) and are very similar to the DFDs of Structured Analysis. The CGs are very similar to Petri Nets, consisting of *nodes* and *control arcs* (see figure 6.26). CG nodes can have DG processors associated with them, this usually being indicated by a hexagonal data processor symbol having the same number as the associated control node. Tokens can be placed on

Fig. 6.24. SARA graphical notation: modules, sockets and interconnections.

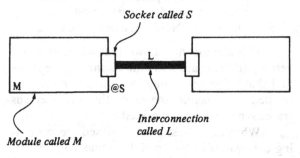

Fig. 6.23. A summary of the SARA design methodology. (From Estrin 1978.)

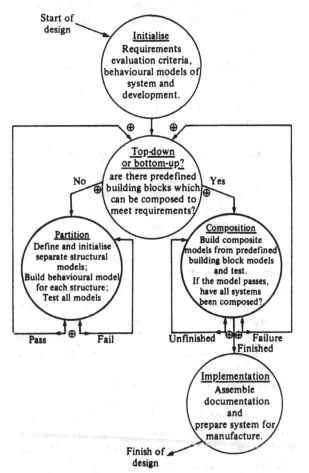

Fig. 6.25. SARA graphical notation: processors, data and datasets.

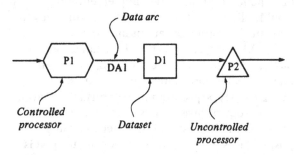

Fig. 6.26. SARA graphical notation: control nodes, control arcs and tokens.

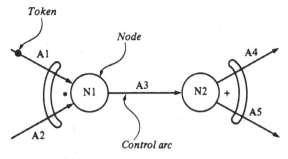

Node N1 fires when tokens are placed on arcs A1 and A2. Node N2 places a token on arc A4 or arc A5

the input control arcs of a node and the node will 'fire' when the tokens satisfy the input control logic of the node (* means AND and + means OR in this logic). The firing of a control node initiates any data processor associated with it and, upon termination of any such processor, tokens will be placed upon the *output* control arcs of the node in accordance with its output logic.

The CG and DG, collectively known as the Graph Model of Behaviour (GMB), are mapped onto the structural model in an attempt to satisfy the requirements. If your Functional Specification contains DFDs, Petri Nets, SADT activity models or similar as part of the specification of functional requirements, then this mapping at the top level should be a natural transition from the Definition to the Design Phase.

Both the GMB and structural model can be

represented in a machine-processable form that can be input to the SARA tools. These allow the model to be experimented with, tested and simulated in order to determine whether it meets the requirements. In particular the flow of data can be simulated and the flow of control analysed for proper termination (e.g. absence of deadlocks).

Once the design has been carried to the point where the overall structure and principal processes and control mechanisms have been defined and have been shown to implement the high-level requirements of the Functional Specification then the System Design Phase can be considered complete. Many modules will still require detailed design during the Production Phase and these modules will have had associated with them detailed requirements that must be satisfied during that phase.

Fig. 6.27. Top-level SARA structure diagram for VISTA and its environment.

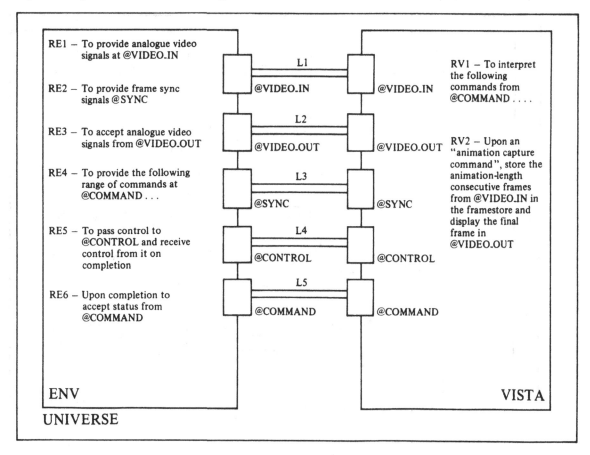

The steps described above can be summarised in the following WBS for the System Design Phase:

3100 System Design Management
3200 Specify System Design
    3210 Map requirements to top-level structural model
    3220 Produce top-level GMB and map to structural model
    3230 Decompose/compose building blocks to satisfy requirements
    3240 Analyse flow of control
    3250 Simulate model
3300 Refine Project Plan
3400 Refine Quality Management Plan
3500 Refine System Models (perhaps part of 3250)

An example

In figure 6.27 we show the top-level structure diagram of the VISTA system and its environment. VISTA and its environment are connected by links for video input/output, command data, frame-synchronisation-control and other control. Onto the two modules in the diagram have been written some of the top-level requirements. In practice there would be a very large number of such requirements that would be referenced by sections of the Functional Specification.

We next map a top-level GMB onto the top-level structure diagram in a first attempt at satisfying the requirements. Such a mapping is shown in figure 6.28. In this diagram, the environment contains four datasets representing a

Fig. 6.28. Top-level SARA GMB for VISTA.

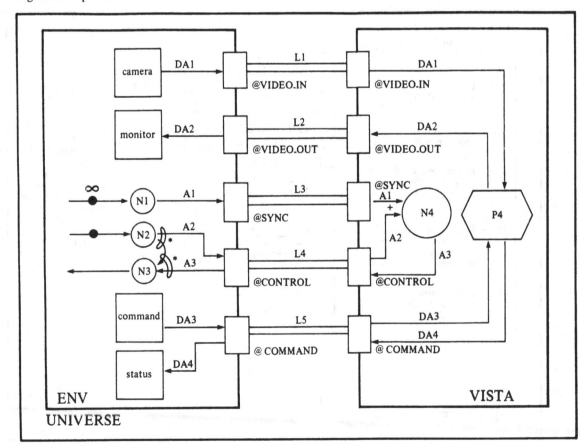

camera, a video monitor and command and status data. It also contains three control nodes. There are initially an infinite number of tokens available on the input arc to N1, representing an indefinite supply of frame syncs. When a token is placed on the input arc to N2, a token is immediately sent to N4, passing control to VISTA, and to N3, preparing it to take back control. Processor P4 is activated by the firing of N4; it inputs video from the camera and commands from @COMMAND and outputs video to the monitor and status to @COMMAND.

We now make our first decision about whether to work top-down or bottom-up. The only predefined building block that we have is the HSD subsystem and this on its own cannot meet all the requirements, so we must proceed top-down, but with one obvious module being the HSD. Our first level of decomposition of the VISTA system is

shown in figure 6.29. This consists of three modules corresponding to items of hardware, namely the HSD, the host computer and the VICE. Onto each of these modules would be mapped requirements which together sum to the requirements for the VISTA module in figure 6.27 and which include requirements relating to the way in which the three modules interact.

Next, the GMB in figure 6.28 must be mapped onto the new modules making up VISTA and, in the process, be refined in order to meet more of the requirements. For simplicity we only consider the requirements RV1 and RV2 in figure 6.27, so in figures 6.30 and 6.31 we only show the GMB for animation capture. In reality, most of this GMB would be contained within the 'animation capture' submodules of the VICE and HOST modules. We have thus skipped one level of decomposition and design.

Fig. 6.29. Second-level SARA structure diagram for VISTA.

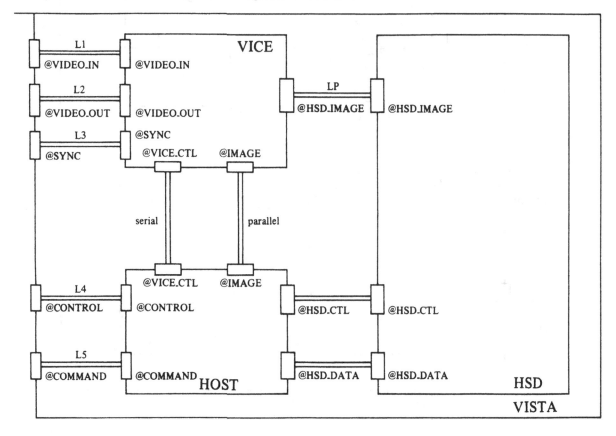

Fig. 6.30. Part of the second-level control flow graph for VISTA.

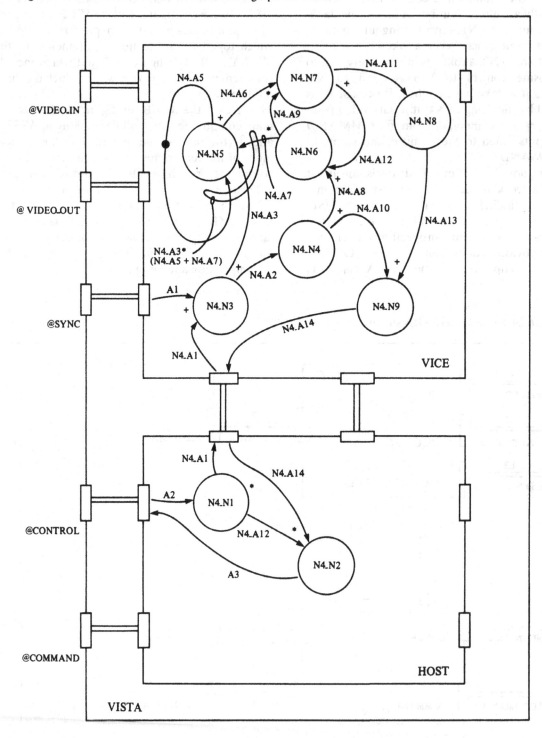

Fig. 6.31. Part of the second-level data flow graph for VISTA.

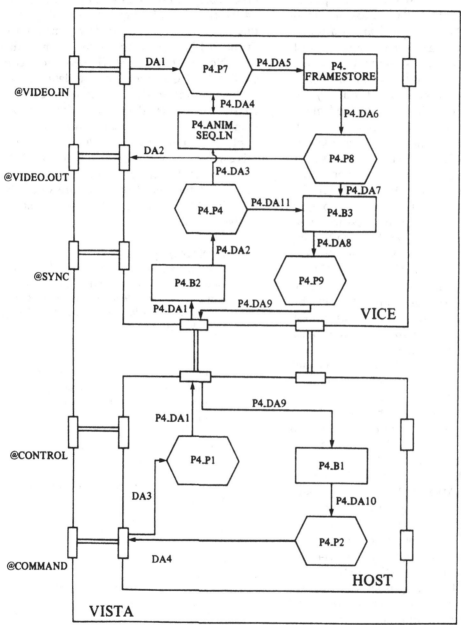

Let us follow the main paths of data and tokens around this GMB. When a token fires node N4-N1, processor P4-P1 is activated and reads in a command, translates it to 'VICE form' and passes it to dataset P4-B2 in the VICE. A token is then passed to node N4-N3 which will fire if a token arrives either because of a command or because of a frame sync. Node N4-N3 results in arbitration of the inputs, giving priority to the command-input. This arbitration could be carried out by an associated processor (not shown) or by the logic of the VICE interrupt system. If N4-N3 has been fired by an incoming command then a token is placed on arc N4-A2, otherwise on N4-A3. A token on arc N4-A2 activates processor P4-P4 which reads the contents of P4-B2 and extracts the animation sequence length. The alternative output is for the case of a command error. Assuming no error, a token is placed on arc N4-A8 firing N4-N6, which in turn places tokens on N4-A7 and N4-A9. If node N4-N5 fires because of tokens on N4-A3 and N4-A7 then a token is placed on N4-A6, otherwise on N4-A5. Tokens on arc N4-A7 can be considered as enabling a frame sync interrupt, for when a token is placed in N4-A3 due to a frame sync, it will be harmlessly absorbed unless N4-A7 is enabled. The logic associated with N4-N5 could be implemented by the VICE interrupt system.

So far we have traced an animation capture command through to the point where it enables a frame sync interrupt. The next frame sync token to arrive at N4-N5 will cause N4-N7 to fire thus activating P4-P7. Processor P4-P7 reads in one frame's worth of video from VIDEO-IN, placing it in dataset P4-FRAMESTORE. The processor then decrements P4-ANIM-SEQ-LN by one. If the result is greater than zero a token is placed on N4-A12, resulting in another frame being captured, otherwise a token is placed on N4-A11 which results in the firing of N4-N8 and the activation of processor P4-P8. This processor displays the last frame captured in VIDEO-OUT and returns status via the output processor P4-P9 and P4-P2 in the HOST.

Before continuing, it is worth noting that the description of the GMB just given is the sort of walkthrough that can be used to check the design even if no automatic tools are available.

The final component of the SARA specifica-

tion of the design at this level is the PLIP interpretation of the processors. For reasons of space we do not give the interpretations of all the data processors but rather choose the relatively simple P4-P4, the PLIP of which is given in figure 6.32. In this figure, the lines preceded by @ are interpreted by the PLIP preprocessor for use in simulation.

Notice that the PLIP definition contains explicit PL/1 data types for the datasets. At this early stage in the design it is more desirable to consider abstract data types for the various datasets, leaving the decision concerning their final implementation until later. A method by which this can be achieved is given in Penedo 1979*b*.

The PLIP interpretations of processors and the SL1 definition of the structure would be fed into the SARA toolset allowing simulation and analysis of the design.

Bibliography

Campos 1978*a* and 1978*b* (descriptions of the SARA methodology with an example), Estrin 1978, Fenchel 1977 and 1979, Gardner 1977, Overman 1977, Penedo 1979*a*, 1979*b* and 1979*c*, Ruggiero 1979, Winchester 1982.

Exercises

1 Compare the SARA and MASCOT design methodologies. Decide which design components are similar and in which ways the methodologies are different.
2 Expand nodes N4-N3 and N4-N5 in figure 6.30 so that they directly implement the logic described in

Fig. 6.32. SARA PLIP for processor P4–P4 in figure 6.29.

```
@template (P4_DA1, P4_DA2) tbuffer char (127);
@template (P4_DA3, P4_DA4) tlen fixed binary (7);
@template (P4_DA7, P4_DA8, P4_DA11) tstatus char (127);

@processor P4-P4;

dcl anim-ln external entry (character(1))
                           returns (fixed binary (7));

    @read P4_B2 @from P4_DA2;
    if substr (P4-B2, 1, 2) = 'AC'
        then do;
            P4-ANIM-SEQ-LN = anim-ln (substr (P4-B2, 3, 3));
            @write P4-ANIM-SEQ-LN @to P4_DA3;
            @output-arcs = 'N4-A8';
            end;
        else do;
            P4-B3 = 'I' | | substr (P4-B2, 1, 2);
            @write P4-B3 @to P4_DA11;
            @output-arcs = 'N4-A10';
            end;
@endprocessor;
```

the text. Decide whether you could implement this logic using the interrupt system of a computer with which you are familiar. If not then modify the GMB to allow implementation using that system.

6.4.7 MASCOT

The key concepts
MASCOT design is carried out in terms of

- *activities*, which process data, and
- *intercommunication data areas* (IDAs), which represent the structures acting as data sources and sinks for activities.

The essential features of activities are that collectively they can run asynchronously and individually they are sequential pieces of program. Thus there is no element of time or synchronisation in an activity.

An IDA is characterised by the *access mechanisms* defined on it and it is the access mechanisms that encapsulate all aspects of parallel processing and the synchronisation of access to data by independent activities. IDAs take two forms:

- *channels*, which are essentially queues of 'unconsumed' messages;
- *pools*, which contain reference data not requiring consumption.

Activities are grouped into *subsystems*, each subsystem approximating to a major functional area in the system, such as 'operator input handling'.

The complete MASCOT development process has three phases that are iterated as necessary: overall software design, detailed design, and implementation and test. The first of these falls reasonably well into our System Design Phase and it is this that we pass on to.

(In our summary we describe MASCOT I. This has subsequently been enhanced to MASCOT II – see the bibliography.)

The MASCOT design process
The primary output from this phase is an activity-channel-pool (ACP) diagram that embodies the entire overall design.

This single (potentially large) diagram is constructed from an analysis of the flow of data from the input devices to the output devices. As the diagram is completed during the analysis the purpose of each element (activity, channel or pool) is justified and recorded.

The data flow is decomposed on the single diagram until the elements are small enough to be easily managed in terms of testability, understandability etc. Thus an activity should be single purpose rather than multi-purpose and situations such as a channel that is read by two or more different activities warrant careful inspection.

Once the data flow has been completely analysed in terms of co-operating asynchronous activities communicating through the IDAs, you consider the performance requirements such as response time. Such considerations may lead you to recombine some activities (according to a set of rules) until the performance of the system model is acceptable. (Compare this with the System Timing and Implementation steps in Jackson's System Development.)

The ACP diagram naturally represents an excellent object from which to derive estimates of the system's size and of the effort that will be required to produce it. It also allows you to determine a test strategy and an implementation sequence compatible with the relationships between the design elements. Furthermore, an ACP network is an appropriate basis on which to construct a prototype, perhaps using a very high level language.

Strictly speaking, MASCOT I does not allow hierarchies of implementable levels. An ACP network is *not* hierarchic. The complexity of an ACP diagram may however force you, for convenience, to draw a summary by inventing *subsystem IDAs* (SIDAs) that act as interfaces betwen subsystems and by producing a summary-level ACP network that treats these SIDAs and the subsystem as elements. This process can be repeated as necessary while the basic ACP diagram appears in full.

One feature of the MASCOT method is the validity checks that can be made on the interfaces between activities. During design, careful control can be kept on the scope of data contained in the system, i.e. on who can access what data. The way those activities then access the data is determined by the precise access mechanisms defined on the individual IDA types. Thus the 'string queue' IDA type might allow the following access mechanisms and these only:

- read string from front of queue or wait if queue is empty,
- add string to end of queue,
- initialise queue to empty state,
- return instantaneous length of queue.

The exact implementation of these operations and their synchronisation are explicitly hidden from accessing activities. This 'hiding' of the design decision as to how a data structure will be implemented accords with Parnas's principle of 'information hiding' as a criterion for decomposition – see the sections on structured programming and control of data in chapter 7. We will see in later chapters that the construction, test and operation functions of MASCOT reinforce the interface relationships at build time and at execution time.

The identification of access mechanisms for IDAs belongs strictly to the second, detailed stage of design in MASCOT but it fits most naturally in our System Design Phase. Initialisation, inspection (for testing purposes) and termination mechanisms should always be considered. Definition of the data structure itself is carried out in the System Production Phase – see chapter 7.

The MASCOT System Design Specification

The following three items would form a System Design Specification for a system designed using MASCOT:

- the single complete ACP network,
- summary level ACP networks as necessary,
- written explanations of the purpose of each element in the ACP network.

Additionally, the following deliverable items can be expected:

- a clarified statement of requirements,
- an implementation plan,

- test strategies for the overall tests, integration tests and ACP network element tests,
- estimates of resource requirements,
- full details of interfaces,
- a prototype for evaluation.

An example of a MASCOT design

ACP diagrams have the simple notation shown in figure 6.33. Figure 6.34 is a summary-level ACP diagram for the VISTA system, covering the VICE, the HSD (purely a hardware device for our purposes here) and the host computer.

Four subsystems are shown, one being the VICE subsystem. From the diagram you will see that peripheral interfaces are shown as IDAs (or, as in this summarised network, SIDAs). This conveniently allows us to consider the handling of interrupts from devices simply as access mechanisms defined on the particular IDA. Thus device drivers do not appear as activities.

Fig. 6.33. MASCOT ACP network notation.

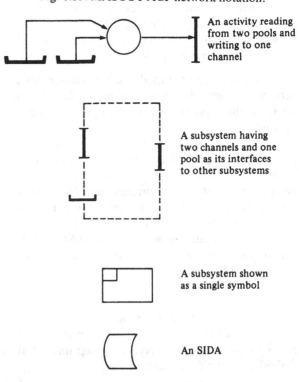

An activity reading from two pools and writing to one channel

A subsystem having two channels and one pool as its interfaces to other subsystems

A subsystem shown as a single symbol

An SIDA

Figure 6.35 shows the ACP diagram for a subsystem in the VICE responsible for the capture of animation sequences. This has been derived from an analysis of the data flow resulting from the input of an animation sequence capture request. Such a request has been processed by the Command Analysis subsystem (say) and reaches the Animation Capture subsystem via a string channel at the subsystem interface.

Entries on this channel are processed by the Initialise-Animation-Capture activity which records the number of required frames in the Animation Pool and triggers the Catch-a-Frame activity by queueing an entry on the Trigger A channel. Such a channel might be defined to have two access mechanisms:

- if queue is empty, activate/schedule nominated activity and queue an entry, otherwise do nothing; and
- consume waiting entry.

The Catch-a-Frame activity now responds to successive frame syncs arriving on its Trigger B channel interface with the Hardware Subsystem. This channel type would also have two access mechanisms, this time a little different:

- if someone is waiting on the other side of the channel, queue an entry, otherwise do nothing; and
- read queue waiting for an entry.

The remainder of the diagram should need little explanation.

From the diagram and the characteristics of the access mechanisms defined for the Trigger B channel we can see that one potential problem is

Fig. 6.34. Summary level MASCOT ACP diagram for VISTA.

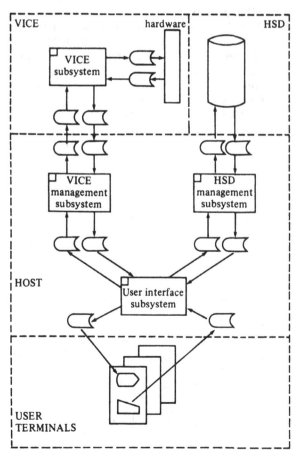

Fig. 6.35. MASCOT ACP network for VISTA animation capture.

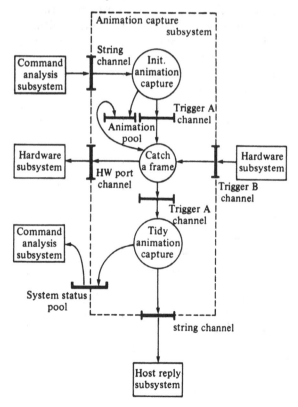

posed by a failure of the Hardware Subsystem to produce frame syncs. Ideally the system should detect such a failure (with time-outs of some duration) and report the fact rather than just hanging up. In this case the Catch-a-Frame activity needs to be notified via the Trigger B channel and we must arrange for this time-out mechanism to be designed into the ACP network of the Hardware Subsystem.

In this example we have several different types of IDA to deal with,

- string channel,
- trigger A channel,
- trigger B channel,
- animation pool,
- system status pool,
- HW port channel,

and we have looked at the access mechanisms that we might require for the trigger channel types. Figure 6.36 shows an example of the diagram that would represent access mechanisms that we might typically expect to require for a channel carrying a queue of strings (e.g. text messages). During testing we will require a mechanism for checking the integrity of the queue, whilst during performance measuring we will require a further mechanism for reading out the instantaneous length of the queue. Similarly, on warm or cold restarts we will need to be able to reset the channel to its empty state.

Finally, we analyse each activity to determine the access mechanisms it will require on the IDAs and record our decisions in a diagram similar to that in figure 6.37.

Work Breakdown Structure

From the preceding paragraphs we can see that we can refine our WBS for the System Design Phase along the following lines when using MASCOT:

3100	System Design Management
3200	Specify System Design
3210	Analyse data flow for ACP network
3220	Draw summary ACP networks
3230	Incorporate performance requirements
3240	Identify IDA access mechanisms
3250	Carry out quality checks
3260	Prototype system from ACP network
3300	Refine Project Plan
3310	Re-estimate effort estimates from ACP network
3320	Plan orders of implementation from ACP network
3400	Refine Quality Management Plan
3410	Define test strategy for system at all levels

Bibliography

MSA 1980 (the official handbook of MASCOT I issued by the Mascot Suppliers Association), RRE 1975 (the definition of MASCOT issued as a Technical Note by the Royal Radar Establishment), Simpson 1979 (a description of the MASCOT software structure and synchronisation), JIMCOM 1983 (the definition of MASCOT II).

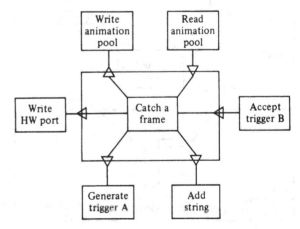

Fig. 6.37. The MASCOT access mechanisms required by an activity.

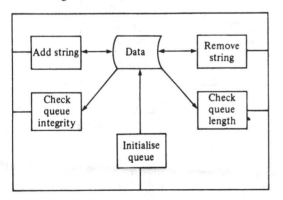

Fig. 6.36. MASCOT access mechanisms for a string channel.

Exercises

1 What sort of problems do you imagine need to be resolved by an access mechanism?
2 What are the benefits of limiting inter-process communications to the two types, channel and pool?
3 Can you think of any design situation where these two are insufficient (i.e. make something impossible)? Can you re-organise your design to use just those two, however, and is this a better design?
4 List the benefits of hidden access mechanisms to the design of a process.

6.4.8 Formal Development Methodology – FDM

Designing through FDM specifications

FDM is one of the few methodologies that we consider that provide the opportunity for the designer to formally prove that the design is correct and that this correctness is maintained not only down through all levels of design but also through into implementation.

Since the proving of the implementation is so strong a continuation of the design process we cover both these phases in this chapter rather than postponing our description of the production phase until chapter 7.

Development of a system with FDM is a process of refinement through a number of levels. At all but the lowest level, FDM models the system as an abstract state machine. Specifying such a model means defining the possible states of the machine in terms of *state variables* and defining the *transformations* that change the machine state, i.e. that change the state variables.

If you are to prove the correctness of your design you must, of course, know what you mean by 'correct'. For this reason, the first stage in the FDM design phase also involves modelling the correctness requirements of the system. For example, a correctness criterion might be that 'no user can access a file without giving a password', or 'all actions that a user can carry out must be constrained so as not to increase their priority'.

Having established the correctness requirements of the system, an overall design specification, known as a *top level specification* (TLS) in FDM terminology, is written and checked against the correctness requirements. Once the TLS has

been verified it is successively refined into lower level specifications, each of which is also checked against the correctness requirements.

FDM specifications are written in a language called Ina Jo, a sample of which is given in figure 6.38. We need not give here a full description of Ina Jo (see Locasso 1980) but simply note below some of the special symbols that we need for our example:

A″	for all
El″	there exists a unique
N″	new value of state variable
T″	type
:	of type
|	or
&	and
→	implies
~	not
==	maps to.

The best way in which we can give the flavour of FDM and Ina Jo in the space available is to consider the meaning of the small example in figure 6.38. This example involves the reservation

Fig. 6.38. Sample top and second-level FDM specification of VISTA.

```
Specification partvista
    Level tls
        Type user,
             vice
        Variable reserved(user, vice): Boolean
        Transform reserve(u:user, v:vice) External
            Effect A"us:user, vs:vice
                    (N"reserved(us, vs) =
                    (us = u & vs = v
                    & A" u2:user(u2 = u
                                |~reserved(u2, vs))
                    |reserved(us, vs)))
        Initial A"vs:vice, us:user(~reserved(us, vs))
        Criterion A"vs:vice(A"us:user(~reserved(us, vs))
                            |E1"u:user(reserved(u, vs))
    End tls

    Level secondlevel under tls
        Type process,
             device
        Constant port0, port1: device
        Type vicedev = T"(port0, port1)
        Variable assigned(process, device): Boolean
        Transform assignVice(p:process, v:vicedev)
            Effect A"ps:process, ds:device
                    (N"assigned(ps, ds) =
                    (ps = p & ds = v
                    |assigned(ps, ds)))
        Initial A"ps:process, ds:device(~assigned(ps, ds))
        Map
            user == process
            vice == vicedev
            reserved(u, v) == assigned(u, v)
            reserve(u, v) == assignVice(u, v)
    End secondlevel
End partvista
```

of a VICE to a user in the VISTA system. Although trivial in nature our example will serve to illustrate the mechanisms of FDM even if it does not do justice to its power.

Consider first the TLS. The state of the abstract machine is defined in terms of a single state Variable 'reserved'. This variable is a function taking two arguments of Type 'user' and 'vice' and returning a Boolean value that is assumed to be true if the VICE is reserved to the user and false otherwise. (Before continuing, try to work out the meaning of the TLS.)

The main element in the TLS is the Transform 'reserve', which describes the Effect on the system state (i.e. the variable 'reserved') of trying to reserve a VICE to a user. The Transform part of the specification can be translated into Structured English as follows:

> The effect of user, u, trying to reserve VICE, v, is as follows:
>> **for all** users and VICEs
>> the **new** answer to the question "is the VICE reserved to the user?" is as follows:
>>> **if** the user is u **and** the VICE is v **and for all** users if **either** the user is u **or** the VICE is **not** reserved to the user
>>> **then** the answer is yes
>>> **otherwise** the answer is as before.

Thus, in particular, the VICE can only be reserved to the user if it is not already reserved to someone else.

The next component of the TLS is a description of the Initial state of the machine. In this case the initial state specification says that all VICEs are initially unreserved.

Before considering the final element of the TLS, namely the Criterion, let us turn to the second-level specification. In this level we move much closer to the method of implementing the reservation mechanism described in the TLS. (Before continuing, try to understand the meaning of the second-level specification. Can you find the error in it?)

The second-level specification deals in terms of much more concrete objects such as 'process', 'device', and 'port'. The state machine is defined in

terms of the state Variable 'assigned' (which relates processes and devices) and a Transform called assignVice which will be implemented directly in terms of a call to the channel assignment system-service in the operating system of the target computer. The Initial state at the second level is defined by stating that no devices are assigned to any processes.

The mapping between the TLS and the second-level specification is given in the Map section. For example, the TLS variable 'reserved' maps to the second-level variable 'assigned' with appropriate arguments determined from the arguments of 'reserved'.

Correctness requirements theorems and proofs

The correctness requirements of the system are modelled using the concepts of *criteria* and *constraints*. Criteria are conditions that must be satisfied by the state variables of the system both before and after each state transformation. Constraints specify relationships that must hold between the new and old values of a state variable. Criteria and constraints only appear in the TLS. They are known collectively as the 'criterion'.

In our example we have modelled the correctness requirement by the Criterion in the TLS which says that for each VICE, either for each user the VICE is not reserved to that user, or the VICE is reserved to a unique user. This, after all, is the reason for reservation: to make sure that only one person at a time uses each VICE.

When the specification is fed into the Ina Jo language processor certain syntax and consistency checks are automatically carried out and a number of theorems are generated. These theorems must be proved in order to establish the correctness of the transforms and the consistency of the specification.

For the TLS, theorems are generated which assert, amongst other things, the following:

(1) all transforms, user-supplied axioms and initial conditions are consistent,
(2) the initial condition satisfies the criteria,
(3) if the criteria are satisfied before a state transformation then they will be satisfied afterwards.

When lower level specifications are submitted to the Ina Jo processor, theorems are generated which are aimed at proving that the lower levels correctly implement the level above them and that they do not violate any of the correctness criteria or constraints imposed at the top level. These theorems are stated in terms of the 'image' under the mapping (Map) of the level above and, amongst other things, they assert the following:

(4) the Initial condition at the lower level is consistent with the image of the Initial condition at the level above it,

(5) any transforms which are not mapped from the level above satisfy theorem 3 with respect to the image of the criteria,

(6) if a transform at a lower level is the mapping of a transform at the level above then the effect of the transform at the lower level is consistent with the image of the effect of the transform in the level above.

Let us consider some of the theorems that would be required in order to prove the correctness of our example.

Theorem 2. Initial Condition → Criterion
This theorem is trivially true since the initial condition says that no VICEs are reserved and this is precisely the first clause of the 'or' statement in the criterion.

Theorem 4. Second Level Initial Condition →
Image (Top Level Initial Condition) The image of the top-level initial condition under the mapping is simply obtained by substitution to be A″vs:vicedevs, us:process (~assigned (us, vs)). This says that all vicedevs are unassigned which is clearly implied by the second-level initial condition which says that all devices are unassigned. So this theorem is satisfied.

Theorem 6 Since there is a mapping between the transforms reserve and assignVice, we must prove the theorem that if the effect of assignVice transpires then so does the image of reserve's effect. That is, we must prove that

A″ ps:process, ds:device (N″assigned
(ps, ds) = (ps = u & ds = v
| assigned (ps, ds))) →

A″ us:process, vs:vicedev (N″assigned
(us, vs) = (us = u & vs = v
& A″ u2:process (u2=u|~assigned
(u2,vs))
| assigned (us, vs)))

This theorem is false. If it were not for the 'and' clause involving u2, it would be true. It is precisely this clause which at the top level ensures that the criterion remains satisfied and that only one user can have a given VICE reserved at a time. Thus the second-level specification does not correctly implement the TLS and we cannot simply rely on the operating system's assignment system-service to implement reservation.

In practice, an automatic tool called the Interactive Theorem Prover (ITP) can be used to assist with the proofs of theorems generated by the Ina Jo processor. The ITP operates by guiding the user to proofs of theorems by the method of proof by contradiction. The ITP documents the proofs in a form suitable for later audit.

From specification to code
The lowest level specifications resulting from the refinement process are the *implementation specifications*. These describe the data structures, identify the elements of code (modules, subroutines, etc.) and map elements of the abstract specification onto those code elements.

Once again these specifications are submitted to the Ina Jo processor which now has two outputs: firstly a set of theorems once more affirming the self-consistency of the specifications, and secondly, for each subroutine, entry and exit and assertions that are required for the correct implementation of the counterpart element in the abstract specification.

The code can now be written in a high-order language using the abstract specifications and the implementation specifications. The code is itself then submitted to the final tool: the Verification Condition Generator (VCG).

This produces conditions that affirm that a coded subroutine satisfies the exit conditions whenever the entry conditions hold. It also produces conditions affirming that the entry conditions do hold at each invocation of the subroutine in the program.

Once these theorems have been proved with the aid of the ITP the process is complete and the program has been verified from top-level specification to code.

The VCG is specific to the implementation language and at the time of writing a VCG for Modula is available.

Work Breakdown Structure
We are now in a position to expand the Design and Production Phase segments of our WBS for FDM:

```
3000    System Design
  3100    System Design Management
  3200    Specify System Design
    3210    Model correctness requirements
    3220    Produce and verify the TLS
    3230    Produce and verify the second-level
            specifications
    3240    ...
  3300    Refine Project Plan
  3400    Refine Quality Management Plan
4000    System Production
  4100    System Production Management
  4200    Produce System for Trial
    4210    Produce and verify implementation
            specifications
    4220    Generate assertions for subroutine code
    4230    Write code for subroutines
    4240    Verify code with VCG
  4300    ... (as usual)
```

Bibliography

Berry 1981 (a case study of FDM applied to database design), Eggert 1980 (an introduction to Ina Jo with an example), Kemmerer 1980 (an overview of FDM), Locasso 1980 (the Ina Jo reference manual), Schorre 1980 (the Interactive Theorem Prover user's manual).

Exercises

1 Attempt to prove the remaining theorems required for the specification in figure 6.38.
2 Think of a way in which the second-level specification in the example could be made consistent with the TLS. Is there a system-service on an operating system with which you are familiar that could be used to implement the TLS transform reserve?
3 FDM hinges on the concepts of layers of abstract machines and refinement by concretisation.

Investigate this notion by mapping, via a number of intervening levels, the filing and editing operations of a word processor onto the physical data storage on a disc. Restricting your attentions to the operations of fetching, storing, deleting and listing documents in a shared environment, model the system as a state machine, identifying the state variables and the allowable transformations. What correctness criteria and state change constraints exist? How do these map down through the levels you have defined?

6.4.9 Hierarchical Development Methodology – HDM

Work Breakdown Structure
HDM provides a very well-defined methodology for proceeding from system conceptualisation through to coding. This is achieved in seven stages which can be summarised as follows

(i) Conceptualisation – identify the problem to be solved and the method by which the system will solve it.
(ii) Extreme Machine Definition – define the external interfaces of the system and the modular structure of the top and bottom abstract machines that provide these interfaces.
(iii) System Structure Definition – define further modular abstract machines between the top and bottom machines.
(iv) Module Specification – write formal specifications, in SPECIAL, of each module.
(v) Data Representation – formally define the data structures in each module in terms of data structures of the modules in the next lower level.
(vi) Abstract Implementation – write ILPL abstract implementations of each module.
(vii) Concrete Implementation – translate the ILPL programs into target language code.

Of these, stage (i) and part of stage (ii) can be considered part of the System Definition Phase. Several of the methods discussed in chapter 5 could be used to produce a Functional Specification that clearly identifies the problem to be solved and the way in which the system is intended to solve it, as well as giving a general definition of the user interface and the primitive machine on which the system is to sit. The part of stage (ii) involved in dividing the extreme abstract machines into modules and stages (iii), (iv) and (v) can be regarded as belonging to the System Design Phase, while stages (vi) and (vii) can be considered as composing the Production Phase and will be considered in the next chapter.

A typical WBS for the System Design Phase of a project using HDM might be

```
3000    System Design
   3100    System Design Management
   3200    Specify System Design
      3210    Review conceptualisation of system
              and complete extreme machine
              definition
      3220    Define system structure
      3230    Module specification
         3231    Specify and verify level 1
                 modules
         3232    Specify and verify level 2
                 modules
                 ⋮
      3240    Data representation
         3241    Specify and verify level 1 data
         3242    Specify and verify level 2 data
                 ⋮
      3250    Verify and prove system design
   3300    Refine Project Plan
   3400    Refine Quality Management Plan
```

An example of the use of HDM

A detailed description of the background to HDM, the definition of its languages and tools and a full worked example fill three fat volumes of the HDM Handbook (SRI 1979). In this book our intention is solely to give a taste of the use of HDM by way of a partial example.

The example that we consider is that of VICE reservation in the VISTA system. This has already been specified using FDM in section 6.4.8 and thus provides an interesting basis for comparison of the two methodologies.

Conceptualisation The user interface of the system is to provide facilities which allow the user to

- log-on to VISTA,
- configure a VICE into VISTA,
- reserve a VICE so that it cannot be used by any other user,

- free a VICE to allow it to be used by other users,
- deconfigure a VICE from VISTA,
- log-off from VISTA.

The HDM methodology includes a number of guidelines, many of which are applicable to any system design approach. One of these guidelines is that all *decisions* should be documented. At this stage we have already made some decisions about facilities that we are *not* going to provide to the user; in particular we are not going to provide facilities for the user to see who is logged-on, which VICEs are configured in and which VICEs are reserved to whom. The design should allow these to be easily added later (see exercise 3).

Also at this stage we make a decision about the primitive abstract machine to be used. In this case we decide that it is the virtual machine provided by the VPL programming language on the WXY computer using the ZOS operating system, which, in particular, provides the following system services:

- create (a process),
- destroy (a process),
- attach (a device to the WXY),
- detach (a device from the WXY),
- assign (a device to a process and return a channel number),
- deassign (a device from a process),
- allocate (a device to a process for its sole use),
- deallocate (a device from a process).

Extreme machine definition We now decompose the extreme machines into modules. The top-level machine involves two quite distinct entities, namely users and VICEs, and a facility to tie them together, namely reservation. We make the decision to isolate the concepts of *users*, *vices* and *reservation* in separate modules bearing those names.

We now decide upon what operations, functions and data must be associated with each module. Consider first module 'vices'. It concerns itself with an abstract data type called 'vice'. Such abstract data types in HDM are known as *designators*. The module must also provide a state function (cf. FDM) which records whether a 'vice' is configured into the system. Such a function is known as a *V-function* as it returns a Value, namely a boolean (TRUE if configured in or else FALSE). Further, the module must contain operations which change the state of a 'vice' by configuring it in or deconfiguring it. Such state changing functions are called O-functions. In a similar way, module 'users' concerns itself with designator 'user' and must contain a V-function to record whether a user is logged-on and O-functions to change this state. Finally, for the top-level machine, module 'reservation' requires a V-function to record whether a 'vice' is reserved to a 'user' and O-functions to change this state. In all of these cases, the value returned by a V-function is not to be made available at the user interface and the V-functions are consequently known as HIDDEN V-functions.

In the case of the primitive machine we decide upon three modules called 'processes', 'devices' and 'assignment', the first and second of which contain designators 'process' and 'device' respectively. It is left to the reader to list all of the functions and operations required and we only note that module 'assignment' must contain an operation 'assign' which not only changes state but which also returns a value (the channel number). Such an operator is known as an OV-function.

System structure definition In reality we would probably need one or more abstract machines between the top and bottom machines; however, for simplicity we have contrived the example in such a way that it is not difficult to see how the top-level machine can be directly implemented in terms of the bottom-level machine. Our example thus has a two-level structure defined by the HSL given in figure 6.39.

Fig. 6.39. HDM structure specification.

```
(INTERFACE level2
   (users)
   (reservation)
   (vices))

(INTERFACE level1
   (process)
   (assignment)
   (devices))

(HIERARCHY partvista
   (level1 IMPLEMENTS level2 USING reservation))
```

Module specification Having decided upon the modules of each of the two machines and upon the facilities that they are to provide we now formally specify each of them in the language SPECIAL. In figure 6.40 we present the module specification for module 'reservation'. The specification is divided into a number of paragraphs. The first paragraph, DEFINITIONS, defines some useful functions. For example, 'nr-reserved' is an integer-valued function which takes as its argument a vice designator and returns as its value the number of users in the set of users having that vice reserved to them.

The EXTERNALREFS paragraph defines all objects in other modules (in the same machine) that are referenced by the 'reservation' module. The ASSERTIONS paragraph contains assertions that must be proved from the module specification. In our case the assertion states that for all vices either no users or one user can have the vice reserved.

Fig. 6.40. HDM specification of module 'reservation'.

```
MODULE reservation
    $(vice reservation module)

    DEFINITIONS

BOOLEAN available (user u, vice v) IS
    NOT (EXIST us : reserved (us, v) AND us ~=u);
INTEGER nr_reserved (vice v) IS
    CARDINALITY ({user u | reserved (u, v)});

    EXTERNALREFS

    FROM vices;
vice : DESIGNATOR;
VFUN configured_in (vice v) → BOOLEAN b;

    FROM users:
user : DESIGNATOR;
VFUN logged_on (user u) → BOOLEAN b;

    ASSERTIONS
FOR ALL vice v : nr_reserved (v) = 0 OR
                 nr_reserved (v) = 1;

    FUNCTIONS

VFUN reserved (user u, vice v) → BOOLEAN b;
    $(b is TRUE if vice v is reserved to user u)
    HIDDEN
    INITIALLY
        b = FALSE;

OFUN reserve (user u, vice v);
    $(if possible reserves vice v to user u)
    EXCEPTIONS
        not_logged_on : NOT (logged_on(u));
        no_vice : NOT (configured_in (v));
        unavailable : NOT (available (u, v));
    EFFECTS
        'reserved (u, v) = TRUE;

END_MODULE
```

The final paragraph, FUNCTIONS, defines all of the functions associated with the module. The specification of the V-function 'reserved' is very simple, saying only that it is a hidden function and that initially it returns the value FALSE (i.e. no vices are reserved to any users). The O-function 'reserve' changes the reservation state by attempting to reserve vice v to user u. The specification starts with an EXCEPTIONS paragraph which lists possible exception conditions and the names that are to be associated with them. For example, an exception called 'unavailable' will be raised if the condition available(u,v) is not true. From the DEFINITIONS paragraph available(u,v) is true if no user other than possibly u has vice v reserved. This then documents a decision that we have made to flag an error (or warning) if a user attempts to

reserve a vice that is already reserved to someone else. If no exceptions occur then the effects documented in the EFFECTS paragraph occur. In this case the effect is that the new value (indicated by the apostrophe) of the V-function 'reserved' when applied to u, v is TRUE. In other words if none of the exceptions are raised then vice v becomes reserved to user u. We leave it to the reader to specify the O-function which frees a vice (see exercise 2).

From the bottom-level machine we give a partial specification of module 'assignment' (figure 6.41). This represents a formal specification of part of the ZOS operating system. It is left for the reader to speculate on the usefulness of the ideal HDM world in which computer manufacturers supply such documentation with their operating systems.

Data representation In this stage we decide how to represent the data in the top-level machine in terms of data in the bottom-level machine. This is achieved by way of a mapping specification an example of which is given in figure 6.42. The two

Fig. 6.41. HDM specification of module 'assignment'.

```
MODULE assignment
    $(OS device assignment and allocation)

    EXTERNALREFS

    FROM process:
process : DESIGNATOR;
VFUN exists (process p) → BOOLEAN b;

    FROM devices:
device : DESIGNATOR;
VFUN attached (device d) → BOOLEAN b;

    FUNCTIONS

VFUN assigned (process p, device d) → BOOLEAN b;
    $(b is TRUE if process p has a channel to device d)
    HIDDEN
    INITIALLY
        b = FALSE;

VFUN allocated (process p, device d) → BOOLEAN b;
    $(b is TRUE if device d is allocated to process p)
    HIDDEN
    INITIALLY
        b = FALSE;

OVFUN assign (process p, device d) → INTEGER chan;
    $(assign device d to process p via channel chan)
    EXCEPTIONS
        no_process : NOT (exists (p));
        no_device : NOT (attached (d));
        already_assigned : assigned (p, d);
    EFFECTS
        'assigned (p,d) = TRUE
        chan = SOME INTEGER | i >= 0 ;

OFUN allocate (process p, device d);
    $(attempt to allocate device d to process p)
    EXCEPTIONS
        no_process : NOT (exits (p));
        no_device : NOT (attached (d));
        already_allocated : EXISTS process ps :
                    allocated (ps, d) AND NOT (ps = p);
    EFFECTS
    'allocated (p, d) = TRUE;

END_MODULE
```

Fig. 6.42. HDM mapping specification.

```
MAP reservation TO assignment;

    DEFINITIONS

nr_assigned (device d) IS
        CARDINALITY ({process p | assigned (p, d)});

    EXTERNALREFS

    FROM reservation:
    ...
VFUN reserved (user u, vice v) → BOOLEAN b;

    FROM assignment:
    ...
VFUN assigned (process p, device d) → BOOLEAN b;
VFUN allocated (process p, device d) → BOOLEAN b;

    FROM users:
user : DESIGNATOR;

    FROM vices:
vice : DESIGNATOR;

    FROM devices:
device : DESIGNATOR;

    INVARIANTS

FOR ALL device d : nr_assigned (d) = 0 OR
                    nr_assigned (d) = 1;

    MAPPINGS

user : process;
vice : device;
reserved (user u, vice v) : allocated (u, v) AND
                    assigned (u, v)

END_MAP
```

paragraphs of most interest are MAPPINGS and INVARIANTS. The MAPPINGS paragraph defines how V-functions, designators etc. in the upper machine are defined in terms of the V-functions, designators etc. of the machine below. In this case we are saying that a user maps to a process, a vice to a device and that a vice is reserved to a user if the device corresponding to the vice is both assigned and allocated to the process corresponding to the user.

The INVARIANTS paragraph places constraints on the way in which the lower level's V-functions etc. are used. Here, the INVARIANTS paragraph is stressing the fact that, although in general an arbitrary number of processes can have a given device assigned, in this case only zero or one process should ever have a device assigned.

From the mapping functions one can derive *map*ped specifications of the upper level modules and consequently entry and exit assertions for the programs that implement the upper level operations. The programs can then be proved correct with respect to these assertions. This process is very similar to that used in FDM as described in section 6.4.8 where the concepts of hierarchical proofs are illustrated in more detail.

Bibliography

Levitt 1980 (pays special attention to the development of secure software using HDM, including useful examples), Millen 1981 (compares HDM with AFFIRM, another formal specification method, in the area of operating system security), Neumann 1983 (describes a number of projects in which HDM has been used), Robinson 1979 (volume 1 of the HDM handbook giving its motivation and basis), Silverberg 1979 (volume 2 of the HDM handbook describing HDM's languages and tools), Silverberg 1981 (a short overview of HDM), SRI 1979 (volume 3 of the HDM handbook giving a fully worked and explained example of the use of HDM).

Exercises

1 Compare the FDM and HDM methodologies and try to come to a decision about which you would rather use.
2 Try to complete the specification given in the example. (Note: you may have to leave some holes unless you have access to the HDM Handbook.)

3 The decision that we made not to provide the user with a means of determining whether a VICE is reserved to a given user has resulted in V-function 'reserved' being a hidden function. Can you think of any other results of this decision in the stages of the example dealt with so far? Consequently do you consider that the design facilitates the later addition of this feature?

6.4.10 Higher Order Software – HOS

The methodology and its implementation

HOS is a methodology that aims at providing a mathematially rigorous basis for design and automatic program generation. This methodology is implemented through a design support tool called USE.IT which has three components:

- a design specification language, AXES,
- an automated design analysis tool, the Analyser,
- an automatic code generator, the Resource Allocation Tool (RAT).

The HOS methodology ensures that a proposed design is consistent with six axioms (see Hamilton 1976) which in turn ensure that the design is internally consistent and that the automatically generated implementation is both consistent with the design and reliable. The axioms were originally obtained from the mathematical properties of a particular type of hierarchical control structure which is the basis of the AXES language.

In its original form (Hamilton 1976 and 1979), HOS required the designer to use the AXES language directly in order to express design specifications in a form in which they could be analysed mechanically. In its current commercial form however, the designer uses the HOS methodology through a graphical form of AXES – the *control map* – so that the AXES language representation is hidden from the user and no mathematical expertise is required. This graphical interaction and the subsequent automatic operations are made available interactively through USE.IT.

The HOS Control Map The central concept is that of the *control map*. This is a hierarchical tree structure used to represent the functional decomposition of a process in graphical form. Each node in the tree represents a function. Each function has a name, takes named input variables and produces named output variables.

If a node is a leaf node (i.e. has no offspring) then it must be one of the following:

- A *defined operation* which has its own control map(s) specified elsewhere and is being 'imported'.
- A *primitive operation* which can either be one of those provided by HOS Inc. or a user-defined application-specific operation. In either case, the operation operates on defined data types and has a corresponding FORTRAN macro. It is the collection of these macros that enables the automatic generation of code from a fully elaborated control map.
- An *external operation* which is external to that part of the system defined via USE.IT – a function of a proprietary package for instance.
- A *recursive operation:* this is a special node type that allows looping. A recursive node references a function that is superior to it in

the control map and thereby makes the repeated performance of an operation possible.

If a node (function) has offspring nodes, these represent subfunctions that together perform the parent function that they compose. The precise control and data flow relationship between subfunctions can take one of seven forms of *control structure* known as *join, include, or, cojoin, coinclude, coor* and *concur*.

In figures 6.43–6.45 we illustrate the first six of these control structures. Each one has a number of rules governing its use – particularly with reference to data flow between sibling functions – these rules ensuring that the control structure satisfies the HOS axioms and hence that provable correctness can be established.

The JOIN and COJOIN control structures represent sequential processing. Under JOIN, all the outputs of the first (right-hand) subfunction become all the inputs of the second (left-hand) subfunction. COJOIN relaxes this rule.

The INCLUDE and COINCLUDE control structures represent independent (i.e. potentially

Fig. 6.43. The JOIN and COJOIN control structures illustrated in a HOS control map fragment.

Fig. 6.44. The INCLUDE and COINCLUDE control structures illustrated in a HOS control map fragment.

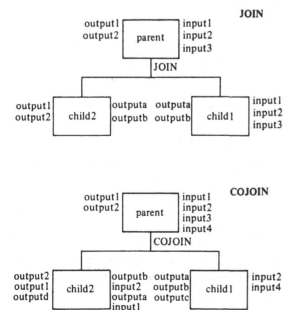

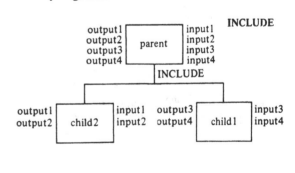

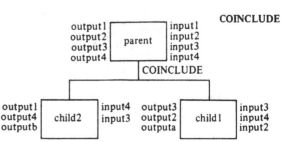

concurrent) processing. There is no data flow between the subfunctions.

The OR and COOR control structures represent branching (i.e. alternative) processing. Under OR, both subfunctions take the same input and produce the same output as the parent function with the exception of the boolean input to the parent that the parent uses to choose between the subfunctions.

The CONCUR control structure combines features of the COJOIN and COINCLUDE structures.

Data typing and data layering. HOS uses *strong data typing.* This means that not only must every item of data appearing in a control map have a *data type* but also, for every data type, there must be explicit specifications of the operations defined on that type and of the relationships between it and other types.

Data layering is the implementation of one data type in terms of other data types. These in their turn can be implemented in terms of yet lower level data types, with the data types at the very lowest level being those supported directly by HOS itself.

Fig. 6.45. The OR and COOR control structures illustrated in a HOS control map fragment.

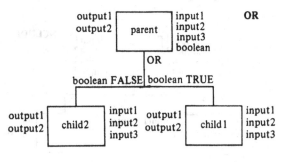

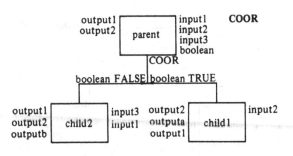

Each *primitive* HOS data type is circumscribed by the operations allowed on it by the system: thus the primitive data type BOOLEAN has the 'natural' primitive operations AND, OR and NOT defined on it:

BOOLEAN = AND (BOOLEAN,
  BOOLEAN)
BOOLEAN = OR (BOOLEAN,
  BOOLEAN)
BOOLEAN = NOT (BOOLEAN)

The type VECTOR has scalar multiplication by a floating point number – type RAT – defined on it:

VECTOR = MUL-VECTOR (VECTOR,
  RAT)

Note how this specifies a relationship between the VECTOR and RAT data types.

A *layered* HOS data type is circumscribed by the operations defined on it by the user: thus, in VISTA, we might consider the data type DIGITISED-FRAME to be an array of elements of type NATural in the range 0 to 255 with the following operations defined:

DIGITISED-FRAME = NEGATIVE
  (DIGITISED-FRAME)

(under which each element of the array is subtracted from 255 to give the corresponding element of the new array)

DIGITISED-FRAME = SCALE
  (DIGITISED-FRAME, RAT)
BOOLEAN = ALL-BLACK
  (DIGITISED-FRAME)
RAT = AVERAGE
  (DIGITISED-FRAME)
NA8 = HISTOGRAM
  (DIGITISED-FRAME)

(where NA8 is the primitive data type consisting of an array of 256 NATurals), and so on.

The definitions of these operations on layered data are given in the form of control maps. By this means new data types can be used in a system without the need for code to be written to handle them – these control maps together with the built in code for system-defined primitive data type operations together enable USE.IT to generate code for operations on the layered data types.

An example Before going on to look at the HOS development methodology it is convenient at this point to give an impression of HOS control maps. To do this figure 6.46 shows the topmost levels of the control map that might be developed for the function of capturing moving sequences of TV frames in VISTA.

The capture-moving-sequence function takes three inputs: the name of the sequence file on the HSDs into which the sequence is to be captured, the frequency of sampling to be used and a boolean saying whether the sequence is to be captured in monochrome or colour. The function has one output: the captured-sequence. Note how the control map is then read from right to left, and how the inputs and outputs of the subfunctions are related according to the control structure they form part of. (Refer to the definitions of JOIN, COINCLUDE and OR above.)

In a full definition all of the data types would be defined and the subfunctions decomposed down to genuine leaf nodes.

Fig. 6.46. A fragment of the HOS control map for the VISTA system.

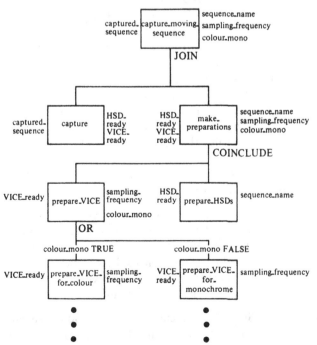

The HOS development methodology phases

The development of a system under HOS takes place, in the general case, in four phases. The first three phases each follow a common sequence of activities which we can summarise thus:

- the control map is prepared,
- the control map is subjected to automated analysis,
- a program is automatically generated from the control map and tested.

The common sequence of activities has, in general, five steps which we now look at in a little more detail:

(i) The first step in producing the control map for an operation is to identify the data elements entering the operation and those leaving it.

(ii) Next the operation is decomposed in terms of a tree of subfunctions showing the control structures that relate sibling subfunctions.

(iii) The products of the first two steps are now combined to produce the control map. This is input to the graphics editor component of USE.IT.

(iv) The control map (now in its internal AXES form) is submitted to the USE.IT Analyser which checks for logical completeness and consistency. The control map is corrected interactively via the editor until the analysis is successful.

(v) Finally the operation's control map is used to steer the generation of code, the linking of code for other defined operations and the test execution of the program component. Operations for which no implementation currently exists can be simulated manually so that partially completed structures can be checked out.

Because of the precise fashion in which functions, data types and the operations on data types are specified it becomes possible for their specifications to be stored for re-use in other applications. Thus, a subtree of a control map (or indeed the entire map) might be re-usable in related programs. The productivity gains are clear.

In the general case the HOS methodology has four phases though the whole process can be tailored for individual applications. (In our brief descriptions of the phases you should note the differences between them and the traditional phases and stages.) We can summarise the phases as follows:

- the production and analysis of a control map for the entire system including non-computerised processes,
- the production, analysis and implementation of a control map for a prototype of each of the computerised processes at subsystem level,
- the production, analysis and implementation of control maps for each of the computerised subsystems to the level of existing library or primitive operations,
- the integration and testing of the system plus the production of documentation.

Phase 1: overall specification In the first phase, the first four of the five general steps take the following form:

(i) Define all the categories of data that the system refers to. In the general case this will include human processes such as manuscript documents and telephone calls as well as computer files.

(ii) Define the overall control structure of the system and the processes (manual, computer and machine) involved, drawing the control map to show the flow of control only.

(iii) Add the data flow to the functional decomposition of step (ii), define the control relationships and identify the computer processes.

(iv) Analyse the resulting overall control map and correct any errors until the analysis is successful.

The fifth step – the generation and testing of a system – is omitted at this stage.

Phase 2: prototype specification
(i) New data types to be used by computer processes are defined in terms of the operations that can be performed on them.

(ii) One of a number of skeleton types is chosen for the application from a library. The control structure of the application is decomposed with the aim of mapping the functions onto primitive, defined or external operations. Existing library support functions, data handling primitives and implemented support functions are identified.

(iii) The prototype control map is input to USE.IT showing the precise control relationships holding between sibling functions and the details of data flow. Unimplemented subsystems are ascribed simulated forms.

(iv) The control map is put through the Analyser and any errors found are corrected.

(v) The code for the prototype is generated, compiled and linked, and the prototype is run in a test harness with test data and simulated subsystems where necessary.

Phase 3: subsystem specification
(i) The data types and operations on them are now built for the *entire* application.

(ii) The control structure of each subsystem is decomposed until all leaf nodes are either existing library functions, external operations or repetitive functions.

(iii) The control map for each subsystem is now constructed to show the data flow and the precise control relationships between the nodes.

(iv) The control maps are analysed by the Analyser and corrected as necessary.

(v) The code for each subsystem is now generated automatically and executed, with test values being prompted for as required.

Phase 4: system integration The final phase is reduced to two steps:

(i) Once the entire system has been built and analysed, actual data files are prepared and the system is run and verified.

(ii) The documentation for the system is produced in the form of hardcopy control maps and narrative description.

Since the logically complete and consistent control maps are mechanically converted into code we have an assurance that the correctness of the specification is not violated in the implementation and this represents one of the major benefits of HOS.

Bibliography

Hamilton 1976 and 1979 (two papers by the originators of HOS which provide a description of the mathematical basis of the methodology), Hamilton 1983, HOS 1983 (describes how USE.IT is applied to the design and specification of business applications), Mimno 1982 (describes the HOS development process and compares it with other methodologies).

Exercises

1 Look at how SADT diagrams representing the functional requirements of a system could be used as input to the HOS methodology. (Programs exist to convert SADT diagrams into HOS control maps – see Mimno 1982.) In particular, study the activation rules of SADT and the way the control relationships between SADT components are related and relate these to HOS's control relationships (JOIN, OR, INCLUDE etc.).
2 Identify a new WBS for HOS development and the deliverable items resulting from the activities.
3 Assess the importance of the direct way that the HOS methodology engages in prototyping. What are the benefits of early prototyping? What are the dangers?
4 Consider to what extent the HOS approach supports the software manager in the allocation of tasks and the structuring of teams.
5 Compare HOS's use of data typing with that available in Modula-2 or object-orientated languages such as CLASCAL and Smalltalk.

6.4.11 Structured Walkthroughs

Once again we bring the technique of the technical review to bear, this time on the products of the System Design Phase. The procedure remains unchanged from that described in the previous chapter.

It is appropriate here to look at how the roles of the reviewers relate to design and to use this as a framework for the issues to be considered at this stage of development.

The Producer has the task during the walkthrough of presenting their product to the participants. Practice shows that it must be possible to do a thorough review in around an hour so the size of the product must be kept down. As examples of suitable products we can cite the ACP diagram for a MASCOT subsystem, the schematic logic for a program generated by JSP or the proof of a theorem produced by FDM.

Besides giving a straightforward walkthrough of the finished design, the Producer/Presenter should consider noting the design decisions that have been made – why this was done this way rather than that. Preferably of course such design decisions should be recorded anyway, but if they can be brought up during a review it is always possible that some misunderstanding could be revealed before the design goes further. And this is precisely the purpose of the review.

Further, the Producer should try in presenting the product to describe any implications of the design chosen. 'This means that we won't be able to use the auto-toggle system-service in the operating system.' 'Anyone needing to access the database at this time may have to wait up to two seconds.' Again, such implications should find their way into an appropriately public part of the design documentation, but there is no harm in raising them at the walkthrough. You have everything to gain.

Now that we are in the Design Phase, the User Representative could well be another member of the team. This might be someone concerned with the design of other parts of the system that have interfaces to the part under scrutiny. Their particular concern would be that interfaces had been fully defined, that they had been adhered to, that the product fulfilled the functions expected of it, that it met any performance requirements imposed on it by its superiors or its peers, and so on.

In some instances the User Representative may indeed represent the *real* user, viz. the organisation that will use the delivered system. This might not be an unusual situation as the users' expectations should have been embodied in the Functional Specification and they may wish to check that the design is implementing that specification. In particular, the User Representative might well be interested in topics such as

• the performance of the system,

- the precise details of user interfaces,
- how well the design models their 'real world' (an important criterion in a methodology such as JSD),
- the resources (hardware and staff) that are implied by the design,
- tradeoffs in design decisions that affect any of these topics.

Decisions made during the Design Phase will have a profound effect on the ease with which the delivered system can be maintained, changed, enhanced and corrected once it has been delivered. For this reason the Maintenance Oracle has a major role to play at this stage.

The Maintenance Oracle needs to pay particular attention to the following questions when preparing for the review:

- Is there a consistent approach to design decisions in the product? Does it have a natural feel?
- Is the product consistent with the rest of the system in the way design decisions are made?
- Is the product well structured?
- Is the structuring determined by a consistently applied approach?
- Does the design preclude likely or definite future enhancements?
- Can the inclusion of such enhancements be eased by some appropriate abstractions now?
- Does the design include sufficient self-checking features and test points to make bug tracing and performance evaluation practical propositions?
- For instance, have software and hardware diagnostics been included where appropriate?

Then there is the Standards Bearer. Since you will have laid down your standards for design in your Quality Plan, this role is well-defined. But let us add one other task to the job. Standards are not written on tablets of stone. It is possible for them to be wrong, so the Standards Bearer should have a sensitive ear for situations where the rules and regulations you have adopted are hindering rather than helping your designers. Have the flexibility to change them if necessary, if not on this project then at least on the next.

Finally, remember that the checklists in this chapter can be used to help walkthrough participants to prepare and you should make it a habit to add your own questions to them from your own experiences and from the literature.

6.4.12 Fagan inspections

For comparison with Structured Walkthroughs, we include here a description of the Fagan inspection taken from Fagan 1976.

A number of checkpoints are defined during development for the various products: the software itself, the test plans, publication material and so on. For each checkpoint, exit criteria are defined. These specify the quality of products passing through the checkpoint. An inspection takes place to check that quality.

An inspection team is reckoned to consist of about four people – a 'moderator' and say three others involved in the product. The moderator is responsible for arranging, chairing and following up the inspection. Where a piece of design is being inspected, Fagan identifies one of the participants as the product's designer, the others being perhaps its implementer(s) and those with interfaces or other interests with the product.

There are four phases. We look at them in the context of the Design Phase, considering an inspection of a piece of design. In the first, the designer presents the whole inspection team with an overview of the product and distributes documentation and any other relevant material. This is used by all the team members in the second phase: their individual preparation. During this they use the accumulated knowledge of past inspections to concentrate on areas where errors are most likely to be found. At the third stage – the inspection proper – a reader nominated by the moderator walks through the product in front of the team, with every piece of logic, every possibility being scrutinised. As in Structured Walkthroughs, the emphasis is on the detection of errors and not their correction. Once an error has been spotted, it is recorded by the moderator, classified by type and given a severity rating.

After the inspection, it is the moderator's responsibility to produce the inspection report. The product then goes back to the producer for the final stage – the reworking – in which all errors and problems raised in the report must be resolved. The moderator checks that this has taken place and then determines whether or not re-inspection is required. Fagan recommends another cycle if more than 5% of the product has been reworked.

There is a strong element of feedback in a Fagan inspection. The records of errors found, their types and severity, are used to draw up and refine 'inspection specifications' – guidelines for inspections designed to improve the error detection rate. Key to this is the identification of which types of error should be looked for the hardest and how they can be looked for. In the section on indicators in this chapter you will find a similar recommendation to keep such records.

Besides the detection of errors, the Fagan inspection displays all the beneficial side-effects of the Structured Walkthrough: shared responsibility, greater common awareness, easier transfer of ownership and so on.

Bibliography
Fagan 1976 (a paper describing the technique and including empirical data collected within IBM).

Exercises
1 Using the relevant source material, draw up a procedure for inspecting products that combines what you consider the best points of Fagan inspections and Structured Walkthroughs.
2 Draft inspection guidelines for finding common and/or expensive errors in design, using your own experiences.
3 Write a paper for your manager justifying your refusal to let him see the statistics that relate errors to individuals.
4 Write a memo to your team convincing them of the benefits to themselves of the public revelation of errors on their part.
5 Draw up forms along the lines of those in Fagan 1976 for recording the results of inspections of design and user handbooks in a form appropriate to your own situation.

6.5 Indicators to be monitored during System Design

6.5.1 What we are looking for
The indicators we discuss below have a wide spectrum of uses. At one end we can identify 'volume metrics' that tell us how much software we are producing for instance, whilst at the other end are the 'quality metrics' that tell us how well we are producing it. Both types are predictive, that is they allow us either to make some predictions about the future, such as how much testing time will be required, or to make a decision that will improve our future performance.

Indicators used during design and production divide roughly into two groups:

- micro-metrics that look at the fine detail of the product and, in particular, require knowledge of the insides of its components;
- macro-metrics that concentrate on the relationships between components.

During design we shall want to have indicators covering the full spectrum at all levels. Each should have one or more of the following characteristics:

- Its performance should correspond closely to our intuition; a complexity metric should for instance ascribe a high complexity value to a design that looks and feels complex to a designer.
- Its performance should in practice correlate with factors that it supposedly influences; again, a complexity metric should rate as highly complex those modules which turn out to be difficult to change or understand.
- It should be sensitive to changes in the system; that is, if a system is changed the change in the value of the indicator should be proportional to the size of the change to the measured property of the system.

6.5.2 An interconnectivity metric
We feel intuitively that the greater the connectivity of modules in a system the more complex the system is and hence the more prone it is to the problems that arise from complexity. This applies to data connections and to control connections. Whilst Myers's module coupling metric restricts itself to data connections, the macro-metric of interconnectivity described by Kafura and Henry in Kafura 1981 covers both.

They define a three-phase analysis of a system to determine the information flow. They describe it as follows. 'The first involves generating a set of relations indicating the flow of information through input parameters, output parameters, returned-values functions and data structures. The second phase generates an information-flow structure from these relations. The third phase analyses the information-flow structure to determine the derived calls, the local flows and the global flows'. A special notation is used to record the result of the first analysis so that automated tools can be used for the second and third phases. The analysis can be carried out on any level of design or production provided a precise enough description is available to allow the connections between components to be deduced.

Four different measurements then yield procedure, module, interface and level complexity metrics derived from the interconnectivity analysis. Figure 6.47 summarises some of the features that these different metrics can point up.

Kafura 1981 gives an interesting example of the metrics as applied to the UNIX operating system.

6.5.3 Myers' module coupling metric

In his book Myers 1975, Myers describes two metrics relating to the quality of module design – module coupling and module cohesion. Module coupling is a micro-metric that measures an 'exter-

Fig. 6.47. Summary of measurements and features using interconnectivity metrics. (From Kafura 1981.)

Measurements	Features
Procedure	1 lack of functionality 2 stress points in the system 3 inadequate refinement
Module	1 poorly designed data structures 2 improper modularization 3 poor module design 4 poor functional decomposition
Interface	1 module coupling 2 measure of modifiability
Level	1 missing level of abstraction 2 comparison of design alternatives

nal' attribute of a group of related modules, namely the degree to which they are bound to each other by data access. If a group of modules forming part or all of your system are strongly bound then you have a poor design – the closeness with which the modules rely on each other for data is likely to lead to difficulties in obtaining correctness, modifiability, good modularity and so on.

Myers identifies six levels of coupling. You will find them listed in the earlier section describing Structured Design. This list can help you in three ways. Firstly, it gives clear guidance to your designers of what sort of decoupling to avoid in their design in the first place. Secondly, it offers a way of choosing between alternative designs. Thirdly, it can be used *post factum* as an indication of the likely difficulties that will be encountered during the production and maintenance phases, particularly giving you guidance on how and in what order to integrate the modules to form the system.

To carry out an analysis of coupling you will need design documentation that is sufficiently detailed for you to establish which modules communicate via data exchange and how that exchange will take place. This information becomes increasingly available as design proceeds and should really all be available once detailed design work has been completed. At the latest, cross reference tables generated by compilers will allow you to assess your module coupling level from the final source code.

Myers 1975 gives definitions and examples of the different levels of coupling. (See also Troy 1981.)

6.5.4 Myers' module cohesion metric

This is the second of the two metrics of module design quality proposed by Myers in Myers 1975. 'Cohesion' is an 'internal' attribute of a single module. It is a macro-metric that measures the relatedness of the different functions performed by and contained within a module. The aim is to produce modules with high cohesion, that is ones in which the constituent functions are closely related.

The earlier section on Structured Design lists the seven levels of cohesion described in Myers 1975. Once again, this measure, like module coupling, can help in three ways: guiding designers on the functional content of the modules they design, providing a criterion for choosing between different distributions of functions over modules and as a mechanism for spotting modules where there may be potential problems.

Although cohesion is an internal metric, the information required to determine cohesion levels will probably be available earlier than that for coupling levels since the distribution of functionality probably represents an earlier design decision than the types of data transfer to be used between modules. You should almost certainly be able to do a cohesion analysis of the modules of your system before launching into detailed design in the next phase. It is a manual operation.

Again Myers 1975 gives definitions of the different cohesion levels and examples. Low cohesion suggests that a module does not hang together well and hence, if it is involved for instance in modification later in design or after, there is an increased chance that functions not related to the change will be affected unwittingly.

6.5.5 Call graph metrics

Given an overall design of a system we can generally, depending on the design technique used, draw a *call graph* showing which components call or activate which other components. This call graph can give us information about the testability of the system by measuring the *accessibility* of individual modules.

Thus, given a module M we can define its accessibility as

$$A(M) = \sum_i \frac{A(M_i)}{C(M_i)}$$

where the modules M_i are the modules that call M and $C(X)$ is the number of modules called by module X.

Given a particular path P through the call graph we can define its *testability*:

$$T(P) = \left\{ \sum_{M_i \in P} \frac{1}{A(M_i)} \right\}^{-1}$$

This in turn can give us a definition for the testability of an entire system of N modules as

$$\left\{ N \sum_{i=1}^{N} \frac{1}{T(P_i)} \right\}^{-1}$$

As with many such metrics it is important not to misinterpret or misuse them. We could in theory increase the testability of the system according to this definition by simply reducing C for as many modules as possible, i.e. by simplifying the call structure of the collection of modules. However it would make little sense to do this by, for instance, having the system in the form of just one module. System testability as defined above needs to be increased in a manner that is consistent with preserving other qualities such as high cohesion and low coupling. Testability also tells us something about how difficult or easy system integration will be and perhaps what order system building should be done in so that the part-systems tested are as testable as possible at each stage.

6.5.6 Error detection metric

This is the phase in which you should start collecting statistics on the errors that you discover in the work you have done to date. The raw data consists simply of the type of error you discover (according to some classification), which component it was found in and at which stage the error was detected. If you have the facilities you can also record the time taken to correct the error – this is covered below. Remember to include errors in the Functional Specification in your records.

Why indulge in this masochism? There are a number of reasons:

- As your error data accumulates, certain activities and certain error types will appear more prominent; these will suggest where you should concentrate extra effort and checking, in other words you will be able to target your inspection and testing better.
- A relatively high error detection rate (EDR) in a particular component of the system can suggest poor quality and the possible need for reworking.
- It can lead to estimates of the number of residual errors in a system and the likely amount of effort required to reduce the error level until it is in some sense acceptable – see section 2.2.6.

- A relatively high EDR in a particular activity or a particular error type can suggest a lack of standards in some area.
- In time, improvements in the experience and skills of your staff and in the techniques they adopt should reveal themselves in reduced EDRs.

All in all, the EDR is a good indicator of quality. Thus if 'incorrect interfaces' seem prevalent take a close look at how you go about defining and enforcing interfaces and tighten up your methods.

Record the data centrally, teach your staff to update it promptly and preferably hold it in machine-processable form to make the generation of fault and exception reports quicker. Take care however not to use the data as a management stick – it is sensitive information that you need in order to get your system right.

6.5.7 Error correction time metric

This is a predictive metric that involves the manual recording of the time spent to clear an error. The data collected can be stored with the error detection metric data. The principal use of this data is to allow you to see the cost of fixing the various types of error discovered on the different stages of development. Error types that demonstrate a high fix cost should cause you to review your techniques to eliminate them earlier, preferably at source.

If you have historical data on error correction times from earlier projects you may also be able to make a judgement on the efficiency of your testing procedures.

The metric applies to all phase of development but you should set up your records now at the same time as those for error detection.

6.5.8 Documentation size metric

A constant management activity is the assessment of the amount of work still required to produce the system. At the various stages of design, the sheer volume of design documentation can help the hard-pressed manager to review his estimates. You will need some historical data to work from and to give you multipliers to get from 'pages of significant design documentation' to 'man-months of effort', or whatever. Though this indi-

cator cannot be used on its own as a predictor it can be a useful second opinion.

If you are using a layered design technique such as SARA and have clear standards of the level of detail to which each layer must go and some historical data from other systems, you may also be able to judge the 'explosion rate' of the system – the rate at which the level of detail is increasing as you pass down through the layers.

6.5.9 Source code size estimate

Depending on how long your system design activity lasts you should be able to make at least one new estimate of the size of the source code that you will finally deliver. If you are developing your design in a layered fashion you may be able to re-estimate on the completion of each layer.

As before you should go to as much detail as is sensible and, to allow you to spot trends at component level, you should also record your estimates at some level (below the entire system) where the breakdown into components is unlikely to change much. This will make comparisons more meaningful. The first level of breakdown will probably suffice.

At some point during the phase it will be possible to switch from estimating in pages of source code (see section 5.5) to estimating in part pages or even lines. The danger in working in lines is that, being such a small unit, it makes it easier to underestimate. If your design technique produces some form of pseudo-code then estimating in lines becomes practical if you have a good conversion factor – perhaps calculated from a small experiment.

Append your estimates to the previous ones and treat a variation of more than 20% as a reason for investigating the situation more closely. Also investigate components that show an inexorable rise in their estimated size even if it is not sudden.

6.5.10 System size indicator

The estimates you made of system size during the Definition Phase will of necessity have been rather coarse. Now that the design is coming off the drawing board followed closely by fresh estimates of the source code size estimate, you should be able to refine your estimate of memory-resident system size and hence re-assess whether your system is at all constrained by the available memory. Remember that, if it is and you do not have buying more memory as an option, your plans will need to take account of the extra work that will be required to ensure a fit – hard optimising, overlaying, recombining functions into new overlays, the use of a better compiler and so on.

6.6 Checklists for the System Design Phase

6.6.1 Topics to be covered in the design process

Irrespective of the design methods you use, your design considerations will need to cover most of the following topics and, where relevant, your decisions will need to be recorded either in the design documentation or in the Project Debriefing Report:

- Overall system structure:
  - What is the process or task structure?
  - How is interprocess communication handled?
  - What is the planned mapping onto memory?
  - What process scheduling algorithm is to be used?
  - How are input/output channels to be used?
  - What is the overall database design?
  - What expectations are there of facilities in the OS?
  - System initialisation, start-up and recovery procedures.
  - Have the critical items of the system been identified?
  - Has their simulation, prototyping or experimentation been planned? If not, why not?
  - Has the memory occupancy been calculated to sufficient granularity and is there sufficient spare room (for errors in estimates, enhancements, etc.)?
  - Has an overall philosophy been determined for the level and nature of internal consistency checking, and the recovery actions to be taken on discovery of an error?

- Subdivision of software:
  - Has the software been subdivided to the point where it can be assigned to individuals for implementation?
  - Are all software components fully specified?
  - Have the consistency checking responsibilities been specified for each component?
  - Have all interfaces between components been defined?
  - Have all functions of the Functional Specification been covered by one or more components?
  - Have all interfaces with the outside world been agreed?
  - What is the overlay structure (if any)?
  - Have existing software components been identified for re-use?
  - Have memory occupancy targets been set for individual component?
  - Have timing targets been set?
- Implementation goals:
  - Has the design been reviewed and agreed by all those with relevant interests?
  - Has it been agreed that the design fully satisfies the requirements?
  - Has it been agreed that the acceptance criteria are satisfactory?
  - Have appropriate simulations been carried out to check timing characteristics and performance?
  - Have estimates of memory utilisation been made to ensure that the software will fit in the memory available with the effort available?
  - Have the staff been trained for the subsequent work?
  - Have the necessary development tools (hardware and software) been procured or planned for development themselves?
  - Have plans been made or reviewed for the implementation phase in the areas of activity management, quality management and configuration management?
- Maintenance facilities:
  - Have appropriate levels of diagnostics

been designed in (tracing, postmortems etc.)?

- Have consistency checking mechanisms such as high-level assertions been designed in?
- Have appropriate maintenance tools been provisioned or planned for, for the maintenance activities (e.g. PROM blowers, maintenance environments, configuration control systems)?
- Hardware aspects:
  - Has the hardware configuration been clearly identified and recorded?
  - Have alternative configurations been considered and, if so, have the reasons for their rejection been recorded?

6.6.2 General properties of the design documentation

Your design documentation should have the following properties, again almost irrespective of which design method you use:

- a hierarchical structure,
- functional completeness,
- traceability back to the Functional Specification (explicitly by cross reference preferably),
- precision (i.e. lack of ambiguity),
- comprehensibility.

On the last property, if you do have to write prose as part of your design documentation take some random samples and determine their 'fog factor'. Here is the algorithm proposed by Robert Gunning in Gunning 1962:

(i) take a sample of around 100 words,
(ii) count the sentences,
(iii) compute the average number of words per sentence (LS),
(iv) count the number of words of three or more syllables but excluding proper names, simple combinations of short easy words and verb forms terminated by -ed, -es and so on,
(v) calculate the percentage of such 'long' words (LW),
(vi) calculate the fog factor as $(LS + LW) * 0.4$.

A fog index of 10 to 12 can be expected for general correspondence whilst 12 to 16 is acceptable for technical reports. Anything over 16 should be considered incomprehensible!

6.6.3 System Design and maintainability

A key property of a design is *integrity*. A design with high integrity is simple, has a consistent philosophy universally applied and naturalness in its structure. An integral design is also a maintainable design. The effect of change or enhancement can be more easily identified and hence is more controllable.

You should ask the following questions at each design review:

- What is the overall design philosophy?
- Is the design philosophy simple?
- Is the design philosophy clearly expressed in the design documentation's higher levels?
- Is the design philosophy consistently applied across the system?
- Are the system's components coupled as loosely as possible?
- Are topics such as error handling and operator interfaces consistently handled across the system?
- Have parameters of the system in areas of likely future change been identified?
- Are the various system resources (memory, disc space, processor time, communications capacity, etc.) sufficiently large for immediate needs and estimated future needs?
- Have existing re-usable components been identified for incorporation into the system?
- Is the entire system adequately documented in a simple structured fashion?
- Are the future system maintainers fully familiarised with the design philosophy?
- Are the future system maintainers satisfied with the extent to which the system design satisfies the maintenance design goals set for it?
- Have features of the design been abstracted and generalised as much as possible?

The involvement of the future maintainers of the system can be significantly beneficial, particularly if they already have experience in maintaining previous systems. They will know how systems change, where generalisations help future change, where new requirements are likely to affect the design, and so on. In his Structured Walkthroughs, Yourdon has a 'Maintenance Oracle' in the cast list. Such an oracle can influence the design beneficially by introducing the following concrete activities into design walkthroughs:

- performing change exercises on the design to test its flexibility;
- evaluating the generality and integrity of the design in terms of its ability to
  - execute on different hardware configurations,
  - operate on different input/output formats,
  - perform a subset of its requirements,
  - perform new requirements suggested as likely during the Definition Phase,
  - operate with different data structures or processing algorithms;
- evaluating how well components likely to change have been decoupled (and even isolated) from the rest of the system;
- determining level of generality of component interfaces;
- checking that the high-level design strategy (rather than just the design itself) has been adequately documented.

6.6.4 Potential design error types

When accumulating your error statistics it is sensible to have a fairly fine classification of types so that you can identify with some accuracy the areas where your development methods are weak. The types should ideally be mutually exclusive. The selection listed below can act as a basis for your own records:

- omission of a required function though stated in the Functional Specification,
- misinterpretation of a stated requirement,
- mishandling of the interface between components,
- mishandling of an interface with the external world (peripherals, users, instrumentation, operating systems, software packages, etc.),
- incorrect representation of design,
- timing problems,
- synchronisation problems,

- space problems (primary or secondary memory),
- incorrect mathematical expressions,
- incorrect boolean expressions,
- error in sequencing of operations,
- indexing error,
- iteration error,
- omission of case,
- incorrect or inconsistent data structuring,
- initialisation error,
- incorrect boundary handling,
- incorrect or absent recovery action,
- incorrect or insufficient self-checking.

6.7 Memorabilia for System Design

Adding to the Project Debriefing Report

At the end of the Design Phase you will be able to record, in the Project Debriefing Report, your findings about this phase and also about the Definition Phase. So, consider the questions in the equivalent *memorabile* in the preceding chapter. Those undiscovered holes and inconsistencies in the Functional Specification are starting to emerge. How could they have been avoided? Once again, the records you keep of your walkthroughs and reviews give an important feedback mechanism and a source of material for the Project Debriefing Report.

Quantifying design goals

In his book Gilb 1976 (see also Gilb 1979), Tom Gilb promotes the idea of giving clear expressions of design goals to a development team as a motivating force. We should, he says, identify important attributes of our design such as 'robustness', 'effectiveness' and 'minimum memory size', define a metric for each, place limits on the measured values to be achieved and describe the relative priorities of the attributes.

The setting of such goals is akin to setting limits on the effort to be expended on a particular task.

Cheap error removal

Much evidence now points to the fact that simply *reading* design documentation with a critical eye is one of the most cost-effective ways of reducing the level of errors in design. Structured walkthroughs *à la* Yourdon and Fagan-style inspections give you a formal basis for reviews by groups but individuals should be encouraged to practise the art on an individual basis too.

Getting errors to raise their heads

None of the techniques described in this book will solve all your problems. You need to recognise that mistakes will be made. This has the important implication that all the techniques you use – especially those for design – and your use of them should increase the *visibility* of errors as soon as possible.

How it might have been

In designing your system using a particular design method it is worth asking yourself how it might have looked if you had used a different methodology. You may discover holes in your design by looking at the system from another viewpoint.

Testing preliminaries

During the Design Phase you will be thinking about and documenting procedures for testing the system both as part of the development of the system and as acceptance testing for your client. You should particularly consider at this stage whether any special tools (both software and hardware) will be required.

The right people for the job

As you produce your design you should give consideration to the type of people that you would like to implement each part of it. You may, of course, have no choice in the matter or it may not make much difference. But if, for example, you are thinking of a change to an operating system interface or some other similarly specialised work package, you had better make sure that you have the right person for the job.

Keeping the client informed

During design, decisions relating to the details of functions beyond what is described in the Functional Specification will inevitably have to be made. If your client is kept in on the decision making process he will have less cause to complain when he sees the finished product!

Drafting tools

Design is by nature a highly iterative process and you should expect many drafts of the design to be produced before the first baseline design document emerges. Pen or pencil and paper is not a good design drafting medium. No matter how clear the writing of your designers (and you will be lucky if at some time you don't get at least one who appears not to have learnt to hold a pen), hand-written documentation is difficult to modify continuously, difficult to read and notoriously difficult to type accurately. The solution to this problem is to enter the design directly into a computer or word processor with suitable editing facilities, and graphic facilities if one of the diagrammatic methodologies is being used. If you are using a design methodology supported by computerised tools then this will be a necessity, but even if you have no intention of carrying out computer verification of your design it is well worth considering using your computer as a drafting and storage system. Once you have the design documentation stored in machine-readable form it is not difficult to produce simple utilities to help validate and maintain it.

7

System Production

7.1 The aims of the System Production Phase

7.1.1 The background to System Production

Let us start by identifying the central purposes of this phase as they relate to *production* of the system. They are:

(i) to take the high-level design resulting from the Design Phase and to elaborate it to the point where all design decisions have been made,

(ii) to take this detailed design and to transform it into code,

(iii) to check that at the detailed level this code correctly implements the detailed design,

(iv) to put the entire system together and prove that it is ready to be submitted for acceptance by your client.

Together these constitute the major stage of this phase, Produce System for Trial, which has as its deliverable item the System Ready for Trial.

In chapter 2 we identified four other stages:

Prepare User Documentation
Prepare Training Schedules
Prepare Acceptance Test Description
Prepare System Conversion Schedule

each with its own component activities. So the segment of WBS for this phase becomes:

4000 System Production
    4100 System Production Management
        4110 Manage detailed (tactical) design
        4120 Manage coding
        4130 Manage unit testing
        4140 Manage system building
        4150 Manage ancillary tasks

4200 Produce System for Trial
    4210 Perform detailed (tactical) design
    4220 Produce code
    4230 Perform unit testing
    4240 Build system
4300 Prepare User Documentation
    4310 Prepare User Guide
    4320 Prepare maintenance documents
    4330 Prepare publicity material
    4340 Prepare management summaries
4400 Prepare Training Schedules
    4410 Prepare Course Materials
    4420 Give training courses
4500 Prepare Acceptance Test Description
4600 Prepare System Conversion Schedule

During the production activities we will be looking for techniques that, even if they do not guarantee, then at least significantly increase our chances of, firstly, correctly transforming the high-level design at the system level into low-level design at component level, and, secondly, correctly transforming that low-level design into code.

Since we rarely have that guarantee we have to add the low-level and integration testing activities to check the correctness of those two transformations. We need to look for techniques that give us a good level of confidence at a reasonable price.

It is with these production activities that we start our review of the aims of the phase.

7.1.2 Elaborating the overall design

Since 'production' as we define it seems simply to continue the design process started in the System Design Phase, one might ask why the two phases are separated and where the separation is made between them. In crude terms, the answer is that the Design Phase produces the strategy whilst the Production Phase fills out this strategy at the tactical level. Hence, the Design Phase defines the system's parts and their relationships, but always doing this from the stance of the system as a whole. There comes a point where those parts are sufficiently defined for them to be considered in isolation and this point marks the end of the Design Phase and the start of the Production Phase.

Detailed design is therefore an activity carried out on components whose interfaces and relationships are clearly defined. It can be undertaken by an individual or small team more or less independently of other individuals or teams working on other components. This does not presuppose top-down working, but it does presuppose some division of the system into relatively small units.

The process of detailed design proceeds to the point where all *design* decisions have been made and only coding (i.e. implementation) decisions remain. There will always be some interaction between design and implementation but a definition of the division is necessary so that you can tell when you have finished design and are ready to proceed with coding.

7.1.3 Transforming correct designs into correct code

With the current state of the art, the act of coding is akin to casting your design in concrete, an act that is very difficult to reverse. It is somehow much harder to throw away unsatisfactory code than unsatisfactory design. The temptation is to knock it about until it is satisfactory. If however we regard code as simply a machine-executable form of our design then we should clearly aim to transform the design into code in a clean single-shot operation. Manipulating the code thereafter in order to make it work (because we did not transform it correctly in the first place) will invariably compromise our original design.

As tools develop – particularly in very high level languages – it will no doubt become increasingly easy to backtrack from code. In the meantime you should check that you really are ready for coding before undertaking it. Some methodologies

currently in use make the transition easier or even try to remove it by writing the design directly into code in some form – Stepwise Refinement and Jackson System Development for instance.

There is another danger in code. As the first apparently tangible evidence that the project team has actually been doing anything for the past months, there is a fairly understandable managerial desire to have the team produce code as soon as possible. You must suppress this desire in yourself and convince others of its perniciousness. The solution is to use *all* your deliverable items as indicators of progress to management. During your planning you must have identified, in particular, deliverable items for the Definition and Design Phases and the early parts of the Production Phase – design documents, review reports, technical reports, system models and so on. Emphasise their importance and announce their completion via your reports. In time, code will be seen as just another step on the road to the final system.

In summary, the relative visibility and irrevocability of code makes it dangerous stuff. Just how dangerous you will find out during testing – the third stage of the Production Phase.

7.1.4 Checking the correctness of the transformation into code

Once you have cast the concrete of code it is unlikely you will have any reason to avoid testing it unless you have carried out a mathematical proof of its correctness. Testing code, by its nature, is an activity which can proceed very quickly – if you got it right – or very slowly – if you did not. Since you cannot assume you got it right, you must assume it will proceed slowly. Of all the stages in software development, testing (both unit and integration) is the one with the largest variation from plan, traditionally *over* plan. There are two ways out of this – plan more realistically using performance data from earlier projects and be thorough in your testing. The first is a managerial problem. The second is dependent on your choice of techniques.

Your aim is to produce software components known to carry out their specification completely and perfectly – a worthy input to the system construction stage.

7.1.5 Putting the system together

There is a basic assumption in our model that you are adopting the divide-and-conquer principle, and that this applies irrespective of whether you are working top-down, bottom-up or in any other fashion. There comes the time therefore when the products of division need to be assembled to form the final system. This activity is variously called 'building' or 'integrating'.

System building is a critical activity as it is likely to be the first time that you will test interfaces between the system components produced by different people or teams.

The pieces will fit together like pieces in a jigsaw if the interfaces were fully defined in the first instance and have been put into code with iron discipline. Integration needs therefore to be performed at a measured pace, piece by piece. The method of integration may vary depending on whether top-down or bottom-up development is used, but whatever integration approach is adopted, it cannot be rushed. Nothing can be gained by throwing the whole system together at once and hoping that it will work, because when it does not you will have no idea which component or (more likely) components are failing.

It is common for this stage to be the point when new hardware is joined to your new software for the first time. Such hardware–software interfaces pose a special danger to the system developer and it is for this reason that we emphasise the need for early simulation of hardware and experimentation with it.

The techniques used in integration are therefore just as much in the nature of good practices as of technical approaches. Once again, they aim for completeness, rigour and cost-effectiveness.

On the bright side, this stage will be the most exciting. What has up to now been PASCAL on the coding sheet or boxes on a structure diagram now starts to emerge as the system you have been working towards. Gradually it emerges from the stubs and dummies, the simulators and debuggers, to take on its own life. Does it look the way you hoped?

7.1.6 Ancillary stages during system production

In chapter 2 we identified a number of other stages in the Production Phase that support the central one: Prepare User Documentation, Prepare Training Schedules, Prepare Acceptance Test Description and Prepare System Conversion Schedule. These are no less demanding than the strictly software production activities and they require special resources and skills. User documentation and training are both highly visible products and the system will be judged by their quality as well as on its own performance. In particular, as much care must go into the preparation of User Manuals and Guides as goes into the design of the user interface to the software. Furthermore, except in the simplest cases, the skills required for producing good, usable manuals are not necessarily to be found in your technical staff. They may well provide the technical input but the orientation and presentation of this for the user may need the services of an experienced technical *author*.

The Acceptance Test Description must be prepared early during System Production – if not earlier – as you will want to use it increasingly as the yardstick against which to measure the system. Ultimately of course during the Acceptance Phase it is *the* yardstick so you will need to have rehearsed it thoroughly before then!

Where your system is replacing an existing one – perhaps a manual version – the conversion from old to new will need to be planned in detail. All the parties affected will need to be involved – shop-floor workers, unions, senior management, computer operations staff, auditors, accountants, legal advisers and so on. Their agreement and commitment to a successful changeover need to be assured if the system is to be smoothly installed in a non-hostile environment.

7.2 The starting point of System Production

From what has been said above you will now be aware that production must proceed on the firm foundation of a strategic design specification. This document can have one of a number of names: High-Level Design Specification, Overall Design Specification, Level 1 Design Document and so on. For convenience we shall refer to any such document generically as the System Design Specification (SDS).

The SDS contains sufficient definition of components and interfaces between components for you to proceed on the divide-and-conquer principle. Individual components can be treated relatively independently by individual workers or teams of workers.

Another important input to the phase is a detailed Project Management Plan. This will, like the design, have been elaborated now to cover low-level activities, at the component level probably. Activities would typically cover the detailed design of subsystem A, the coding of subsystem B, the testing of subsystem C, or the combined testing of subsystems D, E and F with certain items of hardware.

Since this phase does occupy around 50% of the work prior to delivery and since you are now handling manageable pieces of the system, the need and potential for careful monitoring of both schedule and technical quality progress are great. Your plans will be important management tools and records, so you should be sure of having an appropriately detailed Project Management Plan and an equally appropriately developed Quality Management Plan. New revisions of these two will include the use of some of the important indicators for this phase covered later in the chapter.

7.3 The finishing point of System Production

Clearly your major deliverable item is the System Ready for Acceptance – a system that satisfies the Functional Specification and is ready to be proved to do so to your client's satisfaction.

If your project is of the evolutionary variety you will pass through this phase as often as you produce a new incarnation of your evolving system. Direct or evolutionary, your system will need to pass through such a baseline test at least once so that you can issue a system or systems with documented and agreed capabilities before it goes either on to future evolution or into use by your client (or both!).

Your Work Breakdown Structure for this phase will also contain work packages for the production of User Documentation and Training Material and Schedules and these will form subsidiary deliverable items.

7.4 Techniques of use during System Production

During tactical design we will be looking for many of the same features in the methodologies and techniques as we looked for during strategic design. A technique should introduce completeness and rigour into our design; it should generate deliverable items which can be checked, reviewed and analysed for correctness; it should allow us to trace requirements down to the lower levels of the software; it should allow us to break the problem into steps that can be tackled by individuals in short periods of time such as one or two weeks.

In some cases tactical design techniques are continuations of strategic design techniques and there is an obvious progression from one to the other. In other cases you will need to choose a technique or techniques that are appropriate to the type of system you are building. There is no golden road and you may wish to use a combination of techniques, using what each has to offer where it works best.

In the Design Stage we can expect the amount of design documentation to increase rapidly as the level of detail increases and as further staff are brought in to take up the increasing breadth of design activity. This will bring with it all the communication problems one might expect and it is essential that you ensure, whatever techniques you adopt, that you find a representation for your design that carries all the information necessary for communicating design decisions between people. This is a strong reason for formal techniques that give us a good record of our design. During the coding stage a crucial need is to be able to transform the design with the least possible fuss into correct code. In some situations methodologies provide automatic means of generating code directly from the design. Ideally automatic code generation can be performed by your computer from some machine-readable representation of the design. Thus COBOL program source can be generated by software from a design written in Jackson's schematic logic in his methodology. This sort of facility is much to be recommended and even if you do not have the necessary computer software to do the work for you it is often possible to perform the same process manually. This will naturally be slower but the resulting code is more likely to work first time.

After the design techniques that lead into code production we include a short discussion on the choice of language and on the use of macroprocessors. Both of these topics can have significant effects on qualities such as portability, maintainability and productivity. Also of some importance is the topic of programming style but we leave it to you to follow up this (sometimes subjective) area through the literature and restrict ourselves to a short *memorabile* at the end of the chapters.

Finally we pass to some techniques that you can bring to bear on the problem of testing and integration. In an ideal world these two activities would not be problems but until we have tools that produce correct software from our designs the imperfect art of testing will remain with us. Because this area remains so vitally important it is crucial that the system developer has a clear understanding of exactly what can and what cannot be achieved through testing and what the underlying theory is.

7.4.1 Jackson Structured Programming – JSP

Coding a JSP design

In chapter 6 we saw how JSP allows us to generate the design for a program from its input data structures and its output data structures. As a minimum the technique generates 'schematic logic' for each program. This represents a detailed design for a program and to that extent the first stage of production – tactical design – has been done for us. We turn now therefore to coding and unit testing.

JSP schematic logic is in a form of PDL which uses the three basic structured programming constructs – sequence, selection and iteration. Coding this logic into our target language will therefore be more or less easy depending on whether the language syntax supports them. If you have done any backtracking in the schematic logic you will also need to have some form of **goto** available.

Modern 'structured' languages such as PL/1, PASCAL, C, Ada and CORAL all support these facilities and the transformation will be straightforward. If your target language is COBOL it will be less so unless you have available a structured dialect. Tools are available to transform schematic logic into COBOL automatically and these are naturally advantageous in that they remove a major source of error from the production process.

JSP does not concern itself with detailed data representations so that is an area of coding where you will need to act alone.

You will remember from chapter 6 that one of the principal techniques of JSP – program inversion – is in fact carried out on source code rather than on schematic logic. This is an important point. Program inversion is an implementation matter that concerns how you will transform your ideal design to run on the final (probably limited) processor configuration. One result of program inversion (and backtracking) is a proliferation of the hated **goto** statement. Jackson's view is that this is not significant. What is important is the correctness and integrity of the schematic logic; the code is only a mechanically derived and transformed implementation, and the presence of **goto**s in it is of as little consequence as the presence of assembler 'jump' statements in the output of an Ada compiler.

Testing a JSP design

A program can contain errors of logic – errors of design – and errors of coding – typographical and syntactic errors. Testing will not in general find all logic errors nor prove that all have been found. We must therefore try to avoid this type of error in the first place, and we must therefore aim for *correct* design and a *correct* transformation of design into code. In both these activities JSP offers solutions.

As for typographical and syntactic errors, you can reduce the chances of these occurring by using tools to carry out the more mechanical transformations such as schematic-logic-to-COBOL and program inversion. By reducing human intervention, you reduce the possibility of slips.

Since inversion is largely a means to improving the implemented version of a design it makes sense to test a JSP implementation *before* inversion, when testing is much easier. If inversion is then done by hand the inversion also needs to be checked carefully, probably with further tests.

Work Breakdown Structure

JSP can contribute a number of activities to the segment of our WBS for the Production Phase:

4200 Produce System for Trial
    4210 Produce individual programs
        4211 Design detailed data formats
        4212 Transform schematic logic into
             source code
        4213 Carry out necessary program
             inversions
        4214 Prepare code for testing
    4220   (not used)
    4230 Perform unit testing on individual programs
    4240 Build System

(Note that some testing (4230) may be done between 4212 and 4213.)

Exercises

1 Take the schematic logic you constructed in exercise 1 of section 6.4.2 and translate it into any structured language you know. Try to identify mechanical rules for the translation and hence produce a specification for a 'compiler' that produces source code in your chosen language from schematic logic.
2 What help can the Jackson data structure diagrams give you in devising test data for the resulting program? Take account of your answer to exercise 3 of section 6.4.2.
3 When do you think optimisation should be done? On the schematic logic, on the source code before inversion, or after inversion? What would be the impact on the software's maintainability?

7.4.2 Jackson System Development – JSD

The implementation step

The final step in JSD is the 'implementation' step. The five preceding steps – essentially a process of specification – have produced:

- a set of processes that model real world entities and system functions;
- various data streams and state vectors for process communication.

In particular, each process is represented by 'structure text', and the connections between processes are captured in a System Structure Diagram.

The JSD implementation step concerns itself with the conversion of the above material into an implementable form and the production of compilable source code. The third major activity in the Production Phase – Unit Testing – is not covered

by JSD, except in so far as JSD's emphasis on semi-mechanical transformations is designed to produce programs that are correct because of the way they have been designed rather than because they have been subjected to a lot of testing.

This representation of our system could in principle be implemented directly by using one microprocessor for each process and shared memory for communications between them. This is not a practical proposition in general!

Implementation JSD-style is therefore concerned with

- how to share processors amongst processes,
- how to schedule processes, and
- how to share memory amongst parts of a process.

This requires us to transform the *process text* produced so far into *program text* in such a way that processor time and space are effectively shared. Preferably such transformations should be mechanical and JSD supports this preference.

The time has come for our system to be moulded to fit the target environment – the operating system, hardware architecture and so on. From our single target-independent specification we are in a position to derive different implementations depending on the constraints that apply and facilities that are available on the target.

Among the solutions to the problem of sharing processors between processes are all the traditional time-slicing, multi-tasking and multi-programming techniques.

Alternatively, we can also consider ways of reducing the number of processes that we have produced in our system so far. JSD provides such reduction transformations in a mechanical form and in the remainder of this section we look at some of them. The aim, remember, is to reduce the number of processes to the point where the remaining ones can be sensibly accommodated on the target system.

The techniques include:

- those involving 'process inversion';
- those involving 'state-vector separation'.

Under one form of process inversion, two or more processes that communicate through data streams are turned into subroutines subordinate to a 'scheduler'. The scheduler and its subroutines form a single process. This process has the same external interfaces with the outside world as had the original set of processes. Thus, the SID in figure 7.1 becomes the SID in figure 7.2. This act of inversion requires:

- the transformation of the process text for X and Y to
  - make each into a subroutine,
  - replace read-XY by 'suspend back to scheduler remembering suspension point to await write',
  - replace write-XY by 'suspend back to scheduler remembering suspension point to await read';
- the writing of a scheduler root process that calls the new subroutines, arbitrates on the next-to-run according to some 'fair' scheduling algorithm, and receives and passes data records between the subroutines.

Where a pair of processes are connected solely by one data stream and no rough merges are involved, inversion can be achieved without the need for a scheduler simply by making one process into a subroutine subordinate to the other. The latter takes on the role of 'master' and assumes responsibility for the transfer of data between itself and the new subroutine and for the relative scheduling. Figure 7.3 shows the two ways this inversion can be done.

Similar techniques are available for making one process out of a chain of processes communicating through data streams by effectively extending the above techniques with more complex schedulers or scheduling components in the 'master' routine. Where it is impossible to schedule processes in such a way that buffering between processes is unnecessary, buffers can be introduced. These are placed under the control of the scheduler and directly accessible only by the scheduler.

So much for transformations that involve process inversion. The other type of transformation – 'state-vector separation' – is used where we wish to deal with a large (and possibly variable) number of processes modelling identical entities, such as customers of a bank or equipment sensors. We can view this situation as consisting of one

Fig. 7.1. A pair of processes ripe for inversion in JSD.

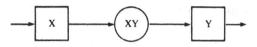

Fig. 7.2. Processes X and Y inverted with respect to the datastream XY.

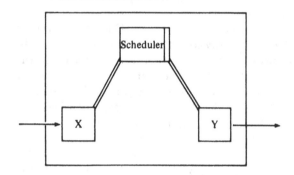

Fig. 7.3. JSD process inversion without a scheduler.

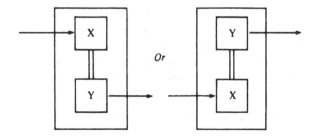

process type with a number of instantiations depending on the number of entities. Each instantiation has its own state-vector (describing the status of that entity in its lifetime) but can share a single copy of the program text.

The transformation here reduces the variable number of processes to a single scheduler process plus the state-vectors, now separated from the process instantiations. The state-vectors are typically stored together, accessed by the scheduler and associated with the process text as and when required.

What we have reached through semi-formal and semi-mechanical means is the traditional transaction-driven database type of system with the state-vectors appearing as records in the database.

The crucial feature of JSD *implementation* is that it primarily consists of taking the design in the form of structure text for processes, and transforming it into code by performing semi-mechanical operations on it. The resulting code (generally packed with the abominated **goto**) is considered to be *object code*, even though it might be, say, COBOL. In other words, although the deliverable item of this phase under JSD is (as with all other procedures) compilable source code, in JSD this code is never written directly or changed – it is only generated from higher level descriptions.

This has an important implication for the testing, maintenance and enhancement activities in the Production and Post-Acceptance Development Phases since all changes to the system are made to the *structure text* of processes, followed by re-application of the appropriate transformations. This distinguishes Jackson System Development from traditional techniques where bug correction and enhancement are typically carried out on the final program source (or even the object code in extreme cases!).

Indicators during JSD

Having completed our brief survey of JSD we can look back at the sorts of indicators that we could use for estimating the size of our system, its complexity, our progress, and so on. The following list can readily be drawn up (Jackson 1983):

- the number of entity types in the model,

- the number of actions in each entity structure,
- the number of nodes in each entity structure,
- the number of functions (perhaps classified by the way they are embedded into the model),
- the number of process types in the SSD,
- the number of processors, real or simulated, to be used,
- the complexity of the necessary transformations, measured by the number of data streams in each inversion.

A JSD Work Breakdown Structure

This is also a convenient moment at which to propose a simple Work Breakdown Structure for JSD to cover the Definition, Design and Production Phases. A point worth noting is the way that JSD provides good modelling facilities right from the beginning.

```
2000 System Definition
     2100 System Definition Management
     2200 Produce Entity/Action Descriptions
          2210 Entity Action step
          2220 Entity Structure step
     2300 Produce Project Plan
     2400 Produce Quality Management Plan
     2500 Produce Acceptance Test Specification
     2600 Perform System Modelling
3000 System Design
     3100 System Design Management
     3200 Specify System Design
          3210 Initial Model step
          3220 Function step
          3230 System Timing step
     3300 Refine Project Plan
     3400 Refine Quality Management Plan
     3500 Refine System Models
          3510 Build prototypes for function
          3520 Build prototypes for performance
     3600 Prepare Acceptance Test Description
4000 System Production
     4100 System Production Management
     4200 Produce System for Trial
          4210 Implementation step
          4220 Carry out detailed tests
     4300 Prepare User Documentation
     4400 Prepare Training Schedules
     4500 Prepare Acceptance Test Description
     4600 Prepare System Conversion Schedule
```

Exercises

1 Compare the two forms of inversion in figure 7.3 with program inversion in JSP.
2 Compare the various schedulers generated by process inversion and state-vector separation with the notion of 'access mechanisms' in MASCOT. Both have responsibility for controlling access by processes to communications data structures and in particular for deciding which processes will run next, i.e. for scheduling.

7.4.3 Finite State Machines – FSM

In section 6.4.4 we described how a system can be designed as a hierarchy of FSMs. The principal product of the Design Phase is likely to be a set of state transition tables along with some form of documentation describing the inputs to the FSMs and the actions that occur under the control of the FSM.

During the Production Phase, each of the modules carrying out the actions will first be designed in detail and then coded and unit tested. A suitable documentation form for the detailed design of action modules is PDL. Since most, if not all, of the decision making in a program designed as an FSM is in the FSM control module (see figure 7.4), action modules will typically contain little or no decision making and consequently are very easily designed, coded and unit tested.

In addition to the action modules, data hiding principles (see section 7.4.10) suggest that modules should exist that hide the precise form of the inputs to and outputs from the FSM. For example, in the FSM considered in section 6.4.4 there was an abstract input 'capture animation sequence'. This abstraction should be maintained

Fig. 7.4. PDL representation of an FSM control module.

```
MODULE fsm_control
    state := initial_state;
    DO WHILE NOT (state = end_state)
        CALL get_input (input);
        action := action_table (input, state);
        new_state := state_table (input, state);
        DO CASE (action)
            /action_1/ CALL action_1;
            ...
            /action_N/ CALL action_N
            ELSE invalid action
        END_CASE;
        state := new_state
    END_WHILE
END_MODULE
```

by a module which hides the fact that this input is implemented by, say, the ASCII string 'STX, 6, 4, ETX' coming over a serial communications link from the HOST.

Finally, when the control module and the action and input/output modules have been integrated, the test sequence generation methods mentioned in section 5.4.7 can be used to check that the program or system as implemented meets its specification.

7.4.4 System Architect's Apprentice – SARA

In section 6.4 we described how SARA is used in top-down, requirements driven system design and how it allows for the bottom-up re-use of existing modules. In the first stage of the Production Phase, the decomposition of the system into modules is continued until a sufficient level of detail is reached for it to be demonstrable that all of the system's requirements will be satisfied. Having reached this stage, the bottom-level modules are coded, using their GMBs as specifications, tested, to ensure that they satisfy their requirements, and integrated into higher level modules. In their turn these higher level modules are tested and integrated. This bottom-up composition continues until the system is complete.

Let us consider these stages in a little more detail. The first stage of top-down decomposition is exactly the same as described in chapter 6 and will not be elaborated on. The production of code from the PLIP interpretations of processors is generally very straightforward (see Campos 1978*b*), especially if coding is performed in PL/1. The implementation of the flow of control as specified in the control graphs can be more difficult when concurrency is involved. Unless a concurrent programming language such as Concurrent PASCAL or Ada is used the facilities of the operating system will generally be heavily relied upon to implement such control graphs (see exercise 1).

Testing of a SARA module involves showing that the module satisfies the requirements that have been mapped onto it. Since the only parts of a module visible to the outside world are its sockets, this testing involves sending data and control in through the module's sockets and checking that the data and control that return satisfy the requirements. If the interface presented at a socket is fairly 'clean', say implemented by procedure calls, then such testing is very straightforward. Moreover, such an interface is very easily 'stubbed', by replacing the interface procedures by dummy procedures.

Exercise
Ignoring the context and nature of the processing of the GMB shown in figures 6.30 and 6.31 decide how you might implement the flow of control and activation of processors using
    (i) a concurrent programming language
    (ii) a non-concurrent programming language and operating system facilities with which you are familiar. (Hint: For example, the token on arc N4-A5 might be implemented by a timer-set event flag.)

7.4.5 MASCOT

System Production under MASCOT
During the Design Phase the MASCOT technique produced a number of deliverable items that form the input to the Production Phase – see section 6.4.7. The principal ones with which we will be concerned here are the Activity-Channel-Pool (ACP) network and the material derived from it, together with the test strategies.

The ACP network embodies the data flow through the system by identifying processing activities communicating data via channels and pools. The remaining steps fall into two groups:

Detailed design:
- designing the intercommunication data areas (IDAs);
- designing the roots, i.e. the activities themselves;
- designing the various levels of tests.

Implementation and test:
- coding the roots and the access mechanisms;
- carrying out the tests.

It is at this point that we introduce the 'MASCOT Machine'. The MASCOT Machine supports application development via a set of construction tools, and collaborates in the running of an application by providing a virtual machine that contains primitives for the control of subsystems and activities. In effect the purpose of the run-time part of the MASCOT Machine is to raise the level of the

virtual machine offered by the host operating system (if indeed there is one) to a standard level appropriate to a MASCOT design.

MASCOT detailed design
1 Designing the IDAs
It is likely that both from system to system and within a single system there will be a number of commonly used IDAs. The first place to look therefore for the design of an IDA and its access mechanisms is in a library of them. MSA 1980 lists a number of standard ones and the implementer would add his own to these.

Since the synchronisation and control of activities are embeddded in the design of the access mechanisms, the designer of IDAs must become familiar with the scheduling and synchronisation primitives supplied by the MASCOT Machine and the scheduling algorithms behind them. These include operations such as STIM which activates another activity via a control queue, WAIT which allows an activity to wait for a corresponding STIM, SUSPEND which permits co-operative scheduling and DELAY which allows an activity to be suspended for a given period. This crucial work therefore requires the designer to have a clear understanding of the synchronisation requirements of his design in order to map them onto MASCOT primitives.

2 Designing the roots
A 'root' is the implemented form of an activity. It is designed as a normal single thread, a sequential program unit, and any design technique can be used that the designer favours.

3 Designing the tests
The overall procedures drawn up in the Design Phase are now refined, and any manual procedures or special software required are defined. Four levels of testing are identified:
- IDA tests. These firstly require the building of a simple ACP network sufficient to guarantee all possible synchronisation situations. Test roots are then devised to initialise, inspect and

access the IDAs via the access mechanisms and to record the sequential data values for verification.

- Root tests. These involve internal path testing of each root using conventional means and the testing of interfaces using simulated IDA access mechanisms.
- Activity tests. The activity is now connected to its channels and pools. External stimuli are generated and their effects monitored by test activities also connected to the IDAs.
- Integration tests. Each subsystem is now put together from its constituent activities and their IDAs. Simulation software (perhaps constituted in part by already-tested subsystems) is placed around the subsystem under test and the subsystem is exercised as a whole.
- Acceptance tests. No special help is available here from the standard MASCOT Machine.

In summary, the outputs of this phase of a MASCOT implementation are detailed design carried to the point where all design decisions have been made and detailed test procedures have been described for all levels of testing.

MASCOT implementation and test Coding proceeds directly from the detailed design and the software source code is then entered into the development system. This will typically not be the same as the target system – for instance, if the software is destined for an embedded micro. However, the development system will also have a MASCOT Machine with its construction tools and facilities for hosting tests.

Construction of a MASCOT-based system takes place in three stages:

- the specification of the elements of the system (roots, channels and pools) and their inclusion ('enrolment') in a Construction Data Base,
- the creation of System Elements,
- the formation of Subsystems from System Elements.

The specification of a System Element (SE) takes the form of a template giving its name, its

connectivity constraints and the places from which its constituent parts can be retrieved. The last is required since an SE may involve programs from a number of sources that require to be combined in some way.

Creation of an SE makes use of the appropriate template to build the root, channel or pool, details of which are also inserted into the Construction Data Base. Subsystem forming makes use of these created SEs to build executable software whose modularity is consistent with the ACP diagram and in which the required connectivity of the SEs (defined by the templates) is assured.

As the system is gradually constructed from the SEs, tests are carried out according to the plans laid in the previous stage: IDAs, roots, activities, subsystem and finally system.

The MASCOT Machine
Figure 7.5 summarises the major elements of

Fig. 7.5. The major elements of the MASCOT machine. (After MSA 1980.)

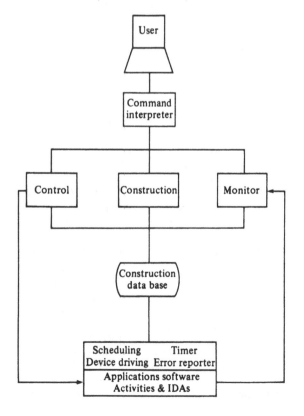

the MASCOT Machine whilst figure 7.6 lists the facilities that it might offer. Exactly which are available on a given implementation will vary but some items are considered mandatory.

Construction tools may be realised by using the development facilities on the host machine – say, those supplied by the manufacturer – or by a specially developed package. They cover compiling, link editing, filing and maintenance of the Construction Data Base.

The real-time tools cover:

- Subsystem control: start, halt, resume and terminate.
- Scheduling: priorities, mutual exclusion, cross stimulation, etc.

- Device handling: perhaps through a host OS.
- Monitoring: the selection of events, their recording and processing during testing.

Like construction tools, real-time tools might either build on host system software or be built especially for a bare machine.

The Work Breakdown Structure

From the above brief description of MASCOT production we can expand the System Production activity of our WBS thus:

```
4000  System Production
      4100  System Production Management
      4200  Produce System for Trial
            4210  Detailed design
                  4211  Design IDAs
                  4212  Design roots
                  4213  Design unit tests
            4220  Implementation
                  4221  Code IDAs
                  4222  Code roots
                  4223  Prepare test environment
            4230  Unit testing
                  4231  Enrol IDAs and roots
                  4232  Create IDAs and roots
                  4233  Test IDAs
                  4234  Test roots
                  4235  Test activities
            4240  Integration
                  4241  Test activities (IDAs and roots)
                  4242  Form Subsystems
                  4243  Test Subsystems
      4300  Prepare User Documentation
      4400  Prepare Training Schedules
      4500  Prepare Acceptance Test Schedule
      4600  Prepare System Conversion Schedule.
```

Fig. 7.6. The facilities of the MASCOT machine. (After MSA 1980.)

Constructing....	Building.........	Compiler, Link Editors ENROL CREATE FORM
	Dismantling.....	CANCEL DESTROY DELETE
Controlling.............................		START TERMINATE HALT RESUME
Scheduling.......	....	Scheduler JOIN WAIT LEAVE STIM
	Synchronising...	
	Timing...........	Timer DELAY TIMENOW
	Suspending & Terminating..	SUSPEND ENDROOT
Device Handling........................		Drivers Handlers CONNECT DISCONNECT STIMINT ENDHANDLER
Monitoring......	Recording....... Selecting.........	RECORD SELECT EXCLUDE
	....	Error Reporter
Interacting.............................		Command Interpreter

Exercises

1 What types of data structure might be suited to an implementation of a MASCOT channel and what features would you ideally want to see in a language in order to handle access mechanisms well?

2 What operations can you imagine that would typically need to be performed on a channel, and hence what access mechanisms might you need?

3 Putting your answers to 1 and 2 together, draw up a 'library' of IDAs and access mechanisms that would be frequently useful.

4 Consider an operating system with which you are familiar and see how far it goes to providing the

functions of a MASCOT Machine. How would you augment and build upon it to produce the functions of a MASCOT Machine described above?

7.4.6 Hierarchical Development Methodology – HDM

Work Breakdown Structure

In section 6.4.9 we saw that the HDM development methodology is divided into seven stages, the last two of which, abstract implementation and concrete implementation, fall within the System Production Phase. A typical WBS for the Production Phase of an HDM project might be

```
4000    System Production
   4100    System Production Management
   4200    Produce System for Trial
      4210    Abstract implementation
         4211 Write and verify ILPL for module A
         4212 Write and verify ILPL for module B
                ⋮
      4220    Concrete implementation
         4221 Code module A
         4222 Code module B
                ⋮
      4230    Carry out program level proof of
              system
      4240    Integrate coded modules
   4300–4600  as normal
```

As we mentioned in section 3.18, the step involving abstract implementation is usually missed in practice. However it is still interesting from the point of view of program proving and is included here as it completes one of the few methods that, in theory, allow continuous proof of correctness from specification to code.

Our HDM example continued

In this section we extend the example of the use of HDM given in section 6.4.9 by giving the abstract implementation of part of the top-level module 'reservation' in terms of the bottom-level module 'assignment' (see figure 7.7).

From the module specification of module 'reservation' (figure 6.40) we see that there is only one function to be implemented, namely the O-function 'reserve'. The V-functions are hidden and consequently do not require implementation. The mapping function (figure 6.42) tells us how the

top-level data is related to bottom-level data and thus guides the writing of the ILPL implementation.

The O-function 'reserve' results in an ILPL OPROG called 'reserve' which, under normal conditions, effects the change of the top-level state 'reserved' to TRUE by using first the bottom-level O-function 'allocate' and then the OV-function 'assign'. The ILPL EXECUTE construct allows us to handle exceptions returned by 'allocate' and to accordingly raise exceptions specified for 'reserve' in its module specification. If 'allocate' returns an exception then neither allocation nor assignment occur and the state of 'reserved' is not changed.

As with most ILPL constructs, it is not difficult to see how to translate OPROG 'reserve' into any structured programming language and we leave this step as an exercise for the reader.

Fig. 7.7. The HDM ILPL implementation of the 'reservation' module of figure 6.40.

```
IMPLEMENTATION reservation IN TERMS OF assignment;

    EXTERNALREFS

    FROM reservation
VFUN reserved (user u, vice v) → BOOLEAN b;

    FROM assignment
VFUN assigned (process p, device d) → BOOLEAN b;
VFUN allocated (process p, device d) → BOOLEAN b;

    FROM users:
user: DESIGNATOR;

    FROM vices:
vice: DESIGNATOR;

    FROM processes:
process: DESIGNATOR;

    FROM devices:
device: DESIGNATOR;

    TYPEMAPPINGS
user: process;
vice: device;

    $(no INITIALISATION paragraph is needed as the lower
      level machine forces the correct initial state for the
      upper level reservation module)

    IMPLEMENTATIONS

OPROG reserve (user u, vice v);
BEGIN
    EXECUTE allocate(u,v) THEN
        ON no_process: RAISE (not_logged_on);
        ON no_device: RAISE (no_vice);
        ON already_allocated: RAISE (unavailable);
        ON NORMAL: END;
    assign (u,v);
END;
END_IMPLEMENTATION
```

7.4.7 Structured programming

Background

As we said in chapter 3, 'structured programming' is a useful umbrella term for a group of techniques and principles applicable to the design and coding of programs. There are, in fact, two strands that run together.

'Stepwise refinement' is about producing programs by making a series of small steps, each step increasing the level of detail and representing some design decision; it is a technique of design that is carried out in a form of high-level language and which can therefore lead you finally straight into code. 'Pure' structured programming is essentially about coding programs in such a way that you can *prove* their correctness.

We start by taking these two strands separately and then go on to look at the benefits of using them in tandem.

Stepwise refinement

In a seminal paper on the topic (Wirth 1971), Niklaus Wirth identified the creative activity of programming as consisting of a sequence of design decisions made about two parallel decompositions: that of tasks into sub-tasks and that of data into data structures. His proposition was that each decomposition step – each successive 'refinement' of a program – should result from a single design decision.

The guidelines proposed for determining the next refinement (i.e. design decision) are that it should:

- decompose decisions as much as possible,
- disentangle aspects which are only seemingly dependent (i.e. reveal the true structure), and
- defer those decisions which concern details of representation (particularly of data) as long as possible.

This third point is important as it leads us to two principles elaborated by other writers. Firstly, it hints at the principle of 'information hiding' described by Parnas in Parnas 1972*a*, 1972*b* and 1976*a*, and which we cover in the next section. This says that the decomposition of a program into modules should be steered not so much according to functionality but more with the aim of restricting knowledge about the representation of data to single modules. Secondly, it hints at Dijkstra's principle of the 'separation of concerns' – particularly the separation of the problem of correctness from the problem of program engineering. We should aim, the principle says, to isolate mere implementation detail from the question of how to structure and write a program that is provably correct.

Linger 1979 reinforces the separation, suggesting that a program produced strictly by stepwise refinement is likely to be inefficient but that the refinement process is concerned with correctness, not efficiency. There should therefore be a second, separate step – 'stepwise re-organisation' – during which the program is re-organised for efficiency, once more in small steps so that the new program can be *proved* to carry out the same function.

Wirth's other criteria for decomposition include efficiency, storage economy, clarity and regularity of structure. Insofar as these are engineering matters, we should aim to isolate them from the more formal problems of program construction.

Wirth notes that stepwise refinement needs a sympathetic notation – FORTRAN, he says, could not be worse, not least because it fails to allow us to give a 'natural' expression to the program and data structure revealed by the refinement process. Some years later, Caine and Gordon (Caine 1975) published a description of a 'Program Design Language' (PDL) better suited to the representation of a design.

The principles of stepwise refinement as applied to writing code are well illustrated in Dijkstra's essay 'Notes on structured programming' in Dahl 1972. In a detailed treatment of the coding of a program to calculate and print the first 1 000 primes he illustrates a number of features of the technique. The program is composed one step at a time with each step deciding as little as possible. A lot of programming is done whilst major decisions remain open, so a subsequent change of mind affects as little as possible of the code written so far.

Although stepwise refinement has an essentially 'top-down' feel about it, iteration must be expected and the process will also be guided by data structuring considerations (q.v.) and program proving (q.v.). The resulting program may have a hierarchical structure but the process of *deriving* it will not necessarily proceed in strict hierarchical fashion.

Program families

Having seen stepwise refinement as a sequence of design decisions we can go on to develop the idea of 'program families', hinted at by Dijkstra 1970 and Wirth 1971 and elaborated in Parnas 1976*a*.

At any given level of refinement we proceed to the next by choosing some point of the design and making a decision on how to refine it. A number of different decisions might be possible and we may not be able (or may not wish) to eliminate all but one at the current stage. The set of possible decisions generates a set of possible programs – a 'program family'. As decomposition proceeds we can imagine a tree of possible programs rooted in the single original statement along the lines of figure 7.8.

This idea has important implications where (when!) a program is modified. Ideally we would like the original program (P1) and the new version (P2) to be members of the same family. If we can recognise their common ancestor in the documentation there is a strong possibility that P1 and P2 will share correctness proofs to a lesser or greater degree, that they will have coding in common, and that the modifications that lead to P2 will be carried out on isolated regions of P1. If we simply regard P1 as a linear series of symbols, modification could become prohibitively difficult.

Pure structured programming

In his essay 'Notes on structured programming', Dijkstra identifies careful program structuring as a consequence of our desire to be able to prove that a program is 'correct', i.e. that there is a correspondence between its action and its intended function. Such structuring, he says, should also anticipate adaptations and modifications of a pro-

Fig. 7.8. A program family.

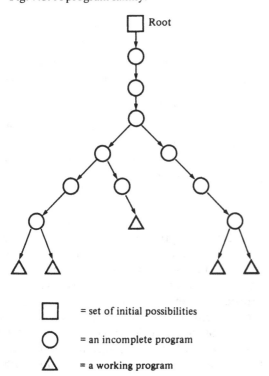

☐ = set of initial possibilities

◯ = an incomplete program

△ = a working program

Fig. 7.9. The preferred constructs of structured programming.

sequence: X; Y

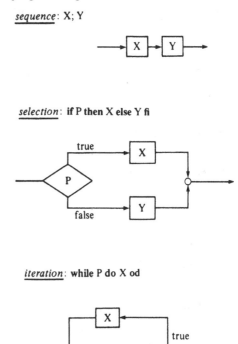

selection: **if** P **then** X **else** Y **fi**

iteration: **while** P **do** X **od**

gram. It should also be clear from the structure what sort of adaptations could be catered for cleanly.

To satisfy these aims, we are asked first to restrict our code to using only three constructs: sequence, selection and iteration. Figure 7.9 illustrates them.

Programs composed of only these three constructs are amenable to a variety of techniques of 'program proving'. Program proving is, at the time of writing, still restricted to smallish programs – perhaps less than a hundred lines. Proofs tend to be large – generally longer than the program itself – and, of course, susceptible to error as much as the original act of coding. However, there will still be situations where the heavy investment in proving is justified by the criticality of the code concerned. Even if you have no intention of doing any program proving, the other benefits of adopting structured programming techniques are considerable and well-known.

A number of approaches to program proving can be found in the literature, Linger 1979 and Dijkstra 1976 for instance. Linger 1979 treats programs as mathematical objects whose correctness is subject to logical reasoning. To assist that

reasoning process, programs are precisely expressed in a 'process design language' (PDL) taking after Caine and Gordon's PDL. This process design language possesses both 'outer syntax' and 'inner syntax'.

Outer syntax (the most important) comprises control, data and system structures with important mathematical properties. In fact it is the control structures that are most important for proving. Inner syntax tends towards greater informality of expression and does not concern us here.

In structured programming, one is restricted to writing 'proper programs' (in their terminology) – i.e. programs that have a single entry and single exit point and in which, for each node (an operation), there is a path from the entry point, through that node, to the exit point. A 'prime program' is then a proper program with no proper non-trivial subprograms. There are an infinity of prime programs including those traditionally employed in structured programming and offered as control constructs in modern programming languages:

> function (i.e. as single operation)
> function; function (sequence)
> **if** . . . **then** . . . (selection)
> **while** . . . **do** . . . (iteration)
> **do** . . . **until** . . . (another sort of iteration).

Linger 1979 then goes on to define a 'structured program' as one obtained by replacing the function nodes of a prime program with prime programs, all the prime programs being chosen from a fixed set. (A moment's reflection will reveal the connection here with stepwise refinement.) In figure 7.10 the function nodes X and Y in an initial prime program are replaced by prime programs, and in these further functions are replaced by yet other prime programs.

Once one has these ideas, a significant theorem can be proved, namely that for any proper program there is a structured program based on the sequence, selection and iteration primes only and with the same function. Once this has been proved, we can restrict our consideration of correctness proving to those three prime constructs. The theory is then developed to show that the correctness of loop-free programs can be verified by an analysis of the different execution paths of

Fig. 7.10. Refining a structured program.

Given the initial prime program

```
if P then X else Y fi
```

we can replace X by the prime program

```
while P1 do X1 od
```

to get the new prime program

```
if P then while P1 do X1 od
        else Y
fi
```

If we then replace X1 by

```
X1A; X1B
```

and Y by

```
if P2 then Y1 else y2 fi
```

we obtain the structured program

```
if P then while P1 do X1A;
                      X1B
                  od
     else if P2 then Y1
                  else Y2
              fi
fi
```

the program, and the verification of looping programs that terminate is reduced to the verification of equivalent loop-free programs. The three results taken together make program proofs a practical proposition, provided we restrict ourselves to writing structured programs.

(As an aside, it is this sort of result that is the motivation behind the proscription of the **goto** statement, a movement triggered by Dijkstra's open letter entitled 'Go to statements considered harmful' (Dijkstra 1968).)

Now that the problem has been reduced to manageable *logical* proportions, a number of techniques can be brought to bear. (The *logistic* proportions will still however be significant in terms of the size of proofs!)

For a program consisting only of a sequence, a *trace table* can be drawn up that simply follows the values of variables to determine (and hence prove) the program's function. The final values of variables (i.e. the outputs) are expressed as functions of the old values (i.e. the inputs). For programs with if–then–else structures we use a *set* of trace tables, each simple trace table corresponding to a particular combination of condition values disjoint from the cases of the other trace tables.

For–do programs are considered to be abbreviations for long repetitive sequence programs with one data item (the control variable) under the control of the for–do. The procedure here is to construct a trace table, hypothesise a program function from early steps and prove it by induction.

(It is important to grasp from all of this the way that stepwise refinement and program proving (based on pure structured programming) are intimately linked.)

Finally, we mention here *program invariants*. These offer an alternative technique for program proving and are particularly important in the handling of for–do loops. A 'loop invariant' for instance is a logical condition that remains true after each execution of the loop body. It can be appreciated that if an invariant is strong enough, it can characterise the program function. Investigation of invariants can therefore be used as a means of proof whilst the initial identification of invariants can be used to guide program construction. These ideas are expanded in great detail in Dijkstra 1976.

Work Breakdown Structure

Because the techniques of structured programming are largely of a detailed nature they do not give us any further breakdown of our Work Breakdown Structure. They can, however, strongly influence the planning and allocation of work.

Stepwise refinement can be expected to give you a basis for dividing the production of a large program amongst a number of people. Information hiding helps to isolate the different parts of a program. Separation of concerns suggests that production should be a two-stage process – the first concerned solely with getting a correct program, the second with optimising that program into a more efficient (yet still correct) program. (See Jackson System Development for a similar attitude.) The level of program proving you decide on will be determined by whether the reliability required of your program justifies the expense.

Whether or not you decide to take on program proving as a technique, all aspects of your development program will benefit from the adoption of the other aspects of structured programming. Much experience and experiment have shown that reliability, maintainability, adaptability and portability are all improved. The dangers that you should be aware of are however that proofs themselves can contain errors and that 'physical' conditions such as limited word lengths, rounding errors and so on will need special handling. Nevertheless professional programmers can considerably improve their skills through an understanding of the underlying theory.

Bibliography
Alagić 1978, Anderson 1974, Berg 1982, Bjorner 1982, Caine 1975 (an early description of Program Design Language (PDL) and some of the tools that were developed commercially to support it), Cichelli 1977 (a paper on the related topic of goal-directed programming), Dahl 1972 (contains lecture notes by Dijkstra covering the structuring constructs, stepwise program composition, program families and layered programs), Dijkstra 1968 (the letter that started the **goto** controversy), Dijkstra 1972 (an early paper containing the seeds of 'program families' and of 'information hiding' ideas covered elsewhere in this chapter), Dijkstra

1976 (a book, at once conversational and theoretical, that covers the formal aspects of correctness proving and program derivation, Hester 1981, Infotech 1976 (a collection of papers and analyses of the topic from a variety of authors), Ledgard 1973, McGowan 1975, Parnas 1972*a* (a paper elaborating the principle of 'information hiding' as the criterion for module decomposition), Parnas 1972*b* (a description of a technique for writing module specifications that are both minimal and sufficient), Parnas 1976*a* (a paper on the use of 'information hiding' as the principle guiding stepwise refinement decisions and leading to 'program families'), Parnas 1977 (a paper discussing how structuring can improve the reliability/robustness of programs), Parnas 1983, Peters 1978*a* (compares stepwise refinement with other design techniques), Reynolds 1981, Sharma 1981, Shneiderman 1976, Wirth 1971 (one of the earliest papers describing stepwise refinement and identifying 'program families' and 'information hiding'), Wulf 1977.

Exercises

1 Using stepwise refinement, write a program in a structured language with which you are familiar to count the number of primes between an arbitrary pair of integers. You must include code that generates primes or tests for primality. At each refinement, note down the design decision you have made as the new branch from the current node in a decision tree. At each revoking of a design decision record the new one as a further branch from the same node.

Note the iterative process producing a hierarchically structured result. Note the family of programs or potential programs you generate via the decision tree. At each refinement carry out an informal proof that the resulting program does/does not work. At each decision determine whether you are refining the control structure or data structure and mark a 'C' or a 'D' on the appropriate branch. Do Cs or Ds appear most at the top of the tree? If Ds, try again this time aiming to get Cs there.

2 What sort of interactive tools would you like to have to support stepwise refinement? Would you want such tools to do some form of consistency and completeness checking as well as being just typographical or graphical aids? Compare your requirements with the tools described in Petrone 1982, Cunningham 1976, Allison 1983 and Feiler 1981.

7.4.8 Control of data

Structured programming as described in the preceding section concerns itself with the control and procedural aspects of programs and does not deal with the data manipulated by them. The control of data in software development can have a considerable impact on such factors as development productivity and program testability, reliability, portability and maintainability. By 'control of data' we mean the control of its specification and documentation, of its implementation and change, and of the way in which it is accessed.

By way of illustrating these concepts, consider the sample 'Data Specification' given in figure 7.11. A system in which all data is itemised in this way might be considered to be quite well documented and indeed documentation of this type or similar is used for describing data in many contemporary software development projects. However, the example is deficient in more than one respect. The natural language description of the use of the data is very imprecise and leaves many questions unanswered (e.g. What is a 'message'? In what order are the bytes of a message stored in a buffer?). This might not be too serious a problem if only one person were ever to use the data item (although with such a vague description it is likely that even the item's implementer might use it inconsistently). In a project involving more than one person such imprecise definition can very

Fig. 7.11. A natural language data specification for the data item BUFFERS.

```
            DATA SPECIFICATION
DATA ITEM        : BUFFERS
IMPLEMENTATION: INTEGER*1 BUFFERS
                 (10,51)
                 COMMON/BUFFERS/
                 BUFFERS
DESCRIPTION      :
```

Provides a pool of 10 buffers for storing messages of lengths up to 100 bytes.
BUFFERS(I,1) contains the number of bytes stored in buffer I. The digits making up the message will be encoded into BCD before being stored in the buffer.

easily lead to inconsistent use of data and thus to testing and reliability problems.

In the example, this problem is exacerbated by the way in which the data item is implemented. The specification of BUFFERS as a FORTRAN COMMON means that more likely than not it is to be accessed from all over the program, Thus a change in requirements leading to a change in the data item (such as an increase in the maximum message size to a value that cannot be represented as INTEGER*1) will require all usages of the data item to be located, so making maintenance difficult.

The problems associated with this example can be classified as problems of *specification* and *access* control. Solutions to both of these problems have been embodied in a number of the 'brand name' methodologies that we have considered (for example HOS and HDM). These methodologies use techniques of information hiding, data abstraction and formal specification developed by Parnas, Hoare and others (see the end of section bibliography). Even if you do not use one of the branded methodologies you should consider using the techniques just mentioned as an alternative to the type of data specification and usage discussed in association with figure 7.11. Let us consider the techniques in more detail.

Information hiding as described by Parnas (1972*a*) generally means the hiding of the details of design decisions within modules in such a way that (most) changes of design will have no effect on the interface that the module presents to the outside world. As applied to data in particular, information hiding means encapsulating all the details of implementation of a data item within a module, only allowing access to the data in a very controlled fashion.

The control of access to data hidden in a module is most naturally performed by way of *data abstraction*. In the example of figure 7.11 we are attempting to describe not a two-dimensional array of integers but rather a collection of abstract objects, namely buffers. The users of a buffer should not need to be aware that we have taken the detailed design decision to implement in a buffer as part of a two-dimensional integer array. All they should need to know are the operations that may be performed on a buffer. Thus, a controlled inter-

face to a module hiding the detailed implementation of buffers might provide operations to assign a free buffer, copy a message to a buffer, read a message from a buffer and de-assign a buffer. If we needed to change our implementation of a buffer (for example by using the operating system to dynamically allocate storage), the interface to the module would remain unchanged.

The way in which data abstraction modules and operations are implemented will depend very much on the programming language that you are using. A number of languages explicitly support abstract data types as language elements: Ada (DoD 1980), ALPHARD (Wulf 1976), CLU (Liskov 1977*a*), Concurrent Pascal (Brinch Hansen 1975), Euclid (Lampson 1977), Madcap (Wells 1976), Mesa (Geschke 1977), Model (Johnson 1976), Modula (Wirth 1977) and SIMULA67 (Dahl 1968). Others add them to existing languages such as the PLUM extension of PL/1 (Zelkowitz 1978) and Enhanced C (Katzenelson 1983*a, b*). In particular, Ada, which will be much used in the future, has drawn on many ideas of earlier data abstraction languages and so typifies many of them. A skeleton implementation of BUFFERS in Ada is given in figure 7.12.

Fig. 7.12. An outline Ada package to implement the abstract data types BUFFER and MESSAGE.

```
package BUFFERS is
    BUFF_DIM: constant :=101;
    MAX_MESSAGE_LENGTH: constant :=50;
    type BUFFER is limited private;
    type MESSAGE is limited private;

    function ASSIGN_BUFFER return BUFFER;
    procedure DEASSIGN_BUFFER (BUFF:MESSAGE);
    function GET_MESSAGE return MESSAGE;
    function MESS_TO_BUFF (MESS:MESSAGE;
                           BUFF:BUFFER) return BUFFER;
private
    type BUFFER is array (1..MAX_MESSAGE_LENGTH) of
                         CHARACTER;
    type BUFFER is array (1..BUFF_DIM) of MESSAGE;
end BUFFERS;

package body BUFFERS is
    MAX_BUFF_NR: constant :=10;
    BUFFER_POOL: array (1..MAX_BUFF_NR) of BUFFER;
    function ASSIGN_BUFFER return BUFFER is
        BUFF_NR: INTEGER:=1;
        begin
            .
            .

            return BUFFER_POOL (BUFF_NR);
        end ASSIGN_BUFFER;
    .
    .
end BUFFERS;
```

There are a number of points worth noting in this example. A data abstraction module in Ada is a 'package'. A package is divided into a package specification and a package body which implements the specification. The first part of the package specification is known as the visible part as it specifies those objects that can be referred to outside the package. In this case the abstract data types BUFFER and MESSAGE and the operators that act on them are specified in the visible part. The data types have been declared as 'limited private' which means that outside the package the only operations allowed on objects of these types are those specified in the visible part of the package. Specifications which follow the keyword 'private' are not visible outside the package and describe how the limited private types are implemented (as arrays). The package body is also not visible outside of the package and it is here that the operators on the abstract types are implemented by manipulating the representations of the types. Thus Ada provides all the constructs that one needs to implement data abstraction and to enforce information hiding and control of access to data.

Even using languages which do not explicitly support abstract data types you can apply a methodology which uses the principles of information hiding and data abstraction. For example, figure 7.13 gives a skeleton for part of a module implementing buffers in the C programming language (Kernighan 1978). In C, 'static' variables defined outside any program block are only accessible within the file in which they are defined. Thus, the detailed implementation of 'message' and 'buffers' as arrays in figure 7.13 is only known within the file BUFFERS. Outside of the BUFFERS module, buffers and messages are referenced by pointers which for clarity have had associated with them the keywords BUFFER and MESSAGE by way of the C 'typedef' construct. Figure 7.14 illustrates the use of these abstract data types by a main program.

A good example of how to use data abstraction in FORTRAN, which supports neither pointers nor sophisticated scoping, can be found in Isner 1982.

The techniques discussed so far solve the problem of access control but still leave open the

Fig. 7.13. An outline implementation in C of the abstract data type BUFFERS.

```
/* FILE BUFFERS - MODULE BUFFERS */

#include "TYPES"
#define MAX_MESS_LENGTH 50
#define MAX_BUFF_SIZE   100
#define BUFF_DIM        MAX_BUFF_SIZE+1
#define MAX_BUFF_NR     10

static char message [MAX_MESS_LENGTH] = {};
static char buffers [MAX_BUFF_NR] [BUFF_DIM] = {};

BUFFER assign_buffer ()
{
    ...
    return (buffers [i]);
}

deassign_buffer (buff)
BUFFER buff;
{
    ...
}

MESSAGE get_message ()
{
    ...
    return message;
}

BUFFER mess_to_buff (mess, buff)
MESSAGE mess,
BUFFER buff;
{
    ...
    return (buff);
}

...

/* END OF MODULE BUFFERS */

/* FILE TYPES */

typedef char *BUFFER;
typedef char *MESSAGE;

/* END OF FILE TYPES */
```

Fig. 7.14. An example of the use of the abstract data types defined in figure 7.13.

```
/*FILE MAIN_PROG */

#include "TYPES"

main ()
{
    BUFFER my_buff, assign_buffer (), mess_to_buff ();
    MESSAGE get_message;
    ...
    my_buff = assign_buffer ();
    mess_to_buff (get_message (), my_buff);
    ...
    deassign (my_buff);
    ...
}
```

question of control of data specification. For, although the operators in figure 7.13 are probably more self-explanatory than the description of the data item in figure 7.11, the user of, for example, mess-to-buff should be able to determine its effect by studying a specification of the abstract data items BUFFER and MESSAGE rather than having to read the code of the BUFFERS module.

Formal specification methods that provide a solution to the problem of imprecise definitions such as that of figure 7.11 and that work hand-in-hand with the ideas of information hiding and data abstraction have been illustrated by the methods of HDM, which arise from the work of Parnas (1972*b*), and HOS, which uses Hoare's (1969) approach to data specification. A good review of such formal specification methods is given in Liskov 1977*b*.

As a further example of formal specification methods, figure 7.15 gives a partial specification of the abstract data type BUFFER using the algebraic specification technique of Zilles (1975). In this example it is assumed that the abstract type MESSAGE has been previously defined. Using such a specification technique one can easily derive desired properties of the abstract objects, such as

BUFF-TO-MESS (MESS-TO-BUFF
(GET-MESSAGE, ASSIGN-BUFFER))
= GET-MESSAGE,

which is needed in the example of figure 7.14.

The formal specification of data also simplifies the testing of its implementation as it is sufficient to show that the data type as implemented specifies the equations of its specification.

The use of formal data specification methods requires a certain amount of mathematical expertise and time for familiarisation. The benefits of such methods over the informal approach illustrated by figure 7.11 make investment in using such methods well worth considering. Without them, many of the advances being made with the advent of languages such as Ada are largely wasted.

Bibliography
Ames 1978, Bentley 1980, Britton 1981, Gehani 1982, Geschke 1977, Guttag 1976, 1978*a*, 1978*b*, 1980, Hester 1981, Hoare 1972*a*, 1972*b*, Johnson 1976, Kutzler 1983 (an extensive bibliography), Lampson 1977, Liskov 1975, 1977*a*, 1977*b*, Moitra 1982, Morris 1980, Musser 1980, Parnas 1972*a*, 1972*b*, 1976*a*, SIGPLAN 1976, Wells 1976, Wulf 1976, Zelkowitz 1978, Zilles 1975.

Exercises
1 Find as many imprecise or undesirable features as possible in the example of figure 7.11. Note how each feature is likely to affect productivity, testability, reliability, portability, maintainability and other such attributes of the project or software.
2 Either complete the example of figure 7.12 or figure 7.13 or implement similar abstract data types in a different programming language. Pay particular attention to trapping errors.
3 The example of the BUFFER and MESSAGE abstraction given in the text is one in which the concept (of a buffer or message) is not very far removed in level of abstraction from the object implementing it. A much higher degree of abstraction is required in representing the concept of Rubik's cube. Write a module similar to that of exercise 2 which implements Rubik's cube as an abstract data type. (Hint: see Druffel 1982.)

7.4.9 Programming languages
The choice of the programming language that is to be used on a project is often over-emphasised in relation to the tools and methods that are to be applied in the earlier System Definition and Design Phases. The decision of whether to use JSD, for example, rather than an *ad hoc* design method is likely to have much more impact on system reliability, maintainability and development productivity than the decision to use PASCAL rather than C.

Also perhaps of more importance than the choice of programming language is the choice of implementation of the language. There is not much

Fig. 7.15. A partial specification of the abstract data type BUFFER.

```
Functionality:
      ASSIGN_BUFFER  : → BUFFER
      MESS_TO_BUFF   : MESSAGE X BUFFER → BUFFER
      BUFF_TO_MESS   : BUFFER → MESSAGE U {BUFFER_ERROR}
Equations :
      BUFF_TO_MESS (MESS_TO_BUFF (m, b)) = m
      BUFF_TO_MESS (ASSIGN_BUFFER) = BUFFER_ERROR
```

point arguing over whether, for example, PAS-CAL is faster than FORTRAN when there might be a factor of 20 in the efficiency of the code produced by any two compilers for each language (see, for example, Gilbreath 1983). As well as considering performance comparisons of different compilers or interpreters the level of support given to the language implementation should be taken into account. For example, being able to obtain rapid bug fixes from the supplier or having available a source level debugger for the language could have a considerable effect on productivity. Figure 7.16 gives a list of implementation-dependent characteristics that you might check.

Of course before settling on the programming language or languages to be used in a system you should give consideration to language features, in particular in relation to:

(i) special system requirements;
(ii) support for good software engineering principles.

In category (i) might be a requirement for portability over a wide range of processors, while in category (ii) might be support for abstract data types (as discussed in section 7.4.8). Figure 7.17 gives a (non-exhaustive) list of language features that may be of importance. A useful example of a detailed comparison of the features of two languages can be found in Feuer 1982.

Unfortunately the choice of programming language used on a project is often made, not by consideration of factors such as those described above, but by default, as the programming lan-guage that everybody on the team knows. While it is true that climbing the 'learning-curve' with a new language can have a negative effect on productivity, this effect is very small compared with other factors on a project. Boehm 1981 shows from data collected at TRW that the effort required to complete a project can increase by a factor of 1.2 if a team of programmers who have no experience in the programming language is used instead of a team of experts in the language. In comparison, there can be a factor of 4.2 increase if a team of very low general capability is used instead of a team of very high capability. The small increase in effort that might be required, for example, to learn and use a 'portable' programming language instead of a non-portable language that everybody knows might be rewarded by a considerable future saving in maintenance effort.

(For an overview of high-level languages see Sammet 1981.)

Fig. 7.16. Implementation-dependent features of programming languages.

Compliance with language standard
Compilation speed
Execution speed of generated code
Memory usage efficiency of generated code
Compiler optimisation features
Extensiveness of compile-time and run-time error checking
Clarity of error messages
Utility of user documentation
Existence of language-specific debug facilities
Level and quality of supplier support
Existence of integrated static analysis package
Existence of integrated instrumentation package

Fig. 7.17. Features to be considered in choosing a programming language.

Application orientation (eg special purpose simulation language)
Existence of international/national language standard (eg ISO, ANSI, BSI, DIN)
Machine-independence and portability
Type checking
Scoping
Readability
Accuracy (support of multi-word and complex arithmetic)
Complexity
I/O capability (eg report generation)
Existence of compatible library packages
Existence of preprocessors (eg for JSP)
Support of:
    structured programming constructs
    abstract data types
    information hiding
    concurrency
    complex data structures
    strings
    bit manipulation
    pointers
    in-line assembly code
    subprograms in other languages
    macros
    recursion
    dynamic storage allocation
    dynamic data dimensioning

Exercises

1 Using Feuer 1982 and figure 7.17 as guides, produce a comparison of your two favourite programming languages (not those compared in Feuer 1982).

2 If you have had experience with more than one implementation of a given programming language, draw up a comparison using figure 7.16 as a guide.

3 Choose two 'very different' programming languages with which you are familiar (e.g. APL and COBOL, or Ada and FORTRAN) and see how short a procedure you can write to compute the Nth Fibonacci number. (The Nth Fibonacci number, $F(N)$, is defined by

$$F(N) = 0 \text{ if } N = 0$$
$$= 1 \text{ if } N = 1$$
$$= F(N-1) + F(N-2) \text{ if } N > 1.$$

See, for example, Zelkowitz 1979, Ch 3.)

What does the difference in size tell you about the two programming languages? Is this important to system software development? Which of the factors in figure 7.17 played a role in determining the size (if any)? Use other samples of code to calculate the Software Science language level for the two languages (see section 7.5.2). Does the difference in language level of the two languages in any way correlate with the difference in smallest size that you have been able to achieve for the Fibonacci program?

7.4.10 Macroprocessors

Although principally just tools, macroprocessors offer the system developer useful ways of achieving certain technical effects and of increasing productivity. A macroprocessor is essentially a text processor. The idea had its origin decades ago when 'macro commands' were used as shorthand in Assembler programs for common sequences of code that varied only slightly from one instance to another. With the more extensive use of high-level languages interest in them has perhaps waned, possibly unjustifiably as they can have more universal application.

In the old Assembler case they were often used to hide some basic hardware implementation detail from the user. For example, a multiply instruction that exists on one processor may need to be emulated by inline code on another. By using a macro for the instruction the programmer need not worry which processor their program will run on – the macroprocessor generates the appropriate Assembler code prior to the assembly process. This old idea extends to the more modern notions of information hiding and virtual machines within software. Macros then become ways of isolating data representation or control structure details from the user. A macroprocessor can thus become a powerful supplement to your compiler to support you in the use of these techniques.

The idea then extends naturally to text processing of any form, with the line between macroprocessors and compilers becoming blurred – indeed, compilers have been implemented using particular macroprocessors with appropriate macro definitions!

In its simplest form a macroprocessor takes two input files and produces one output file. The two input files contain respectively the definitions of the macros and the text to be processed containing 'macro calls'. The output file is the resulting processed text with all macro calls resolved. A macro definition will typically consist of a template by which a macro call can be identified, definitions of parameters that can be expected and the text that is to be generated, i.e. a description of how a macro call is to be 'expanded' and how it is to vary with different values for the parameters.

Macrodefinitions are frequently recursive and contain both conditional statements to control the expansion process and macro variables that are used by the macroprocessor itself. Figure 7.18 contains an imaginary macro definition for a macro that multiplies two numbers to produce a third. If the target processor has a multiply instruction then

Fig. 7.18. An imaginary multiplication macro.

```
define macro mult $A, $B, $C
    if @multiply_unit_fitted = yes
    then ("can generate using available MPY instruction"
         if $C not present
         then ("leave result in first parameter"
             MPY  $A, $B
             )
         else ("leave result in third parameter"
             MOVE $A, $C
             MPY  $C, $B
             )
         )
    else ("have to call a subroutine to do it"
         CALL SYSMPY $A, $B, $C
         )
end macro
```

that is used; otherwise, a system subroutine is called. If the result parameter is not specified the result is written to the first parameter by default.

Amongst the generally available established macroprocessors you will find GPM (Strachey 1965), STAGE-2 (Poole 1970 and Waite 1967) and ML/1 (Brown 1967). The compilers and assemblers on your computers may offer some level of macro-processing but it is unlikely to offer the power and generality of GPM or STAGE-2. For a thorough description of the topic see Brown 1974 and Cole 1981.

7.4.11 Program libraries and re-usability

The ever increasing cost of producing new software and the shortage of skilled software engineers available to produce it have led to a realisation of the importance of re-using existing software. Unfortunately in most organisations this aim has only been partly met, if at all. The reason for this is threefold.

Firstly there is usually a lack of communication about what software already exists in an organisation. For example, Fred in the Birmingham office will invest two man-years of effort in writing X25 communications software for an XYZ computer completely unaware that Joe in the San Francisco office has produced such a software package that has already been operational in the field for a year. The solution to this problem should be simple. Whenever a software package which might be of general use is produced its existence should be made known to all those in the organisation who might be interested in using it. This is probably best done via the Project Debriefing Report described in chapter 9.

Having decided to tell everyone about a particular piece of software you are faced with the second problem. How do you describe your software sufficiently well that a potential user can firstly judge precisely what it will do and secondly decide how to use it? This may not be too difficult for a self-contained piece of software like an X25 package, satisfying the CCITT standard and having a single interface to applications, but for more specialised pieces of software it may be very difficult. Before discussing solutions to this problem we consider the third related problem.

The final major reason why more software is not re-used is that not much re-usable software is produced. For a piece of software, henceforth called a *component*, to be re-usable it must at least satisfy the following requirements:

- It must be possible to isolate the component as carrying out a distinct function or set of related functions. The isolated component must have a simple interface to other software.
- The component must be portable from its original virtual machine environment to other virtual machines, or at least the non-portable pieces of code should be relatively small, easily isolated and well documented to allow rewriting for other virtual machines.
- The component should be sufficiently general to allow operation in slightly different applications from that for which it was originally designed. This might be via configuration parameters or at least by isolated pieces of code which have been designed to allow reworking for enhancement.

Software satisfying these requirements has, in the past, been very scarce.

Part of the solution to both of the problems just described is to use good design and production methods as described elsewhere in this book. Design methods which rely on information hiding invariably produce designs which isolate functions to distinct modules, isolate non-portable pieces of code and allow a well-defined enhancement path.

There is, perhaps unfortunately, only one solution to the problem of adequately describing the function and use of a re-usable software component and that is to use rigorous formal methods of description. The reason for this is simple; it is impossible to give a precise and unambigous description of a component using natural language. Natural language is useful to give an informal précis of the functional and usage description of a component but when it comes to deciding how to use a component in building a system there is no room for the vagueness of natural language.

Some of the methodologies that we have described particularly aim at the development of re-usable components and their incorporation into new systems. Particularly notable are HOS, which makes use of libraries of predefined, application oriented abstract data types specified by formal methods and the SARA design methodology which is particularly geared to a combination of top-down functional decomposition and bottom-up re-use of existing modules. The use of these methods or the adoption of ideas incorporated in them is well worth considering if you wish to benefit from the cost savings obtainable by software re-use.

The adoption of good software re-use practices should start with their use within the confines of each and every individual software development project. An example of bad practice is typified by the system with five different procedures or code segments for converting binary numbers to binary coded decimal. Such a situation, which wastes effort (and memory space) and which is very non-maintainable, results from precisely the problems described above but in microcosm. The five pieces of conversion code probably result from five programmers who do not communicate with one another and, even if they did, their description of their code in natural language would probably be too vague to make it of use. Further, each of the conversion routines would probably be insufficiently general for use by others (e.g. only dealing with a fixed number of BCD digits).

Precisely the same solutions apply within the confines of a given project as in the more general situation. A mechanism for circulating information on potentially useful procedures should be instigated within the project. The use and function of such procedures should be defined in a rigorous and formal manner. The procedures should be designed so that they are reasonably general and flexible. Once tested they should be made readily available to all those who need to use them and placed under change control. Probably the best place to put such procedures is in an object code library of the variety supported by most modern development oriented operating systems. Either one library for all common procedures can be maintained or several libraries for different classes of procedures can be used. You should also consider whether all such common procedures should be re-entrant so that only one copy of each need be

maintained in the system's executable image, thereby saving memory space.

7.4.12 Walkthroughs and inspections

As in earlier phases, Structured Walkthroughs, Fagan inspections and similar review mechanisms can prove valuable in ensuring the quality and correctness of the products of the Production Phase. During this phase you are most likely to hold reviews of the following material,

- tactical design documentation,
- code,
- test cases and test output,

although reviews of other output from the phase, such as Acceptance Test Descriptions, can also be useful.

The amount of design, code and test documentation produced on even a moderately sized project is likely to be so large that it is only possible to hold full Structured Walkthroughs or Fagan inspections of a very small part of it. You should aim, however, to hold full walkthroughs of the documentation of the most critical portions of the system and at least one walkthrough of some part of the produce of each person in the team.

For the parts of the documentation for which full walkthroughs are not held you should consider using 'peer reviews', at least for samples of the material. In such a review, the producer of the material walks through his work with one of his peers from the development team. The same rules as are applied for full Structured Walkthroughs or Fagan inspections can be applied to such reviews. In many cases, particularly in code reviews, it is the producer rather than the reviewer who spots most of the errors. The act of having to explain their code to someone else makes them see errors that they ignored before. In this respect it would make little difference whether the review consisted of one or more reviewers.

In choosing sections of material to be reviewed it is well worth considering using the indicators for the material as a guide to potential risk areas as discussed in section 7.5. Thus, for example, you might schedule a review of the testing of any module for which the number of test cases fell below or close to the cyclomatic number of the code for the module. Such a review would take as its input the code and the test cases and would check that the test cases sufficiently exercised the code.

An interesting controlled experiment which compares code walkthroughs with other forms of program testing is described in Myers 1978*b*. The conclusion of this experiment was that walkthroughs are an effective way of finding errors but are not as cost-effective as some other methods. An important point to note regarding this experiment is that, because of the experiment's particular aim, none of the error detection methods included the author of the program. For code walkthroughs this is not an approach that we would recommend because of the observation made above that it is very often the program's author who finds most errors in a walkthrough. Indeed so effective is author review of code that we strongly recommend the practice of source code desk checking.

This is arguably one of the simplest and most cost-effective ways of finding bugs in source code. Once the programmer has written and keyed in their source code they take a listing of it before doing anything further with it – even compilation – and read through it checking for all the common coding faults: syntax errors, spelling mistakes, missing brackets and semi-colons, wrongly nested conditional statements, wrongly used variables, badly terminated loops, inverted conditional jumps, incorrectly executed arithmetic, and so on.

Experience has repeatedly shown that this one-person walkthrough will quickly show up faults that would otherwise mean aborted compilations and wasted test shots. The technique (if it warrants such a grand title) can be further improved by adopting the idea of 'inspection specifications' from Fagan inspections: namely, a detailed list of the most common and/or critical bugs and how to spot them. To get the best out of these, ensure that your programmers record and classify in the module history the errors they find so that you can produce improved guidelines for future projects from the Project Debriefing Report for this one. We cover this topic in more detail in the indicators section for this phase.

Exercise

The need for source code desk checking should largely disappear as development machine CPU time becomes an increasingly less valuable commodity and as programming languages and compilers become more 'intelligent' in trapping or picking up errors. This is certainly not the case with most contemporary development environments.

Draw up a list of error types that your favourite compiler does not spot but that you could easily look for in source code desk checking. (For example, with FORTRAN: variable used before it is initialised, misspelled variable name, missing code.)

7.4.13 Static analysis

Given the source code of a program it is possible to carry out various forms of (preferably automated) analysis without executing the program. The following are examples of the sort of static analysis that can be carried out:

- Information can be gathered for guiding test data generation (a topic with its own section later).
- Non-standard or dubious programming practices can be identified – 'anomaly analysis'. Such anomalies will suggest (if not identify) logical faults. Examples are uninitialised variables, unreachable code, incorrectly calculated array bounds, badly coerced data types, and variables that are set but not read.
- Compliancy with interfaces can be checked for at both syntactic and semantic levels.
- Cross reference tables (for both data and procedures) can be drawn up. These will suggest points of over-coupling, unintended coupling, and misuse of global variables, and will help in interface analysis.

Static analysis will tend to be suggestive rather than yield yes–no answers to questions of whether a program works. In particular, static analysis is powerless where pointers and array variables are used as it is unable, for instance, to distinguish one array element from another. Furthermore, static analysis alone cannot discriminate between paths through a program that are syntactically possible and those that are semantically possible; in other words, it cannot identify *infeasible* paths that no input data can cause the program to follow. This is not a matter of practicality but of mathematical fact: it can be proved that there is no algorithm that, given an arbitrary program, can determine whether a given syntactic path through it is feasible. We will be meeting this 'undecidability result' frequently in the sections on program testing.

Nevertheless, the checks that are possible with static analysis make it a valuable component in an overall testing strategy, and probably explain the number of packages that are available to carry out the different analyses. (See Stucki 1977*a* and Miller 1977*b* for instance.) Some of these analyses are being incorporated into the syntactic passes of compilers for obvious reasons.

In the absence of automated tools, static analysis becomes impractical for modules of any significant size but may still yield benefits if specific aspects are applied to critical modules. Anomaly analysis and interface analysis could easily form part of review programmes or be included in the Fagan inspection specification for certain parts of your system.

A description of a static analysis package for ANSI FORTRAN programs to be found in the literature is that of DAVE in Osterweil 1976. DAVE uses data flow analysis to reveal suspicious or erroneous use of data, in particular to spot two types of data access anomaly:

- reference to data not preceded by definition of the data;
- definition of data not followed by a reference to the data.

It works on whole or part programs and handles subprograms and the data flow between them by working leaf-up from the program call graph. Faced by the undecidability of infeasible paths it is prone to pointing out apparently anomalous data usage on infeasible paths (i.e. paths through the program that cannot be achieved on real data). Amongst its output, DAVE includes error and warning messages, general information about the program and data usage information.

Static analysers like the QUAY package for FORTRAN marketed by Logica employ database and interactive query techniques to expand the types of analysis possible. The program is first analysed in detail and the results are transferred to a relational database (in this case, RAPPORT).

(RAPPORT is a registered trademark of Logica Limited.) The database query facilities then allow both standard and *ad hoc* analyses to be carried out.

Another example is the LINT program available for checking for simple (non-dynamic) anomalies in programs written in C.

Bibliography
Fairley 1978, Gannon 1979, Meeson 1979, Miller 1977*a*, *b*, Osterweil 1976, Taylor 1980, Voges 1980, Woodward 1980, Zeil 1981, Zelkowitz 1976.

7.4.14 Symbolic execution

Symbolic execution represents a mid-point between running a set of individual test inputs through a program and carrying out a proof of its correctness. It involves using a special program that takes the target program's source code as its input and *interprets* it whilst carrying symbolically all the inputs to the program – its parameters, globally shared data, own variables and so on. With a single symbolic execution you can achieve as much as a large (if not unbounded) number of individual test runs.

During interpretation, the symbolic evaluator handles the evaluation of expressions (in assignments for instance) by manipulating them algebraically. Thus, if I is an input and the following two statements are executed:

$$M := 1.6$$
$$L := (M+5.2)/(I+6)$$

then the result is

$$M = 1.6$$

and

$$L = 6.8/(I+6).$$

At decision points within the target program the interpreter must evaluate predicates. Both forks of an **if** . . . **then** . . . **else** . . . statement will in general need to be explored via parallel executions. The forking of syntactic paths forms an 'execution tree' at each of whose nodes is a predicate representing the accumulated decisions in getting to that point in the execution – see figure 7.19. Once more however we meet the undecidability problem that says that our interpreter cannot in general tell when it is chasing down an infeasible path, i.e. one which no input data can cause the program to traverse in reality.

Once the interpreter has carried out symbolic evaluation along each syntactic path of the target program, the output of the target program for each path will be expressed in (symbolic) terms of the inputs plus the predicate that defines the conditions that the inputs must satisfy for that path to have been traversed. Collectively, this output effectively contains the definition of the function of the program as written together with functional definitions for infeasible paths. In the ideal situation this derived function could be compared automatically with a machine-processable definition of the function the program was *intended* to have. Otherwise, manual comparison is necessary.

Fig. 7.19. A simple program and its execution tree.

```
S1;
if P1
then begin
        if P2
        then begin
                S2;
                S3
            end
        else S4;
        S5
    end
else begin
        S6;
        if P3
        then S7;
        S8
    end
```

A structured program

Execution tree for the program

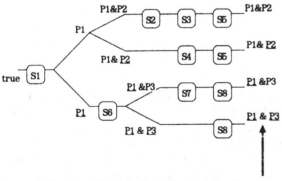

The accumulated predicates for the syntactic paths

key: P̲x = not(Px)

Since the number of syntactic paths may be very large, with many of them infeasible, the only option may be to – perhaps interactively – prune the 'execution tree' of paths in order to make the task manageable. There is of course an attendant risk here that an 'important' path is pruned unwittingly. A further problem arises from the fact that to the interpreter, the execution tree will be infinite if the target program contains a loop whose termination is somehow dependent on the values of the inputs. Once again some form of dynamic pruning may be necessary to bring the interpretation back under control. (Alternatively, if a program contains loop-invariant assertions along the lines of those discussed in the section on structured programming, the interpreter can be assisted in handling loops.)

On the brighter side, the accumulated predicates for the different syntactic paths output by symbolic execution define a set of equivalence classes each of which in turn defines the inputs that cause a given syntactic path to be traversed. This information can be used as a guide in choosing test data. It can only be a *guide* because, as we have seen, finding good test data means finding *semantic* (i.e. feasible) paths – a subset of the syntactic paths.

In some situations the concept of symbolic execution can offer a 'test coverage' metric. We could say that a set of test cases 'covers' a program if the disjunction of their path predicates is **true**. Where it is not, the negation of the disjunction will indicate which are the untested areas of the input space of the program. Although this is not a perfect measure (simple counter-examples are easily constructed) it does represent another way of getting a handle on 'good coverage' – one of the central notions of testing along with 'representativeness', 'thoroughness' and so on.

In his paper Howden 1978b, William Howden describes the results of an experiment designed to compare the effectiveness of symbolic execution with that of other program techniques. He concludes that, within the context of the experiment, symbolic execution should be seen as *one* technique available to the software tester, one that has its own strengths particularly when applied to low-level modules.

Two symbolic execution systems that have

been reported in the literature are DISSECT (Howden 1977 and 1978*c*) and SELECT (Boyer 1975). These and others are available commercially or are in the public domain, though, in common with many testing tools, they are generally restricted to use on programs written in FORTRAN.

Bibliography
Boyer 1975 (a description of SELECT), Cheatham 1979 (a general discussion), Clarke 1976, Darringer 1978 (a clear summary of the topic of symbolic evaluation), Howden 1977 (a description of DISSECT), Howden 1978*b* (the results of an experiment into the effectiveness of the technique), Howden 1978*c* (a subsequent description of DISSECT), King 1976.

Exercise
Take a small (one or two page) high-level language program and carry out a symbolic execution of it manually. (Have a large piece of paper handy.) If the program has fixed length loops and no array references you should have no trouble. Compare the definition of the program that you obtain with the actual specification of the program. Which is better? Which is right? How would you use your results to choose test data for the program?

7.4.15 Assertion checking
In the simplest case of program testing we select test values for the inputs of the program, run the program and compare the actual output with the expected output. It is as if we were to make the assertion at the end of the program that a certain relationship should apply between the input and the outputs. For instance, at the end of a program that calculates square roots, we can assert that the square of the output should equal the input to some degree of accuracy. If this assertion fails, the program has failed.

During testing we would like to be able to tell with greater precision *where* the program has failed and the obvious move is to make more frequent and detailed assertions within the body of the program. If these assertions are made an executable part of the program during testing we get a firm handle on the debugging process. (There is often a case for leaving them in the operational program if further code can be included to invoke

some form of error recovery should the assertion fail, but this is really outside the scope of this book.)

Assertions also have a natural place at the entry point of a module. The module's action will be defined for a given subset of the possible values of its inputs – the domain of the module. An entry point assertion can be made to the effect that the actual inputs received at run-time lie within the domain. If they do not, something has failed before the module was called or the module's domain has been wrongly defined.

Given the power of assertions as a debugging tool in particular, it is becoming more common for an assertion mechanism to be incorporated into the syntax of languages. They can be used however even if the language does not support them directly, for instance by preprocessing the program source code with some form of macroprocessor which can transform embedded assertions either into comments or into executable code.

This really only makes sense for what we might call 'instantaneous assertions', i.e. those checked for validity only at the point at which they are invoked. 'Running assertions' generally require the co-operation of the compiler, an example being the use of range specifications for variables supported by PASCAL compilers: when an integer is declared it might also be specified as only having a value in the range [1,100]. Wherever that integer has a value assigned to it this running assertion about its range is automatically made after the assignment and checked for validity. This is a particularly valuable technique during debugging but is less likely to be of use in an operational program precisely because of its non-selective nature and the considerable overheads the continual checking is likely to impose.

A further use to which assertions can be put is that of the metric described in Andrews 1981 which proposes that the 'number of assertion violations' be used to steer the generations of test data and the isolation of faults during program testing.

The strong link with the program proving techniques described in the section on structured programming should be clear. An assertion at a point in a program encapsulates a theorem that should be true at that point no matter what path has been followed to reach it – a 'loop invariant' for instance. At the end of a loop that removes one entry from a bi-directional chain on each iteration we could, for instance, assert that the chain is logically intact, that the required entry has been deleted and that the others remain in the same order; the iteration in a square root routine could be asserted to generate monotonically improving approximations, and so on.

This idea gives us the notion of 'inductive assertion' as a means of program proving. Suppose we place assertions at the start of the program and at the end of each atomic segment of code (i.e. a group of consecutive instructions not containing a branch). Suppose we can now prove that each assertion A is true if all the assertions met prior to A were true irrespective of the path taken to A. We can then inductively prove that if the input assertion at the start of the program is true, the exit assertion at the end of the program is also true. If this exit assertion is strong enough we will have proved our program (see Anderson 1974 or 1979).

Bibliography
ACM 1972, Alagić 1978, Anderson 1979 (has a good bibliography), Andrews 1981, Chow 1976, Katz 1976, Oppen 1975.

7.4.16 Test data selection

When testing a module, the difficult question always arises as to what test data will be 'enough' to test the module. In general there is no complete yet practical answer to this question so it is important to understand exactly what *is* achievable in the selection of test data and what the residual risks are. This section is therefore of a somewhat philosophical nature, providing pointers and ideas to help you develop your own testing strategy appropriate to your environment.

Firstly we should point out that in the remainder of this section we ignore the extreme case of *exhaustive testing* where a module is subjected to all possible inputs. Where this is possible it should be done, but combinatorial explosion almost invariably makes it quite impracticable.

Two useful notions relating to test data selection are *reliability* and *validity*. A selection criterion is reliable if *any* set of test data it selects will reveal any incorrectness of the program. A selection criterion is valid if it is simply *able* to select a test data set that will demonstrate the incorrectness of the program. An ideal selection criterion is one that is both valid and reliable, in that it guarantees that any incorrect program will be shown to be so by the test data it selects.

Such a criterion would amount to a proof of correctness which, in the general case, is unfortunately unattainable, so we need to be aware exactly what is attainable with imperfect techniques.

There are two orthogonal but complementary approaches to test data selection:

- black box treatment, and
- white box treatment.

Black box or *functional* treatment consists essentially of looking at the set of inputs for which the module's action is specified – its *domain* – and choosing a finite subset on which to test the module. This might for instance be done by splitting the domain into disjoint subdomains reflecting the structure of the domain in some way, and then choosing one test case from each subdomain. Another criterion might be based on identifying the boundaries of the module's domain and generating test data corresponding to them (White 1980). The test inputs are submitted to the black box module and its outputs are compared with expectations derived from the specification. Black box testing is therefore driven from the module's specification.

In *white box* treatment we look inside the module for inspiration and base our tests on the contents of the box, that is, on the module's internal workings. Criteria of this sort generally rely on an analysis of the predicates in the module and the iterations it performs in order to generate test cases that exercise the various paths through the module.

Four traditional white box criteria are the following:

- *path testing* where each executable path through a program is tested at least once,
- *branch testing* which exercises all outcomes of each predicate,
- *structured testing* where loops are tested to some upper bound of iterations,
- *special values testing* where 'singularities' and boundaries in the input space are

explored and potential exception or end-point conditions in the code are targeted at by the choice of input data.

Both white box and black box criteria can be found that are valid in that they have the *potential* to choose test data for which a faulty module behaves incorrectly. What we need however are criteria that are also reliable, in other words that realise that potential every time.

Unfortunately, a simple example (Gerhart 1977) is easily constructed to show that, although valid, a black box criterion can easily be unreliable (see the exercises below). Furthermore, the commonly used white box criteria will not detect certain classes of errors (Goodenough 1979 and Howden 1976).

This inability of either white box or black box testing to solve our problems simply suggests two general principles: when choosing our test data we need to consider the specification of what the program is to do *and* how it works; and we need to combine a number of techniques – a number of criteria – to increase our coverage.

Let us return to the definition of an ideal selection criterion as one of which a program is faulty in its domain if and only if it fails for some input defined by the criterion. We have seen that such a criterion would amount to a proof and we could guess therefore that finding it will be exceedingly difficult. In fact, a programmer cannot in general know if he has an ideal criterion unless he already knows the errors in the program or at least that they are of specified types; moreover, reliability and validity are not independent properties of a criterion and it can be shown (Weyuker 1980) that one way to ensure that a criterion has one property is to ensure it does not have the other!

One partial solution of this dilemma is that of using *revealing subdomains*.

A subset of a program's input domain is revealing if the existence of one incorrectly processed input [in the subset] implies that all of the subset's elements are processed incorrectly. The intent of this notion is to partition the program's domain in such a way that all elements of an equivalence class are either processed correctly or processed incorrectly. A test set is then formed by choosing an arbitrary element from each class. For a practical testing strategy, the domain is partitioned into subdomains which are revealing for errors considered likely to occur. (Weyuker 1980)

This 'revealing partition' is formed from the intersection of two other partitions: the first (the *path domain partition*)

separates the domain into classes of inputs which *are* treated the same way by the program [white box analysis] while the second (the *problem domain partition*) separates the domain into classes which *should be* treated the same way by the program [black box analysis]. Intersecting these classes yields subdomains with the desired property.

Weyuker 1980 gives three examples of revealing subdomain construction. The revealing subdomains technique provides a useful handle on the manual testing of small programs particularly as it combines both black and white box criteria. Its extension to larger programs will probably require assistance from hitherto undeveloped tools.

It should be clear from the above discussion that choosing test data is an area with few fixed points. If for no other reason, you are therefore well advised to monitor carefully the performance of the selection criteria (and combinations thereof) that you use. Howden 1978*a* expresses the view that we are likely to learn more about testing by observing than theorising.

The unit test description

The only place for intuition and subjectivity in thorough testing is as *adjuncts* to objective techniques. For this reason, if no other, no testing should start until a full description has been produced of the expected results. You must ensure that precisely what is expected of a piece of software is defined before testing begins. Only then can you tell, when it is declared 'tested', whether it is of the quality you require as defined by the tests you describe.

For every unit of software that is to be individually tested, there should therefore be produced a *unit test description*. Precisely who produces this is an organisational matter. It is often the programmer who wrote the software. In larger organisations there may be an entire department with the responsibility for third-party testing and independent of the production department.

Either way, it will need to be produced *after*

the code has been written. You may feel that it snould/could be written immediately after the module has been specified, i.e. once its function has been set down and before a word of code is written. However, you will see from the discussion above that tests based purely on what a program *should* do are insufficient on their own and need to be combined with tests based on what the program *does* do, i.e. on the code.

Later in this chapter you will find a checklist of the items that should be considered for inclusion in a unit test description. You should aim to standardise on some format that is appropriate to your design technique, the implementation language and the development environment – particularly test tools – that your testers have at their disposal.

Unit test descriptions immediately become important (internal) deliverable items of this phase and your Quality Management Plan should reflect this by identifying them clearly as such and by defining the standard to which they are to be produced. Like any other deliverable items the descriptions become suitable subject matter of reviews.

Bibliography

Beizer 1983 (recommended), Chandrasekaran 1981, Clarke 1976, Gerhart 1977, Goodenough 1975, 1979, Howden 1976, 1978a, 1980 and 1982b, Infotech 1979b, Miller 1978, 1979a, Myers 1979 (recommended), Panzl 1978, Ramamoorthy 1975, Rapps 1982, Ruby 1975, Tai 1980, Voges 1980, Weyuker 1980, White 1980, Zeil 1981.

Exercises

1 Convince yourself that no black box criterion will reliably produce test data that shows that the following program does not correctly determine whether its three input integer values are equal:

  procedure pathological (**input** integer A, B, C;   **output** boolean R):

  begin

      R := ((A+B+C)/3 = A)

  end;

2 Use your normal techniques to choose test data for the program you looked at in the exercise in the section on symbolic execution. How did you go about it? Did you use both black and white box criteria? Get someone to seed a bug or two in the program and see if your test data detects them.

7.4.17 Test coverage analysis and software metrication

Since we have no magic formula for generating test cases we need to look at ways of analysing the effectiveness of different criteria and to investigate where some criteria are more effective than others.

Coverage is an important metric that measures the extent to which the test data generated by a given criterion (or set of criteria) exercise the program under test. Traditional coverage metrics are

- the percentage of source code instructions executed,
- the percentage of partial paths traversed, where a partial path is a section of code connecting two decision points and not containing any decision points itself, and
- the percentage of predicate outcomes exercised.

Even 100% coverage of any given feature gives us no guarantees of program correctness, but criteria giving less than 100% coverage are still useful provided that they are used in conjunction with complementary criteria and that their limitations are recognised.

An extension to the second metric above can be found in Woodward 1980 where a hierarchy of metrics is discussed that can be used to *guide* the selection of test cases and monitor the coverage of test paths. A 'ladder' of metrics relates to coverage of increasingly long partial paths – that is, paths with 0, 1, 2, 3 . . . intermediate decisions. The tester proceeds up the ladder, testing ever longer partial paths, finally giving up once all entry-to-exit paths have been tested (unlikely) or the number of infeasible paths increases so fast as to confound. Once more the undecidability result defeats us in the general case by showing that for an arbitrary program it will be impossible to tell whether a path is infeasible. However, for short partial paths the ladder of metrics does give guidance in the choice of test data.

Determining the degree of coverage requires the program to be *instrumented* before the selected test data is submitted. The purpose of the instrumentation is to record, to some level of detail, the history of the program executions caused by the test data. From this history one or more degrees of coverage can be determined for that test data and, by implication, for the selection criterion that selected it. Although the insertion of *probes* into a program can be done manually there is clearly much to be said for automatic instrumentation. This is generally done either by a special option in the compiler or by preprocessing the program.

What probes are placed where is clearly important in determining what metrics of coverage can be used. It will also depend on the language syntax since the instrumentation program needs to carry out some form of static analysis in order to place the probes sensibly. As an example, Probert 1982 gives an algorithm for inserting the minimal number of probes in a program that is written in a language with delimited constructs (e.g. **if** . . . **endif**) and where branch testing coverage is to be measured.

Voges 1980 describes a tool called SADAT that combines three forms of test data generation with run-time instrumentation to try to combine a number of ideas. Test data can be either generated automatically to provide full decision-to-decision path coverage, or derived from path/predicate evaluation or specified by the tester (who might be aware of 'dangerous' corners in the system). After the insertion of 'instrumentation' into the code, the program is executed with the test data thereby allowing execution coverage to be determined.

Instrumentation mechanisms have been developed for FORTRAN (Holthouse 1979), PL/1 (Zelkowitz 1976) and COBOL (Sorkowitz 1979) amongst others. A scan of available software tools will reveal a number of test coverage analysis programs for a variety of languages available commercially and in the public domain.

Ohba 1982 extends the potential usefulness of test coverage analysis by using it in conjunction with a program's accuracy in the tests to give a measure of the overall quality.

As a further spin-off of metrication, the frequency with which the various parts of a program are traversed can be established and this information used to decide where optimisation of the program would be most cost-effective. This is very much in line with the philosophy of optimising the program *after* it has been developed rather than complicating implementation with optimisation.

Bibliography
Chow 1978, Foster 1980, Geiger 1979, Holthouse 1979, Howden 1981, Huang 1978, Panzl 1978, Power 1983, Probert 1982, Sorkowitz 1979, Stucki 1977*a*, Voges 1980, Zelkowitz 1976.

7.4.18 Development environments

Requirements for development environments

So far we have discussed tools and methodologies and what they can do for you, with little or no discussion of the environment in which they are used. The development environment in which a system is produced can have a major effect on development productivity and system quality (Boehm 1981). By the development environment we mean both the physical working environment for the development of software and the setting for the tools that are available to help in its production. In this section we concentrate primarily on the computer setting for development tools, the development system, and refer the reader to the references (e.g. Matsumoto 1981 and McCue 1978) for more discussion of the physical environment.

The principal requirements for a development system that is to encourage productivity are as follows:

- it must be easy to use effectively,
- it must be readily available and give a good response time,
- it must be stable,
- it must ensure security of data.

Additional requirements for an environment that is to encourage software quality are that:

- it should be highly controlled;
- it should facilitate the provision of indicator data.

Let us consider the significance of each of these requirements in more detail.

For a development system to be easy to use it must

- be easy to learn or be already known to the user,
- provide a 'friendly' and informative user interface,
- be appropriate to the task being undertaken and the methodology being used.

All of these points are related to the ergonomics of the development system (e.g. Spier 1981). The final point also relates to the choice of tools that are available on the development system. An obvious example of degrees of appropriateness of tools is the difference between a source language debugger as opposed to an assembly language debugger for debugging a high-level language. In considering the appropriateness of an environment for the support of a given methodology you should also consider how well integrated the tools are that will be used with the methodology. If the methodology has a number of stages that run into one another, do the tools for each stage interface easily with one another?

The relationship between productivity and development system availability and response time is obvious. You should ensure that your development system will be available sufficiently early in development to allow familiarisation before actual production begins. If you are using top-down development (see section 7.4.19) you will require your development system earlier than if you use top-down design and bottom-up production. You should also consider the availability of the development system once you start using it. Will it be available for after-normal-working-hours usage? Will you have to compete with other user groups for connect-time or CPU time? Will it support enough terminals reliably and with good response time?

Related to the availability of the development system is its stability. In the crudest form the stability of the system is a matter of how often it is going to break down and how long it takes to fix when it does. Slightly more subtle and potentially more important is the stability of the development software running on the system. You should ask yourself questions such as: How often will new versions of the tools be released? Will data produced with different versions of the tools be compatible? In general, is the development environment sufficiently mature for use on my project?

The final major requirement affecting productivity is data security. Programmers must be able to produce work on the development system without interference from other users and with the confidence that their produce will remain on the system as long as they need it. Ensuring this depends on a combination of good procedures (e.g. back-up or archiving schedules) plus proper support and protection from the development system.

Many of the features required above are provided by any powerful computer with a good operating system, in other words a good program development environment. Perhaps what separates a good system development environment from a good program development environment is the requirement for the encouragement of software quality. The requirement that the environment should be highly controlled recognises the fact that in system development there may be large numbers of software engineers working on many pieces of software in different states of development or even in different versions. Keeping track of the state of software components in such a way that they can finally be brought together in a consistent system introduces a requirement for configuration control upon the development environment (see section 2.4.4).

Finally, if the environment is truly integrated with the development methodology being employed it should provide management with indicator data of the type mentioned throughout this book relating to progress and quality.

Choosing a development system that satisfies these requirements could be one of the most important decisions that you make on a project and the reasons for your choice should be well documented. Such documentation could well appear with your software cost estimation, as many estimation models contain parameters which allow for features of the development environment.

Types of environment

One of the first decisions to be made in choosing a development environment for a project is whether to use the target computer system, that is the computer on which the software produced is ultimately to run, as the development system. The alternative is to use a separate system for development of the software and to finally load the software onto the target computer. We shall call this latter environment a *host–target* environment.

The decision of whether or not to use a host–target environment should be based on the satisfaction of the requirements of the previous subsection as well as financial considerations. Let us turn to some of these considerations.

If you are using a wide variety of target computers it is very unlikely that they will all support environments that satisfy all of the requirements of a desirable development system. This is particularly the case where the target computer is a microcomputer (or even a minicomputer) which is to be embedded in some larger system (e.g. an avionics system). Such microcomputers are unlikely to have most of the support features that are required of a good development system as these are not required in the final embedded application. In such circumstances it is far preferable to develop the microprocessor software on a host computer and carry out as much testing as possible on the host, possibly using target computer simulators, before loading the software into the embedded microcomputer for final testing. Cross-development tools, such as high-level language compilers that produce both host and target object code, are widely available for many microcom-

puters. A typical host–target environment is shown in figure 7.20. (See also Matsumoto 1981, Rauch-Hindin 1982.)

Even if your different target computers do support good development environments it is quite likely that they will all have different user interfaces and will require some time for the user to become familiar with their use. If the same host is used for all development, software engineers become familiar with its user interface thereby increasing their productivity.

A further, related, advantage of a host–target development environment is that it is available independently of the timetable for delivery of the target computer both into and out of the project. Thus, development can commence on the host prior to delivery of the target and post-delivery development can continue on the host once the target computer has been delivered to its end user.

The use of the same host for all software development is only a partial solution to the problem of software engineers continually requiring

Fig. 7.20. A host–target development system based on a local area network.

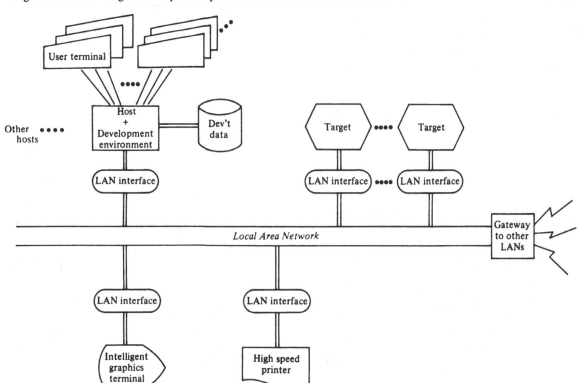

retraining as they encounter new environments. A more complete solution is a standard environment which can run on all hosts.

The environment which probably comes closest to providing such a universal, standard operating environment is the UNIX (UNIX is a trademark of Bell Telephone Laboratories) operating system (Bell Laboratories 1978, Ritchie 1978, Kernighan 1981, Feldman 1979). UNIX with Programmer's Work Bench (PWB/UNIX) provides many of the features that one would expect of a host–target development system (see, for example, Mitze 1981 for a critique and Ivie 1977 for a description). In particular PWB/UNIX provides facilities for job submission to a target and processing of returned results, configuration management (via its Source Code Control System – SCCS), document production and input/output device simulation.

While the UNIX system has developed as a widely used 'standard' environment in a largely informal and uncontrolled fashion (although there are now moves to formalise a standard), the United States Department of Defense is carefully orchestrating an effort to produce a standard Ada Programming Support Environment (APSE), the requirements of which are laid down in the 'Stoneman' document (Buxton 1980). An APSE will provide a host–target development environment with an architecture which can well be represented as a series of concentric layers as illustrated in figure 7.21. The functions of the layers as defined in 'Stoneman' are as follows:

level 0: Hardware and host software support as appropriate.
level 1: Kernel Ada Program Support Environment (KAPSE), which provides database, communication and run-time support functions to enable the execution of an Ada program (including a MAPSE tool) and which presents a machine-independent portability interface.
level 2: Minimal Ada Program Support Environment (MAPSE), which provides a minimal set of tools, written in Ada and supported by the KAPSE, which are both necessary and sufficient for the development and continuing support of Ada programs.
level 3: Ada Program Support Environments (APSEs)

which are constructed by extensions of the MAPSE to provide fuller support of particular applications or methodologies.
(From Buxton 1980, with permission)

The portability of APSE tools will be achieved by the standardisation of the interface to the KAPSE in terms of Ada package specifications and abstract data types in the true spirit of information hiding (see section 7.4.8). This will provide a standard virtual machine for use by Ada programs including tools.

Development databases and configuration control

At the heart of even the crudest development system must be some form of filing system or database containing program source, object code and perhaps documentation and other project data. The facilities provided for manipulating and controlling this database become extremely important on a large project with large numbers of people, files and software versions. Development environments such as UNIX and APSE recognise this by having (or proposing) features explicitly for configuration control.

Fig. 7.21. The architecture of the APSE. (After Buxton 1980.)

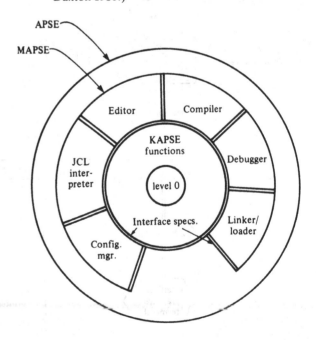

In an APSE environment all activities centre on the APSE database in which all project data resides. 'Stoneman' defines the APSE database as containing *objects*, such as Ada program units. Several objects can be related as belonging to a particular *version group*, typically formed of different versions of a given abstract object. A *configuration* consists of a given grouping of objects from the database. Tools will be provided in an APSE for the generation, release and control of configurations. In particular the history of all objects in the database and the constitution of configurations will be maintained. The approach taken to configuration control in one prototypical APSE, the Gandalf system, is described in Haberman 1981.

The ideas of software engineering databases such as that in the APSE are likely to become increasingly central to future development environments. Many of the features of such databases are likely to be similar to those of SDS, described in section 5.4.10, and CADES (see Snowdon 1981 and references cited therein). The use of a single database as a controlled and integrated repository of project data from all stages of software development is particularly desirable.

The PWB/UNIX environment provides an example of a minimal satisfactory configuration control system without the sophistication and complexity of a full software engineering database. The UNIX Source Code Control System (SCCS – see Rochkind 1975) stores the original version of a file and consequently only stores the changes, called *deltas*, to the file. To effect a change to a file under SCCS control the 'get' command is used to retrieve the file, the modification is made and the change recorded using the 'delta' command. If required a new version number will be assigned to the modified file. Facilities are also provided to store commentary on each change, such as who made it and why.

The incremental change method allows any version of a file to be re-created using 'get', allowing different configurations of a system composed of different versions of its component parts to be readily created. This is aided by the UNIX 'make' tool which builds a program according to information in a control file. This file specifies dependencies between the source files involved in building the system. 'Make' uses these dependencies to ensure that necessary recompilations of changed files and their dependants are carried out during the build process.

Many of the features for configuration control found under PWB/UNIX can easily be implemented on other operating systems using facilities provided by their filing systems and command languages. Doing this could prove a simple but effective step to easing configuration control problems on your project.

Bibliography
Anderson 1982, Hausen 1981*a* (short characterisations of a selection of 20 environments are given), Hausen 1981*b*, Howden 1982*c*, Huenke 1981 (this book contains a large number of papers on various aspects of software engineering environments as well as a very complete bibliography), Riddle 1980*a* and 1980*b*, Snowdon 1978 and 1981, Tseng 1982.

Exercises
1 Consider a development environment that you have used against the requirements for a good environment given in this section. Are there any simple ways in which it could be improved?
2 Design a configuration control system based on an operating system with which you are familiar, preferably only using its command language (i.e. no special programs). Features should include those of the 'get' and 'delta' and 'make' commands of UNIX plus commands to place a file under control, include commentary with a change, read commentary, remove a delta, and undo a previous get on a file.

7.4.19 Techniques for system integration
As mentioned in section 7.1.5, we have assumed that for any reasonably sized system it will be necessary for you to divide the system into components of a manageable size. This assumption raises the following questions:

When should you start putting the components together? In what order should the components be assembled? How can you be sure that the resulting assemblage is working correctly?

The answers to these questions define your system integration procedure. Your choice of integration procedure should have such an important effect on the way in which you develop the system that we might have alternatively titled this section 'Approaches to system production'.

Once your System Design is complete there are basically three ways in which you can produce the system, namely, 'top-down', 'sideways' or 'bottom-up'.

Bottom-up integration

Probably the most conventional form of production approach is to carry out top-down tactical design and bottom-up integration. In this approach the components produced as a result of the System Design Phase (e.g. subsystems) are further divided into successively smaller components. The smallest components are coded and are then gradually integrated into increasingly large components until the system is complete.

In this approach, integration starts late in the development lifecycle. This can be a disadvantage as it means that the most serious types of errors such as requirements not satisfied (e.g. functions missing) and major interface mismatches are not discovered until the project is meant to be drawing to its conclusion. It is these problems that are most often used as arguments for top-down development rather than bottom-up integration (e.g. Gane 1979). However, if you have used good System Definition and Design methods as described in earlier chapters you should not run into these problems and the use of bottom-up integration should not be ruled out on these grounds alone.

An advantage of a late start to integration is that you will be less constrained by requirements of early availability of computer time or special equipment.

The order in which to integrate components should be clear if a well structured design approach has been used. The order of integration will, in general, be the reverse of the order of decomposition. For example, referring to the structure diagram in figure 6.3 for the host software in the VISTA system, we would first integrate and test the lowest level modules such as 'Send command to VICE' by using a test harness to drive the module and perhaps a VDU in place of the VICE to monitor the serial link. We would then proceed to integrate the next lowest level of modules with those below them and so on until we come to integrate the top-level VISTA module and thus the whole of the host software. We would similarly integrate the VICE software in a bottom-up manner and finally integrate the host and VICE subsystems to form the entire VISTA system.

At each stage of bottom-up testing it is necessary to test that the part of the system that has been integrated is working properly. As recognised above, at all but the final stage of integration a test harness will be required to drive the tests. A test harness is typically first used during unit testing to test a component in isolation with 'stubs' substituted for subordinate components. In integrating the component the same test harness and probably even the same tests that were used during unit testing can be applied, the only difference being that the stubs are replaced by the fully integrated subordinate components that they represent.

Top-down integration

Having coded and unit tested all the components in the system, there is no particularly compelling reason why the order of integration should be from the bottom up. An alternative approach is to start from the top and work down. Referring again to figure 6.3, this approach would involve first testing the VISTA module, with stubs representing the first-level modules being gradually replaced by the first-level modules themselves but with second-level modules stubbed and so on.

This top-down integration approach involves starting integration at the same point in the development path but can have a number of advantages over bottom-up integration. Firstly, in most cases, test harnesses will not be required during integration, although stubs, which may well be generated automatically, will. Secondly, the tests that are applied might well be a subset of the tests that will be applied for acceptance testing, rather than special purpose tests for a given stage of integration. Thus, for example, at each stage of top-down integration in the VISTA system, a test involving a 'User request' to capture a moving sequence might be required. If the first stage of integration involved simply replacing the 'Read user input' and 'Write user output' stubs by the actual modules, then the result of this test would simply result in the display of a 'System response' generated from dummy 'Capture attributes' and 'Process response' data returned by the 'Capture video' and 'Process image' stubs. As integration continued the result of issuing the test would be more and more complete until it involved the actual capture of a moving sequence via the VICE and HSD subsystems.

A related advantage is that, although integration starts at the same time as in bottom-up integration, the system becomes visible to the user near the beginning of the integration process rather than at the end in bottom-up integration. For example, in the top-down VISTA system integration described above, the user could be invited at an early stage in integration to experience the user interface to the system by running through some of the acceptance tests.

A final potential advantage of top-down integration is that it tends to test the machine-dependent aspects of the system last. This can be very useful if the target hardware is not available early enough. For example, in top-down integration of the VISTA host software we would not have to worry about what we can put on the parallel and serial links to take the place of the VICE and HSD. The top-down integration of the VICE software would proceed in parallel with the integration of the host software. The final stage of integration would involve the incorporation of the bottom-level modules that drive the links and the physical interconnection of the host and VICE to form a complete system. Balancing this advantage, there is a danger in testing the machine-dependent aspects of the system last in that these are often the most difficult and problematic areas. This point is discussed later.

Top-down development

Top-down *development* involves working through the complete production process from the top down. That is, the top-level components are first designed in detail, coded, unit tested and integrated with stubs replacing lower-level components. Then the next-level components are designed, coded, unit tested and integrated in and so on. Top-down development can be considered as a form of incremental development as described in section 7.4.7.

The advantages of top-down development, which have been discussed in detail by, for example, Yourdon, include the early testing of major system interfaces and the early visibility of the system to the user. The reason for this is that with

top-down development the first tests of the system take place at a point in the development lifecycle not long after the completion of the System Design Phase. With the more conventional approach discussed previously only tactical design will be taking place at this point.

This early start to coding and testing also means that computer usage is more evenly distributed over the Production Phase. This can be a considerable advantage provided that the computer facilities are available early enough.

Sideways integration or development

We have seen above that bottom-up integration leaves the integration of major interfaces and the user visibility of the system to last while top-down development usually leaves the potentially tricky hardware interfaces to last. For a given system one of these aspects may not matter (e.g. there may be no tricky hardware interfaces) and a selection of top-down or bottom-up can be made based on other considerations such as availability of the target computer. In some systems, however, there may be a need for an early proving of both the user interface and some special hardware, or the desire to give an early test to a given complete function of the system. Neither the top-down nor the bottom-up approach caters for these requirements and for this reason the sideways integration or development approach is introduced.

In the sideways approach the system is integrated or developed as a series of top-to-bottom sections. The choice of sections and the order in which they are integrated or developed will depend on the design methodology used and on what is considered to be the most sensitive and risky aspect of the system. The order of integration of components making up a section can be chosen to be top-down or bottom-up based on the considerations of the previous sections or can be in any order that seems appropriate.

As an example, let us return to the Structured Design example illustrated in part by the structure diagram in figure 6.3. Let us suppose that we are particularly concerned to demonstrate at an early stage that it is possible to transfer a frame from the host to the VICE. This might be because we are worried about the timing of handshaking on the parallel and serial links. But it would also provide an early visual demonstration of the system to the user. We thus want to test a complete function of the system.

To do this we need to find the section or 'thread' (Dreyfus 1976) through the system that is involved in carrying out this function. This is done by tracing the command from the user interface through the system. The resulting section is shown in figure 7.22. The modules drawn with broken lines would only be partially tested at this stage of sideways integration or would only need to be partially implemented at this stage of sideways development.

Some system design methodologies make sideways integration or development very natural if not essential. For example, MASCOT does not provide a hierarchical decomposition of the system

that can be used in guiding top-down or bottom-up procedures in the way that the Structured Design method does. Rather, it provides subsystems which implement a functional area of the system and that can be used as sections in the sideways integration or development of the system. If, for example, in the MASCOT design based production of the VICE software we wished to provide early testing of the animation capture and replay functions, we would first complete the integration of the Animation Capture Subsystem (see figure 6.35) and the Animation Replay Subsystem (as sections through the system) and then integrate these two subsystems to test the complete function. Stubs would be needed for some of the other subsystems such as the Command Analysis Subsystem (see figure 6.35).

Fig. 7.22. The thread through the structure diagram in figure 6.3 invoked when a frame is transferred from the VISTA HOST to the VICE.

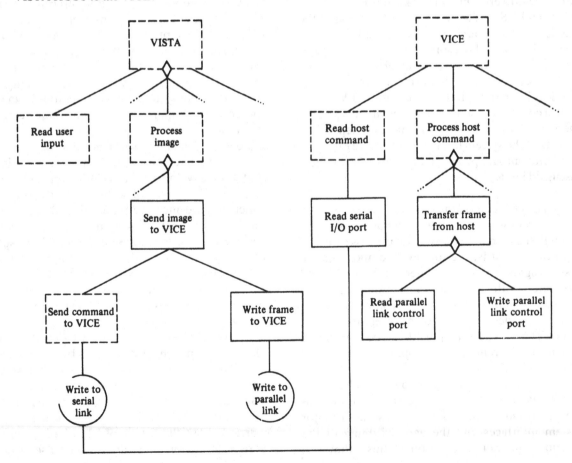

An integration approach based on sections through the system each of which implements a different function has a major advantage in that it allows functional testing of the system. That is, at each stage of integration, the tests that are applied test a new function that is being added into the system. These tests may well be based on the Acceptance Tests for the system so that upon completion of integration you can be certain that the system will pass its Acceptance Tests.

Bibliography
Top-down integration or development
Gane 1979, McGowan 1975, Mills 1971, Yourdon 1979b.
Bottom-up integration
Zelkowitz 1979.

Exercises
1 For each of the system design methods described in chapter 6, decide how you would apply each of the production approaches described in this section.
2 Describe the integration of a system with which you have been involved. Which of the approaches to production described in this section most closely approximates the approach used on your system? How might the other approaches have been applied and might they have been better?

7.4.20 System developer psychology
The quality of the people involved in system development is one of the most important factors affecting development timescales and system quality. But, no matter how good the people, if they are not happy or motivated the expected results will not be achieved. The psychology of the system developer is consequently an important matter for consideration in a successful project and, although it is somewhat removed from the mainstream of topics dealt with elsewhere in this book, we mention below three of its most important aspects. For a thorough treatment of the topic we strongly recommend Weinberg's (1971a) perceptive and amusing book *The Psychology of Computer Programming*.

Choosing people
During a software development project you will, if you are lucky, be able to choose staff to work on the project. If you are unlucky they will be thrust upon you, although you might try resisting this by quoting the work of people like Boehm (1981) to show how disastrous it might be to have the wrong people on the job.

Assuming that you are able to choose your staff, how do you do it? The choice of systems analysts and senior designers will probably be made on past experience in the applications area and in the methods being used, so let us concentrate on the choice of programmers, of whom there will be the largest number.

In employing programmers many organisations use programmer aptitude tests. Such tests have come in for considerable criticism on the grounds both that they are not relevant to the programmer's task and that performance in the tests increases rapidly with practice. We do not wish to add to this debate here but offer one thought for consideration if you do use aptitude tests. This is that the performance of programmers on projects should be monitored and included in the Project Debriefing Report (PDR) for correlation with the scores that they obtained in the aptitude test.

This leads to choosing staff from within your organisation. If the past performance of staff has been recorded in the PDRs of previous projects that they have worked on then you can consult these documents in deciding on whether a particular programmer is suitable for your project.

What performance data should be recorded concerning a programmer? The answer to this is simple. As you record indicator data for inclusion in the PDR you should tabulate it against programmers. Thus you might record the average productivity of each programmer, the average cyclomatic complexity of their code or the cohesion and coupling of their subsystem structure. If you tabulate indicators against programmers it is even more important to record circumstances which might affect the indicators, such as 'Joe's productivity dropped to 5 lines/day in subsystem S following his being concussed when falling off his horse'. If indicators are recorded fairly in this way you should not meet resistance from staff and it is likely that they will take an active interest in their track record.

If you are employing a builder it is very likely that you would look at some of their previous constructions. Why not then, when employing a programmer, look at some of their code? A program, if properly read, can reveal a great deal about the person who wrote it and the circumstances under which it was written (Weinberg 1971*a*, chapter 1). Unfortunately, very few managers either bother to read, or are capable of reading, the code produced by their staff. By reading some code produced by a programmer before you take them onto your project you might avoid some unpleasant surprises later on.

Programming teams

Having chosen the individuals to work on your project, how should you form them into a team or teams? The main reason for forming a team structure is to define the function of individuals on the project, the communication channels between them and between the project and the outside world. In particular the members of a project may be broken down into a number of teams in order to reduce the total number of communication channels in the project and thus the communications overhead (see section 2.2.5).

Much has been written on different team structures and their benefits, or otherwise, for the software development process. We shall not repeat discussion of particular team structures but rather refer the reader to the bibliography and turn to making a number of general points about setting up teams.

The functions to be carried out by the team as a whole should be clear and the first step in setting up a team or teams is to assign functions or roles to job slots to be filled by people working on the project.

Once job slots have been decided upon, control and data flow paths between the job slots should be decided. The distinction between control and data flow on a project is important. It does not follow that because person A controls person B that all of B's reporting should be to A. As an example consider the (partial) control and data flow of the hypothetical team structure in figure 7.23. Although the project manager directly con-

Fig. 7.23. Simplified control and data flow in a typical team structure.

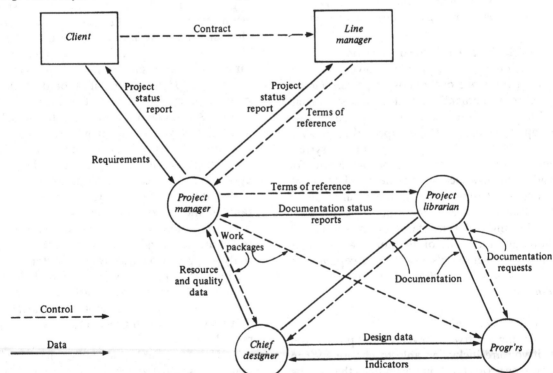

trols the programmers they report their indicator data to the chief designer who has no control over them. This way the programmers are more likely to provide their data in a spirit of co-operative striving towards design quality rather than with the feeling that 'Big Brother is watching'.

Having established a team structure most suitable for the project it is necessary to assign people to the job slots. In doing this it may be necessary to adapt the team structure to the people available.

In assigning people to a team it is worth categorising each of them as most closely falling into one of three types (Sommerville 1982):

- Task oriented: if motivated mainly by the challenge of the task at hand.
- Interaction oriented: if motivated mainly by interactions with other people.
- Self oriented: if motivated mainly by a desire for personal success.

One of the most useful things that you can ask a previous manager of a member of staff whom you are thinking of using, is for a decision as to which of the three types the person belongs to. In assigning people to job slots it is not only important to ensure the right type of person for each slot but also to ensure that there is a balance of types on the team.

Team motivation and morale

In order to obtain the best out of members of a project it is necessary to know what motivates each individual and to attempt to put them in a position where they are motivated. For example a task oriented individual may be most motivated by being given the opportunity to make the XYZ operating system run on the ABC computer, while a self oriented individual may be motivated by being given the job of deputy project manager with the ultimate aim of taking over from the project manager. Of course it may not always be possible to achieve such a happy match, in which case this should be discussed with the individual with the aim of reaching a reasonably happy compromise. (For example, with the task oriented individual: 'You can get down to putting the XYZ operating system on the ABC computer as soon as you have given the preliminary training course to the client'.)

One of the best ways of improving project morale is to use good methodologies such as those described in this book. No one likes working on a system which is badly specified, badly designed or for which there are insufficient tools to do a good job of development, and morale can drop dramatically as a project finds itself in trouble for these reasons. What is worse, as morale drops staff are likely to leave, thereby making things even worse. Avoidance of this situation can make it well worth investing in tools and methods and in seeking feedback from staff on their feelings about the tools and methods being employed.

Of all the methods that we have described there is one that warrants a special mention in relation to its effect on team performance and morale. This is the Structured Walkthrough. Structured Walkthroughs have the following particular benefits as far as the team is concerned:

- everyone's work enters the public domain (in the spirit of 'egoless programming' – Weinberg 1971*a*),
- good pieces of work are admired and praise given where due,
- weaker team members may be inspired by better members,
- there is less chance of a team member being left to struggle out of their depth,
- the chance of a team member becoming 'indispensable' is reduced by their work being reviewed. (The dangers of a team member becoming indispensable are obvious and the remedy severe: 'If a programmer is indispensable, get rid of him as soon as possible' – Weinberg 1971*a*.)

Generally, Structured Walkthroughs help to promote a team spirit which is one of the most important factors in maintaining a happy, successful project.

Bibliography
Baker 1972, McClure 1981, Shneidermann 1980, Sommerville 1982, Weinberg 1971*a*.

7.5 Indicators to be monitored during System Production

The Production Phase is arguably the most important time for you to use indicators. During this phase the project is likely to be most heavily staffed and new material (detailed design documentation, code, test data and documentation) is being produced at the highest rate. The high quality of this material is crucial to ensure easy integration, successful acceptance and trouble-free operation and maintenance. How can you be sure of the quality of all of this new material which is being produced by a potentially large number of people including perhaps relatively inexperienced programmers?

One answer is to use walkthroughs of the material as discussed in section 7.4.12. However, because of schedule or effort constraints it may only be possible to walk through the more critical material in detail, and some automatic or semi-automatic means of reviewing all material produced is still required. Indicators can provide just such a reviewing mechanism. A quick scan of indicators collected for all sections of design, code or other material can be used to isolate potentially troublesome areas for more detailed walkthroughs.

In the following subsections we discuss a sample of the indicators that can be used at various stages in the Production Phase. The literature on the subject of *software metrics* provides a further rich source of potential indicators, some of which may be specially appropriate to the circumstances of your particular project.

7.5.1 Detailed design indicators

During the System Design Phase we were particularly interested in indicators relating to the overall structure of the software being designed (see section 6.5). During the Production Phase we are more interested in the content of the modules that make up this structure and consequently are most concerned with micro-metrics. As usual, the sooner you can spot potential problems the less effort will be involved in remedying them and in this case it is far better to find problems in the detailed design of a module than to wait until it is coded and possibly tested and under integration.

The indicators that can be used in the detailed design stage will depend on the methodology that you are using although, in general, the same indicators that are used in the coding stage

can be applied during detailed design. For example, if program design language (PDL) is being used to document module design then precisely the same indicators as are used for code can be used. Thus, if the cyclomatic number (see below) of a module's PDL is too high then that of the resulting code will be as bad or worse.

The gathering of indicators from module design documentation is greatly aided if the documentation is held in a machine-readable form. Regular printouts of indicator data for completed module specifications can then be obtained allowing early action to be taken in trouble areas. This may be particularly important if it allows you to provide early guidance to a programmer who might otherwise have produced large quantities of low quality work which would only have been detected at a later walkthrough.

In addition to giving a guide to the likely quality of code to be produced for a module, detailed design indicators can be used in conjunction with historical data to provide a very accurate estimate of the likely coding and testing effort required for each module.

Empirical measurements have revealed (Chen 1978) that the relationship between complexity and time-taken-to-produce is not linear, indeed that there is in fact a level of complexity at which productivity falls off markedly or, to put it another way, the program becomes simply too difficult for efficient implementation!

7.5.2 Coding indicators

Indicators obtained during the coding stage can be used in a number of different but related areas:

- in assessing module attributes such as testability, comprehensibility, reliability and performance,
- in predicting effort required for testing, integration and maintenance of the module,
- for addition to historical data for use in assessment and prediction in future systems.

As discussed in section 2.3.2 there are three possible methods of use for indicators, namely

- direct comparison against plan (e.g. actual coding time against planned coding time),

- comparison against plan using historical data (e.g. number of executable statements to be tested against planned testing effort),
- comparison against historical data (e.g. cyclomatic number against number of executable statements).

The usefulness of an indicator in these respects depends both on how easily it may be obtained and on how well it correlates with the 'management' quantities against which it is compared.

In figure 7.24 we give a selection of indicators against a list of such management quantities with which comparison might be useful. In some cases the correlation between the indicator and management quantity is obvious. In other cases it has been supported in experiments reported in the literature, while in others you will have to use your own historical data to determine whether you can expect a correlation in your particular circumstances.

Most of the indicators in the table are self-explanatory and will not be commented upon further. However, the indicators E, $V(G)$ and 'control entropy', which are members of the quite large family of *complexity measures*, require some definition. Curtis 1979*a* and 1979*b* contain the results of experiments to determine how well E,

$V(G)$ and simple line counting reveal the 'difficulty' of a module.

McCabe's $V(G)$

McCabe (1976) introduced the cyclomatic number of the control flow graph of a program as a measure of program complexity. The cyclomatic number of a graph counts the number of linearly independent cycles in the graph and thus gives the number of basic paths through a program.

The cyclomatic number of a connected graph G can be calculated using the formula

$$V(G) = e - n + 2$$

where e is the number of edges and n is the number of nodes in the graph. For example, the program segment in figure 7.25(*a*) gives rise to the control flow graph in figure 7.25(*b*) which has $e = 9$ and $n = 8$ giving a cyclomatic number $V(G) = 3$. Alternatively it can be shown that for structured programs the cyclomatic number can be obtained by adding one to the number of predicates in the program segment. This latter method is clearly the more useful for computer generation of the cyclomatic numbers of modules stored in machine-readable form.

The cyclomatic number has been shown to

Fig. 7.24. Indicators concerning a number of useful management quantities.

Management quantity	CT	S	O	P	CB/S	S/CT	C/S	D/S	E	V(G)	O/S	CE
Planned CT	×	×							×	×		
Planned S		×							×	×		
Planned test time	×	×							×	×		×
Planned memory occupancy			×									
Planned CPU utilisation				×								
Historical CB/S					×				×	×		
Historical S/CT						×			×	×		
Historical C/S							×					
Historical D/S								×				
Historical O/S											×	

key
CT = coding time
O = number of object bytes
CB = number of compiler detected errors
C = number of comment lines
D = number of units of module design documentation

S = number of executable source instructions
P = size of path lengths (instructions or seconds)
E = Halstead's effort metric
$V(G)$ = McCabe's cyclomatic number
CE = control entropy

correlate quite well with the number of errors found in code and with programming time. It can also clearly be used as an indicator of the number of test cases that should be applied to a module to test all basic paths.

McCabe's initial definition of cyclomatic number is expanded in Myers 1977 and discussed in Elshoff 1978.

Control entropy

Given the control flow graph of a module or program we can also get some indication of the *control entropy* of the module by looking at the number of nodes in the graph on each path through the module. Consistent with maintaining acceptable values of other metrics for the module we would like to minimise the following function:

$$\sum_p P(p) \log_2 (P/P(p))$$

Fig. 7.25. A short segment of code and its associated control flow graph used for determining the cyclomatic number of the segment.

(a)

```
1.   B = C;
2.   DO WHILE A < B;
3.       IF (A = Z) THEN
4.           A = A + 1;
         ELSE DO;
5.           A = H (Z);
6.           Z = M (A);
         END;
7.       C = C + A;
     END;
8.   B = Z;
```

(b)

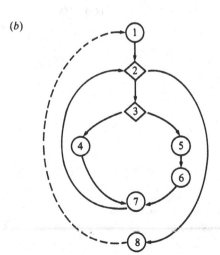

where

$$P = \sum_p P(p)$$

and $P(p)$ the number of nodes on path p. It should be clear from the discussion of 'semantic' (i.e. feasible) paths earlier in the chapter that deciding which paths to count is critical.

Halstead's E

Halstead's (1977) *Software Science* provides a number of useful indicators which have both theoretical and empirical connections with management quantities of interest in monitoring software development. In the following we provide a very brief summary of *Software Science* indicators and refer the reader to the bibliography (in particular Halstead 1977 and Fitzsimmons 1978) for more details.

Given a module or complete program, the following measures are defined

η_1 = number of unique operators
η_2 = number of unique operands
N_1 = total occurrences of operators
N_2 = total occurrences of operands.

As an example, figure 7.26 lists the unique

Fig. 7.26. Counts of operators and operands used in calculating *Software Science* indicators for the code segment in figure 7.25.

Operator	Number of occurrences
;	10
=	7
DO ... END or (...)	4
DO ... WHILE ... END	1
IF ... THEN ... ELSE	1
+	2
<	1

Operand	Number of occurrences
A	7
B	3
C	3
Z	4
H	1
M	1

operators and operands of the program segment in figure 7.25(*a*). This example has $\eta_1 = 7$, $\eta_2 = 6$, $N_1 = 26$, $N_2 = 19$.

The *vocabulary size* of the program is defined as

$$\eta = \eta_1 + \eta_2$$

and the length of the program as

$$N = N_1 + N_2$$

From these basic measures a number of more complex measures are defined. The program *volume*

$$V = N \log_2 \eta$$

is a measure in 'bits' of the size of the program. The *potential volume*, V^*, is defined as the smallest possible encoding of the program and leads to definitions of the *program level*

$$L = V^*/V$$

and *program difficulty*

$$D = 1/L$$

Halstead hypothesises that for a given language the quantity

$$\lambda = LV^* = L^2V$$

is a constant. This constant is termed the *language level* and has typical values of 1.53 for PL/1, 1.21 for Algol, 1.147 for FORTRAN and 0.88 for CDC assembly language (Shen 1983). Finally, the *effort* measure is defined as

$$E = V/L$$

and represents the total number of elementary mental discriminations required to generate the program.

Dividing E by the rate at which the brain can perform such elementary discriminations (the Stroud number, S, between 5 and 20) gives the time required to produce the program

$$T = E/S$$

In order to allow estimation of the program level (and hence potential volume) directly from the basic measures, Halstead has hypothesised and validated the following equation

$$L = 2(\eta_2/\eta_1)N_2$$

(where $\hat{L}$ denotes the estimated value of L).

The measures E, V and D all provide useful indicators of program complexity. In particular the theoretically derived number of delivered bugs in a program is

$$B = V/E_0$$

where E_0 is a constant with a value of about 3000. Alternatively this can be shown to be approximately equivalent to

$$B = E^{2/3}/E_0$$

From these results a useful rule of thumb follows: for a module to have a reasonable chance of being bug free it should have V less than $0.5E = 1500$. This can be shown to be equivalent to having a length N less than 260.

As an example, for FORTRAN N is approximately 7.5 times the number of executable statements which means that the rule of thumb implies that there should be no more than 35 executable statements per module. If we assume that there are about 50% non-executable statements per module then this relates well to the rule of thumb that a module should fit on a single listing page.

7.5.3 Testing indicators

Indicators are collected during testing primarily to determine the thoroughness of the testing and as a means of predicting such quantities as

- the number of remaining bugs,
- the mean time to failure (MTTF) of the system,
- the likely maintenance effort.

Many of the indicators discussed in the sections on System Design and coding indicators are related to these quantities and can be used as predictors. During testing, indicators relating to the number and type of tests applied, the test coverage achieved (see section 7.4.17) and the number and type of errors detected and the rate at which they are detected should be collected. Thus, for example, if a module has a cyclomatic number of ten and only two sets of test data have been applied to it you should be very suspicious. Similarly if the *Software Science* bug prediction equation (perhaps recalibrated against your historical data) indicates that a subsystem should contain about 200 bugs and only 20 have been detected by the end of integration testing then you should be equally suspicious.

As mentioned in section 2.2.6, theories of software reliability are still fairly young and are areas of current research. It is still of use to attempt to apply reliability models to your system in order to give at least some idea of its MTTF and likely maintenance effort. As an example, Shooman (1973) proposes a reliability model in which the MTTF of a program after *t* man-months of debugging is given by

$$\text{MTTF} = \{K[E/I - rt]\}^{-1}$$

where *K* is a constant that can be estimated by

K = number of catastrophic errors detected/total number of errors detected,

and where *E* is the total number of errors in the program, *I* is the total number of instructions in the program, and *r* is the error detection rate (errors detected per man-month of debugging time). The ratio *E/I* (errors/instruction) and the rate *r* are determined from historical data and are obvious

quantities for you to collect during all debugging and maintenance stages.

Bibliography
Abe 1979, Bail 1978, Bowen 1979, Chapin 1979, Chen 1978, Curtis 1979*a*, *b*, Fitzsimmons 1978, Gilb 1976, 1979, Gordon 1979, Halstead 1977, Henry 1981, Jones 1978, Lassez 1981, Lipow 1982, Littlewood 1980, McCabe 1976, McClure 1978, Mendis 1979, 1982, Mohanty 1979, Perlis 1981, Remus 1979, Schick 1978, Schneidewind 1979, Shen 1983, Shooman 1973, Sunohara 1981, Tai 1980, Woodfield 1979, 1981, Woodward 1979, Yin 1978.

7.6 Checklists for the System Production Phase

In addition to the checklists given here, the reader is referred to the excellent book *Characteristics of Software Quality* (Boehm 1978, see also Boehm 1976) in which a large number of checklists for the evaluation of the quality of software are given. The checklists are used to assess software against a number of attributes which are shown to have a correlation with high quality software. The attributes for which checklists are provided are those at the bottom level of the characteristics tree in figure 7.27. The tree shows how these basic

Fig. 7.27. Quality attributes and their relationships. (From Boehm 1978.)

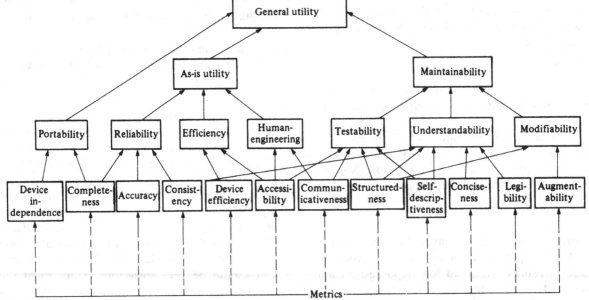

attributes relate to higher level characteristics of the software and eventually to its general utility.

7.6.1 Checklist for detailed design

- Have the design standards in the Quality Management Plan been adhered to?
- Have all the higher level functional requirements been fully devolved onto the lower level components? Traceably?
- Is the decomposition of the system into modules/components precisely recorded in the documentation?
- Have the components been decided upon in line with the quality criteria? E.g., with low coupling, high cohesion, manageable size, manageable logical complexity etc.?
- Have the interfaces that modules present been precisely defined?
- Have the system-wide principles for defensive programming and error handling been kept to?
- Have accesses to shared data been correctly controlled and co-ordinated, perhaps via data hiding modules?
- Has the implementation language been chosen? How?
- Have the timing constraints for the subsystems been correctly implemented via the module breakdown?
- Have any execution time constraints on individual modules been satisfactorily handled in their design? Have timing estimates been made and how do they compare with the timing budget?
- Have the memory requirements for modules been estimated and how do they compare with any memory budgets for the modules?
- Have any numerical techniques used been analysed for accuracy, termination and correctness? And do they demonstrate that the module complies with the requirements on it?
- Does the module design require any new pre-conditions, qualifications or restrictions that have an impact anywhere else in the system?

7.6.2 Checklist for coding

- Have the coding standards and conventions laid down in the Quality Management Plan been adhered to?
- Has the module been coded into units of a testable size (e.g. with low McCabe complexity value)?
- Have appropriate instrumentation and assertions been embedded for testing and performance checking to be carried out adequately?
- Is all the code reachable?
- Has the module interface as specified been implemented precisely so in the code?
- Does the module compile cleanly?
- How does the actual compiled code size compare with any memory budget for the module?
- Are the comments meaningful to a third party familiar with that part of the system?
- Have all unnecessary esoteric constructions been purged?
- Has the code been successfully walked through to establish that the required functionality of the module is achieved?
- Have all pointers been correctly referenced?
- Have conventions for machine register allocations been recorded and abided by?
- Is all the arithmetic dimensionally correct?
- Is all data being accessed with its correct type in mind?
- Have rounding and truncation errors been accounted for?
- Are initialisation and exit conditioning properly defined and executed?

7.6.3 Checklist for unit testing

- Does the unit test description identify the following:
  - the name of the unit to be tested,
  - the files where source is to be taken from,
  - the test stubs required and their function,
  - any test harnesses and simulation required,
  - the criteria used in generating the test data,
  - the test data to be input and the expected output,
  - any hardware required for testing, both to host the test and to test interfaces with special hardware,

- any special software (or versions) required (compilers, OSs, database managers . . .)?
- Has the termination of all loops been satisfactorily established for a range of input values?
- Have arithmetic operations been checked at the limits of the computer's resolution?
- Have all variables and pointers been exercised at the limits of their ranges?
- Has the module been validated for null or empty data structures such as empty queues, cleared stacks and null input?
- Has the module been exercised on data that is bad but within its input domain?
- Has the module been timed and the timings compared with any timing budget?
- Has the testing been witnessed when required (say for external auditing purposes)?
- If test results are to be kept have they been annotated and labelled and do they observably record the inputs and outputs of the test?
- Does the module test need to check for repeatability of result?
- Does the test exercise the module over an 'acceptably representative' subset of its input domain?

For additional background reading, volume **SE-6** number 3 (May 1980) of the *IEEE Transactions on Software Engineering* contains a Special Collection from a Workshop on Software Testing and Test Documentation.

7.6.4 Checklist for User Documentation

The users' opinions of your system will be considerably influenced by the quality of the documentation you give them and the ease with which it gets them using the system efficiently. Given this, the User Documentation is always a prime candidate for a walkthrough or review of some form. An obvious participant is a representative of the future users, together with any staff responsible for training, technical authors whose skill is in presenting technical information to the non-technical reader and a system development team member.

The following list presents some of the questions such a review could address itself to:

- Have the user interfaces been fully described?
- Have all default inputs been listed?
- Have the ranges or permitted values of all inputs been specified?
- Has the system's response to each type of erroneous input been specified?
- Has any back-up or recovery mechanism requiring human intervention been fully covered?
- Have emergency procedures been detailed, including emergency contact personnel?
- Is there a glossary of jargon and special terms?
- Is there a good index?
- Is the manual well cross referenced?
- Has the manual actually been used from end to end to try it out for correctness and usability? In other words has the manual been tested?
- Are there good worked examples throughout?

7.6.5 Checklist for the System Conversion Schedule

The introduction of a new system can be a difficult and trying experience for both the system's developers and its users. It is therefore important to draw up a System Conversion Schedule which smooths, as far as possible, the replacement of an existing system by a new one. Here is a checklist of points for consideration in drawing up the schedule:

- Will a period of parallel running of the old and new systems be required? Such a period might be required to allow training of staff or for the final validation of the output of the new system by comparison with that of the old.
- If a period of parallel running is required, are sufficient staff and accommodation available? Have manual methods which will support both systems been derived?
- Will all utilities required for the new system be available when needed? Such utilities might include power supplies, air

conditioning, leased communications lines, reinforced flooring etc. Is a site survey required to determine these needs?

- How much disruption to operations can be tolerated in the conversion to the new system? Will out-of-operational-hours working by installation staff be required?
- How will data from the old system be transferred and converted to that required by the new system? Do the systems have compatible communications or removable storage media? Can the conversion of data take place at a sufficient rate to ensure that it is not out-of-date by the time it comes to be used? Does this require data transfer outside operational hours? Have methods for validating the transferred data been devised?
- Have all manual procedures for use with the new system been specified and will staff be trained in their use in time for the introduction of the new system? Will all required consumables (special forms etc.) be available in time?

Your system may not be replacing an existing automated or manual one but may be breaking new ground. In this case many of the same questions need to be asked about the installation of your system.

7.6.6 Checklist for the Training Schedule

If a new system is to be a success with its users it is essential that they should be well trained in its use. To this end, your Training Schedule should be carefully thought out so as to ensure that training is carried out when it is needed and that the necessary resources will be available. Here is a checklist of items for consideration in drawing up the schedule:

- What are the different types of users that may require separate special training? Examples are
  - Management (Overview),
  - System Manager,
  - User systems support staff,
  - User operations staff,
  - Applications users.
- Are training courses to be held only once or will regular courses be required to train new users?

- Will user manuals be available for distribution either before or during training courses?
- Do the user manuals include introductory instruction manuals (primers) as well as reference manuals?
- Would a computer-aided instruction program be appropriate for any of the training?
- Is a system simulator necessary for training? If so how will the simulator be constructed from the real system?
- Will worked examples with sample input and output forms etc. be available for training?
- The quality of the training courses depends crucially on both the pedagogical skills of the trainers and their knowledge of the material being taught. Will suitable trainers be available?
- Will it be necessary to impose prerequisites for any of the courses (e.g. attendance at a particular course given by the computer manufacturer)?

7.6.7 Checklists for the Acceptance Test Description

A The content of the Acceptance Test Description

- Is every function in the Functional Specification covered in the Acceptance Test?
- Have any tests covering items *not* in the FS been agreed as such by both parties?
- Is each test possible?
- Can each test be completed in the scheduled time allowing for a reasonable measure of hold-ups, etc.?
- Are the system's initial state and the required inputs defined and in sufficient detail for each test?
- Are the system's required final state and output defined and in sufficient detail for each test?
- Have all parties agreed in writing to the Acceptance Test Description?
- If the tests are not exhaustive, has their actual extent and coverage been recorded?

Fig. 7.28. Fragment of the Acceptance Test Description for VISTA.

VISTA ACCEPTANCE TEST DESCRIPTION ISSUE 2.3 DATED 83-10-27

TEST SEQUENCE DESCRIPTION for sequence number *29*

Functions tested: A1B, Parameter defaults on A1A [operating envelope on *single-shot-capture-request (*SSCR) and its parameter defaults]

Sequence preconditions and Resource Requirements

1 Two users logged onto system
2 Test card 3 RGB inputs attached to SFS
3 SFS attached to computer and using 13.5 MHz rate
4 RGB monitor attached to SFS outputs
5 Test sequences 16, 17, 23 and 28 successfully completed.

Estimated Test Duration: 12 minutes

Test Sequence: (A: action, R: expected response)

A1 (test framestore reserved to user A)
     Issue *SSCR (SFSO, 320, 320) from user A
     Issue *SSCR (SFSO, 320, 320) from user B
R1 User A request accepted. User B request rejected.

(Exercise request for typical and limiting values of window parameters)

Repeat A2/R2 for each parameter pair in the following table:

DPPW	720	16	128	240	352	464	576	688
DPPH	576	344	288	232	176	120	64	1

A2 Issue *SSCR (SFSO, DPPW, DPPH) from user A
R2 Image captured and displayed on monitor in correct dimensions (check using known specification of test card 3)

. . .

(check defaults on *DPP-width and *DPP-height parameters)

A7 Present test card 4 on RGB input to SFSO
     Issue *SSCR (SFSO, 0, 0) from user A
R7 Image of width 720 and height 576 captured and displayed (check using known specification of test card 4)

. . .

Figure 7.28 gives an extract from what might be the Acceptance Test Description test sequence for the part of the VISTA system defined in the example of Structured English in section 5.4.

B Checklist for the Acceptance Test environment

- Have all necessary personnel been identified for operating test equipment and the system itself?
- Has all the necessary equipment been identified?
  - Computers,
  - peripherals,
  - storage media,
  - output media,
  - electronic test equipment,
  - measurement devices,
  - hardware simulators and emulators,
  - communications facilities.
- Has all necessary software been identified?
  - The system under test,
  - software probes and measurement tools,
  - software simulators and emulators,
  - ancillary software: operating systems, database management systems, compilers, linkers, loaders, etc.
- Have all necessary 'soft' materials been identified (e.g. preset files and databases)?

C Endurance as a feature of acceptance testing
The following steps should be remembered:

- determine the system's operating envelope from the Functional Specification,
- test the program to the boundaries of that envelope,
- determine, in particular, the system's required reaction to failure of whatever type,
- test the program in those failure regions,
- where feasible, test the system over 'significant' time boundaries, e.g. run it for 25 hours.

D Static analysis as a feature of acceptance testing
You should not assume that acceptance testing always consists solely of testing the system

dynamically, i.e. running it. Certain required properties, such as adaptability, cannot be checked in this way and static analysis may be needed. This might take the form of a formal review or measurement of some attribute.

Defining acceptability via a formal review is difficult in that subjective evaluation may creep in to cloud the issue; on the other hand, objective measurement of an attribute of the software – module coupling for instance – will give a binary acceptability criterion. If there are requirements on the system that can only be checked statically it is vitally important that the *means* of checking are clearly stated in the Functional Specification.

7.6.8 Potential coding error types

During the Production Phase, errors will be revealed in the detailed design. The checklist in section 6.6.4 can be used to classify these errors as well as those in the Design Phase. The additional checklist below gives a starter set for coding error types against which you can accumulate coding error statistics:

- misunderstanding of design,
- mishandling of interface between components,
- mishandling of interface with the external world,
- misnaming of variables,
- inconsistent data handling (e.g. type, size, width),
- syntax error,
- incorrect evaluation of arithmetic expression,
- incorrect evaluation of boolean expression,
- wrong action on test outcome,
- incorrect loop handling (premature or absent termination),
- actions in wrong order,
- action missing,
- incorrect branching,
- indexing error,
- missing declaration or specification (in program or data),
- incorrect comment,
- insufficient or absent self-checking code,
- initialisation error,
- termination error (e.g. variables left in wrong state).

7.7 Memorabilia for the Production Phase

Maintaining the information flow

Whether you keep your design and production output (specifications, source code, etc.) on paper or computer, a good information flow around the project team must be not only encouraged but also supported with a good distribution system. When changes are made to public documents, copies should reach the desks of interested parties within a working day if possible, particularly if changes are collected over a period of time prior to re-issue of the document. The larger the project team the more important formal control of distribution – let alone of the changes – will become. This applies as much to module libraries on disc as to the System Design Specification.

Manning the Production Phase

Our definition of the split between the Design and Production Phases tells us something very definite about the relative manning of the two phases. The Design Phase clearly needs a small kernel of experienced personnel co-operating closely to find that coherent strategy for the whole system. The detailed design performed at the start of Production can then be undertaken by individuals or teams who can work largely independently of each other. Within each of these teams we would expect the same single-minded search for coherent design as took place at the strategic level.

Controlling change on the System Design Specification

Although you should expect to start the phase with a fully consistent and complete System Design Specification (SDS) it need not be considered untouchable. During the Production Phase you may discover errors in it, errors that are revealed during the tactical elaboration of the strategy. The SDS will then need to be changed. The higher the level of change the greater the danger of inconsistency, error and ambiguity that can creep into the document and hence into the design. Make changes only after thorough analysis of the implications. Treat a high level of change as an indication of possible deep-rooted problems.

Estimating the duration of testing

The simple fact that this testing activity is necessary tells us that in general we cannot be certain that we designed and coded the system correctly. The techniques available during testing are therefore largely concerned with checking the correctness of the software in a reliable and rigorous way. The temptation for programmers testing their software is to random-walk around the space of test cases choosing to do the easy/interesting/less obvious testing without any consideration for thoroughness. As a result, some errors may be found and corrected and the extent of the testing performed may be determined by the number of man-days allocated rather than by the logic of the software.

Herein lies one of the great pitfalls of testing. Whilst estimating its duration is difficult during the planning phase, estimating how much there is left to do once it has started is no easier. If the software works, testing proceeds smoothly and quickly.

If it does not, there is no telling how much work you may have on your hands to get it to work. As a result, testing activities are notorious for overrunning. To try and regain a hold on the situation we recommend above some indicators which will help you assess the progress of testing and, by implication. the quality of the work that has gone before.

Adopting or adapting?

There are often significant benefits to be had by selecting individual features from techniques if they suit your purposes. Methodologies are naturally presented by their inventors as complete and self-consistent techniques but you should never feel obliged to take them in their entirety. Select what you can use and adapt it to your situation.

Adding to the PDR

During the Production Phase you will have been using various techniques and you should once again consider the questions in the equivalent *memorabile* for the Definition Phase. You are now having to live with the strategic decisions made during the Design Phase. Take a cynical, cold-blooded look at those decisions and record for yourself and your successors what went right and what went wrong. In addition:

- Are the system and its components the sizes you predicted?
- Were they as easy/difficult to produce as you expected?
- Did you set up as good a development environment as you could have?
- Would development have been easier/better if you had used/not used the techniques that you did not/did?

Spotting the bad apples

A useful idea is that of using the error detection metric (perhaps in conjunction with others that are measured at module level) to identify very error-prone or poor quality modules with a view to scrapping them entirely and reworking them from scratch, rather than continuing to patch them up.

Such low quality modules frequently lead to disproportionate amounts of testing and maintenance work downstream and corrective action now where it counts most can be a good investment.

Artificial bug insemination

Called variously 'bug seeding', 'bebugging' and 'artificial bug insemination', this is a technique for determining (to low accuracy) the number of residual bugs in a system. It should ideally be used from the start of the testing phase but can be used *post factum* on a tested system.

It works on the following well-known idea. Suppose you seed s bugs in a program and then test the program, recording *all* the bugs that are found and removed. Suppose you find f bugs of which k were originally seeded. Then you could estimate that before seeding there were $f*s/k$ bugs in the system if you make certain assumptions about randomness, homogeneity and so on.

Such matters are never so simple of course. The types of bug you seed, the types of bug that are detected by your tests, the size of your system (this is after all a statistical process) – all these have an effect. But the results can be qualified if these things are known. It is not obvious how synchronisation problems or other *architectural* errors can be seeded – perhaps they cannot be handled and the technique should be restricted to single large programs. Furthermore, the results are in a significant way dependent on the thoroughness of your testing and probably say as much about that as about the bug density of your software.

Descriptions of the technique can be found in Gilb 1976 and references therein.

Independent testing of systems

There are good reasons for having the development and testing of software carried out by different personnel. The developers have a natural defensive attitude to their product whilst the desire to find errors is probably stronger in an independent party without such parental feelings. If you have not got the staff to support this idea you are well advised to use walkthroughs to establish the thoroughness of the testing as it is documented in the test descriptions.

Keeping software static during testing

Make sure you test the version of the software – be it module or system – that you intend delivering from the relevant work package. Changing a module 'slightly' to make testing more convenient can amount to not testing the module at all.

Programming style

Discussion of programming style probably wastes more time in teams than any other topic of aesthetics. Legislation on style can be difficult both to formulate and to adjudicate on. Nevertheless it is worth the effort of developing a house style, one that is recorded in written form. You could start from something like Kernighan 1974 and build on that. Help is also available in Weinberg 1971b and 1977, and Ledgard 1975a and 1975b.

8

System Acceptance and Post-Acceptance Development

8.1 The aims of System Acceptance

The system resulting from the Production Phase must now be tested against the Functional Specification to your client's satisfaction. There are two principal reasons for giving the System Acceptance process a phase of its own:

- firstly, to emphasise the importance of careful preparation for it and proper orientation of the preceding phases towards it;
- secondly, because possibly for the first time since System Definition and the production of the Functional Specification, your client will once more play a major role.

Formal acceptance of the system by your client – in other words, a signature – is as important as his formal acceptance of the Functional Specification. It records his agreement that you have carried out your commitment to build his system.

It is likely that, if you have a commercial contract with your client, payment of some portion of the contract price will be dependent on the system's successfully passing an agreed Acceptance Test.

Throughout the preceding phases we have emphasised the need to prepare for Acceptance well ahead of the date of handover. The earlier the Acceptance Test is defined, for instance, the earlier the system can be checked out against it by its implementers. Above all, however, acceptance will not always be simply a matter of running some tests on the system and walking away. You may

well be involved in a major handover operation requiring the conversion of the user's organisation and operational procedures, cutover from an existing system, conversion of existing databases to new formats, periods of parallel running, training of staff and so on. Whilst acceptance is to you almost the end of your work, to your client it is only the beginning of working with the system you have produced and it is in your interest to ensure that the handover takes place in a receptive environment and as smoothly as possible.

Finally, one of the most important prerequisites for a smooth handover and start-up of the new system is to have the receiving organisation well trained and familiar with the system as soon as possible. Although we have left it until now to detail this need there is no reason why it should not start as early as is practicable in the lifecycle. If you have chosen an evolutionary approach or have adopted prototyping as a procedure earlier on, the education of your future users will already be well under way.

In summary, therefore, the aims of this phase are:

(i) to prove to your client's satisfaction that the system works,
(ii) to install it and put it into operation as efficiently as possible,
(iii) to train its new users.

8.2 The starting point of System Acceptance

This phase takes the following deliverable items as its inputs:

- the System Ready for Trial,
- the Acceptance Test Specification,
- the Acceptance Test Description,
- the System Conversion Schedule,
- Training Schedules,
- User Documentation.

8.3 The finishing point of System Acceptance

The deliverable items from System Acceptance fall into two groups: those that are presented to your client and those that you retain for yourself. Your client will receive the Accepted System, Training and the User Documentation. You will wish to retain the project files, particularly all the plans and reports together with all the statistics that you have collected through the project – what we might collectively term the Project Fact File. This will form the basis of your work during the Project Debriefing, as described in chapter 9.

8.4 Carrying out the Acceptance Test

Most of the spade work for the Test should have already been done by now. The purpose, environment, organisation and 'rules of conduct' for its execution have been set down in the Acceptance Test Specification and agreed by the parties concerned. The detailed tests to be performed have been set down in the Acceptance Test Description and also agreed. All test equipment (software and hardware), test data and personnel have been identified well in advance and prepared. The schedule for tests has been drawn up, dates have been fixed and the system is being prepared for its trial.

Good luck.

8.5 Managing Post-Acceptance Development

8.5.1 Preparing for change

It is now a widely appreciated fact that the software engineer's task is not complete with system handover. Indeed, in some cases, before the system becomes obsolete it may cost its users as much (or more) to maintain as it cost them to implement in the first place (see figure 2.8).

It is often suggested that software does not wear out and does not need repair in the same way that hardware does. Perhaps this is true strictly speaking but software does need maintenance. We can identify a number of reasons for this:

- the user's requirements change (typically they increase),
- the system's environment changes,
- the system is found to contain faults.

With time, this process of change and repair can degrade the system's quality to the point that replacement is the only solution. Often this happens before the system becomes obsolete through being no longer needed. We can draw an important conclusion from this: if the system is to have a long life its original development must be managed with this as an aim. This means that positive action must be taken at each phase of development. The maintenance process can be seen as an extension to good practices in the development process.

There are some activities which must be carried out during development or, at latest, shortly thereafter, which are aimed solely at preparing for maintaining the system. These activities involve deciding how potential changes and errors will be monitored, how changes will be accepted for implementation, rejected or postponed and the approach that will be taken to the implementation of changes including likely resource (people and equipment) requirements. The outcome of these decisions, guidelines for which are set out in the following subsections, should be written down in a Maintenance Plan, which ideally should be part of the Project Plan, forming a plan for the entire life of the system.

8.5.2 Monitoring and assessing change

The starting point of the maintenance cycle is the determination that a change to the system may be necessary. There are essentially three types of change that can be made to a system (Swanson 1976): corrective, adaptive and perfective. The first are changes to correct errors in the system, while the second are to adapt the system to changes in its environment and the third are to improve the system's functionality.

It is important to decide the type of each potential change that confronts the system and to deal with it in the framework of the maintenance philosophy laid down in the Maintenance Plan.

For example, a most extreme maintenance philosophy might be to carry out only corrective changes to the system. Whatever the maintenance philosophy it is likely that the different categories of change will be treated with different priorities and will become justified at different thresholds of assessment criteria.

Criteria which should be considered in justifying a change are (McClure 1981):

- Can the system's functionality be tolerated without the change?
- What is the total cost of the change?
- What resources are required to implement the change?
- What is the elapsed time needed to implement the change?
- For how long will the current service be disrupted by the change?
- Will retraining of operations staff and users be required following the change?
- Can software quality be maintained in implementing the change?
- What is the likely effect of the change on the future maintainability of the software?
- Is the implementation of the change compatible with the software lifecycle plan? In particular, is the system due for replacement in the near future?
- Will the implementation of the change require multiple versions of the system to be maintained for different user groups? If so, the extra maintenance effort required to do this should be assessed.

The mechanism for requesting a change and planning its implementation should be the configuration control procedure discussed in section 2.4.4. In order to maintain the quality of the system's software and thus to help ensure its longevity, it is important that configuration control procedures are rigorously applied. Before it is possible to assess a change request against the criteria given above to decide how the change should be implemented, if at all, it will generally be necessary to carry out quite a lot of design and, in the case of perfective and adaptive changes, possibly requirements and functional specification. Structured Walkthroughs of the documents produced at the completion of each of these activities

should be carried out to review them against the criteria established in the Maintenance Plan.

In the case of corrective changes it may be necessary to implement an immediate concessionary change to provide an emergency solution to a problem that is disrupting normal system operation. Such a change should be carefully documented and the normal change control and review procedures applied to it after the emergency is over. If necessary the concessionary change may be removed and replaced by a permanent change which satisfies the Maintenance Plan criteria.

8.5.3 The specification, design and implementation of changes

The specification, design and implementation of changes should take place within the same framework, using the same methods and tools, as the original development project. Indeed, in order to maintain the system's integrity it is very important that the design approach and design decisions taken during development are taken account of in making changes. This aim will be made much easier if design decisions have been carefully recorded during development.

The obvious difference between the development phases and the maintenance phase is that in the latter existing code is being changed and the potential effects of change and the difficulty of implementing it must be assessed. This assessment procedure can be greatly aided by indicator data collected during development. For example, data on the coupling of modules and use of Myers' program stability model can give a good indication of the likely implications for other modules of changing a given module. This ripple effect and its consequences for software maintenance are considered in Yau 1978. Similarly, indicators such as McCabe's cyclomatic number can be used to assess how difficult it will be to change and re-test a given module.

Before the design of a change is decided upon, alternative design approaches should be reviewed and compared using indicator data for the modules affected. The design which adheres most closely to the original design philosophy of the system and is simplest when assessed using indicator data is likely to be the best candidate for implementation.

The implementation of a change should be carefully planned so as to cause as little disruption as possible to the normal operation of the system (unless, of course, disruption is not a problem). All of the intended changes should be written and reviewed and all test cases planned before anyone starts changing the system. Needless to say, a copy of the unchanged system should be held in case there are problems with the change.

The testing of changed software is extremely important. An error introduced deep into the software during a change may be very difficult to locate without returning to the unit test stage; a hopeless task in a large system. The tests applied to changed software should be based on the tests performed during system development. For this reason it is important that test descriptions and test data and harnesses used during development are made available to the maintenance staff and are sufficiently well documented as to be usable. The changed software should go through all of the

stages of testing that occur during development from unit testing through integration to acceptance testing. Of course not all of the tests need necessarily be applied and some new tests will need to be generated. Indicator data collected during initial testing should be a guide to what tests should be applied given the change that has been made. If you are using a method that involves proving the correctness of your design or code (such as FDM) you will have to be careful to revalidate a sufficient amount of the design or code to ensure that the original integrity is maintained. During the changing and re-testing of a system, indicator data should be collected as in the original development so as to aid in future maintenance.

Bibliography
Ebert 1980, Glass 1981, Harrison 1982, Lientz 1978 and 1980, McClure 1981, Martin 1983, Parikh 1981, Parnas 1979, Swanson 1976, Yau 1978 and 1980.

9

Project Debriefing

9.1 The purpose of Project Debriefing

Now that the development project is over and your system is installed it is time to make sure that future projects will benefit from what you have achieved and learnt. This is the purpose of Project Debriefing; to record your experiences in carrying out the project in a way that will be of benefit to other projects and which will add to your organisation's collective database of project statistics.

The way in which the results of Project Debriefing can most help your organisation is in planning future projects. Such planning may be at the start of a new project or as part of a tendering activity. In either case the collected experiences of previous projects are of inestimable value in producing accurate project plans. For this reason, Project Debriefing should be strongly related to the topics of estimation and indicators discussed in chapter 2.

If you have been recording indicators throughout the project it will require little effort to organise, summarise and record these indicators as part of Project Debriefing. Of special importance will be indicators related to attributes used in arriving at the project plan (those of type (ii) on page 19). These indicator values can be used in updating the calibration of your cost estimation model or in pin-pointing weaknesses in the model. Weaknesses in the model or its use may show up in the form of input parameters to the model whose estimated values consistently bear no resemblance to their final values. Such difficult-to-estimate parameters are best eliminated from the model

unless better procedures for estimating them can be found.

Project Debriefing for a well organised project should take very little time and will provide invaluable input to the continuing improvement of your organisation's software development approach.

9.2 The framework for Project Debriefing

In order that your organisation can most benefit from Project Debriefing it is highly desirable that a common approach be taken for all projects. This should be the case no matter whether you maintain written Project Debriefing Reports or a computerised debriefing database linked to cost estimation models.

It is especially important that common definitions are used for indicators; for example, a common definition of a line of code. Equally important is the accuracy of the information produced in debriefing. In particular the project manager should be under no pressure to hide mistakes made in the project or to provide inaccurate statistics which are closer to plan than in reality.

As well as containing statistics, the Project Debriefing Report format should accommodate more subjective analysis of the project. Thoughts on the usefulness of the particular programming languages or hardware used or the integration approach adopted may be of value to other project teams. Also thoughts on why problems occurred and how they might have been avoided or, on the other hand, on why the project was so successful will usefully add to your organisation's collective project management wisdom. Such thoughts should be collected from everyone on the project team, not just the project manager. The perspective of problems as seen by a programmer may be quite different to that of the project manager and of more use to programmers on future projects.

Project Debriefing Reports produced in this way are valuable resources of your organisation which must be fully exploited. To achieve this they must not be locked away for ever more, but rather be circulated wherever they may be of use. Of course, the best way to ensure their exploitation is to use them as input to cost estimation and project planning models which are routinely employed at the start of projects or in tendering activities. Whatever approach you adopt, it is most important that you obtain strong management support for it and use it widely and routinely.

9.3 Contents of a Debriefing Report

In this section we give possible contents for a Project Debriefing Report. The precise contents and format of the report will vary from organisation to organisation and will be affected by such matters as whether the data is to be entered into a computerised system. Remember, however, that the contents should be standardised throughout your organisation.

Project description
You should give a brief qualitative description of the project in terms of the client, the application, the hardware and systems software used and hardware and software developed.

Project attributes history
This section should give the estimated and actual values of project attributes used in project modelling (cost estimation etc.). The results of applying these values to your estimation models should then be given and compared with actual values.

The contents of this section are determined solely by your estimation models so as to facilitate recalibration of these models. For example, if you used bottom-up effort estimation based on the estimated number of lines of code in each software unit, you should record:

- a progressive history of estimates of number of lines of code in each unit,
- the final number of lines of code in each unit,
- the progressive history of effort estimates produced by the model for each unit,
- the actual effort for each unit.

You should also record anything that might affect the accuracy of the results such as:

In the final month of the project everyone was working 18 hour days.

Indicator history
Having recorded in the previous section all indicator data which is directly relevant to your estimation model you now record all remaining indicator data collected during the project. This data may be of use in improving or adding to your existing models.

As well as noting anything relevant to the accuracy of the data you should note any trends or observations relating to the data, such as:

We should have seen that the high module coupling coefficient inherent in the design of subsystem C would lead to the integration problems which resulted in the schedule overrun for this subsystem. We should have redesigned this subsystem to reduce the coupling indicator value.

Evaluation of techniques and systems
In this section you should provide a qualitative judgement of all the techniques and systems used, including

- the virtual machine (hardware and systems software),
- methods and tools used in each of the phases,
- project team structure,
- indicators, monitoring and reporting methods,
- client liaison and change control methods,
- subcontractor monitoring and control methods.

If it is desired, these judgements can be quantified by the assignment of grades to each item.

Potentially re-usable items

You should list any items of hardware or software that may potentially be re-usable in other projects. Such items should especially include any useful tools that you developed during the project but might also include general items of hardware or software. Each item should be cross referenced to the Project Fact File.

General words of wisdom

This section provides a catch-all for useful comments that do not fit in elsewhere in the report. For example you might wish to record your experiences on the best way of getting a large computer into your tenth-floor development area, or relate how you would run the project if you did it again.

It must be noted that the Project Debriefing Report is *not* the place to record comments on the future lifecycle of the system. Anything regarding maintenance, enhancement or potential problems with the system should be recorded in the system's documentation archive (Project Fact File) in a form which is easily accessible to maintenance staff.

Keyword abstract

Finally you should produce a keyword abstract to the report which is either filed separately from the report in an index of reports or used to provide keys in a database retrieval system. This abstract might include:

- client type,
- application type,
- hardware used,
- systems software used,
- names of methods used in each phase,
- re-usable software types.

9.4 A checklist for the Project Debriefing Report

- Is it in your organisation's standard format?
- Are all estimated and actual inputs and outputs to your estimation models included?
- Have any areas of inaccuracy been noted?
- Are standard terminology and definitions used except where explicitly stated?
- Have the thoughts of all project members been sought and included?

- Have all problems, no matter how embarrassing, been honestly analysed and recorded?
- Have all outstanding successes been honestly analysed and recorded?
- Has the report been properly filed and widely circulated?

9.5 Sample Project Debriefing Report

The following pages give excerpts from a sample PDR for the development of the VISTA system used throughout the remainder of the book as an example. The PDR is largely fictitious. Certain of the statistics given in the report are, however, drawn from a project very similar to the VISTA development (see Ould 1982, Birrell 1984).

Title	VISTA PROJECT DEBRIEFING REPORT
Authors	N. D. BIRRELL AND M. A. OULD
Keywords	(Client type) Research Establishment
	(Application type) Image Processing Digital Television
	(Hardware used) XAV/075 Host Micro 999 processor based purpose-built hardware HSD001 High speed discs
	(Systems software used) XAV–VOS Operating System WSO C compiler and cross compiler

Contents
1 PROJECT DESCRIPTION
2 PROJECT ATTRIBUTES HISTORY
3 INDICATOR HISTORY
4 EVALUATION OF TECHNIQUES AND SYSTEMS
5 POTENTIALLY RE-USABLE ITEMS
6 FINAL THOUGHTS

1 Project description

[The project description given in section 4.10 would be suitable as a basis for this section of the PDR if supplemented by information on the client and hardware and systems software.]

2 Project attributes history

The manpower estimates were derived primarily using the linear cost estimation model

$$M = I/p$$

where M is the total manpower in days for all of the development work packages listed below, I is the number of lines of deliverable code including comments and p is the coding rate in lines/man-day.

The total numbers of lines of code were estimated in a bottom-up fashion with the software units used for estimating being subsystems. Brief descriptions of the subsystems into which the software was divided are as follows:

A Host Diagnostics: software responsible for host diagnostics and the control of VICE diagnostics.
B HSD Management: software responsible for control of and transfer of data to/from the HSDs
C The parallel line device driver.
⋮

All of the subsystems with the exception of C, which was written in assembler, were written in the high-level C programming language. For all but subsystem C the value $p = 7$ was used in the cost estimation equation based on the value given in the PDR for the very similar VUIM project. For subsystem C a value of $p = 4$ was used based on the indicators given in the XSYSTEM project PDR for a similar driver.

The initial estimate of I for each subsystem along with the final count at the end of system acceptance were as follows:

SUBSYSTEM	INITIAL ESTIMATE	FINAL COUNT
A	840	546
B	960	1294
C	1500	0
E	660	898
F	900	2252
G	450	1705
H	600	451
J	390	1381
N	600	28
P	660	1022
Q	1200	603
R	360	246
S	600	742
TOTAL	9720	11168

The final count for subsystem C is zero because we found that an unsupported manufacturer-supplied driver would do the job. Intermediate estimates of line numbers for each subsystem are given in figure 9.1 [only part given] while the cumulative count for the entire system is shown in figure 9.2.

Fig. 9.1. Intermediate estimates of line numbers for each subsystem (VISTA PDR).

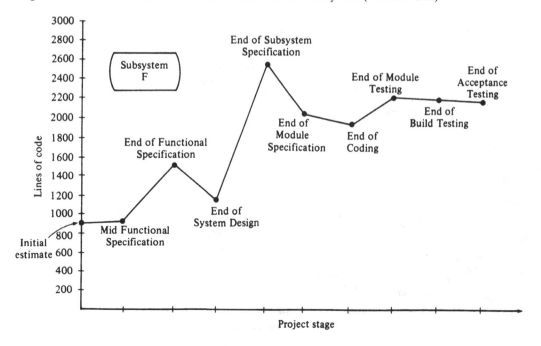

Based on these figures the cost estimation model gives a total manpower required acrss the project of 1549 man-days. This was divided across work packages based on percentages given in the VUIM PDR. Figure 9.3 shows these figures alongside the final actual values. A more detailed breakdown by subsystem for the production phase is given in figure X [not included here]. It should be noted that, as in the VUIM project, all project management effort is recorded against work package 8000 although it was generally evenly divided between phases and overall project management.

From the final count of lines of code and the final number of man-days expended an actual value of $p = 8.0$ is obtained for the project.

3 Indicator data

Each of the following subsections covers one of the indicators measured through the project.

3.1 Cyclomatic number

The cyclomatic number of modules in each subsystem was measured and used as a guide to the number of test cases to be applied. The results are summarised in figure 9.4. Any subsystem for which the number of test cases was not greater than or equal to the cyclomatic number was subjected to special scrutiny.

3.2 Bug counts

The number of bugs detected for each module was maintained and categorised by type of bug and stage of detection. The results are tabulated in figure 7 [not included] and the total for each type is graphed against stage in figure 9.5 [only part included].

3.3 Code expansion

The ROM requirements for the Micro 999 microprocessor were calculated using an expansion factor for bytes of object code/line of C of 15 obtained from the WAM project PDR. The values obtained for each of the microprocessor subsystems in our system are given in figure Z [not included]. The average of 17.9 bytes/line is probably a more useful figure than that of the WAM project which was based on a smaller sample.

The expansion factors for the host were of less importance because of the virtual memory capability but are given . . .

3.3 Evaluation of techniques used

3.3.1 The virtual machine

The XAV/075 with XAV–VOS operating system proved an excellent development environment for the project and was praised by all who used it. The operating system user interface was learnt rapidly by programmers.

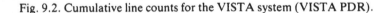

Fig. 9.2. Cumulative line counts for the VISTA system (VISTA PDR).

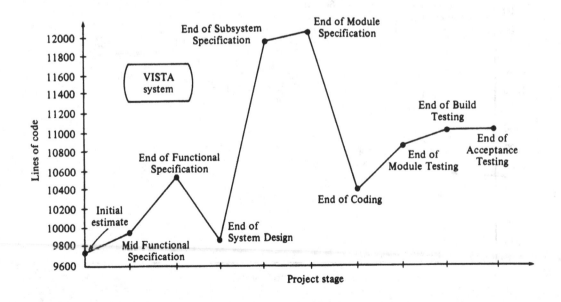

Fig. 9.3. Actual vs estimated manpower requirements (VISTA PDR).

WBS activity	activity name	original estimate		final outturn	
		man-days	percentage	man-days	percentage
2000	System Definition	201	13	189	13
3000	System Design	139	9	164	12
4000	System Production	805	52	717	51
5000	System Acceptance	108	7	79	6
8000	Project Management	294	19	256	18
	totals	1547	100	1405	100

Fig. 9.4. Cyclomatic sizes of subsystems (VISTA PDR).

subsystem	cyclomatic number	number of test cases
A	103	71
B	236	142
C	—	—
E	158	107
F	260	946
G	249	274
H	86	157
J	208	398
N	3	5
P	92	213
Q	74	72
R	25	394
S	130	210
totals	1624	2989

Fig. 9.5. Logic error bugs vs time of detection (VISTA PDR).

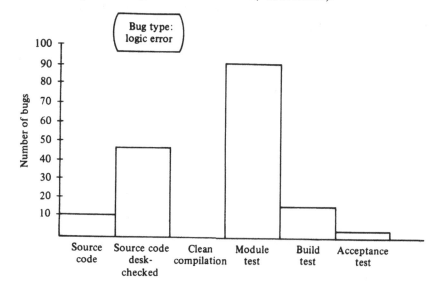

The use of the XAV/075 as the development computer for the VICE microprocessor proved to be very successful. The WSO native compiler and Micro 999 cross compiler running on the XAV/075 allowed most VICE software to be module tested on the XAV/075.

⋮

A number of bugs were found in the WSO cross compiler as follows:

i Double assignment statements of the form A = B = C did not compile to produce correct code

⋮

3.3.2 *Methods and tools used*
Structured Analysis was used for the production of the Functional Specification of the system and Structured Design for the overall system design and subsystem design of the host software. Finite State Machines were used in the subsystem design of the VICE software.

Structured Analysis worked well for the production of the Functional Specification with the following exceptions. Firstly a manual data dictionary was used which proved to be too difficult to maintain and control properly. We should have developed a very simple automated system on the XAV using supplied XAV–VOS tools. Secondly, the Functional Specification method did not aid greatly in the modelling of the system operation or analysis of performance. Use of a method such as SREM, even without tools, could have been more appropriate. Alternatively we could have additionally used Finite State Machines in the Functional Specification and used the FSM testing tool (see below) to model operation.

Use of structured design for the host software was adequate. In retrospect, the project would have been a good one to pilot a more rigid design methodology such as HOS, FDM or HDM. We suggest that suitable pilots are sought at the start of future projects.

Use of FSMs as the subsystem design method on the VICE was very successful, particularly in conjunction with the Chow test sequence generator and test harness. All major design bugs were eliminated by completion of subsystem design by use of this tool.

⋮

3.4 Potentially re-usable items

3.4.1 *HSD001 control software*
The HSD discs are not supported by the XAV–VOS operating system. Subsystem B provides directory and other support functions which could be used on other systems using the HSDs. About 200 lines of the code are machine-dependent and would need to be rewritten if the code were to be used on other than an XAV with XAV–VOS.

⋮

3.5 Final thoughts

3.5.1 *Staff training*
Each person who joined the project once it was underway was put through a familiarisation course involving study of fundamental documents with questions to answer and a coding exercise in C. This proved to be very successful. In particular the code produced in training was of a generally lower standard than the deliverable code produced after the course and so it proved appropriate to train on non-critical code.

3.5.2 *Power availability*
The HSDs required a 100 Amps three-phase power supply. This was not available at all of the commissioning sites without the electricity board being required to dig up the street.

⋮

Other bibliographies

Management of software development
Axelrod 1982, Bentley 1982, Bratman 1975, Bruce 1981,
Couger 1980, De Marco 1983, Donaldson 1978,
Fox 1982, Glass 1979, Gourd 1982, Gunther 1978,
Hice 1978, Keen 1981, Myers 1976, Paster 1981,
Rullo 1980, Steward 1981, Weinwurm 1970,
Yourdon 1982.

**Costing of software development
(further references)**
Black 1977, Boehm 1980, Chrysler 1978, Farr 1965,
Frederic 1974, Herd 1977, James 1978, Johnson
1977, Kustanowitz 1977, Liklider 1969, Nelson
1966, Nelson 1976, Nelson 1978, Parr 1980,
Schneider 1978, Shooman 1979, Suding 1977,
Wolberg 1982, Wolverton 1974.

Other development techniques
Decision Tables: Chvalovský 1983, Hurley 1983,
Metzner 1977, Montalbano 1974.
DREAM: Riddle 1980*d*, Wileden 1979.
HIPO: Stay 1976.
Nassi–Shneiderman charts: Nassi 1973.
PAD: Ehrenberger 1976, Futamura 1981.
Pearl: Martin 1979.
SPECK: Gilbert 1981, Quirk 1977, Quirk 1978.
VDM: Bjorner 1982, Jones 1980.
Verification Graphs: Belford 1976*a*, Belford 1976*b*.
WELLMADE: Boyd 1978.

References

[Abe 1979]
Abe, J., Sakamura, K., & Aiso, H. (1979). An analysis of software project failure. In *Proceedings of the 4th International Conference on Software Engineering*, pp. 378–85. New York: IEEE Computer Society Press.

[ACM 1972]
Proceedings of an ACM conference on proving assertions about programs. *ACM SIGPLAN Notices*, **7**, 1, entire issue.

[AFSC 1975]
Government/Industry Software Workshop Summary Notes. Air Force Systems Command, Electronic Systems Div., USA.

[Alagić 1978]
Alagić, S., & Arbib, M. A. (1978). *The Design of Well-Structured and Correct Programs*, Berlin: Springer-Verlag.

[Alford 1977]
Alford, M. W. (1977). A requirements engineering methodology for real-time processing requirements. *IEEE Transactions on Software Engineering*, **SE-3**, 60–9.

[Alford 1978a]
Alford, M. (1978). Requirements for distributed data processing design. In *Proceedings of the 1st International Conference on Distributed Computer Systems*, pp. 1–14.
New York: IEEE Computer Society Press.

[Alford 1978b]
Alford, M. W. (1978). Software Requirements Engineering Methodology (SREM) at the age of two. In *Proceedings of the 2nd International Computer Software and Applications Conference*, pp. 332–9. New York: IEEE Computer Society Press.

[Alford 1980]
Alford, M. W. (1980). Software Requirements Engineering Methodology (SREM) at the age of four. In *Proceedings of the International Computer Software and Applications Conference*, pp. 866–74. New York: IEEE Computer Society Press.

[Alford 1981]
Alford, M. W., & Davis, C. G. (1981). Experience with the software development system. In Huenke 1981.

[Allison 1983]
Allison, L. (1983). Syntax directed program editing. *Software – Practice and Experience*, **13**, 453–65.

[Ames 1978]
Ames, S. R., & Millen, J. K. (1978). Interface verification for a security kernel. In *Infotech State of the Art Report on System Reliability and Integrity*, pp. 1–23. Maidenhead: Infotech.

[Anderson 1974]
Anderson, R. (1974). *Proving Programs Correct*. London: Wiley.

[Anderson 1978]
Anderson, T., & Shrivastava, S. K. (1978). Reliable software: a selective annotated bibliography. *Software – Practice and Experience*, **8**, 59–76.

[Anderson 1979]
Anderson, R. B. (1979). *Proving Programs Correct*. New York: Wiley.

[Anderson 1982]
Anderson, G. E., & Shumate, K. C. (1982). Selecting a programming language, compiler, and support environment: method and example. *Computer*, **15**, August, 29–36.

[Andrews 1981]
Andrews, D. M., & Benson, J. P. (1981). An automated program testing methodology and its implementation. In *Proceedings of the 5th International Conference on Software Engineering*, pp. 254–61. New York: IEEE Computer Society Press.

[Appleton 1983]
Appleton, D. S. (1983). Data-driven prototyping. *Datamation*, November 1983, 259–68.

[Aron 1969]
Aron, J. D. (1969). Estimating resources for large programming systems. In *Software Engineering Techniques, Report on a Conference Sponsored by the NATO Science Committee, Rome, Italy, 27th to 31st October 1969*, pp. 68–79. Brussels: NATO Science Committee.

[Axelrod 1982]
Axelrod, C. W. (1982). *Computer Productivity*. New York: Wiley.

[Bail 1978]
Bail, W. G., & Zelkowitz, M. V. (1978). Program complexity using hierarchical abstract computers. In *Proceedings of the National Computer Conference 1978*, pp. 605–8. Montvale, N.J.: AFIPS Press.

[Bailey 1981]
Bailey, J. W., & Basili, V. R. (1981). A meta-model for software development resource expenditure. In *Proceedings of the 5th International Conference on Software Engineering*, pp. 107–16. New York: IEEE Computer Society Press.

[Baker 1972]
Baker, F. T. (1972). Chief programmer team management of production programming. *IBM Systems Journal*, **11**, 56–73.

[Balkovich 1976]
Balkovich, E. E., & Engelberg, G. P. (1976). Research towards a technology to support the specification of data processing system performance requirements. In *Proceedings of the 2nd International Conference on Software Engineering*, pp. 110–15. New York: IEEE Computer Society Press.

[Basili 1975]
Basili, V. R., & Turner, A. J. (1975). Iterative enhancement: a practical technique for software development. *IEEE Transactions on Software Engineering*, **SE-1**, 390–6.

[Basili 1978]
Basili, V. R. (Chairman) (1978). A panel session – user experience with new software methods. In *Proceedings of the National Computer Conference, 1978*, pp. 629–39. Montvale, N.J.: AFIPS Press.

[Basili 1981]
Basili, V. R., & Reiter, R. W. (1981). A controlled experiment quantitatively comparing software development approaches. *IEEE Transactions on Software Engineering*, **SE-7**, 299–320.

[Beizer 1983]
Beizer, B. (1983). *Software Testing Techniques*. New York: Van Nostrand Reinhold.

[Belford 1976a]
Belford, P. C., Bond, A. F., Henderson, D. G., & Sellers, L. S. (1976). Specifications: a key to effective software development. In *Proceedings of the 2nd International Conference on Software Engineering*, pp. 71–9. New York: IEEE Computer Society Press.

[Belford 1976b]
Belford, P., & Taylor, D. S. (1976). Specifications verification – a key to improving software reliability. In *Proceedings of the MRI Symposium on Computer Software Engineering, 1975*. New York: Polytechnic Press.

[Belford 1978]
Belford, P. C. (1978). Experience utilising components of the Software Development System. In *Proceedings of the 2nd International Computer Software and Applications Conference*, pp. 340–5. New York: IEEE Computer Society Press.

[Bell 1976]
Bell, T. E., & Thayer, T. A. (1976). Software requirements: are they really a problem? In *Proceedings of the 2nd International Conference on Software Engineering*, pp. 61–8. New York: IEEE Computer Society Press.

[Bell 1977]
Bell, T. E., Bixler, D. C., & Dyer, M. E. (1977). An extendable approach to computer-aided software requirements engineering. *IEEE Transactions on Software Engineering*, **SE-3**, 49–60.

[Bell Laboratories 1978]
UNIX time-sharing system. *Bell System Technical Journal*, **57**, 6, 2. Issue devoted to this topic.

[Bentley 1980]
Bentley, J. L., & Shaw, M. (1980). An Alphard specification of a correct and efficient transformation on data structures. *IEEE Transactions on Software Engineering*, **SE-6**, 572–84.

[Bentley 1982]
Bentley, C. (1982). *Computer Project Management*. London: Heyden.

[Berg 1982]
Berg, H. K., Boebert, W. E., Franta, W. R., & Moher, T. G. (1982). *Formal Methods of Program Verification and Specification*. Englewood Cliffs, N.J.: Prentice-Hall.

[Bergland 1979]
Bergland, G. D., & Gordon, R. (1979). *Software Design Strategies*. New York: IEEE Computer Society Press.

[Bergland 1981]
Bergland, G. D. (1981). A guided tour of program design methodologies. *Computer*, **14**, October, 13–37.

[Berry 1981]
Berry, D. M. (1981). The application of the Formal Development Methodology to data base design and integrity verification. *UCLA Computer Science Department Quarterly*, **9**, 63–96.

[Bersoff 1981]
Bersoff, E. H., Henderson, V. D., & Siegel, S. G. (1981). *Software Configuration Management. An Investment in Product Integrity*. Englewood Cliffs, N.J.: Prentice-Hall.

[Birke 1972]
Birke, D. M. (1972). State-transition programming techniques and their use in producing teleprocessing device-control programs. *IEEE Transactions on Communications*, **COM-20**, 569–75.

[Birrell 1984]
Birrell, N. D., & Blease, D. H. S. (1984). Increasing productivity in embedded microprocessor software development. *Proceedings of the 11th Australian Computer Conference*. Sydney: Australian Computer Society.

[Bjorner 1982]
Bjorner, D., & Jones, C. B. (1982). *Formal Specification and Software Development*. Englewood Cliffs, N.J.: Prentice-Hall.

[Black 1977]
Black, R. K. D., Curnow, R. P., Katz, R., & Gray, M. D. (1977). *BCS Software Production Data*. Boeing Computer Services. (RADC-TR-77-116; NTIS No. AD-A039852).

[Boehm 1975]
Boehm, B. (1975). *Software design and structuring*. In Horowitz 1975.

[Boehm 1976]
Boehm, B. W., Brown, J. R., & Lipow, M. (1976). Quantitative evaluation of software quality. In *Proceedings of the 2nd International Conference on Software Engineering*, pp. 592–605. New York: IEEE Computer Society Press.

[Boehm 1977]
Boehm, B. W. (1977). Seven basic principles of software engineering. In *Infotech State of the Art Report on Software Engineering Techniques*, pp. 79–113. Maidenhead: Infotech.

[Boehm 1978]
Boehm, B. W., Brown, J. R., Kaspar, H., Lipow, M., MacLeod, G. L., & Merritt, M. J. (1978). *Characteristics of Software Quality*. Amsterdam: North-Holland.

[Boehm 1980]
Boehm, B. W., & Wolverton, R. W. (1980). Software cost modelling: some lessons learned. *Journal of Systems and Software*, **1**, 195–201.

[Boehm 1981]
Boehm, B. W. (1981). *Software Engineering Economics*. Englewood Cliffs, N.J.: Prentice-Hall.

[Boehm 1983]
Boehm, B. W., Gray, T., & Seewaldt, T. (1983). Prototyping vs specifying: A multi-project experiment. *UCLA Computer Science Department Quarterly*, **11**, 93–105.

[Bowen 1979]
Bowen, J. B. (1979). A survey of standards and proposed metrics for software quality testing. *Computer*, **12**, August, 37–41.

[Boyd 1978]
Boyd, D. L., & Pizzarello, A. (1978). Introduction to the WELLMADE design methodology. In *Proceedings of the 3rd International Conference on Software Engineering*, pp. 94–100. New York: IEEE Computer Society Press.

[Boyer 1975]
Boyer, R. S., Elspas, B., & Levitt, K. N. (1975). SELECT – A formal system for testing and debugging programs by symbolic execution. In *Proceedings of the International Conference on Reliable Software, 1975*, pp. 234–45. Published as *ACM SIGPLAN Notices*, **10**, 6 (June 1975), 221–7 by ACM, New York.

[Bratman 1975]
Bratman, H. (1975). Automatic techniques for project management and control. In Horowitz 1975.

[Braun 1981]
Braun, R. D., & Givone, D. D. (1981). A generalised algorithm for constructing checking sequences. *IEEE Transactions on Computers*, **C-30**, 141–4.

[Brinch Hansen 1975]
Brinch Hansen, P. (1975). The programming language Concurrent Pascal. *IEEE Transactions on Software Engineering*, **SE-1**, 199–207.

[Britton 1981]
Britton, K. H., Parker, R. A., & Parnas, D. L. (1981). A procedure for designing abstract interfaces for device interface modules. In *Proceedings of the 5th International Conference on Software Engineering*, pp. 195–204. New York: IEEE Computer Society Press.

[Brooks 1975]
Brooks, F. P. (1975). *The Mythical Man-Month*. Reading, Mass.: Addison-Wesley.

[Brown 1967]
Brown, P. J. (1967). The ML/1 macro processor. *Communications of the ACM*, **10**, 618–23.

[Brown 1974]
Brown, P. J. (1974). *Macroprocessors and Techniques for Portable Software*. London: Wiley.

[Bruce 1981]
Bruce, P., & Pederson, S. M. (1981). *The Software Development Project: Planning and Management*. New York: Wiley-Interscience.

[Buck 1971]
Buck, F., *et al.* (1971). *A Cost-by-Function Model for Avionics Computer System*, volume 1. Naval Air Development Centre, NADC-SD-7088.

[Buckley 1979]
Buckley, F. (1979). A standard for software quality assurance plans. *Computer*, **12**, August, 43–9.

[Buxton 1980]
Buxton, J. N. (1980). *Requirements for Ada Programming Support Environments (Stoneman)*. Washington: United States Department of Defense. (Also subsequently republished in 1981 by US DoD, Ada Joint Program Office.)

[Caine 1975]
Caine, S. H., & Gordon, E. K. (1975). PDL – A tool for software design. In *Proceedings of the National Computer Conference 1975*, pp. 271–6. Montvale, N.J.: AFIPS Press.

[Campos 1978a]
Campos, I. M., & Estrin, G. (1978). SARA aided design of software for concurrent systems. In *Proceedings of the National Computer Conference 1978*, pp. 325–36. Montvale, N.J.: AFIPS Press.

[Campos 1978b]
Campos, I. M., & Estrin, G. (1978). Concurrent software system design supported by SARA at the age of one. In *Proceedings of the 3rd International Conference on Software Engineering*, pp. 230–42. New York: IEEE Computer Society Press.

[Celko 1982]
Celko, J. (1982). Time token design methodology. *Software – Practice and Experience*, **12**, 889–95.

[Chand 1980]
Chand, D. R., & Yadav, S. B. (1980). Logical construction of software. *Communications of the ACM*, **23**, 546–55.

[Chandrasekaran 1981]
Eds. Chandrasekaran, B., & Radicchi, S. (1981). *Computer Program Testing. Proceedings of Summer School on Computer Program Testing*, Sogesta, Urbino, Italy. Amsterdam: North-Holland.

[Chapin 1979]
Chapin, N. (1979). A measure of software complexity. In *Proceedings of the National Computer Conference, 1979*, pp. 995–1002. Montvale, N.J.: AFIPS Press.

[Cheatham 1979]
Cheatham, T. E., Holloway, G. H., & Townley, J. A. (1979). Symbolic evaluation and the analysis of programs. *IEEE Transactions on Software Engineering*, **SE-5**, 402–17.

[Chen 1978]
Chen, E. T. (1978). Program complexity and programmer productivity. *IEEE Transactions on Software Engineering*, **SE-4**, 187–94.

[Cho 1980]
Cho, C. (1980). *An Introduction to Software Quality Control*. New York: Wiley.

[Chow 1976]
Chow, T. S. (1976). A generalised assertion language. In *Proceedings of the 2nd International Conference on Software Engineering*, pp. 392–9. New York: IEEE Computer Society Press.

[Chow 1978]
Chow, T. S. (1978). Testing software design modelled by finite-state machines. *IEEE Transactions on Software Engineering*, **SE-4**, 178–87.

[Chrysler 1978]
Chrysler, E. (1978). Some basic determinants of computer programming productivity. *Communications of the ACM*, **21**, 472–83.

[Chvalovský 1983]
Chvalovský, V. (1983). Decision tables. *Software – Practice and Experience*, **13**, 423–9.

[Cichelli 1977]
Cichelli, R. J., & Cichelli, M. J. (1977). Goal directed programming. *ACM SIGPLAN Notices*, **12**, 7, 51–9.

[Clarke 1976]
Clarke, L. (1976). A system to generate test data and symbolically execute programs. *IEEE Transactions on Software Engineering*, **SE-2**, 215–22.

[Cole 1981]
Cole, A. J. (1981). *Macro Processors*. Cambridge: Cambridge University Press.

[Collins 1982]
Collins, G., & Blay, G. (1982). *Structured Systems Development Techniques: Strategic Planning to System Testing*. London: Pitman.

[Comer 1979]
Comer, D., & Halstead, M. H. (1979). A simple experiment in top-down design. *IEEE Transactions on Software Engineering*, **SE-5**, 105–9.

[Connor 1980]
Connor, M. F. (1980). *SADT. Structured Analysis and Design Technique Introduction.* SofTech report 9595-7. Waltham, Mass.: SofTech, Inc.

[Cook 1982]
Cook, M. L. (1982). Software metrics: an introduction and annotated bibliography. *ACM SIGSOFT Software Engineering Notes*, **7**, 2, 41–60.

[Coolahan 1983]
Coolahan, J. E., Jr, & Roussopoulos, N. (1983). Timing requirements for time-driven systems using augmented Petri Nets. *IEEE Transactions on Software Engineering*, **SE-9**, 603–16.

[Cooper 1979]
Eds. Cooper, J. D., & Fisher, M. J. (1979). *Software Quality Management.* New York: Petrocelli.

[Couger 1980]
Couger, J. D., & Zawacki, R. A. (1980). *Motivating and Managing Computer Personnel.* New York: Wiley.

[Coulter 1983]
Coulter, N. S. (1983). Software Science and cognitive psychology. *IEEE Transactions on Software Engineering*, **SE-9**, 166–71.

[Cunningham 1976]
Cunningham, R. J., & Pugh, C. G. (1976). A language-independent system to aid the development of structured programs. *Software – Practice and Experience*, **6**, 487–503.

[Curtis 1979a]
Curtis, W., Sheppard, S. B., Milliman, P., Borst, M. A., & Love, T. (1979). Measuring the psychological complexity of software maintenance tasks with the Halstead and McCabe metrics. *IEEE Transactions on Software Engineering*, **SE-5**, 96–104.

[Curtis 1979b]
Curtis, W., Sheppard, S. B., & Milliman, P. (1979). Third time charm: stronger prediction of programmer performance by software complexity metrics. In *Proceedings of the 4th International Conference on Software Engineering*, pp. 356–60. New York: IEEE Computer Society Press.

[DACS 1979]
Data and Analysis Center for Software (1979). *AIAA Tools Survey.* New York: Grifiss AFB.

[Dahl 1968]
Dahl, O. J., Nygaard, K., & Myhrhuag, B. (1968). *The SIMULA 67 Common Base Language.* Oslo: Norwegian Computing Centre.

[Dahl 1972]
Dahl, O. J., Dijkstra, E. W., & Hoare, C. A. R. (1972). *Structured Programming.* London: Academic Press.

[Darringer 1978]
Darringer, J. A., & King, J. C. (1978). Applications of symbolic execution to program testing. *Computer*, **11**, April, 51–60.

[Davis 1977]
Davis, C. G., & Vick, C. R. (1977). The Software Development System. *IEEE Transactions on Software Engineering*, **SE-3**, 69–84.

[Davis 1978]
Davis, C. G. (1978). Requirements problems in large real-time systems development. In Infotech 1978, volume 2, pp. 77–97.

[Davis 1983]
Davis, W. S. (1983). *Systems Analysis and Design. A Structured Approach.* Reading, Mass.: Addison-Wesley.

[Dearnley 1983]
Dearnley, P. A., & Mayhew, P. J. (1983). In favour of system prototypes and their integration into the systems development cycle. *Computer Journal*, **26**, 36–42.

[de Bono 1971]
de Bono, E. (1971). *The Use of Lateral Thinking.* Harmondsworth, Middlesex: Penguin.

[De Marco 1978]
De Marco, T. (1978). *Structured Analysis and System Specification.* New York: Yourdon Press.

[De Marco 1983]
De Marco, T. (1983). *Controlling Software Projects.* New York: Yourdon Press.

[Dickinson 1980]
Dickinson, B. (1980). *Developing Structured Systems.* New York: Yourdon Press.

[Dickover 1978]
Dickover, M. E., McGowan, C. L., & Ross, D. T. (1978). Software design using SADT. In Infotech 1978, volume 2, pp. 99–114.

[Dijkstra 1968]
Dijkstra, E. W. (1968). Go to statements considered harmful. Letter to editor, *Communications of the ACM*, **11**, 147–8.

[Dijkstra 1970]
Dijkstra, E. W. (1970). Structured programming. In *Software Engineering Techniques*, eds. J. N. Buxton & B. Randell, pp. 84–7. Brussels: NATO Scientific Affairs Division.

[Dijkstra 1972]
Dijkstra, E. W. (1972). Notes on structured programming. In Dahl 1972.

[Dijkstra 1976]
Dijkstra, E. W. (1976). *A Discipline of Programming.* Englewood Cliffs, N.J.: Prentice-Hall.

[DoD 1980]
Reference Manual for the Ada Programming Language,

Proposed Standard Document. US Department of Defense (1980). Also New York: Springer-Verlag (1981).

[Dodd 1980]
Dodd, W. P. (1980). Prototype programs. *Computer*, **13**, February, 81.

[DoI 1981]
Ada-based system development methodology, study report, volume 1. London: Department of Industry.

[Donaldson 1978]
Donaldson, H. (1978). *A Guide to the Successful Management of Computer Projects.* London: Associated Business Press.

[Dreyfus 1976]
Dreyfus, J. M., & Karacsony, P. J. (1976). The preliminary design as a key to successful software development. In *Proceedings of the 2nd International Conference on Software Engineering*, pp. 206–13. New York: IEEE Computer Society Press.

[Druffel 1982]
Druffel, L. E. (1982). The potential effect of Ada on software engineering in the 1980's. In *EASCOM 1982 Conference Record*, pp. 161–6. New York: IEEE Computer Society Press.

[Dunn 1982]
Dunn, R., & Ullman, R. (1982). *Quality Assurance for Computer Software.* New York: McGraw-Hill.

[Ebert 1980]
Eds. Ebert, R., Luegger, J., & Goecke, L. (1980). *Practice in Software Adaption and Maintenance.* Amsterdam: North-Holland.

[Eggert 1980]
Eggert, P. R. (1980). *Overview of the Ina Jo Specification Language.* Santa Monica, Calif.: System Development Corporation.

[Ehrenberger 1976]
Ehrenberger, E., Rauch, G., & Chroy, K. (1976). Program analysis – a method for the verification of software for the control of a nuclear reactor. In *Proceedings of the 3rd International Conference on Software Engineering*, pp. 611–16. New York: IEEE Computer Society Press.

[Elshoff 1978]
Elshoff, J. L., & Marcotty, M. (1978). On the use of the cyclomatic number to measure program complexity. *ACM SIGPLAN Notices*, **13**, 12, 29–40.

[Estrin 1978]
Estrin, G. (1978). A methodology for design of digital systems – supported by SARA at the age of one. In *Proceedings of the National Computer Conference, 1978*, pp. 313–24. Montvale, N.J.: AFIPS Press.

[Fagan 1976]
Fagan, M. E. (1976). Design and code inspections to reduce errors in program development. *IBM Systems Journal*, **15**, 182–211.

[Fairley 1978]
Fairley, R. E. (1978). Tutorial: Static analysis and dynamic testing of computer software. *Computer*, **11**, April, 14–23.

[Falla 1977]
Falla, M. (1977). System development systems. In *Infotech State of the Art Report, Software Engineering Techniques*, volume 2, pp. 169–87. Maidenhead: Infotech.

[Farr 1965]
Farr, L., & Zagorski, H. J. (1965). Quantitative analysis of programming cost factors: a progress report. In *ICC Symposium Proceedings, Economics of Automatic Data Processing, 1965*. Amsterdam: North-Holland.

[Feiler 1981]
Feiler, P. H., & Medina-Mora, R. (1981). An incremental programming environment. In *Proceedings of the 5th International Conference on Software Engineering*, pp. 44–53. New York: IEEE Computer Society Press.

[Feldman 1979]
Feldman, S. L. (1979). MAKE – A program for maintaining computer programs. *Software – Practice and Experience*, **9**, 255–65.

[Fenchel 1977]
Fenchel, R. S. (1977). *System Architect's Apprentice (SARA) System Reference Manual.* Los Angeles: UCLA Computer Science Department.

[Fenchel 1979]
Fenchel, R. (1979). *SARA System Tutorial Reference Manual.* Los Angeles: UCLA Computer Science Department.

[Feuer 1982]
Feuer, A. R., & Gehani, N. H. (1982). A comparison of the programming languages C and Pascal. *Computing Surveys*, **14**, 73–92.

[Fitzgerald 1973]
Fitzgerald, J. M., & Fitzgerald, A. F. (1973). *Fundamentals of System Analysis.* London: Wiley.

[Fitzsimmons 1978]
Fitzsimmons, A., & Love, T. (1978). A review and evaluation of Software Science. *ACM Computing Surveys*, **10**, 3–18.

[Floyd 1971]
Floyd, R. W. (1971). Toward automatic synthesis of

programs. In *Proceedings of the 1971 IFIP Congress*. Amsterdam: North-Holland.

[Foster 1980]
Foster, K. A. (1980). Error sensitive test cases analysis (ESTCA). *IEEE Transactions on Software Engineering*, **SE-6**, 258–64.

[Fox 1982]
Fox, J. M. (1982). *Software and its Development*. Englewood Cliffs, N.J.: Prentice-Hall.

[Frederic 1974]
Frederic, B. C. (1974). *A provisional model for estimating computer program development costs*. Tecolote Research Inc. Report TM-7/REV-1.

[Freedman 1979]
Freedman, D. P., & Weinberg, G. M. (1979). *Ethnotechnical Review Handbook*. Lincoln, Nebraska, USA: Ethnotech Inc.

[Freeman 1979]
Freeman, P. (1979). Requirement analysis and specification. In Infotech 1979*a*, volume 2, pp. 41–56.

[Freeman 1980*a*]
Eds. Freeman, H., & Lewis, P. M. (1980). *Software Engineering*. Proceedings of the workshop (Albany, Troy, and Schenectady, New York, May 30–June 1 1979). New York: Academic Press.

[Freeman 1980*b*]
Eds. Freeman, P., & Wasserman, A. (1980). *Software Design Techniques*. New York: IEEE Computer Society Press.

[Freeman 1982]
Freeman, P., & Wasserman, A. I. (1982). *Software Development Methodologies and Ada*. US Department of Defense – Ada Joint Program Office.

[Freiman 1979]
Freiman, F. R., & Park, R. D. PRICE software model – version 3: an overview. In *Proceedings of IEEE – PINY Workshop on Quantitative Software Models*, pp. 32–41. New York: IEEE Computer Society Press.

[Futamura 1981]
Futamura, Y., Kawai, T., Horikoshi, H., & Tsutsumi, M. (1981). Development of computer programs by Problem Analysis Diagram (PAD). In *Proceedings of the 5th International Conference on Software Engineering*, pp. 325–32. New York: IEEE Computer Society Press.

[Gane 1979]
Gane, C., & Sarson, T. (1979). *Structured Systems Analysis: Tools and Techniques*. Englewood Cliffs, N.J.: Prentice-Hall.

[Gannon 1979]
Gannon, C. (1979). Error detection using path testing and static analysis. *Computer*, **12**, August, 26–31.

[Gardner 1977]
Gardner, R., Overman, W., & Ruggiero, W. (1977). *GMB System Reference Manual*. Los Angeles: UCLA Computer Science Department.

[Gardner 1981]
Gardner, A. C. (1981). *Practical LCP*. Maidenhead: McGraw-Hill.

[Gehani 1982]
Gehani, N. (1982). Specifications: formal and informal – a case study. *Software – Practice and Experience*, **12**, 433–44.

[Geiger 1979]
Geiger, W., Gmeiner, L., Trauboth, H., & Voges, U. (1979). Program testing techniques for nuclear reactor protection systems. *Computer*, **12**, August, 10–18.

[Gerhart 1977]
Gerhart, S. L. A unified view of current program testing and proving: theory and practice. In *Proceedings of the State of the Art Conference on Reliable . Software, London, 1977*, pp. 65–94. Maidenhead: Infotech.

[Geschke 1977]
Geschke, C., Morris, J. H., & Satterthwaite, E. (1977). Early experience with Mesa. In *Proceedings of the ACM Conference on Language Design for Reliable Software*, pp. 138–52.

[Gilb 1976]
Gilb, T. (1976). *Software Metrics*. Lund, Sweden: Studentlitteratur.

[Gilb 1979]
Gilb, T. (1979). Structured design methods for maintainability. In Infotech 1979*a*, pp. 85–98.

[Gilbert 1981]
Gilbert, M. H., Quirk, W. J., Winsborrow, R. P. J., & Langsford, A. (1981). *Application of SPECK to the Design of Digital Hardware Systems*. Harwell: AERE (AERE-R10257).

[Gilbreath 1983]
Gilbreath, J., & Gilbreath, G. (1983). Eratosthenes revisited: once more through the sieve. *BYTE*, Jan 1983, 283–326.

[Gildersleeve 1970]
Gildersleeve, T. R. (1970). *Decision Tables and their Practical Application in Data Processing*. Englewood Cliffs, N.J.: Prentice-Hall.

[Gill 1962]
Gill, A. (1962). *Introduction to the Theory of Finite State Machines*. New York: McGraw-Hill.

[Glass 1977]
Glass, R. L. (1977). *The Universal Elixir and Other*

Computing Projects which Failed. Seattle: Computing Trends.

[Glass 1979]
Glass, R. L. (1979). *Software Reliability Guidebook*. Englewood Cliffs, N.J.: Prentice-Hall.

[Glass 1980]
Glass, R. L. (1980). A benefit analysis of some software reliability methodologies. *ACM SIGSOFT Software Engineering Notes*, **5**, 2, 26–33.

[Glass 1981]
Glass, R. L., & Noiseux, R. A. (1981). *Software Maintenance Guidebook*. Englewood Cliffs, N.J.: Prentice-Hall.

[Glass 1982]
Glass, R. L. (1982). *Modern Programming Practices. A Report from Industry*. Englewood Cliffs, N.J.: Prentice-Hall.

[Goel 1980]
Goel, A. L. (1980). A summary of the discussion on 'an analysis of competing software reliability models'. *IEEE Transactions on Software Engineering*, **SE-6**, 501–2.

[Gomaa 1981]
Gomaa, H., & Scott, D. B. H. (1981). Prototyping as a tool in the specification of user requirements. In *Proceedings of the 5th International Conference on Software Engineering*, pp. 333–9. New York: IEEE Computer Society Press.

[Goodenough 1975]
Goodenough, J. B., & Gerhart, S. L. (1975). Toward a theory of test data selection. *IEEE Transactions on Software Engineering*, **SE-1**, 156–73.

[Goodenough 1979]
Goodenough, J. (1979). A survey of program testing issues. In *Research Directions in Software Technology*, Ed. P. Wegner, pp. 316–40. Cambridge, Mass.: MIT Press.

[Gordon 1977]
Gordon, R. L., & Lamb, J. C. (1977). A close look at Brooks' Law. *Datamation*, **23**, June, 81–6.

[Gordon 1979]
Gordon, R. D. (1979). Measuring improvements in program clarity. *IEEE Transactions on Software Engineering*, **SE-5**, 79–90.

[Gotlieb 1978]
Gotlieb, C. C., & Gotlieb, L. R. (1978). *Data Types and Structures*. Englewood Cliffs, N.J.: Prentice-Hall.

[Gouda 1976]
Gouda, M. G., & Manning, E. G. (1976). On the modelling, analysis and design of protocols – a special class of software structures. In *Proceedings of the 2nd International Conference on Software Engineering*, pp. 256–62. New York: IEEE Computer Society Press.

[Gourd 1982]
Gourd, R. S. (1982). A self-assessment procedure dealing with software project management. *Communications of the ACM*, **25**, 883–7.

[Griffiths 1978]
Griffiths, S. N. (1978). Design methodologies – a comparison. In Infotech 1978, pp. 133–66.

[Gunning 1962]
Gunning, R. (1962). *How to Take the Fog out of Writing*. Chicago: Dartwell Press.

[Gunther 1978]
Gunther, R. C. (1978). *Management Methodology for Software Product Engineering*. New York: Wiley.

[Guttag 1976]
Guttag, J. V., Horowitz, E., & Musser, D. R. (1976). The design of data type specifications. In *Proceedings of the 2nd International Conference on Software Engineering*, pp. 414–20. New York: IEEE Computer Society Press.

[Guttag 1978a]
Guttag, J. V., Horowitz, E., & Musser, D. R. (1978). Abstract data types and software validation. *Communications of the ACM*, **21**, 1048–64.

[Guttag 1978b]
Guttag, J. V., & Horning, J. J. (1978). The algebraic specification of abstract data types. *Acta Informatica*, **10**, 27–52.

[Guttag 1980]
Guttag, J. (1980). Notes on type abstraction: version 2. *IEEE Transactions on Software Engineering*, **SE-6**, 13–23.

[Haberman 1981]
Haberman, A. N., & Perry, D. E. (1981). System composition and version control for Ada. In Huenke 1981.

[Halstead 1977]
Halstead, M. (1977). *Elements of Software Science*. New York: Elsevier North-Holland.

[Hamer 1982]
Hamer, P. G., & Frewin, G. D. (1982). M. H. Halstead's Software Science – a critical examination. In *Proceedings of the 6th International Conference on Software Engineering*, pp. 197–206. New York: IEEE Computer Society Press.

[Hamilton 1976]
Hamilton, M., & Zeldin, S. (1976). Higher Order Software – a methodology for defining software. *IEEE Transactions on Software Engineering*, **SE-2**, 9–32.

[Hamilton 1979]
Hamilton, M., & Zeldin, S. (1979). The relationship between design and verification. *Journal of Systems and Software*, **1**, 29–56.

[Hamilton 1983]

Hamilton, M., & Zeldin, S. (1983). The functional life cycle model and its automation: USE.IT. *Journal of Systems and Software*, **3**, 25–62.

[Harrison 1982]

Harrison, W., Magel, K., Kluczny, R., & De Kock, A. (1982). Applying software complexity metrics to program maintenance. *Computer*, **15**, September, 65–79.

[Hausen 1981a]

Hausen, H. L., & Muellerburg, M. (1981). Software engineering environments – a bibliography. In Huenke 1981.

[Hausen 1981b]

Hausen, H. L., & Muellerburg, M. (1981). Conspectus of software engineering environments. In *Proceedings of the 5th International Conference on Software Engineering*, pp. 34–43. New York: IEEE Computer Society Press.

[Henderson 1975]

Henderson, P. (1975). Finite state modelling in program development. *ACM SIGPLAN Notices*, **10**, 6, 221–7.

[Henry 1981]

Henry, S. M., & Kafura, D. G. (1981). Software structure metrics based on information flow. *IEEE Transactions on Software Engineering*, **SE-7**, 510–18.

[Herd 1977]

Herd, J. R., Postak, J. N., Russell, W. E., & Stewart, K. R. (1977). *Cost Estimation Study – Study Results*. RADC-TR-77-220 Vol. 1. Rockville, Md.: Doty Associates Inc.

[Hershey 1975a]

Hershey, E. A., & Bastarache, M. (1975). *PSA – Command Descriptions*. ISDOS Working Paper 91. University of Michigan.

[Hershey 1975b]

Hershey, E. A., Winters, E. W., Berg, D. L., Dickey, A. F., & Kahn, B. L. (1975). *Problem Statement Language – Language Reference Manual*. ISDOS Working Paper 68. University of Michigan.

[Hester 1981]

Hester, S. D., Parnas, D. L., & Utter, D. F. (1981). Using documentation as a software design medium. *Bell System Technical Journal*, **60**, 1941–77.

[Hice 1978]

Hice, G. F., Turner, W. S., & Cookwell, L. F. (1978). *System Development Methodology*. Amsterdam: North-Holland.

[Higgins 1979]

Higgins, D. A. (1979). Structured programming with Warnier–Orr diagrams. In *Software Design*

Strategies. New York: IEEE Computer Society Press.

[Hoare 1969]

Hoare, C. A. R. (1969). An axiomatic basis for computer programming. *Communications of the ACM*, **12**, 576–80.

[Hoare 1972a]

Hoare, C. A. R. (1972). Notes on data structuring. In *Structured Programming*, eds. O. J. Dahl, E. W. Dijkstra & C. A. R. Hoare. New York: Academic Press.

[Hoare 1972b]

Hoare, C. A. R. (1972). Proofs of correctness of data representations. *Acta Informatica*, **1**, 271–81.

[Holthouse 1979]

Holthouse, M. A., & Hatch, M. J. (1979). Experience with automated testing analysis. *Computer*, **12**, August, 33–6.

[Horowitz 1975]

Ed. Horowitz, E. (1975). *Practical Strategies for Developing Large Software Systems*. Reading, Mass.: Addison-Wesley.

[HOS 1983]

Building Systems with USE.IT. Cambridge, Mass.: Higher Order Software, Inc.

[Houghton 1980]

Eds. Houghton, R. C., & Oakley, K. A. (1980). *NBS Software Tools Database*. NBSIR 80-2159. Washington D.C.: National Bureau of Standards.

[Houghton 1981]

Houghton, R. C. (1981). *Features of Software Development Tools*. NBS Special Publication 500-74. Washington D.C.: National Bureau of Standards.

[Houghton 1982]

Houghton, R. C. (1982). *Software Development Tools*. NBS Special Publication 500-82. Washington D.C.: National Bureau of Standards.

[Houghton 1983]

Houghton, R. C. (1983). Software development tools: A profile. *Computer*, **16**, May, 63–70.

[Howard 1980]

Howard, P. C. (1980). Productivity in system development. *EDP Performance Review*, **8**, 1–7.

[Howden 1976]

Howden, W. E. (1976). Reliability of the path analysis testing strategy. *IEEE Transactions on Software Engineering*, **SE-2**, 208–15.

[Howden 1977]

Howden, W. E. (1977). Symbolic testing and the DISSECT symbolic evaluation system. *IEEE Transactions on Software Engineering*, **SE-3**, 266–78.

[Howden 1978*a*]
Howden, W. E. (1978). Theoretical and empirical studies of program testing. In *Proceedings of the 3rd International Conference on Software Engineering*, pp. 305–11. New York: IEEE Computer Society Press.

[Howden 1978*b*]
Howden, W. E. (1978). An evaluation of the effectiveness of symbolic testing. *Software – Practice and Experience*, **8**, 381–97.

[Howden 1978*c*]
Howden, W. E. (1978). DISSECT – A symbolic evaluation and program testing system. *IEEE Transactions on Software Engineering*, **SE-4**, 70–3.

[Howden 1980]
Howden, W. E. (1980). Functional program testing. *IEEE Transactions on Software Engineering*, **SE-6**, 162–9.

[Howden 1981]
Howden, W. E. (1981). Completeness criteria for testing elementary program functions. In *Proceedings of the 5th International Conference on Software Engineering*, pp. 235–43. New York: IEEE Computer Society Press.

[Howden 1982*a*]
Howden, W. E. (1982). Life-cycle software validation. *Computer*, **15**, February, 71–9.

[Howden 1982*b*]
Howden, W. E. (1982). Weak mutation testing and completeness of test sets. *IEEE Transactions on Software Engineering*, **SE-8**, 371–9.

[Howden 1982*c*]
Howden, W. E. (1982). Contemporary software development environments. *Communications of the ACM*, **25**, 318–29.

[Huang 1978]
Huang, J. (1978). Program instrumentation and software testing. *Computer*, **11**, April, 25–32.

[Huenke 1981]
Ed. Huenke, H. (1981). *Software Engineering Environments*. Amsterdam: North-Holland.

[Hughes 1979]
Hughes, J. W. (1979). A formalisation and explication of the Michael Jackson method of program design. *Software – Practice and Experience*, **9**, 191–202.

[Hurley 1983]
Hurley, R. B. (1983). *Decision Tables in Software Engineering*. New York: Van Nostrand Reinhold.

[IBM 1970]
General Purpose Simulation System/360 Users' Manual. White Plains, N.Y.: IBM Technical Publication Department.

[IBM 1975]
HIPO – A Design Aid and Documentation Technique. IBM publication GC20-185-1. New York: IBM.

[Infotech 1976]
Infotech State of the Art Report on Structured Programming. Maidenhead: Infotech.

[Infotech 1978]
Infotech State of the Art Report on Structured Analysis and Design. Maidenhead: Infotech.

[Infotech 1979*a*]
Infotech State of the Art Report on Structured Software Development. Maidenhead: Infotech.

[Infotech 1979*b*]
Infotech State of the Art Report on Software Testing. Maidenhead: Infotech.

[Ingevaldsson 1979]
Ingevaldsson, L. (1979). *JSP – A Practical Method of Program Design*. Bromley: Chartwell-Bratt.

[ISDOS 1981]
ISDOS Project (1981). *PSL/PSA – User's Reference Manual*. Ann Arbor, Mich.: University of Michigan.

[Isner 1982]
Isner, J. F. (1982). A FORTRAN programming methodology based on data abstraction. *Communications of the ACM*, **25**, 686–97.

[Ivie 1977]
Ivie, E. (1977). The programmer's workbench – a machine for software development. *Communications of the ACM*, **20**, 746–53.

[Jackson 1975]
Jackson, M. A. (1975). *Principles of Program Design*. New York: Academic Press.

[Jackson 1983]
Jackson, M. (1983). *System Development*. Englewood Cliffs, N.J.: Prentice-Hall.

[James 1978]
James, T. G. (1978). Software cost estimating methodology. In *Proceedings of the National Aerospace Electronics Conference*, pp. 22–8. New York: IEEE Computer Society Press.

[JIMCOM 1983]
Joint IECCA and MUF Committee On MASCOT (1983). *The Official Handbook of MASCOT II Issue 2*. Malvern: RRE.

[Johnson 1976]
Johnson, R. T., & Morris, J. B. (1976). Abstract data types in the model programming language. In *Proceedings of the Conference on Data: Abstraction, Definition and Structure, ACM SIGPLAN Notices*, **11**, special issue, 34–46.

[Johnson 1977]
Johnson, J. R. (1977). A working measure of productivity. *Datamation*, February 1977, 106–10.

[Jones 1978]
Jones, T. C. (1978). Measuring programming quality and productivity. *IBM Systems Journal*, **17**, 43–50.

[Jones 1980]
Jones, C. B. (1980). *Software Development: A Rigorous Approach*. London: Prentice-Hall.

[Kafura 1981]
Kafura, D., & Henry, S. (1981). Software quality metrics based on interconnectivity. *Journal of Systems and Software*, **2**, 121–31.

[Katz 1976]
Katz, S. M., & Manna, Z. (1976). The logical analysis of programs. *Communications of the ACM*, **19**, 188–206.

[Katzenelson 1983a]
Katzenelson, J. (1983). Introduction to Enhanced C (EC). *Software – Practice and Experience*, **13**, 551–76.

[Katzenelson 1983b]
Katzenelson, J. (1983). Higher level programming and data abstraction – a case study of using Enhanced C. *Software – Practice and Experience*, **13**, 577–95.

[Keen 1981]
Keen, J. (1981). *Managing Systems Development*. London: Wiley.

[Kemmerer 1980]
Kemmerer, R. (1980). *FDM – A Specification and Verification Methodology*. System Development Corporation Report SP-4088/000/00.

[Kernighan 1974]
Kernighan, B. W., & Plauger, P. J. (1974). *The Elements of Programming Style*. New York: McGraw-Hill.

[Kernighan 1978]
Kernighan, B. W., & Ritchie, D. M. (1978). *The C Programming Language*. Englewood Cliffs, N.J.: Prentice-Hall.

[Kernighan 1981]
Kernighan, B. W., & Mashey, J. R. (1981). The UNIX programming environment. *Computer*, **14**, 12–24.

[King 1976]
King, J. C. (1976). Symbolic execution and program testing. *Communications of the ACM*, **19**, 385–94.

[Kustanowitz 1977]
Kustanowitz, A. L. (1977). System Life Cycle Estimation (SLICE): a new approach to estimating resources for application program development. In *Proceedings of the 1st International Conference on Computer Software and Applications*, pp. 226–32. New York: IEEE Computer Society Press.

[Kutzler 1983]
Kutzler, B., & Lichtenberger, F. (1983). *Bibliography on Abstract Data Types*. Berlin: Springer-Verlag.

[Lampson 1977]
Lampson, B. W., Horning, J. J., London, R. L., Mitchell, J. G., & Popek, G. J. (1977). Report on the programming language Euclid. *ACM SIGPLAN Notices*, **12**, 2, entire issue devoted to report.

[Lano 1979]
Lano, R. J. (1979). *A Technique for Software and Systems Design*. Amsterdam: North-Holland.

[Lassez 1981]
Lassez, J. L., van der Knijff, D., Shepherd, J., & Lassez, C. (1981). A critical examination of software science. *Journal of Systems and Software*, **2**, 105–12.

[Ledgard 1973]
Ledgard, H. F. (1973). The case for structured programming. *BIT*, **13**, 45–7.

[Ledgard 1975a]
Ledgard, H. F. (1975). *Programming Proverbs*. Rochelle Park, N.J.: Hayden Book Co.

[Ledgard 1975b]
Ledgard, H. F. (1975). *Programming Proverbs for Fortran Programmers*. Rochelle Park, N.J.: Hayden Book Co.

[Levitt 1980]
Levitt, K. N., Neumann, P. G., & Robinson, L. (1980). *The SRI Hierarchical Development Methodology (HDM) and its Application to the Development of Secure Software*. Washington D.C.: National Bureau of Standards.

[Lewis 1982]
Lewis, T. G. (1982). *Software Engineering: Analysis and Verification*. Reston, Va.: Reston Publishing Co. Inc.

[Lientz 1978]
Lientz, B., Swanson, E., & Tompkins, G. (1978). Characteristics of application software maintenance. *Communications of the ACM*, **6**, 466–71.

[Lientz 1980]
Lientz, B. F., & Swanson, E. B. (1980). *Software Maintenance Management. A Study of the Maintenance of Computer Application Software in 487 Data Processing Organisations*. Reading, Mass.: Addison-Wesley.

[Liklider 1969]
Liklider, J. C. R. (1969). Under-estimates and over-expectations. *Computers and Automation*, **18**, 48–52.

[Linger 1979]
Linger, R. C., Mills, H. D., & Witt, B. I. (1979). *Structured Programming: Theory and Practice*. Reading, Mass.: Addison-Wesley.

[Lipow 1982]
Lipow, M. (1982). Number of faults per line of code. *IEEE Transactions on Software Engineering*, **SE-8**, 437–9.

[Liskov 1975]
Liskov, B. H., & Zilles, S. N. (1975). Specification techniques for data abstraction. *IEEE Transactions on Software Engineering*, **SE-1**, 7–19.

[Liskov 1977a]
Liskov, B., Snyder, A., Atkinson, R., & Schaffert, C. (1977). Abstraction mechanisms in CLU. *Communications of the ACM*, **20**, 564–76.

[Liskov 1977b]
Liskov, B., & Zilles, S. (1977). An introduction to formal specifications of data abstractions. In Yeh 1977, pp. 1–32.

[Littlewood 1980]
Littlewood, B. (1980). Theories of software reliability: How good are they and how can they be improved? *IEEE Transactions on Software Engineering*, **SE-6**, 489–500.

[Locasso 1980]
Locasso, R., Scheid, J., Schorre, V., & Eggert, P. (1980). *The Ina Jo Specification Language Reference Manual.* System Development Corporation Report TM-(L)-6021/001/00.

[McCabe 1976]
McCabe, T. J. (1976). A complexity measure. *IEEE Transactions on Software Engineering*, **SE-2**, 308–20.

[McClure 1978]
McClure, C. L. (1978). A model for program complexity analysis. In *Proceedings of the 3rd International Conference on Software Engineering*, pp. 149–57. New York: IEEE Computer Society Press.

[McClure 1981]
McClure, C. L. (1981). *Managing Software Development and Maintenance.* New York: Van Nostrand Reinhold.

[McCue 1978]
McCue, G. M. (1978). IBM's Santa Teresa laboratory – architectural design for program development. *IBM Systems Journal*, **17**, 4–25.

[McGowan 1975]
McGowan, C. L., & Kelly, J. R. (1975). *Top-Down Structured Programming Techniques.* New York: Petrocelli/Charter.

[McGowan 1977]
McGowan, C. L., & Kelly, J. R. (1977). A review of decomposition and design methodologies. In *Infotech State of the Art Conference on Reliable Software, 1977*, pp. 37–63. Maidenhead: Infotech.

[Marmor-Squires 1977a]
Marmor-Squires, A. B. (1977). An annotated bibliography on software engineering. In *Infotech State of the Art Report on Software Engineering Techniques*, vol. 2, pp. 161–221. Maidenhead: Infotech.

[Marmor-Squires 1977b]
Marmor-Squires, A. B. (1977). On methodologies and programming environments to support the development of verified software. In Infotech 1979a, pp. 165–76.

[Martin 1979]
Martin, T. (1979). Pearl at the age of three. In *Proceedings of the 4th International Conference on Software Engineering*, pp. 100–109. New York: IEEE Computer Society Press.

[Martin 1982]
Martin, J. (1982). *Application Development without Programmers.* Englewood Cliffs, N.J.: Prentice-Hall.

[Martin 1983]
Martin, J., & McClure, C. (1983). *Software Maintenance: The Problem and its Solution.* London: Prentice-Hall.

[Mason 1983]
Mason, R. E. A., & Carey, T. T. (1983). Prototyping interactive information systems. *Communications of the ACM*, **26**, 347–54.

[Matsumoto 1981]
Matsumoto, Y., Sasaki, O., Nakajima, S., & Takezawa, K. (1981). SWB system: a software factory. In Huenke 1981.

[Meeson 1979]
Meeson, R. N., & Gannon, C. (1979). An empirical evaluation of static analysis and path testing. In *Proceedings of AIAA Computers in Aerospace Conference II, Los Angeles, October 1979.*

[Melliar-Smith 1982]
Melliar-Smith, P. M., & Schwartz, R. L. (1982). Formal specification and mechanical verification of SIFT: a fault-tolerant flight control system. *IEEE Transactions on Computers*, **C-31**, 616–30. ·

[Mendis 1979]
Mendis, K. S., & Gollis, M. L. (1979). Software error history and projection, a case study. In *Proceedings, NSIA Software Conference*, pp. 30–7. National Security Industrial Association.

[Mendis 1982]
Mendis, K. S. (1982). Quantifying software quality. In *Proceedings of ACM '81 Conference*, pp. 268–73. New York: ACM.

[Metzner 1977]
Metzner, J. R., & Barnes, B. H. (1977). *Decision Table*

Languages and Systems. New York: Academic Press.

[Millen 1981]
Millen, J. K., & Drake, D. L. (1981). An experiment with Affirm and HDM. *Journal of Systems and Software*, **2**, 159–76.

[Miller 1977a]
Miller, E. F. (1977). Program testing: art meets theory. *Computer*, **10**, July, 42–51.

[Miller 1977b]
Miller, E. F. (1977). Program testing tools – a survey. In *Proceedings of MIDCON, Chicago, 1977.*

[Miller 1978]
Miller, E., & Howden, W. E. (1978). *Tutorial: Software Testing and Validation Techniques.* New York: IEEE Computer Society Press.

[Miller 1979a]
Ed. Miller, E. (1979). *Programming Testing Techniques.* New York: IEEE Computer Society Press.

[Miller 1979b]
Miller, E. F. (1979). *Automated Tools for Software Engineering.* New York: IEEE Computer Society Press.

[Mills 1971]
Mills, H. D. (1971). *Debugging Techniques in Large Systems.* Englewood Cliffs, N.J.: Prentice-Hall.

[Mimno 1982]
Mimno, P. (1982). A new technology for mathematically provable software. *Computerworld*, **16**, 41.

[Misra 1983]
Misra, P. N. (1983). Software reliability analysis. *IBM Systems Journal*, **22**, 262–70.

[Mitze 1981]
Mitze, R. W. (1981). The UNIX system as a software engineering environment. In Huenke 1981.

[Miyamoto 1978]
Miyamoto, I. (1978). Toward an effective software reliability evaluation. In *Proceedings of the 3rd International Conference on Software Engineering*, pp. 46–55. New York: IEEE Computer Society Press.

[Mohanty 1979]
Mohanty, S. N. (1979). Models and measurements for quality assessment of software. *ACM Computing Surveys*, **11**, 251–75.

[Mohanty 1981]
Mohanty, S. N. (1981). Software cost estimation: present and future. *Software – Practice and Experience*, **11**, 103–21.

[Moitra 1982]
Moitra, A. (1982). Direct implementation of algebraic

specification of abstract data types. *IEEE Transactions on Software Engineering*, **SE-8**, 12–20.

[Montalbano 1974]
Montalbano, M. (1974). *Decision Tables.* Science Research Associates.

[Morris 1980]
Morris, J. B. (1980). Programming by successive refinement of data abstraction. *Software – Practice and Experience*, **10**, 249–63.

[MSA 1980]
Mascot Suppliers Association (1980). *The Official Handbook of Mascot.* Malvern: Mascot Suppliers Association.

[Mullery 1979]
Mullery, G. P. (1979). CORE – A method for controlled requirement specification. In *Proceedings of the 4th International Conference on Software Engineering*, pp. 126–35

[Musser 1980]
Musser, D. R. (1980). Abstract data type specification in the AFFIRM system. *IEEE Transactions on Software Engineering*, **SE-6**, 24–32.

[Myers 1975]
Myers, G. J. (1975). *Reliable Software through Composite Design.* New York: Van Nostrand Reinhold.

[Myers 1976]
Myers, G. J. (1976). *Software Reliability – Principles and Practices.* London: Wiley.

[Myers 1977]
Myers, G. J. (1977). An extension to the cyclomatic measure of program complexity. *ACM SIGPLAN Notices*, **12**, 10, 61–4.

[Myers 1978a]
Myers, G. J. (1978). *Composite/Structured Design.* New York: van Nostrand Reinhold.

[Myers 1978b]
Myers, G. J. (1978). A controlled experiment in program testing and code walkthroughs/inspections. *Communications of the ACM*, **21**, 760–8.

[Myers 1979]
Myers, G. J. (1979). *The Art of Software Testing.* London: Wiley.

[Nassi 1973]
Nassi, I., & Shneiderman, B. (1973). Flowchart techniques for structured programming. *ACM SIGPLAN Notices*, **8**, 8, 12–26.

[NBS 1981]
Software Development Tools: A Reference Guide to a Taxonomy of Tool Features. US Department of Commerce, National Bureau of Standards,

Center for Programming, Science and
Technology.

[Nelson 1966]
Nelson, E. A. (1966). *Management Handbook for the Estimation of Computer Programming Costs.* Systems Development Corporation report AD-A648-750.

[Nelson 1976]
Nelson, E. (1976). Developing a software cost methodology. In *Proceedings of COMPCON Fall, 1976*, pp. 144–5. New York: IEEE Computer Society Press.

[Nelson 1978]
Nelson, R. (1978). *Software Data Collection and Analysis at RADC.* Rome, N.Y.: Rome Air Development Center.

[Nelson 1983]
Nelson, R. A., Haibt, L. M., & Sheridan, P. B. (1983). Casting Petri Nets into programs. *IEEE Transactions on Software Engineering*, **SE-9**, 590–602.

[Neumann 1983]
Neumann, P. G. (1983). Experiences with a formal methodology for software development. In *Software Factory Experiences*, eds. D. Ferrari, M. Bolognani, & J. Goguer. Amsterdam: North-Holland.

[Ohba 1982]
Ohba, M. (1982). Software Quality = Test Accuracy × Test Coverage. In *Proceedings of the 6th International Conference on Software Engineering*, pp. 287–93. New York: IEEE Computer Society Press.

[Ohno 1982]
Ed. Ohno, Y. (1982). *Proceedings of the International Symposium on Current Issues of Requirements Engineering Environments, 1982.* Amsterdam: North-Holland.

[Oppen 1975]
Oppen, D. C., & Cook, S. A. (1975). Proving assertions about programs that manipulate data structures. In *Seventh Annual ACM Symposium on the Theory of Computation, 1975*, pp. 107–16. New York: ACM.

[Orr 1977]
Orr, K. T. (1977). *Structured Systems Development.* New York: Yourdon Press.

[Orr 1978]
Orr, K. T. (1978). Introducing Structured Systems Design. In Infotech 1978, pp. 215–29.

[Orr 1979]
Orr, W. D. (1979). *Structured Requirements Definition.* Langton, Kitch & Associates Inc.

[Orr 1981]
Orr, K. T. (1981). *Structured Requirements Specification.* Topeka, Kan.: Orr Associates, Inc.

[Osterweil 1976]
Osterweil, L. J., & Fosdick, L. D. (1976). DAVE – A validation error detection and documentation system for Fortran programs. *Software – Practice and Experience*, **6**, 473–86.

[Ottenstein 1979]
Ottenstein, L. M. (1979). Quantitative estimates of debugging requirements. *IEEE Transactions on Software Engineering*, **SE-5**, 505–14.

[Ould 1982]
Ould, M. A., Birrell, N. D., Radford, P., Tucker, N., & Crawford, D. I. (1982). A workbench for computer simulation of picture coding schemes. In *Proceedings of the IEE 1982 International Conference on Electronic Image Processing*, pp. 199–203. London: IEE (Conference Publication number 214).

[Overman 1977]
Overman, W. (1977). *PLIP Reference Manual.* Los Angeles: Computer Science Department, UCLA.

[Pagnoni 1983]
Eds. Pagnoni, A., & Rozenberg, G. (1983). *Applications and Theory of Petri Nets.* Berlin: Springer-Verlag.

[Palmer 1979]
Palmer, P. F. (1979). Structured programming techniques in interrupt–driver routines. *ICL Technical Journal*, November 1979, 247–64.

[Panzl 1978]
Panzl, D. J. (1978). Automatic software test drivers. *Computer*, **11**, April, 44–50.

[Parikh 1981]
Ed. Parikh, G. (1981). *Techniques of Program and System Maintenance.* Cambridge, Mass.: Winthrop Publishers.

[Parnas 1972a]
Parnas, D. L. (1972). On the criteria to be used in decomposing systems into modules. *Communications of the ACM*, **15**, 1053–8.

[Parnas 1972b]
Parnas, D. L. (1972). A technique for software module specification with examples. *Communications of the ACM*, **15**, 330–6.

[Parnas 1976a]
Parnas, D. L. (1976). On the design and development of program families. *IEEE Transactions on Software Engineering*, **SE-2**, 1–9.

[Parnas 1976b]
Parnas, D. L., & Wurges, H. (1976). Response to

undesired events in software systems. In *Proceedings of the 3rd International Conference on Software Engineering*, pp. 437–46. New York: IEEE Computer Society Press.

[Parnas 1977]
Parnas, D. L. (1977). The influence of software structure on reliability. In Yeh 1977.

[Parnas 1979]
Parnas, D. L. (1979). Designing software for ease of extension and contraction. *IEEE Transactions on Software Engineering*, **SE-5**, 128–37.

[Parnas 1983]
Parnas, D. L. (1983). A generalised control structure and its formal definition. *Communications of the ACM*, **26**, 572–81.

[Parr 1980]
Parr, F. N. (1980). An alternative to the Rayleigh curve model for software development effort. *IEEE Transactions on Software Engineering*, **SE-6**, 291–6.

[Paster 1981]
Paster, D. L. (1981). Experience with application of modern software management controls. In *Proceedings of the 5th International Conference on Software Engineering*, pp. 18–26. New York: IEEE Computer Society Press.

[Pedersen 1978]
Pedersen, J. T., & Buckle, J. K. (1978). Kongsberg's road to an industrial software methodology. In *Proceedings of the 3rd International Conference on Software Engineering*, pp. 85–93. New York: IEEE Computer Society Press.

[Penedo 1979a]
Penedo, M. H. (1979). *SL1 System Reference Manual*. Los Angeles: Computer Science Department, UCLA.

[Penedo 1979b]
Penedo, M. H. (1979). *A Design Example Using the SARA Methodology*. Los Angeles: Computer Science Department, UCLA.

[Penedo 1979c]
Penedo, M. H., & Berry, D. M. (1979). The use of a module interconnection language in the SARA system design methodology. In *Proceedings of the 4th International Conference on Software Engineering*, pp. 294–307. New York: IEEE Computer Society Press.

[Perlis 1981]
Perlis, A., Sayward, F., & Shaw, M. (1981). *Software Metrics: An Analysis and Evaluation*. Cambridge, Mass.: MIT Press.

[Peters 1977]
Peters, L. J., & Tripp, L. L. (1977). Comparing software design methodologies. *Datamation*, November 1977.

[Peters 1978a]
Peters, L. J., & Tripp, L. L. (1978). Some limitations of current design methods. In Infotech 1978, pp. 249–64.

[Peters 1978b]
Peters, L. J., & Tripp, L. L. (1978). A model of software engineering. In *Proceedings of the 3rd International Conference on Software Engineering*, pp. 63–70. New York: IEEE Computer Society Press.

[Peters 1979]
Peters, L. J. (1979). Software design: current methods and techniques. In Infotech 1979a, volume 2, pp. 240–62. Maidenhead: Infotech.

[Peterson 1977]
Peterson, J. L. (1977). Petri Nets. *Computing Surveys*, **9**, 223–52.

[Peterson 1981]
Peterson, J. L. (1981). *Petri Net Theory and the Modelling of Systems*. Englewood Cliffs, N.J.: Prentice-Hall.

[Petri 1962]
Petri, C. A. (1962). Kommunikation mit Automaten. Ph.D. dissertation, University of Bonn.

[Petrone 1982]
Petrone, L., DiLeva, A., & Sirovich, F. (1982). DUAL: An integrated tool for developing documented programs by stepwise refinement. In *Proceedings of the 6th International Conference on Software Engineering*, pp. 350–7. New York: IEEE Computer Society Press.

[Poole 1970]
Poole, P. C., & Waite, W. M. (1970). *The STAGE 2 Macroprocessor User Reference Manual*. Abingdon: UKAEA Research Group, Culham Laboratory.

[Popek 1977]
Popek, G. J., Horning, J. J., Lampson, B. W., Mitchell, J. G., & London, R. L. (1977). Notes on the design of Euclid. In *Proceedings of an ACM Conference on Language Design for Reliable Software, 1977*, published as *ACM SIGPLAN Notices*, **12**, 3, entire issue.

[Power 1983]
Power, L. R. (1983). Design and use of a program execution analyser. *IBM Systems Journal*, **22**, 271–94.

[Pressman 1982]
Pressman, R. S. (1982). *Software Engineering: A Practitioner's Approach*. New York: McGraw-Hill.

[Probert 1982]
Probert, R. L. (1982). Optimal insertion of software probes in well delimited programs. *IEEE Transactions on Software Engineering*, **SE-8**, 34–42.

[Putnam 1978]
Putnam, L. H. (1978). A general empirical solution to the macro software sizing and estimating problem. *IEEE Transactions on Software Engineering*, **SE-4**, 345–61.

[Putnam 1979]
Putnam, L. H., & Fitzsimmons, A. (1979). Estimating software costs. *Datamation*, 1979; September, 189–98; October, 171–8; November, 137–40.

[Quirk 1977]
Quirk, W. J., & Gilbert, R. (1977). *The Formal Specification of Requirements of Complex Realtime Systems*. UKAEA report AERE-R8602. Harwell: UKAEA.

[Quirk 1978]
Quirk, W. J. (1978). *The Automatic Analysis of Formal Real-time System Specifications*. UKAEA report AERE-R9046. Harwell: UKAEA.

[Ramamoorthy 1975]
Ramamoorthy, C. V., & Ho, S. F. (1975). Testing large software with automated software evaluation systems. *IEEE Transactions on Software Engineering*, **SE-1**, 46–58.

[Ramamoorthy 1977]
Ramamoorthy, C. V., & So, H. H. (1977). Survey of principles and techniques of software requirements and specifications. In *Infotech State of the Art Report on Software Engineering Techniques*, volume 2, pp. 265–318. Maidenhead: Infotech.

[Ramamoorthy 1981]
Ramamoorthy, C. V., Mok, Y.-K. R., Bastani, F. B., Chin, G. H., & Suzuki, K. (1981). Application of a methodology for the development and validation of reliable process control software. *IEEE Transactions on Software Engineering*, **SE-7**, 537–55.

[Ramamoorthy 1982]
Ramamoorthy, C. V., & Bastani, F. B. (1982). Software reliability – status and perspectives. *IEEE Transactions on Software Engineering*, **SE-8**, 354–70.

[Ramsey 1979]
Ramsey, H. R., Atwood, M. E., & Campbell, G. D. (1979). *An Analysis of Software Design Methodologies*. US Army, Research Institute for the Behavioral and Social Sciences, Technical Report 401. Springfield, Va.: US Dept of Com-

merce, National Technical Information Service.

[Rapps 1982]
Rapps, S., & Weyuker, E. J. (1982). Data flow analysis techniques for test data selection. In *Proceedings of the 6th International Conference on Software Engineering*, pp. 272–8. New York: IEEE Computer Society Press.

[Rauch-Hindin 1982]
Rauch-Hindin, W. (1982). Software tools: New ways to chip software into shape. *Data Communications*, April 1982, 83–115.

[Reifer 1981]
Software Tools Directory. Torrance, Calif.: Reifer Consultants Inc.

[Remus 1979]
Remus, H., & Zilles, S. (1979). Prediction and management of program quality. In *Proceedings of the 4th International Conference on Software Engineering*, pp. 341–50. New York: IEEE Computer Society Press.

[Reynolds 1981]
Reynolds, J. C. (1981). *Correctness Proving: The Craft of Programming*. Englewood Cliffs, N.J.: Prentice-Hall.

[Riddle 1978a]
Riddle, W. E., Wilden, J. C., Sayler, J. H., Segal, A. R., & Stavely, A. M. (1978). Behaviour modelling during software design. In *Proceedings of the 3rd International Conference on Software Engineering*, pp. 13–22. New York: IEEE Computer Society Press.

[Riddle 1978b]
Riddle, W. E., & Wileden, J. C. (1978). Languages for representing software specifications and designs. *ACM SIGSOFT Software Engineering Notes*, **3**, 4, 7–11.

[Riddle 1980a]
Eds. Riddle, W. E., & Fairley, R. E. (1980). *Software Development Tools*. Berlin: Springer-Verlag.

[Riddle 1980b]
Riddle, W. E. (1980). Panel: Software development environments. In *Proceedings of the 4th International Conference on Computer Software and Applications*, pp. 220–4. New York: IEEE Computer Society Press.

[Riddle 1980c]
Riddle, W. E., & Wileden, J. C. (1980). *Tutorial on Software System Design: Description and Analysis*. New York: IEEE Computer Society Press.

[Riddle 1980d]
Riddle, W. E. (1980). An assessment of DREAM. In Huenke 1981.

[Ritchie 1978]
Ritchie, D. M., & Thomson, K. (1978). The UNIX time-sharing system. *Bell System Technical Journal*, **57**, 1905–29.

[Robinson 1977]
Robinson, L., Levitt, K. N., Neumann, P. G., & Saxena, A. R. (1977). A formal methodology for the design of operating system software. In Yeh 1977.

[Robinson 1979]
Robinson, L. (1979). *The HDM Handbook Volume 1: The Foundations of HDM*. Menlo Park, Calif.: SRI International.

[Rochkind 1975]
Rochkind, M. J. (1975). The Source Code Control System. *IEEE Transactions on Software Engineering*, **SE-1**, 255–65.

[Ross 1977a]
Ross, D. T., & Schoman, K. E. (1977). Structured analysis for requirements definition. *IEEE Transactions on Software Engineering*, **SE-3**, 6–15.

[Ross 1977b]
Ross, D. T. (1977). Structured Analysis (SA): A language for communicating ideas. *IEEE Transactions on Software Engineering*, **SE-3**, 16–34.

[Royce 1975]
Royce, W. W. (1975). Software requirements analysis: sizing and costing. In Horowitz 1975.

[RRE 1975]
Jackson, K., & Simpson, H. R. (1975), *MASCOT – A Modular Approach to Software Construction, Operation and Test*. RRE technical note 778. Malvern: RRE.

[Ruby 1975]
Ruby, R. J., Dana, J. A., & Biche, P. W. (1975). Qualitative aspects of software validation. *IEEE Transactions on Software Engineering*, **SE-1**, 150–5.

[Ruggiero 1979]
Ruggiero, W., Estrin, G., Fenchel, R., Razouk, R., Schwabe, D., & Vernon, M. (1979). Analysis of data flow models using the SARA graph model of behavior. In *Proceedings of the National Computer Conference 1979*, pp. 975–88. Montvale, N.J.: AFIPS Press.

[Rullo 1980]
Ed. Rullo, T. A. (1980). *Advances in Computer Programming Management*. Philadelphia: Heyden.

[Salter 1976]
Salter, K. G. (1976). A methodology for decomposing

system requirements into data processing requirements. In *Proceedings of the 2nd International Conference on Software Engineering*, pp. 91–101. New York: IEEE Computer Society Press.

[Sammet 1981]
Sammet, J. E. (1981). An overview of high-level languages. In *Advances in Computers; volume 20*, ed. M. C. Yovits, pp. 199–259. New York: Academic Press.

[Schach 1982]
Schach, S. R. (1982). A unified theory for software production. *Software – Practice and Experience*, **12**, 683–7.

[Schick 1978]
Schick, G. J., & Wolverton, R. W. (1978). An analysis of competing software reliability models. *IEEE Transactions on Software Engineering*, **SE-4**, 104–20.

[Schneider 1978]
Schneider, V. (1978). Prediction of software effort and project duration – four new formulas. *ACM SIGPLAN Notices*, **13**, 6, 49–59.

[Schneidewind 1979]
Schneidewind, N. F., & Hoffman, H. M. (1979). An experiment in software error data collection and analysis. *IEEE Transactions on Software Engineering*, **SE-5**, 276–86.

[Schorre 1980]
Schorre, V., & Stein, J. (1980). *The Interactive Theorem Prover (ITP) User Manual*. System Development Corporation Report TM-6889/000/01.

[Sharma 1981]
Sharma, D. K. (1981). McDonald's problem – an example of using Dijkstra's programming method. *Bell System Technical Journal*, **60**, 2157–65.

[Shen 1983]
Shen, V. Y., Conte, S. D., & Dunsmore, H. E. (1983). Software Science revisited: a critical analysis of the theory and its empirical support. *IEEE Transactions on Software Engineering*, **SE-9**, 155–65.

[Shneiderman 1976]
Shneiderman, B. (1976). A review of design techniques for programs and data. *Software – Practice and Experience*, **6**, 555–67.

[Shneiderman 1980]
Shneiderman, B. (1980). *Software Psychology*. Cambridge, Mass.: Winthrop Publishers.

[Shooman 1973]
Shooman, M. L. (1973). Operational testing and software reliability estimation during program

development. In *Proceedings of the 1973 IEEE Symposium on Computer Software Reliability*, pp. 51–7. New York: IEEE Computer Society Press.

[Shooman 1976]
Shooman, M. L. (1976). Structural models for software reliability prediction. In *Proceedings of the 2nd International Conference on Software Engineering, 1976*, pp. 268–80. New York: IEEE Computer Society Press.

[Shooman 1979]
Shooman, M. L. (1979). Tutorial on software cost models. In *Proceedings of Workshop on Quantitative Software Models*, pp. 1–19. New York: IEEE Computer Society Press.

[SIGPLAN 1976]
Proceedings of Conference on data: abstraction, definition and structure. *ACM SIGPLAN Notices*, **11**, special issue.

[Silverberg 1979]
Silverberg, B. A., Robinson, L., & Levitt, K. N. (1979). *The HDM Handbook Volume II: The Languages and Tools of HDM*. Menlo Park, Calif.: SRI International.

[Silverberg 1981]
Silverberg, B. A. (1981). An overview of the SRI Hierarchical Development Methodology. In Huenke 1981.

[Simpson 1979]
Simpson, H. R., & Jackson, K. (1979). Process synchronisation in MASCOT. *Computer Journal*, **22**, 332–45.

[Snowdon 1978]
Snowdon, R. A., & Henderson, P. (1978). The TOPD system for computer-aided system development. In Infotech 1978, pp. 283–305.

[Snowdon 1981]
Snowdon, R. A. (1981). CADES and software system development. In Huenke 1981.

[SofTech 1976]
SofTech, Inc. (1976). *An Introduction to SADT. Structured Analysis and Design Technique*. SofTech report 9022-78R. Waltham, Mass.: SofTech, Inc.

[Sommerville 1982]
Sommerville, I. (1982). *Software Engineering*. London: Addison-Wesley.

[Sorkowitz 1979]
Sorkowitz, A. R. (1979). Certification testing: a procedure to improve the quality of software testing. *Computer*, **10**, August, 20–4.

[Spier 1981]
Spier, M. J., Gutz, S., & Wasserman, A. I. (1981). The ergonomics of software engineering – description of the problem space. In Huenke 1981.

[SRA 1981]
Software Engineering Automated Tool Index. San Francisco: Software Research Associates.

[SRI 1979]
The HDM Handbook Volume III: A Detailed Example in the Use of HDM. Menlo Park, Calif.: SRI International.

[SSL 1981]
Concepts and Facilities for SDS Project Control. Macclesfield: Software Sciences Limited.

[SSL 1982a]
Introduction to SDS. Macclesfield: Software Sciences Limited.

[SSL 1982b]
Concepts and Facilities for SDS Design Control. Macclesfield: Software Sciences Limited.

[Stay 1976]
Stay, J. F. (1976). HIPO and integrated program design. *IBM Systems Journal*, **15**, 143–54.

[Stevens 1974]
Stevens, W. P., Myers, G. J., & Constantine, L. L. (1974). Structured Design. *IBM Systems Journal*, **13**, 115–39.

[Stevens 1978]
Stevens, S. A., & Tripp, L. A. (1978). Requirements expression and verification aid. In *Proceedings of the 3rd International Conference on Software Engineering*, pp. 101–8. New York: IEEE Computer Society Press.

[Stevens 1981]
Stevens, W. P. (1981). *Using Structured Design. How to Make Programs Simple, Changeable, Flexible, and Reusable*. New York: Wiley.

[Stevens 1982]
Stevens, A. C. (1982). *User Assessments of Software Tools: SDS. Report No 1 on Software Development System*. London: Department of Industry.

[Steward 1981]
Steward, D. V. (1981). *Systems Analysis and Management: Structures, Strategy and Design*. New York: Petrocelli.

[Strachey 1965]
Strachey, C. (1965). A general purpose macrogenerator. *Computer Journal*, **8**, 225–41.

[Stucki 1975]
Stucki, L. G. (1975). Coding and testing – tools for software development. In Horowitz 1975.

[Stucki 1977a]
Stucki, L. (1977). New directions in automated tools for improving software quality. In Yeh 1977.

[Stucki 1977*b*]
Stucki, L. G. (1977). Software development tools – acquisition considerations. In *Proceedings of the National Computer Conference, 1977*, pp. 267–8.

[Suding 1977]
Suding, A. D. (1977). Hobbits, dwarfs and software. *Datamation*, June 1977, 92–7.

[Sunohara 1981]
Sunohara, T., Takano, A., Uehara, K., & Ohkawaka, T. (1981). Program complexity measure for software development management. In *Proceedings of the 5th International Conference on Software Engineering*, pp. 100–6. New York: IEEE Computer Society Press.

[Sunshine 1982]
Sunshine, C. A., Thompson, D. H., Erickson, R. W., Gerhart, S. L., & Schwabe, D. (1982). Specification and verification of communication protocols in AFFIRM using state transition models. *IEEE Transactions on Software Engineering*, **SE-8**, 460–89.

[Sunshine 1983]
Sunshine, C. A., Thompson, D. H., Erickson, R. W., Gerhart, S. L., & Schwabe, D. (1983). Correction to 'Specification and verification of communication protocols in AFFIRM using state transition models'. *IEEE Transactions on Software Engineering*, **SE-9**, 113.

[Swanson 1976]
Swanson, E. B. (1976). The dimensions of maintenance. In *Proceedings of the 2nd International Conference on Software Engineering*, pp. 492–7. New York: IEEE Computer Society Press.

[Symons 1980]
Symons, F. J. W. (1980). Introduction to numerical Petri Nets, a general graphical model of concurrent processing systems. *Australian Telecommunication Research Journal*, **14**.

[Symons 1982]
Symons, F. J. W. (1982). *The application of Petri Nets and numerical Petri Nets*. Telecom Australia Research Laboratories, Report 720. Clayton, Victoria: Telecom Australia Research Laboratories.

[Tai 1980]
Tai, K.-C. (1980). Program testing complexity and test criteria. *IEEE Transactions on Software Engineering*, **SE-6**, 531–8.

[Taylor 1980]
Taylor, R. N., & Osterweil, L. J. (1980). Anomaly detection in concurrent software by static data flow analysis. *IEEE Transactions on Software Engineering*, **SE-6**, 265–77.

[Teichroew 1977]
Teichroew, D., & Hershey, E. A. (1977). PSL/PSA: A computer-aided technique for structured documentation and analysis of information processing systems. *IEEE Transactions on Software Engineering*, **SE-3**, 41–8.

[Terrio 1981]
Terrio, F. J., & Vreeland, J. J. (1981). *Task Oriented User Requirements and Program Design*. IBM Technical Report TRO3.111.

[Thayer 1978]
Thayer, T. A., Lipow, M., & Nelson, E. C. (1978). *Software Reliability – A Study of Large Project Reality*. Amsterdam: North-Holland.

[Thomas 1978]
Thomas, M. (1978). Functional decomposition: SADT. In Infotech 1978, volume 2, pp. 335–54.

[Troy 1981]
Troy, D. A., & Zweben, S. H. (1981). Measuring the quality of structured designs. *Journal of Systems and Software*, **2**, 113–20.

[TRW]
A New Approach for Software Success. Brochure published by TRW, Defense and Space Systems Group, USA.

[Tseng 1982]
Tseng, V. (1982). *Microprocessor Development and Development Systems*. New York: McGraw-Hill.

[Voges 1976]
Voges, U. (1976). Aspects of design, test and validation of the software for a computerised reactor protection system. In *Proceedings of the 2nd International Conference on Software Engineering*, pp. 606–10. New York: IEEE Computer Society Press.

[Voges 1980]
Voges, U., Gmeiner, L., & Amschler, A. (1980). SADAT – An automated testing tool. *IEEE Transactions on Software Engineering*, **SE-6**, 286–90.

[Waite 1967]
Waite, W. M. (1967). A language independent macro processor. *Communications of the ACM*, **10**, 433–40.

[Walston 1977]
Walston, C. E., & Felix, C. P. (1977). A method of programming measurement and estimation. *IBM Systems Journal*, **16**, 1, 54–73, and 4, 422–3.

[Ward 1981]
Ward, A. O. (1981). A consistent approach to the development of system requirements and software design. In *AGARD Conference*

Proceedings No 303, pp. 15-1–15-16.
Neuilly-sur-Seine: AGARD, NATO.

[Warfield 1973]
Warfield, J. N. (1973). Binary matrices in systems
modeling. *IEEE Transactions on Systems, Man
and Cybernetics*, **SMC-3**, 441–9.

[Warnier 1974]
Warnier, J. D. (1974). *Logical Construction of
Programs*. Leiden, Netherlands: Stenport
Kroese.

[Warnier 1981]
Warnier, J. D. (1981). *Logical Construction of Systems*.
New York: Van Nostrand Reinhold.

[Weinberg 1971*a*]
Weinberg, G. M. (1971). *The Psychology of Computer
Programming*. New York: Van Nostrand
Reinhold.

[Weinberg 1971*b*]
Weinberg, G. M. (1971). *PL/1 Programming: A
Manual of Style*. New York: McGraw-Hill.

[Weinberg 1977]
Weinberg, G. M., Wright, S. E., Kauffman, R., &
Goetz, M. A. (1977). *High Level COBOL
Programming*. Cambridge, Mass.: Winthrop
Publishers.

[Weinberg 1978]
Weinberg, G. M. (1978). *Structured Analysis*. New
York: Yourdon Press.

[Weinwurm 1970]
Weinwurm, G. F. (1970). *On the Management of
Computer Programming*. New York: Auerbach.

[Wells 1976]
Wells, M. B., & Cornwell, F. L. (1976). A data type
encapsulation scheme utilizing base language
operators. In *Proceedings of the Conference on
Data: Abstraction, Definition and Structure, ACM
SIGPLAN Notices*, **11**, special issue, 170–8. New
York: ACM.

[Wensley 1976]
Wensley, J. H., Green, M. W., Levitt, K. N., &
Shostak, R. E. (1976). The design, analysis and
verification of the SIFT fault tolerant system. In
*Proceedings of the 2nd International Conference
on Software Engineering*, pp. 458–69. New York:
IEEE Computer Society Press.

[Weyuker 1980]
Weyuker, E. J., & Ostrand, T. J. (1980). Theories of
program testing and the application of revealing
subdomains. *IEEE Transactions on Software
Engineering*, **SE-6**, 236–46.

[White 1980]
White, L. J., & Cohen, E. I. (1980). A domain strategy
for computer program testing. *IEEE Transactions
on Software Engineering*, **SE-6**, 247–57.

[Wig 1978]
Wig, E. D. (1978). *PSL/PSA Primer*. Ann Arbor,
Mich.: University of Michigan.

[Wileden 1979]
Wileden, J. C. (1979). DREAM – An approach to
designing large scale, concurrent software
systems. In *Proceedings of the 1979 ACM Annual
Conference*, pp. 88–94. New York: ACM.

[Winchester 1982]
Winchester, J. W., & Estrin, G. (1982). Requirements
definition and its interface to the SARA design
methodology for computer-based systems. In
*Proceedings of the National Computer
Conference, 1982*, pp. 369–79. Arlington, Va.:
AFIPS Press.

[Winters 1979*a*]
Winters, E. W. (1979). An analysis of the capabilities of
Problem Statement Language: a language for
system requirements and specifications. In
*Proceedings of the 3rd International Conference
on Computer Software and Applications*, pp.
283–8. New York: IEEE Computer Society Press.

[Winters 1979*b*]
Winters, E. W. (1979). Experience with Problem
Statement Language: a tool for Structured
Documentation. In *Proceedings of the
Application Development Symposium, Monterey,
California, 1979*, pp. 137–141.

[Wirth 1971]
Wirth, N. (1971). Program development by stepwise
refinement. *Communications of the ACM*, **14**,
221–7.

[Wirth 1977]
Wirth, N. (1977). Modula: a language for modular
multi-programming. *Software – Practice and
Experience*, **7**, 3–36.

[Wolberg 1982]
Wolberg, J. R. (1982). A costing model for software
conversions. *Software – Practice and Experience*,
12, 1043–9.

[Wolberg 1983]
Wolberg, J. R. (1983). *Conversion of Computer
Software*. Englewood Cliffs, N.J.: Prentice-Hall.

[Wolverton 1974]
Wolverton, R. W. (1974). The cost of developing large
scale software. *IEEE Transactions on Computers*,
C-23, 615–36.

[Woodfield 1979]
Woodfield, S. N. (1979). An experiment on unit
increase in program complexity. *IEEE
Transactions on Software Engineering*, **SE-5**,
76–9.

[Woodfield 1981]
Woodfield, S. N., Shen, V. Y., & Dunsmore, H. E.

(1981). A study of several metrics for programming effort. *Journal of Systems and Software*, **2**, 97–103.

[Woodward 1979]
Woodward, M. R., Hennell, M. A., & Hedley, D. (1979). A measure of control flow complexity in program text. *IEEE Transactions on Software Engineering*, **SE-5**, 45–50.

[Woodward 1980]
Woodward, M. R., Hedley, D., & Hennell, M. A. (1980). Experience with path analysis and testing of programs. *IEEE Transactions on Software Engineering*, **SE-6**, 278–86.

[Wulf 1976]
Wulf, W. A., London, R. L., & Shaw, M. (1976). An introduction to the construction and verification of Alphard programs. *IEEE Transactions on Software Engineering*, **SE-2**, 253–64.

[Wulf 1977]
Wulf, W. A. (1977). Languages and structured programs. In Yeh 1977.

[Yau 1978]
Yau, S., Collofello, J., & MacGregor, T. (1978). Ripple effect analysis of software maintenance. In *Proceedings of the 2nd International Conference on Computer Software and Applications*, pp. 60–5. New York: IEEE Computer Society Press.

[Yau 1980]
Yau, S. S., & Collofello, J. S. (1980). Some stability measures for software maintenance. *IEEE Transactions on Software Engineering*, **SE-6**, 545–52.

[Yeh 1977]
Ed. Yeh, R. T. (1977). *Current Trends in Programming Methodology, Volume 1*. Englewood Cliffs, N.J.: Prentice-Hall.

[Yeh 1979]
Yeh, R. T., Araya, A., Mittermeir, R., Mao, W., & Evans, F. (1979). Software requirement engineering: a perspective. In Infotech 1979*a*, pp. 313–42.

[Yin 1978]
Yin, B. H., & Winchester, J. W. (1978). The establishment and use of measures to evaluate the quality of software designs. In *Proceedings of the ACM Software Quality and Assurance Workshop, SIGSOFT Software Engineering Notes*, **3**, 5, 45–52. New York: ACM.

[Yourdon 1978]
Yourdon, E., & Constantine, L. L. (1978). *Structured Design*. Englewood Cliffs, N.J.: Prentice-Hall.

[Yourdon 1979*a*]
Yourdon, E. (1979). *Structured Walkthroughs*. New York: Yourdon.

[Yourdon 1979*b*]
Yourdon, E., & Constantine, L. L. (1979). *Structured Design: Fundamentals of a Discipline of Computer Program and Systems Design*. Englewood Cliffs, N.J.: Prentice-Hall.

[Yourdon 1979*c*]
Yourdon, E. (1979). *Managing the Structured Techniques*. Englewood Cliffs, N.J.: Prentice-Hall.

[Yourdon 1982]
Yourdon, E. (1982). *Managing the System Life-cycle: Software Development Methodology*. New York: Yourdon Press.

[Zave 1981]
Zave, P., & Yeh, R. T. (1981). Executable requirements for embedded systems. In *Proceedings of the 5th International Conference on Software Engineering*, pp. 295–304. New York: IEEE Computer Society Press.

[Zeil 1981]
Zeil, S. J., & White, L. J. (1981). Sufficient test sets for path analysis testing strategies. In *Proceedings of the 5th International Conference on Software Engineering*, pp. 184–91. New York: IEEE Computer Society Press.

[Zelkowitz 1976]
Zelkowitz, M. V. (1976). Automatic program analysis and evaluation. In *Proceedings of the 3rd International Conference on Software Engineering*, pp. 158–63. New York: IEEE Computer Society Press.

[Zelkowitz 1978]
Zelkowitz, M. V., & Larsen, H. J. (1978). Implementation of a capability-based data abstraction. *IEEE Transactions on Software Engineering*, **SE-4**, 56–64.

[Zelkowitz 1979]
Zelkowitz, M. *et al.* (1979). *Principles of Software Engineering and Design*. Englewood Cliffs, N.J.: Prentice-Hall.

[Zelkowitz 1980]
Zelkowitz, M. V. (1980). Advances in software engineering: resource estimation. In *Advances in Computer Programming Management*, ed. T. A. Rullo. Philadelphia: Heyden.

[Zelkowitz 1982]
Eds. Zelkowitz, M., & Branstad, M. (1982). Working Papers from the ACM SIGSOFT Rapid Prototyping Workshop, Columbia, Maryland, 19–21 April 1982. *ACM SIGSOFT Software Engineering Notes*, **7**, 5, entire issue.

[Zilles 1975]
Zilles, S. N. (1975). *Abstract Specification for Data Types*. San Jose, Calif.: IBM Research Laboratory.

Index

Page numbers in boldface represent the main entry or entries for a topic